Portable City

The City as Place

Emotions, Experiences, and Meanings

Series Editors

Professor Rebecca Madgin, Urban Studies,
University of Glasgow
and
Professor Nicolas Kenny, History,
Simon Fraser University

Volume 2

Stephen Bowman and Kieran Taylor (eds)

Portable City

Modern Glasgow's Transatlantic Connections

PETER LANG

Oxford · Berlin · Bruxelles · Chennai · Lausanne · New York

Bibliographic information published by die Deutsche Nationalbibliothek
Die Deutsche Nationalbibliothek lists this publication in the Deutsche Nationalbibliografie; detailed bibliographic data is available on the Internet at http://dnb.d-nb.de.

A catalogue record for this book is available from the British Library.

Library of Congress Control Number: 2025049699

Cover image: Renfield Street towards St Vincent Street, Glasgow (Stephen Bowman, 2023)

ISSN 2632-0924
ISBN 978-1-80374-281-6 (Print)
ISBN 978-1-80374-282-3 (ePDF)
ISBN 978-1-80374-283-0 (ePUB)
DOI 10.3726/b21091

Published by Peter Lang Ltd, Oxford (United Kingdom)

info@peterlang.com

This publication has been peer reviewed.

www.peterlang.com

Contact for General Product Safety Regulation (GPSR): gpsr@peterlang.com

I dedicate this book to my children, Fraser Elliot and Margo Rosa Joy, neither of whom were born when I first started writing my parts of it, and to my wife Fiona, whose love and support I could not do without. I also want to dedicate the book to each of my grandparents, whose own lives were entangled with the City of Glasgow, and to my Aunt Elizabeth, who is with them now once again.

Stephen Bowman

To my wife, Jasmeena. Without your love and patience this book would never have been written.

Kieran Taylor

Contents

Photographs

Tables and Charts

Acknowledgements

We would like to thank the many people who assisted in guiding this book through publication, in particular Series Editors Nicolas Kenny and Rebecca Madgin, who provided much-needed guidance while also giving us the freedom to attempt to produce the book we wanted to produce. Sincere thanks are also due to Laurel Plapp, Senior Acquisitions Editor at Peter Lang, who so patiently and clearly addressed our queries at various points in the process, and to Marta Podvolotskaya, Peter Lang's Publishing Success Manager, for so efficiently overseeing the final production of the book. We also thank the anonymous reviewers who provided such fulsome feedback on our original proposal and on earlier drafts of the work. Finally, we offer our heartfelt thanks to our contributors, without whom this book would be much shorter.

LC23 ZVE

SARAR
BROAD

Transatlantic Avenues of Exchange

Stephen Bowman and Kieran Taylor

Glasgow is Scotland's metropolis. It has long been the country's largest city and is the place where all the challenges and changes wrought by modernity emerged most clearly. *Portable City* is about the tangible and intangible significance of this metropolis as muse, as site of personal and collective memory, as imperial and industrial centre, as home for new immigrants, as bigoted slum, and as pioneering provider for the poor. More than that, it is about how Glasgow – a transatlantic city in ways that more celebrated destinations like London and Edinburgh have never been – has been defined by its historical entanglements with North America. In this knowledge, this book is a collective attempt to trace, analyse, and explain the vital and various transatlantic linkages that together constitute modern Glasgow.

Glasgow has been Scotland's gateway to the world and the world's gateway to Scotland. An Atlantic port city of sorts and 'Workshop of the World' by 1914, it sent its ships and machinery around the globe. Glasgow was also a place of Enlightenment-era learning, culture, art, music, and entertainment, and would play host to no fewer than four international exhibitions between 1880 and 1938. The city's reputation for innovation and industry was enhanced by a local political culture historically rooted in a liberal unionist tradition. Crucially, this was heavily influenced by a progressive Presbyterianism and envied by civic activists in New York and Chicago in the 1890s and 1900s. Yet the flip side of this vision of urban utopia was the deprivation of the city's slums, a criminal court system that dealt with more cases than anywhere in Britain outside of London, and the exploitation of the enslaved and colonised people whose labour had contributed to the city's growth in the first place.[1] The egalitarian ethos of Glasgow's political culture says nothing about how the city's wealth was created through empire and capitalism or their attendant miseries, obscuring the fact that 'Glasgow' has been a byword for poverty as much as it was a symbol of reformist progress. Writing in 1913 novelist and playwright Charles McEvoy depicted Glasgow as a 'fine clean city', but the citizenry he encountered as he stepped off the train

1 David G. Barrie and Susan Broomhall, *Police Courts in Nineteenth-Century Scotland, Volume 1: Magistrates, Media and the Masses* (London, 2016), 12.

were 'physical wreckage', 'barefooted', 'emaciated' and 'half naked'.[2] Glasgow's underclass: ignorant, exploited and relegated to precarious employment and inadequate housing were regarded as the human detritus of the city. In this light, the 'Glasgow Effect' – public health terminology for the way in which the city's population continues to die younger than its peers in other post-industrial British cities such as Liverpool or Manchester – takes on a new and more ambivalent meaning, raising questions about the lingering aftershocks of Scotland's collision with urban modernity.[3]

Our book neither reproduces booster accounts of Glasgow nor does it diminish the significance of Glasgow as an international city. It begins from the assumption that histories of Glasgow, and to some extent Scotland itself, are best understood with reference to their transnationalism. This transnational approach to urban history is of course pertinent to many other cities across continents. Liverpool, Mumbai, Lagos, Johannesburg, Rio De Janeiro, and Shanghai, to name a few, all share similarly diverse narratives of global connectivity shaped by their historical international influence.[4] The histories of place are thus interconnected through migration and language as well as those processes associated with colonialism and trade. These complex social and economic forces have shaped relationships between people and the connection and exchange of ideas. In acknowledgement of the fact that the national context is not always as important as the more geographically and culturally specific, transnational urban histories like the ones *Portable City* addresses are better termed 'transurban', as Richard Rodger suggests.[5] This book focuses on Glasgow's transurban relationships with parts of the USA, with Bernard Aspinwall's unsurpassed but imperfect *Portable Utopia: Glasgow and the United States, 1820–1920* providing the inspiration for its editors and authors. Published in 1984, Aspinwall's book traces Glasgow's determining influence on the transatlantic exchange of apparently shared Scotto-American ideas and values about democracy, Protestant moral theology, political

2 Charles McEvoy, *Brass Faces* (Boston: Houghton and Mifflin Company, 1913), 229.

3 'No City for Old Men', *The Economist* (25 August 2012).

4 These cities' histories have been influenced by colonialism, trade, and rapid urban growth. Like Glasgow, these second cities have served as commercial hubs, entry or exit points for migrants or places of tourism. Most importantly these metropolises have similarly influenced other places through diaspora and culture.

5 Richard Rodger, 'Putting the "Trans" into Transnational Urban History', in Nicolas Kenny and Rebecca Madgin, eds, *Cities Beyond Borders: Comparative and Transnational Approaches to Urban History* (London: Routledge, 2015), 211.

reform, and civic governance.[6] As fascinating and richly detailed as *Portable Utopia* is, it also has several important shortcomings. Upon its publication, J. M. Bumsted described Aspinwall's book as 'curiously comprehensive, if exasperating'.[7] John Schultz called it 'unmade history, without much in the way of structure or methodology'.[8] In its critics' views, the book's argument 'remains a suggestion only', leaving 'the nature, extent, and impact of the North Atlantic link … elusive' and the wider 'achievements' of the 'Scottish diaspora … abandoned'.[9] *Portable Utopia's* lack of a conventional index does not help the case for the defence and the reader has the impression that Aspinwall's earlier journal article on 'Glasgow trams and American politics' benefited from the discipline imposed by its publication in the *Scottish Historical Review*. Although influenced by Aspinwall's detailed survey of Glasgow's entanglement with 'transatlantic culture', our book deviates from the roadmap set out in *Portable Utopia* and seeks to amount to more than 'a suggestion'. By comparison, *Portable City* provides a succinct and evidential exploration of Glasgow's transatlantic relationships, one shaped by recent European and North American influences on urban history writing and diaspora studies. This collection is concerned with examining historical relationships, exchange and interaction between Glasgow and North America as filtered through the cities of the United States' East Coast. New York necessarily dominates these historical relationships, but Boston and Philadelphia are important too, as is Chicago in the Midwest.[10]

Glasgow's history was shaped by cultural and economic exchange which followed the avenues carved out by shipping routes, migration, trade, and empire. An inspection of the destination lists for Glasgow's passenger and merchant shipping fleets at the turn of the twentieth century reveals that they reached a

---

6 Bernard Aspinwall, *Portable Utopia: Glasgow and the United States, 1820–1920* (Aberdeen: Aberdeen University Press, 1984).

7 J. M. Bumsted, 'Reviewed Work(s): Portable Utopia: Glasgow and the United States, 1829–1920 by Bernard Aspinwall', *Journal of American History* 71/2 (1984), 393.

8 John Schulz, '*Portable Utopia: Glasgow and the United States, 1820–1920*, by Bernard Aspinwall', *Canadian Journal of History* 20/1 (1985), 131–132.

9 Ibid., p. 131; David Smith, 'Reviewed Work(s): Portable Utopia: Glasgow and the United States 1820–1920 by Bernard Aspinwall', *Albion: A Quarterly Journal Concerned with British Studies* 17/1 (1985), 123–124.

10 Jean Gottmann, 'Megalopolis or the Urbanization of the Northeastern Seaboard', *Economic Geography* 33/3 (1957),189–200. These are the cities of what Gotmann called the Megalopolis, the expansive urban region which in 1957 was home to almost 30 million Americans. While Glasgow, a city which has shrunk, is by no means a megalopolis, the wider region of greater Glasgow or the former Strathclyde holds almost 2 million people.

diverse array of locations. Glasgow's trade and merchant shipping crossed not only the Atlantic, but the Pacific and Indian Oceans arriving at strategically important ports and major population centres.[11] The interconnected nature of Glasgow's industry meant that seafaring was central to the city's economy. By the early twentieth century there were 120 merchant and passenger shipping companies operating on the Clyde. The city's shipping firms specialised in trade with the two key areas with which the west of Scotland had historical ties to: North America and South Asia.[12] These ties originated in empire, most obviously with the infamous Glasgow 'Tobacco Lords' made wealthy by the work of the enslaved on the plantations in Virginia and the West Indies. The Tobacco Lords' period of ascendancy was relatively brief, dating only from Scotland's union with England in 1707 to the American War of Independence (1775–1783). But as Craig Lamont establishes in this volume, this was a formative time best regarded as one of the multiple 'waves of empire' that have washed over the city. With its fortunes so bound to the colonial economy, it is noteworthy that Glasgow raised its own loyalist regiment to fight against the Continental Army in the Americas and, in 1819, would dedicate the first statue in George Square to one of its leading soldiers, Sir John Moore. As Lamont shows, waves of imperialism left their mark on the built environment and have had a determining influence on the city's identity. The statue of King William of Orange, erected in 1735 and commissioned by a member of the British East India Company is an early example of a trend in imperial mythmaking and memorial-building by Glasgow's elite. Over the course of the following two centuries, this trend toward imperialism would lead to the erection in the city of statues of Napoleonic War leaders Lord Horatio Nelson and the Duke of Wellington, as well as Earl Roberts, Field Marshall of the British Army and veteran of the 1857 Indian Mutiny.[13] Similarly, the Doulton Fountain, designed

---

11 Glasgow City Archive (GCA) Clyde Navigation Trust and Glasgow Chamber of Commerce, *True Reciprocity*, (Glasgow: Clyde Navigation Trust and Glasgow Chamber of Commerce, 1939), 2. TD 329/20/5. Glaswegian ships reached New York, Boston, Philadelphia, San Francsico, Newfoundland, Montreal, Vancouver, Jamaica, Georgetown, Lagos, Egypt, Nairobi, Durban, Cape Town, Hong Kong, Colombo, Bombay, Calcutta, Rangoon, Singapore, New Guinea, Perth, Christchurch and Auckland.

12 T. M. Devine and John M. MacKenzie, 'Scots in the Imperial Economy' in John M. MacKenzie and T. M. Devine, *Scotland and the British Empire* (Oxford: Oxford University Press, 2012), 240.

13 Victoria Cross Winner, Roberts had been involved in the Abyssinian Expedition, the Second Anglo-Afghan War and the Boer War. Despite few direct connections to Glasgow he was awarded an honorary degree by Glasgow University in 1913.

for the 1888 International Exhibition, celebrated the Canadian, South African and Australian dominions as well as the arts and industry of India, through physical representations of trappers, farmers and artisans. Yet, and though anti-imperialist activists launched an unsuccessful petition to remove the city's statue of Earl Roberts in 2017, Glasgow did not witness a violent reappraisal of its imperialist monuments comparable to the toppling of the Colston statue in Bristol in 2020. Yes, the nature and memory of Glasgow's early connections to North America and other parts of the world have been increasingly scrutinised, but, as Lamont shows, the high-water marks created by 'waves of empire' are still in evidence across Glasgow's cityscape.

The prevalence of statues to imperialist figures did not mean, however, that Glasgow was an undesirable location for visitors from Britain's former American colonies in the nineteenth century. Kevin James' chapter in this volume focuses especially on leisure travellers' embodied experiences of the oceanic voyage between Glasgow and New York. Using published accounts and diaries of middle-class American and Canadian travellers making the journey to Europe, James finds evidence of cultural tropes and discourses that were specific to the New York-Glasgow crossing and rooted in a sense of place. Though Glasgow was not the primary point of arrival for American visitors to Britain, there was something distinctive and evocative about sailing into the Scottish metropolis. As one writer observed in 1882, there were 'some curious facts connected with this entering of Europe by the Glasgow door ... Glasgow is nearly a thousand miles to the north of New York City'.[14] Another traveller described his 'mingled feelings of pleasure and sadness' as he 'saw the land fade out leaving a vague indistinct line on the distant horizon' on his outward journey from New York in 1889, but was similarly emotional upon first sighting the Irish and then the Scottish coast at the other end of the journey. As his ship made its way up the Clyde estuary and passed Dumbarton Castle, this traveller 'thought of the old associations of Scottish history' and 'began to realize that we were indeed nearing sacred historic ground'. This attraction to Scotland's ancient past, however, existed alongside a fascination with the modern City of Glasgow, whose 'lights ... presented a fine picture, which we sat and watched for a long time'.[15] James' assessment of these travellers' accounts opens a revealing porthole onto the transatlantic voyage to Glasgow.

---

14 E. A., 'New York to Glasgow', *The Literary World* 13/16 ('whole no., 198'), 12 August 1882, 264.

15 'Anonymous Travel Diary, 1889', Doc. 983, 6 & 24, Winterthur Library, Delaware.

In addition to welcoming people travelling to Scotland for leisure, Glasgow was home to individuals born in the United States too. Using evidence from census records for the period c. 1850–c. 1900, Tahitia McCabe's chapter provides invaluable and hitherto-unanalysed detail about Glasgow's American-born population in the nineteenth century. In truth, Americans represented only a small proportion of the city's alien residents, the majority of whom were Italians or Ashkenazi Jews many of whom were in transit to the New World. The relatively small number of Americans offers one explanation for the ease with which they assimilated into, and were welcomed by, the city's native population, certainly compared to the more voluminous and religiously 'other' Catholic Irish. The fact that most Americans in the city could be accommodated within prevailing notions of Scottish-British or Anglo-Saxon Protestant ethnicity eased their integration, though tensions did emerge in relation to the construction of Confederate ships by Glaswegian firms during the American Civil War, a reminder that geopolitics were not always conducive to good relations. Despite the relatively small numbers involved, McCabe's analysis of Americans in Glasgow sheds new light on the transience of the people involved in the population movements of the first era of globalisation.[16] Importantly, most of McCabe's Americans were 'Generation 0.5', people born in the United States to Scottish parents who had since returned to Glasgow, or 'twice migrants', Americans born to Irish parents who had moved to Glasgow.[17] These included Jane Walker, born in New York in 1844 to parents married in Glasgow in 1841, and her brother John Alexander, born in Connecticut in 1846. The Walker family returned to live in Glasgow in 1861, when Jane initially found work as a cotton weaver and her brother became a tinsmith. Other examples from McCabe's research include the Kings, American sisters born to Irish parents, and New York-born letterpress printer Gavin Connell who returned with his parents to their Glaswegian origins in the 1850s. This should all be one sentence: Business and family underpinned Glasgow's migratory transatlantic connections, for example, the Singer Sewing Machine Company agent Alonzo Kimball who moved to Glasgow in 1859 to act as his New York-based company's representative in the west of Scotland, and New Yorker and manager of Glasgow's famous Britannia Music Hall from the 1860s, Hubert Thomas Rossborough.

---

[16] Guillaume Daudin, Matthias Morys and Kevin H. O'Rourke, 'Globalization, 1870–1914', in Stephen Broadberry and Kevin O'Roarke, eds., *The Cambridge Economic History of Modern Europe: Volume 2: 1870 to the Present* (Cambridge: Cambridge University Press, 2010), 6, 16.

[17] Parminder Bhachu, *Twice Migrants*, (Sydney: Law Book Co of Australasia, 1985).

Business and trade between Scotland and the United States assume central importance in Kieran Taylor's chapter on Glasgow's 1938 Empire Exhibition. An attempt by the Scottish Development Council (SDC) to encourage inward investment into a city and national economy badly shaken by the Depression of the 1930s, the Exhibition in Glasgow's Bellahouston Park sought to showcase the best of Scottish industry and culture. Even though this was an event couched in the language of Scottish and British imperial connection, the Exhibition's organisers had more than one eye on American markets. It was no coincidence that transatlantic shipping company the Anchor Line was one of the Exhibition's sponsors, or that the event incorporated an 'America Day' on 4 July 1938. Taylor uncovers evidence of perhaps the most compelling demonstration of Glasgow and Scotland's attempt to court the United States in 1938: the SDC's appointment of Marie Kane as a good will ambassador, tasked with travelling to cities across the US and Canada to publicise the Exhibition and to counter American reticence to invest in Britain due to concerns about the likelihood of European war. Kane, a Dundonian born into an Eastern European Jewish family, was by her mid-20s familiar with the United States having been an art student in New York. Taylor's chapter argues that Kane's tour, along with Glasgow Lord Provost Patrick Dollan's official visit to the New York World Fair in 1939 and relationship with Mayor Fiorello La Guardia, placed Glasgow and Scotland at the heart of an evolving UK-US relationship in the immediate lead up to the Second World War.

Ideas as well as people and trade flowed along the various avenues of exchange between Glasgow and the urban United States. As scholars such as Frank Ninkovich and Daniel Rodgers have stablished, the nineteenth and early twentieth centuries witnessed the development of a new interconnectedness between liberal elites in Europe and North America.[18] This included the interest shown by American progressives such as Albert Shaw in the municipal reforms occurring in Glasgow (which Bernard Aspinwall wrote about), but also in Birmingham, Liverpool, Paris, and Berlin. The industrial cities of the old world which had contended with ill health and social disorder may have offered a blueprint for American city planners. In his chapter on public wash-houses from the 1870s to the 1950s in this volume, James Smyth adds new layers to understandings of such transatlantic conversations about health and public services. In considering the nostalgia associated with these services – through Tony Roper's 1980 splay

[18] Frank Ninkovich, *Global Dawn: The Cultural Foundation of American Internationalism, 1865–1890* (Harvard: Harvard University Press, 2009); Daniel T. Rodgers, *Atlantic Crossings: Social Politics in a Progressive Age* (Cambridge, MA: Belknap Press of Harvard University Press, 1998).

The Steamie – Smyth identifies the importance of notions of public service to the cultural memory of Glasgow. Smyth argues that it was empathy for the poor, rather than Foucauldian social control which underpinned urban reform. Frank Cohen, Glasgow's retired Master of Works, was shocked by what he regarded as a lack of basic public amenities when he visited New York in 1912. Chief among New York's shortcomings in his eyes were that it had no publicly owned laundry rooms, instead citizens were required to dry their washing outdoors in the polluted Manhattan air. Cohen contrasted this with Glasgow, where people could not only wash and dry their clothes in public facilities but could also clean their bodies in the municipal baths and swimming 'ponds'. Albert Shaw had urged the authorities to follow Glasgow's lead in providing wash-houses with adjoining baths. While the New York Tenement House Committee built a number of swimming baths it was unconvinced about the value and utility of wash-houses. Ironically, Smyth posits that the lack of public wash-houses in New York may have been the result of lessons learned from Glasgow's experience. For one, Shaw had reported that Glasgow's wash-houses were in fact under-utilised. There was perhaps also less of a need for such facilities in New York. The Tenement House Committee was shocked to learn in 1894 that so many tenements in Glasgow were single room homes and expressed relief that tenements in New York were generally larger and comparatively more comfortable. As incredibly dense as New York's streets were, overcrowding inside rooms was worse in Glasgow. In light of this, it seems likely that washing and drying clothes at home was a much more palatable option to New Yorkers than it was to Glaswegians. As Smyth indicates, this complicates – but does not obliterate – Frank Cohen's picture of Glasgow's much-vaunted and well-meaning provision of public cleaning facilities.

Graham MacSporran's chapter adds further nuance to histories of welfare in Glasgow and New York by exploring the relationship between economic fluctuations and indicators of health from 1900 to 1939. MacSporran divides his period into three distinct segments: 1900–1914, 1914–1919 and the Depression-hit 1930s charting the public health in the poorest districts of both cities. MacSporran identifies a paradox in his analysis of the health, questioning why morbidity and mortality rates did not worsen as a consequence of the mass unemployment and hardship of the Great Depression. MacSporran considers this question through discussion of the relief efforts that were implemented to assist the able-bodied unemployed in Glasgow and New York in this period, tracing changes in attitudes toward poverty across the first half of the twentieth century. This research adds greater detail to Aspinwall's and Rodgers' general picture of transatlantic progressivism, evidencing the varied successes of municipal authorities in Glasgow and

New York in navigating the interwoven challenges of public health and living standards in capitalist economies.

Similarities, differences, and interconnections between Glasgow and New York also emerge in Cameron McKay's research. McKay assesses the similarities and differences between the two cities' experiences of sectarianism in his chapter, asking why anti-Irish and anti-Catholic sentiment lingered long into the twentieth century in Glasgow. This was despite violent sectarianism in America lasting until the late nineteenth century. After the death of nearly 170 people during riots around an Orange parade in New York in 1871, the *New York Herald* observed that:

> in every large city in the world where Irishmen of the opposite creed do congregate peace is disturbed, property is imperilled, life is endangered once a year. This is true in Belfast and Dublin. It is true in Glasgow and Liverpool. It is true in New York, in Boston, in Chicago, in Saint Louis, in San Francisco.[19]

McKay reveals some striking and distinct contrasts between responses to the immigration of large numbers of Catholic Irish in the nineteenth century in the cases of Glasgow and New York. Though in both cities sectarianism was underpinned by a dominant nativist Protestantism (with its own Scottish American connections and characteristics, as established by Aspinwall) and was given renewed impetus by the arrival of Ulster Protestant religious organisations like the Orange Order, McKay's history tells of an improving situation for Irish Catholics in New York and a worsening situation for their counterparts in Glasgow, at least until the 1930s. Glasgow never experienced violence comparable to the 1871 Orange Parade Riots in New York. Nor did the Catholic Irish represent an organised and formidable political force as they did in New York through Tammany Hall. By the twentieth century American distaste for British imperialism encouraged popular support for Irish Home Rule. Further, immigration from Eastern Europe, Asia, Latin America and the increasing presence of African Americans within New York meant that the Irish, including Catholics, were tentatively accepted as American. The reverse was true in Scotland and in Glasgow, where the Catholic Irish were to an ever-greater extent regarded as an ethnically and religiously other. Like Smyth's and MacSporran's chapters, McKay's provides answers to questions left unanswered by *Portable Utopia*.

In 'Parallel Cities', Stephen Bowman explores modern Glasgow's historiography, explaining how the 'dear green place' should be considered as being in

---

19 'Religious and Political Reforms – Progress and Triumph of Popular Ideas', *New York Herald* (17 July 1871), 4.

correspondence with the world's most famous transnational city: New York. The chapter spans the latter half of the nineteenth century and the entirety of the twentieth to identify key discourses that – like those emphasising the 'light and darkness' or 'pleasure and pain' of city life – recur in the historiographies of both cities. The most important of these discourses centre on how Glasgow and New York have been at points embraced and rejected in their respective country's national histories, and on typically urban modernist concerns about 'decay' and 'rebirth'. Bowman uses scholarly as well as cultural material to assess why writers have chosen to analyse Glasgow's and New York's pasts in the ways they have often done. As Bowman notes, Patrick Dollan came away from his 1939 trip to the New York World's Fair with a lasting impression of a similarity between Glasgow and New York, in its architecture, culture, municipal politics and people. Bowman also examines Glasgow and New York's association with violence, something that has shaped cultural depictions of both cities transnationally. The Glasgow depicted in McCarthur and Kingsley-Long's *No Mean City* famously presented Glasgow's 1920's slums as blighted by violence perpetrated by angry young men in flat caps. *No Mean City* seemed to pre-empt *West Side Story* and its tale of ethnic and gang rivalry, set in the then dilapidated buildings of the Upper West Side.[20]. In the late twentieth century, poor living conditions, deindustrialisation and drugs would feed a cycle of crime in both cities. Just as the Big Apple came to terms with its reputation as 'Fear City' in the 1970s, Glasgow would too aim to address its own reputation for gangsterism, violence, drugs and murder. The 'Murder Capital of Europe' aimed to reduce homicide through initiatives such as the Violence Reduction Scheme in the new millennium.[21] Glasgow has also emulated New York in having a reputation for the seedy. Indeed, Glasgow's inclination toward a puritanical Presbyterianism was precisely in response to the presence and extent of vice throughout its history. The immorality of the city was embodied at various points by the myriad of brothels, shebeens, vaudeville theatres, bookies, dancehalls, and like New York later in the twentieth century, a network of X-rated cinemas. It was no coincidence, therefore, that the publicity

20 Avram Taylor, '"Are You a Billy, or a Dan, or an Old Tin Can?": Street Violence and Relations between Catholics, Jews and Protestants in the Gorbals during the Inter-War Years', *Urban History* 41/1 (2014), 124–140; Alistair Fraser, 'The Gorbals – Past and Present', *Sunday Feature*, BBC Radio 3, 10 October 2021, https://www.bbc.co.uk/sounds/play/m0010fyb.

21 DCI John Paterson, *Tackling Youth Crime, Violence & Disorder: A Partnership Approach* (Strathclyde Police & Fullbright Commission, 2013), 17. The Violence Reduction Scheme itself was modelled on the Boston Ceasefire Project, an initiative which assisted in reducing youth gun violence.

slogan 'Glasgow's Miles Better' took direct inspiration from the 'I♥NY' rebranding campaign.

Bowman is interested in Glasgow's transatlanticism. Whereas his first chapter focuses on historical and historiographical imaginings – that is to say on how historiography acts as another 'avenue of exchange' – his second chapter reflects on his own personal relationship to the city and its history. Inspired by Walter Benjamin, 'A Glasgow Imaginarium' explores the emotional dimension to writing about place. Bowman's focus is less on how people in the past experienced the city and more on how historians bring emotion, meaning, and experience to academic research and writing. He places himself and other contributors to *Portable City* at the centre of this inquiry, examining how their biographies have shaped this project. A reflective and autobiographical impetus has also informed the decision to include new photography in the book. On the surface, these photographs depict scenes that speak to the content of this chapter and others. Importantly, however, they reflect Bowman's sense of space, place and emotion.

Transnationalism is central to this volume and a transnational approach underpins the themes within each chapter. As indicated above, this transnational approach subscribes to a view of 'urban history as comparative and transnational practice'.[22] The people and ideas explored in this book were portable across national, local and urban boundaries, moulded by their transplantation across the Atlantic. Without denying the role of national identity among portable people and diasporic groups, Tanja Bueltmann's epilogue outlining a manifesto for 'translocal Scottish diaspora studies' underscores how more specific place-based connections interweave and overlap with national and transnational discourses. This is perhaps most obviously the case with 'the city', and the translocalism of Glasgow's portability is revealed by this book to lie in particular meanings attached to the transatlantic voyages of Kevin James' travellers and by the real and imagined connections and contacts between Glasgow and New York explored by Bowman, Smyth, MacSporran and McKay. Bueltmann's epilogue conceptualises the translocal – a term hitherto unapplied in Scottish historiography – and considers its precise meaning of Glasgow's 'portability'. She takes Allan Pinkerton, the Glasgow-born Chartist who emigrated to the United States and became famous for his private detective agency and strike-breaking activities. Pinkerton was a portable Glaswegian whose many social and political contradictions raise questions about the extent to which the cultural ideas that he took with him to the United States were locally or nationally framed. As such, Glasgow's

---

[22] Nicolas Kenny and Rebecca Madgin, '"Every Time I Describe a City": Urban History as Comparative and Transnational Practice', in Kenny and Madgin, eds, *Cities Beyond Borders*.

transatlanticism is defined not only by exchange between Scotland – or the United Kingdom – and the United States, but by the journeys back and forth between specific locales on either side of the Atlantic Ocean.

The book has been divided into three sections (and the chapters do not appear in the order in which they have been summarised here), each contributing a distinctive layer to our interpretation of Glasgow's connections with North America. *Part I: Impressions* includes those chapters that examine how Glasgow has been perceived, interpreted, and portrayed by people in the past. It includes Kevin James' chapter 'Ocean-Bound Travel from New York to Scotland in the Late Nineteenth Century'; Kieran Taylor's chapter '"You Americans have the wrong impression of Great Britain": Glasgow, the Empire Exhibition of 1938 and Transatlantic Relations', and Stephen Bowman's chapter 'Parallel Cities: Glasgow and New York'. *Part II: Experiences* focuses on the lives of residents and migrants to the city and includes Tahitia McCabe's chapter 'Americans in Glasgow, 1850–1900'; James Smyth's chapter '"Man, we fear, is naturally a dirty animal and so is woman": Keeping Clean in the City, c. 1870s–1950s'; Graham MacSporran's chapter 'Health and Wealth in Glasgow and New York,1900–1939'; and Cameron McKay's chapter 'Sectarianism in the City: A Comparison of Glasgow and New York in the Nineteenth Century'. *Part III: Imaginings*, considers the layers of meaning scaffolding Glasgow's urban history and cityscapes, and further conceptualises the city's emotional dimension, the importance of empire, and the precise nature of its transnationalism. It includes Bowman's second chapter 'A Glasgow Imaginarium: Portable Emotions, Experiences, and Meanings', Craig Lamont's chapter 'Glasgow and the British Empire'; and Tanja Bueltmann's epilogue 'People Make Glasgow Portable – and Portable People Make Glasgow: The Case for Translocal Scottish Diaspora Studies'.

At its heart, this book is about unpicking the historical avenues of exchange (which are trans*local* as much as trans*national*) that have made Glasgow feel, look, and exist the way it does. *Portable City* is emphatically not an exercise in simple comparison, as though drawing parallels between Glasgow and North American urbanism was an attempt at historiographical novelty. Comparison necessarily forms a part of this undertaking, but only in pursuit of a broader intellectual agenda that sees comparison and transnationalism (along with translocalism, transurbanism, and all such variations) as 'overlapping and mutually constitutive', for the researcher and the subject of research alike.[23] This book therefore seeks to explore how Glasgow's connections with other places acted as a proactive

[23] Kevin Ward quoted in Kenny and Madgin, 'Urban History as Comparative and Transnational Practice', 9.

influence on the history of the city and the people who live in it. Such an aim should interest anyone who has happened to see Glasgow city centre when it has been quite deliberately made to look American. With Hollywood film crews descending on Scotland's largest urban centre to shoot movies including *World War Z*, *Indiana Jones and the Dial of Destiny*, *The Running Man*, *Spiderman* and *Batman* (its derivatives) various city streets have been dressed with US-style fire hydrants, traffic lights, shop fronts, and automobiles. Of course, even before the set designers started their work, Glasgow's dense tenement housing, imposing public buildings adorned with classical features, and the network of overground railway bridges and arches give the city an architectural similarity to urban American counterparts, as shown by some of the photographs in this book. An *Economist* article from 2012 commented on some of these perceived similarities:

> Wander out into the streets of Glasgow after a whisky-soaked summer evening and it is possible to mistake the place for an unexplored corner of New York. The grand converted warehouses of Wilson Street might be SoHo; the reddish sandstone buildings of the West End were built while brownstone was cheap and fashionable on Manhattan.[24]

Crucially, however, Glasgow's historical interconnectedness with North America runs deeper than a mere passing resemblance to Gotham. As this book makes apparent, architecture is only the most visible feature of Glasgow's connections with North America. Hollywood actor Brendan Fraser's comments after his time filming the cancelled *Batgirl* film in the city perhaps said more than he realised: 'Gotham never looked better cast as Glasgow, Scotland. It's decaying and just gorgeous, and it looks like it's Gotham City. It's perfectly cast. You believe it no matter where you look at the town if you light it the right way.'[25] Fraser's remarks demonstrate not just that Glasgow 'looks like' DC Comics' fictional metropolis or that it only *appears* to embody the various economic and moral crises so characteristic of urban modernity; they also suggest that Gotham itself represents a particular version of Glasgow. Fraser presumably meant to say that Glasgow was 'cast as' Gotham, but the formulation appears to work just as well the other way around. His are remarks conditioned by the city's historical avenues of transatlantic exchange explored in this book.

---

24 'No City for Old Men', *The Economist* (25 August 2012). The article takes the comparison further: 'another is that Glasgow, for all its charms, is sick – and not metaphorically. Glaswegians die younger than other Britons and nobody knows why.'

25 Nicole Mitchell 'Brendan Fraser says Glasgow was "perfectly cast" as Gotham in Batgirl', *Glasgow Times* (8 February 2023).

PART I

Impressions

Ocean-Bound Travel from New York to Scotland in the Late Nineteenth Century

Kevin James

In 1870, jeweller Robert Dayton Williams of Albany, NY, set off on a three-month European tour, contending that the same journey 100 years ago would have presented few similarities with the one he now enjoyed – thanks to intervening 'modern improvements in steam communication on the mighty deep, and the network of railroads on land'.[1] Williams' reflections, penned in a short, humorously illustrated travel diary, are a rich source for exploring embodied dimensions of ocean-borne travel as he recounted a voyage across the North Atlantic, from New York to Glasgow. This chapter explores travel narratives along this route, anchoring its analysis in Williams' account, and interweaving descriptions of departures and shipboard life with wider evaluations of the Clyde and landfall as travellers drew close to, and reached, Scotland's metropolis. This chapter draws on three manuscript diaries written by American travellers: Williams' 1870 account, Martin Howard's 1874 travel narrative, and the account of an unnamed traveller in 1889. It also utilises three printed accounts: one a short article in a periodical in 1882 by an author identified only by the initials 'E. A.', another comprising two serialised letters by the scholar and one-time Swarthmore University President Edward H. Magill from 1889, and the last a book of serialised accounts of travel published by Canadian educator J. E. Wetherell in 1892. I argue that the overarching narrative of disruption, dislocation and discomfort attended the sea voyage. I also contend that far from being de-territorialised, narratives of shipboard travel such as Williams' depended on spatial framing practices centred on New York, Ireland, the Clyde, Greenock and Glasgow.

The cultural history of ocean travel has received significant recent attention from scholars, unmooring it from its traditional berth in transport history and economic history, as well as popular histories characterised by lavishly illustrated volumes, in order to explore the sensations and spectacles of seaborne travel, as

[1] Robert Dayton Williams travel journal 1870, 'Yankee Vandals Abroad, or Our Trip to Europe. 1870', Mclmss002299, William Clements Library, University of Michigan, Ann Arbor.

well as the place it occupied in the public imaginary.[2] The intersecting interests of global history, blue humanities and mobilities studies are evident in efforts to historicise the experience of movement across oceans and explore embodied experiences of sea travel, as well as complex regimes of sociability that were sited shipboard. The resulting scholarship has emphasised the cultural history of steam travel, and shown oceanic steam passages as essential, vital connections

---

2 An example of this approach to an early crossing is Stephen R. Berry, *A Path in the Mighty Waters: Shipboard Life and Atlantic Crossings to the New World* (New Haven: Yale University Press, 2015); Crosbie Smith, *Coal, Steam and Ships: Engineering, Enterprise and Empire on the Nineteenth-Century Seas* (Cambridge University Press, 2018); Douglas R. Burgess Jr, *Engines of Empire: Steamships and the Victorian Imagination* (Stanford: Stanford University Press, 2016); Anyaa Anim-Addo, '"The Great Event of the Fortnight": Steamship Rhythms and Colonial Communication', *Mobilities* 9/3 (2014), 43–57.; Ben Marsden and Crosbie Smith, *Engineering Empires: A Cultural History of Technology in Nineteenth-Century Britain* (Basingstoke: Palgrave Macmillan, 2005); Jonathan Stafford, 'Home on the Waves: Domesticity and Discomfort Aboard the Overland Route Steamship, 1842–1862', *Mobilities* 14 (2019), 578–95; Jonathan Stafford, 'A Sea View: Perceptions of Maritime Space and Landscape in Accounts of Nineteenth-Century Colonial Steamship Travel', *Journal of Historical Geography*, 55 (2017), 69–81; Frances Steel, *Oceania under Steam* (Manchester: Manchester University Press, 2017); Jonathan Stafford, *Imperial Steam: Modernity on the Sea route to India, 1837–74* (Manchester: Manchester University Press, 2023); Edward Gillin, 'Prophets of Progress: Authority in the Scientific Projections and Religious Realizations of the "Great Eastern" Steamship', *Technology and Culture* 56/4 (2015), 928–956. Roland Wenzlhuemer and Michael Offermann, 'Ship Newspapers and Passenger Life Aboard Transoceanic Steamships in the Late Nineteenth Century', *The Journal of Transcultural Studies* 3/1 (2012), 77–121; Mark A. Russell, *Steamship Nationalism: Ocean Liners and National Identity in Imperial Germany and the Atlantic World* (Abingdon: Routledge, 2020); Paul Ashmore, 'Slowing Down Mobilities: Passengering on an Inter-war Ocean Liner', *Mobilities* 8/4 (2013), 595–611. There has been a related interest in the cultural history of 'trust': see Crosbie Smith and Anne Scott, '"Trust in Providence": Building Confidence into the Cunard Line of Steamer', *Technology and Culture* 48/ 3 (2007), 471–96, and literary cultures of the ocean: see Shawna Ross, '"History, Mystery, Leisure, Pleasure": Evelyn Waugh, Bruno Latour, and the Ocean Liner', in Robert T. Tally, Jr, ed., *Literary Cartographies: Spatiality, Representation, and Narrative* (New York: Palgrave Macmillan, 2014), 111–125. Another notable area of interest, and departure from interest in the heavy engineering aspects of design history, has been on interior spaces and labour and their gendered dimensions. See Anne Massey, '"A Feminine Touch": Gender, Design and the Ocean Liner', *Journal for Maritime Research* 17/2 (2015), 169–181; Anne Wealleans, *Designing Liners: A History of Interior Design Afloat* (Abingdon: Routledge, 2006); Francesca Lanz, 'The Interior Decoration of Ocean Liners: A Chapter in Italian Design History', *Interiors* 3/3 (2012), 247–269; Frances Steel, 'Waitresses at Sea: Gender, Race and Service Labour on Ocean Liners, c. 1930s–1960s', *Women's History Review* 30/2 (2021), 223–240. Seaboard cultural sociabilities have been explored by George Burrows, 'Anything Goes on an Ocean Liner: Musical Comedy as a Carnivalistic Heterotopia', *Studies in Musical Theatre* 7/3 (2013), 327–45; Marlis Schweitzer, 'Networking the Waves: Ocean Liners, Impresarios, and Broadway's Atlantic Expansion', *Theatre Survey* 53/2 (2012), 241–67.

in an increasingly global network of mobility.[3] It has also identified the shipboard environment as a place of distinctive social, inter-cultural and class-conditioned experiences: it was a vital socially generative space, rather than a space 'in between'.

By its very nature, much of seaborne travel is de-territorialised, and scholarship has tended to chart a similar path, focusing on liminal experiences associated with the unusual regimes of sociability and mobility that took place on the azure main. While this chapter adopts a frame that encompasses shipboard activities and sensations at sea, it pays close attention to the specificity of the New York-to-Glasgow axis, which produced specific tropes in narratives of travel. There were many other places from which ships left the United States of America, and Canada, on their way to Scotland. In fact, Glasgow was not the primary port of arrival: in the nineteenth century, Britain's principal ports were London and Liverpool. As the leisure sector of transatlantic travel grew, Liverpool and Southampton were major passenger ports for both pleasure travellers, and Liverpool was a principal port for emigrants. But Glasgow was, like New York, also a transnational metropolis – a long-standing and growing centre of manufacture and commerce, and a gateway city for travellers to Britain and beyond (just as it too was a major port for emigrants).[4] In charting journeys between the Americas' largest metropolis to Scotland's largest city, this study engages with a particular subset of travel – journeys that were not connected to permanent migration. Embarking at, and disembarking from, these two sprawling cities framed the overall experience of travel: passengers' encounters with land and sea shaped accounts of farewells at bustling New York piers; of malady, monotony and fellowship at sea; and of encounters with Scotland mediated by views of Ireland, then travel through the Clyde estuary and disembarkation at Greenock.

3 See, for instance, Anyaa Anim-Addo, William Hasty, and Kimberley Peters, 'The Mobilities of Ships and Shipped Mobilities', in Anyaa Anim-Addo, William Hasty, and Kimberley Peters, eds, *The Mobilities of Ships* (London: Routledge, 2017), 11–23. Studies of onboard communications and reading practices have also underscored the networked nature of the shipboard experience: see Roland Wenzlhuemer, 'The Ship, the Media, and the World: Conceptualizing Connections in Global History', *Journal of Global History* 11/ 2 (2016), 163–86; Bill Bell, 'Bound for Australia: Shipboard Reading in the Nineteenth Century', *Journal of Australian Studies* 25/68 (2001), 5–18; Susann Liebich and Laurence Publicover, *Shipboard Literary Cultures: Reading, Writing, and Performing at Sea* (Cham: Palgrave Macmillan, 2021).

4 Sarah Palmer, 'Ports', in Martin Daunton, ed., *The Cambridge Urban History of Britain*, vol. 3 (Cambridge: Cambridge University Press, 2001), 133–50; Gordon Jackson and Charles Munn, 'Trade, Commerce and Finance', in W. H. Fraser and Irene Maver, eds, *Glasgow*, vol. 2, *1830–1912* (Manchester: Manchester University Press, 1996), 52–95; Forbes Munro and Tony Slaven, 'Networks and Markets in Clyde Shipping: The Donaldsons and the Hogarth, 1870–1939', *Business History* 43/2 (2001): 19–50.

Narratives of the North Atlantic Journey

Writing in the Boston periodical *The Literary World* in August 1882 of a July journey from New York to Scotland, 'E. A.' observed dryly that 'Nine hundred and ninety-nine letters have probably been written describing the Atlantic voyage. Can a thousandth furnish anything new? Hardly; and yet the old story can sometimes be made a little fresh by strange lips that try to tell it'.[5] There were indeed many such accounts, taking many different forms – manuscript diaries, pre-printed books with spaces for passengers to fill out observations in their own hand, and published narratives that appeared in newspapers, periodicals and books. Sometimes they were enfolded within wider narratives of travel, as the seaborne journey served as a prelude and a coda to wider travels. Robert Dayton Williams' account of shipboard travel, while ending somewhat jarringly with an accounting of his barber's expenses upon his arrival in Glasgow, constitutes a discrete account of the sea voyage. Notwithstanding a title on the front cover 'Yankee Vandals Abroad, or Our Trip to Europe. 1870' – that seems to promise a more geographically expansive compass, the book's bound form suggests that it was produced, and was intended to be read, as an account of his outbound ocean travels alone.

There are a number of ways of approaching the study of the ocean crossing, including the analysis of a single voyage.[6] Prosopographical approaches, by contrast, are hindered by the absence of multiple accounts of a single voyage. By proposing a particular crossing as its focus, and by analysing different treatments of it produced over nearly a quarter century, this chapter underscores the textual matrix of ocean travel. Narratives were prefigured by a widely circulating textual field.[7] No one narrative of travel was divorced from that field, as 'E. A.' underscored when referring to the vast ocean of extant accounts. Each narrative, then, must be read with this wider constellation of influences in mind. And elements

---

5 E. A., 'New York to Glasgow', *The Literary World* 13/16 ('whole no., 198'), (12 August 1882), 264.

6 Sarah Sharp Wenzlhuemer, 'A Place to Mourn?: Emotion, Genre, and Child Death in the Lady Egidia Shipboard Diaries', *Victorians: A Journal of Culture and Literature* 133/ 1 (2018), 30–43.

7 Tamson Pietsch, 'Bodies at Sea: Traveling to Australia in the Age of Sail', *Journal of Global History* 11/2 (2016), 209–28. There is a comparatively large body of scholarship exploring emigrant passenger diaries. See Sarah Sharp, 'A Place to Mourn?'. While the experiences of the recreational traveller have received attention in important works such as Cecilia Morgan's *A Happy Holiday': English-Canadians and Transatlantic Tourism, 1870–1930* (Toronto: University of Toronto Press, 2008), work remains to be done on the collective experience of specific routes and journeys.

of these accounts – notably ways in which the embodied experience of travel was narrated – were not unique to this route. Even along the same route, experiences were shaped by such factors as the size of a ship, which could alter the route of travel, impact the embodied experience of travel, and reduce time spent at sea. But there are important ways in which travel across this route fostered a particular set of sensations and dispositions. First, there was a trajectory that engendered heightened ideas of 'northernness' in comparison to other more travelled lines (notably from New York to Liverpool). As E. A. observed:

> There are some curious facts connected with this entering of Europe by the Glasgow door. How many readers of this letter realize the geographical position of Glasgow, and the effects of it? Glasgow is nearly a thousand miles to the north of New York City. A line run due west from Glasgow would pass within three hundred miles of the southern extremity of Greenland, cut the coast of Labrador well north of the Strait of Belle Isle, traverse Hudson's Bay, and strike the lower regions of Alaksa. The same line run due east would leave Moscow to the south as it crossed Russia, and traverse Siberia well to the north of Irkutsk, coming out at Kamschatka. Glasgow, then, is emphatically in the Northern regions.[8]

This path of travel brought the traveller in contact with peculiar spectacles: the climate was tempered by the Gulf Stream and the Northern Lights were on prominent display. And while all transatlantic travellers' experiences of temporal disruption involved a gain of time requiring a daily change of watches, this trajectory introduced more dramatic differences in the lengths of days.[9]

Experiences of seaborne travel were intermediated by the segregated spaces of sleep and sociability. They could produce very different physical, mental and emotional responses to travel, with steerage passengers in the more spartan, shared spaces of the ship liable to feel the violent movement of ships when they were caught up in storms (Robert Dayton Williams recorded twenty-five cabin and seventy-five steerage passengers on board his journey). Shipboard life encompassed a broad variety of experiences shaped by gender, social class and nationality. While it was not uncommon, especially in the early decades of the twentieth century, for whole ships to be given over to tourists, recreational travellers often shared the crossing with emigrants, frequently of many nationalities (especially if they were coming *to* North America in this period), as well as ships' crews drawn from many backgrounds. Some passengers were leaving home, others returning. Some had deep connections to one or both of the cities that marked the beginning and end of the ocean journey, while others had only a fleeting encounter with

8 E. A, 'New York to Glasgow', 264.
9 Ibid., 264.

them as they arrived in New York to depart by ship or disembarked in Glasgow to quickly move on to other places. For some it was their first trip across the ocean. Others had travelled the same route, or another, before and therefore their travels were prefigured not only by a broad textual field, but also by personal experience. Recreational travel constituted one motivation for travel, but it could well be mixed with others (business abroad and health-related travel, for instance). With these caveats in mind, however, key themes unite accounts explored here: sensorial 'captivity' by the sea, unique forms of social engagement shaped by the affordances of the ship and the liminal spaces of the sea travel; and an arrival in Glasgow mediated by initial encounters with Ireland and then the Clyde estuary.

Kinetic Dimensions of North Atlantic Travel

Robert Dayton Williams remarked that 'modern improvements in steam communication' had transformed modern oceanic travel. They had certainly accelerated travel and, in a period of intensive immigration from Britain and Europe to continental Europe, as well as extensive commercial links and growing recreational travel, more people were crossing the ocean than ever before. The growth of the firm – the Anchor Line – on whose ship Williams travelled, and the level of traffic on that path generally, testified to the growth of the popular New York-to-Glasgow crossing. The route was plied by several companies in the nineteenth century, carrying both post and packets: notably the Glasgow and New York SS Company Ltd (1851–1859). From 1852, Captain Thomas Henderson became a partner in the sailing-ship line Handysides & Co of Glasgow (established in 1838). Its first months operating steam engine routes under the Anchor Line name between Glasgow and New York, starting in October 1856, began inauspiciously with the loss of a vessel in February 1857, but by the 1870s it was a dominant firm on the Glasgow-to-New York route. Its routes and fleet expanded, and the firm was taken over by the Cunard Line in 1911.[10] The firm was not the only service connecting the two cities along a route that stopped in the north of Ireland (leading to the rapid development of Moville in Co. Donegal, on the north-western coast of Lough Foyle, as a point of embarkation and disembarkation). By the end of the nineteenth century, three lines were plying the route between the two cities: the Anchor and Allan Lines carrying passengers and freight (each with one, and sometimes two sailings weekly), and the Donaldson Line, which,

10 See R. S. McLellan, *Anchor Line, 1856–1956* (Glasgow: Anchor Line, Ltd., 1956).

unlike the other two, specialised in freight.[11] The larger and more powerful ships could move directly from port to northern port, ploughing (as E. A. noted of the 1,200 horse-powered *Alaska*) through 'fogs and icebergs' to reach Queenstown, Co. Cork from New York more speedily than the slower *Circassia* heading to Glasgow.[12] The embodied experience was correspondingly varied too, as sights, temperatures, winds and waves all impacted in different ways on the ship, and on passengers' experiences of the journey.

Overall, the crossing was becoming much faster. Steam power had greatly increased the speed of crossings, especially by the largest ships that were driven at high horse-power, consuming vast quantities of coal. By 1896 the record holder on the New York-to-Glasgow route was listed in the *World Almanac and Encyclopaedia* as the Anchor Line's *City of Rome* steamship, which in August 1886 had completed the journey in six days, twenty hours and thirty-five minutes (over two hours less time by the same ship in the opposite direction one year earlier).[13] Robert Dayton Williams was acutely aware of the comparative speed with which he travelled along the Atlantic. In the time that it might have taken 'one of our old ships, the Constitution' to sail across the Atlantic, Williams marvelled that an 1870 traveller could 'cross the ocean [,] visit England, Ireland, Scotland – cross the channel and take a peep at many of the principal cities on the Continent. Then [sic] return to America'. Even the Yankee, whose nature Williams insisted was to link inseparably time and money, would 'throw aside cares of business' for the sake of such travels, in light of such efficiency.

Suggesting that the efficiency of steam had induced even Americans to prise themselves away from work and embrace a transatlantic holiday, Williams also revealed the motivations behind his travels. Styling himself a 'Yankee under the weather', Williams proclaimed that one goal was to see whether, through 'a few excursions through the Bogs of Ireland – A peep at the 'Highland' scenery, while feasting on Scottish oatmeal, and a glimpse at Old H'england, through smoked glass – or its equivalent – a LONDON fog', might not 'around up to healthy action the dormant blood, and infuse new life and action into every muscle and

---

11 *Highways of Commerce: The Ocean Lines, Railways, Canals, and Other Trade Routes of Foreign Countries*, vol. 12. Issued from the Bureau of Statistics, Department of State, in 1895. Reissued, with Supplementary Reports of Ocean Routes for Steam Vessels, from the Bureau of Foreign Commerce, Department of State, in 1899 (Washington: Government Printing Office, 1899), 202.

12 E. A., 'New York to Glasgow', 264.

13 *The World Almanac and Encyclopaedia 1896*, 3/28 (January 1896). ('Issued by the Press Publishing Co., New York), 214.

limb'.[14] His wife, Anna, hoping that her own health might benefit from a change of climate, concurred, and so they set their sights on a tour of Britain and Ireland, in search of rejuvenation.

In his whimsically illustrated narrative, narrated in a jocular tone, Williams described a departure from Pier 22 aboard the SS *Australia*. It did not begin auspiciously, with the loss of a trunk. Williams captured the episode in verse:

> 'By jove' it is hard, as everyone knows
> For a girl to see Europe without any clothes
> For how can she travel in comfort when there
> If her trunk, left behind, she has nothing to wear.[15]

In a description that broke with the otherwise whimsical and often exaggerated-seeming tone of the narrative, Williams, who was accompanied to the pier by his daughter Maggie, as well as by his wife, wrote in a poignant vein of fond farewells whispered in their ears by 'Father, Mothers, Sisters & friends accompanied by Kisses and a few silent tears'. He and Anna then began their journey across the ocean to Scotland.

If Williams declared himself to be a 'Yankee under the weather', the sea voyage only amplified his maladies. The seaborne voyage engendered a variety of emotional and physiological responses which Williams captured in dramatic illustration and prose. The North Atlantic, with its strong winds, dark storms and rolling waves, cultivated violent bodily reactions. Cold winds often limited passengers' time on deck and necessitated 'protection' from the elements as they scrambled below deck. Williams described episodes of seasickness – 'Everybody (excepting one or two old salts)' – and remained below deck for a day amid violent seas, with lashing rain and surging waves.[16] This confinement, while physically isolating passengers from each other, was, paradoxically, not altogether socially isolating. The atomisation of passengers forged its own shared experience, for the crossing was undergirded by a common encounter with *mal de mer*. Queasiness and seasickness linked individual bodies to a wider social world at sea. The pitching back and forth, the noises that the wind and waves engendered: all these external forces produced remarkable sensorial experiences onboard. Williams wrote at one point of the ship being caught up in nature's fury as it found itself in the middle of a 'terrible equinox gale', the ship creaking, the dining china rattling, and water infiltrating the cabins – 'Vast mountains of waves

[14] Williams, Travel Journal 1870, np.
[15] Ibid.
[16] Ibid.

following each other in quick succession with an inexpressible sort of motion – dashing over decks with a crash – one moment the bow under water – next moment the stern in a similar predicament', with crew members on board thrown violently about.

Williams also underlined how the tempestuousness of nature undermined planned activities, from games to meals. The day after the extraordinary violence of movement described above, entertainments on deck could not rouse the couple from a prone position. By the third day they 'were allowed to crawl up on deck ... where we enjoyed the fresh sea air, and drank our health, with considerable gusto, in copious draughts of Gruel, and by the afternoon he began to feel well again'.[17] As the ocean crossing continued, Williams reported 'our digestive organs getting a little stronger', and shifted his remarks to the ship that conveyed him.[18] A passing familiarity with the route of passage, perhaps gleaned onboard, provided some sense of orientation, even as Williams jokingly professed ignorance of the geography of the 'Banks' they were due to pass.[19] But, for the most part, they were engulfed by the sea as far as they could train their eyes, which induced levels of disorientation and dislocation to match the unfamiliar and unsettled bodily experiences.

As the seas calmed, Williams recorded a remarkable change of temper, focus and routine, reflecting by 23 September (a week into the journey) that 'about all we have to think of is when will the next meal be ready for us' and then 'if we will ever be in a condition to eat again'. He had not felt settled since coming aboard. 'A dog's life is this sea business' he wrote on his seventh day at sea. Backgammon and a well-stocked library occupied his time. When halfway to Derry, he wrote humorously but with clear sincerity that the travails of his voyage led him to eagerly await landfall: 'This "Auld" Ireland indeed I never knew how much I loved you. Why I would be willing to kiss the "Blarney Stone" – or any other brick bat could I but press its greeny sods'.[20] This yearning to be on *terra firma* reflected unsettling physical and psychic responses to the unpredictability and unsettling nature of life at sea.

When Rev. Martin S. Howard embarked upon a similar journey on 14 May 1874, his manuscript journal, 'A Bell Line Through Gt. Britain', shared some appraisals of the voyage, though in some respects he and Williams were markedly different

---

[17] Ibid.
[18] Ibid.
[19] Ibid.
[20] Ibid.

travellers.[21] If Williams was motivated to return to vigorous health Howard's professed purpose was to enlarge the mind: 'The advantages of travel are manifold', he wrote:

> It quickens the intellect, enlarges the field of observation, and if one is gifted with a reasonable degree of common sense, it makes a man extremely modest and unpretending. The little he sees and enjoys is but a small taste of the unbounded delights which lie hidden out of his sight.

With this observation, Howard set out under sunshine from New York, 'steamed along the picturesque shores of New Jersey', and headed out to sea, where he marvelled at the Atlantic spreading out 'in wondrous infinity', and the sonorous beating of the 'ship's heart' that carried them forward: 'nights coming down, day creeping over the waters, with now and then some stoppage of engines, or flight of birds, or sound or sight mysterious' to break the monotonous and regular path forward. Howard also fell victim to the same *mal de mer* from which Robert Dayton Williams suffered. Indeed, it constituted to Howard 'one of the great drawbacks of the sea'. In remarks that hinted at his familiarity with other accounts of the crossing, Howard remarked that a 'record of this kind' was 'incomplete without allusion to it':

> You have all heard of sea sickness. It is general topic of remark on shipboard almost as common as the weather is on land. It is not an agreeable sensation. Indeed, it may be termed disagreeable even. There is something peculiarly uniting about it, so that with however light a step and elastic spirits a man sets forth on deck, he often experiences a considerable revolution of feeling before many hours have passed.[22]

Writing with euphemism, and in the third person, of how a man under the 'full state of this malady' is 'not in a state of high enjoyment', Howard cautioned that it would inflict a depressed condition on the sufferer and undermine his anticipation of a 'pleasurable' voyage. A cleric himself, he recorded his displeasure with the captain surmising that a 'rough and strong' passage had been foreshadowed by numerous ministers on board. In fact, the presence of clerics on board was commonly remarked upon by travellers.[23] Men of the cloth were part of a vibrant transatlantic clerical community engaged in intensive interaction and coordination

---

21 Travel journal, Martin S. Howard Papers, c. 1870–1880s, SCO 00847, SC Box 48, Swem Libraries Special Collections Research Centre, College of William and Mary. The journal is not paginated. The first leg of travel, across the Atlantic, is entitled 'A Bee Line Through Gt. Britain'.

22 Travel journal, Martin S. Howard Papers, np.

23 Ibid.

in the Victorian period.[24] As we shall see, they were amongst passengers who were called to perform their conventional 'work', especially on Sundays. They were critical to defining the unusual rhythm of life that broke with conventional diurnal experiences and were also entangled in a narrational strategy through which writers trained their eyes on certain occupational types aboard.

An unidentified traveller in 1889 found space in his manuscript account of the crossing from New York to Glasgow to remark on the number of ministers present, enumerating 'only seven ... three Presbyterian, two Methodist, and one Universalist' (perhaps his own membership in this group was revealed by the omission of one of this number in their denominational enumeration, and by his involvement in a heated theological debate on the second day at sea). This traveller, journeying with his companion, a 'Mr Roy', to Great Britain and France from 29 April 1889 to 12 June 1889, produced a manuscript account that included his journey from Oakland, Maine. He had visited family in Biddeford before returning to Portland and embarking on a steamer for a rough journey to Boston.[25] A short sightseeing visit there preceded a trip to New York aboard a steamer: he awoke to apprehend a vista of the 'vast and extended city'.[26] After inspecting their steamship and making preparations for the trip, he and his companion set about exploring the city.[27] His account reminds us that many passengers were departing from a city as unfamiliar to them as the one that they were crossing the sea to visit. Like Robert Dayton Williams, this traveller professed to be deeply affected by the sight of farewells offered to passengers as they boarded the ship on 2 May: 'Some of them', he wrote, 'it seemed as though they never could say the last word. It was cry, and laugh and kiss, again and again till word was given that the plank was to be drawn'.[28] Passengers and those on the wharf waved handkerchiefs to signal goodbye, and the vessel steamed away.

As their ship set off from the pier, the *Nebraska* arriving from Glasgow passed them by. The traveller admitted that in three months he was certain to share the glad feelings of those returning home on that ship.[29] Like other accounts, the close-up view of the Statue of Liberty supplied a novel experience as he sailed out to sea, and '[i]t was with mingled feelings of pleasure and sadness that I saw

[24] Andrew T. N. Muirhead, 'We Have an anchor that keeps the soul: Religious Observance on Glasgow's Anchor Line and Other Scottish Emigrant Ships, 1870–1900', *Scottish Church History* 40/1 (2010), 159–184.

[25] Anonymous Travel Diary, 1889, Delaware, Doc. 983, 1, Winterthur Library, Delaware.

[26] Ibid., 2.

[27] Ibid., 3.

[28] Ibid., 4.

[29] Ibid., 5.

the land fade out leaving a vague indistinct line on the distant horizon'.[30] Now as the sun set, from his set on the deck, his gaze took in nothing 'but a world of water'; his thoughts turned to 'that little house in Maine, where the idols of my heart are treasured', and he bowed his head in prayer.[31] While he expressed confidence as the ship went to sea that he would not join those passengers and his own companion in illness 'unless it became very much rougher', by the next day he succumbed, though the seas were calm. He recounted his determination that seasickness should not prevent him from eating.[32] By 4 May sea conditions had changed and many passengers were now ill.[33] At one point, several days into the voyage, as calm seas helped to restore all but the most ill passengers to health, evening brought strong winds, and as the ship rolled, he found himself lying on the floor, and went on deck 'to pay my morning tribute to the sea'.[34] The affliction continued and became an overarching narrative uniting his diurnal entries in a continuous index of wellbeing (in which his travelling companion's condition featured prominently, too).

The Sabbath was an important marker in shipboard life. Sunday, 5 May, gave the writer occasion to reflect on his own church and Sunday school, and to participate in a service in the dining saloon led by a Methodist. Shipboard life often bred an ecumenical culture. Sundays supplied a yardstick by which travel was measured temporally, when so many days bled into each other. The trope of Sabbath days as ways of counting the voyage's length appeared prominently in travel accounts, in part because divine services were significant markers of the shipboard calendar, which partly suspended the conventional diurnal practices (indeed the diary itself helped to locate a writer within the week, and the prominence of the Sabbath anchored their narratives). They also offered distinctive moments for class mixing onboard.[35]

The next day, the passengers were 'beginning to get acquainted',[36] and he recorded the passengers' activities as if capturing them in a picture: 'a party of ladies playing cards, a sad faced young man reading a book, an old pleasant faced Presbyterian minister reading, three or four children at play and making things lively, a Methodist minister's wife looking with a sad face and pained expression at the ladies playing cards, two cabin waiters asleep, a young lady quite pretty

30 Ibid., 6.
31 Ibid., 6.
32 Ibid., 10.
33 Ibid., 11.
34 Ibid., 14.
35 Muirhead, 'We Have an Anchor'.
36 Anonymous Travel Diary, 1889, Doc. 983, 13.

doing some sort of fancy work in a loop'.[37] This self-representation of the diarist as a kind of arm's-length ethnographer was common to many diaries, and reveals much about authorial self-positioning, as well as regimes of shipboard sociability.

Social Dimensions of the Transatlantic Crossing

The observational lens described above supplied a means through which writers narrated distance, applied critical faculties and recounted shipboard life in a semi-comical vein by assembling a cast of characters for readers – each member a representative occupational or national type. If travellers such as Robert Dayton Williams explored the departure from New York, the sea voyage was the focus of E. A.'s brief 1882 account of her voyage in *The Literary World*. E. A. remarked that the 140 or 150 passengers on the Anchor Line's *Circassia* would transform popular understandings of 'Circassian beauties' from the 'veiled females of the East' to 'belles of New York, Boston and Chicago, very much wrapped up as to the feet as well as to the head, and with hair given to the winds and generally dishevelled'.[38] E. A.'s article focused on peculiar regimes of sociability that characterised the crossing. The nameless passengers became a suite of representative types: 'The tall and military-looking Canadian', who had been ejected from home as a boy, and now is captaining a boat of which 'he never trod a stiffer and steadier' example; and two large excursion parties, one, numbering fifteen to twenty belonged to 'Jenkins', former manager of Cook's Agency in New York. In addition to these 'excursionists', who formed one body of traveller in E. A.'s assessment, there was the 'usual assortment of figures and characters on board, the study of whom is an endless entertainment'.

This narrative exercise, which constituted the writer as a distant observer, was used to assemble passengers into a suite of types. E. A. counted eleven men of the cloth ('enough, it was well said, to sink the ship'); a 'handsome young Swede from Boston' travelling to spend summer in his native country 'a heavily bronzed young Scotchman from Edinburgh' returning from North American travels; another 'older and fatherly Scotchman from Edinburgh, with three quiet daughters', returning from a tour of Asia; a Presbyterian doctor of divinity from Orange, New Jersey, with a 'clever gift at sketching, and a remarkable sketch-book as a result of it'; a 'young Scottish mother, the married daughter of an eminent Scotch divine', travelling with her husband and baby to visit her parents; Professor C. O. Thompson of Worcester, Massachusetts, with a family party of five, heading out

[37] Ibid., 13.

[38] E. A., 'New York to Glasgow', 264.

to study English and Continental technical schools ahead of assuming charge of one in Indiana; a young Methodist divinity professor heading for a year to study in Greece; a Baptist professor from Newton and Brown University doing the same thing; and the son of a Congregational minister in Manchester, England about to matriculate at Oxford; 'and so forth and so on'.[39] E. A. also engaged in an observational and narrational practice that was by no means unique to this account – one in which the prominence of 'Scotch' men and women reflected the distinctive geography of the crossing

In his serialised account of travel from New York to Scotland aboard the Anchor Line's *Circassia* published in 1889 in the Philadelphia-based *Friends' Intelligencer and Journal*, Edward H. Magill, president of the Quaker-founded Swarthmore College, opined, as E. A. had, that '[a] voyage by sea is perhaps too common now, and too monotonous to be of special interest to your readers'. Nonetheless, he contended that 'I believe that there are many among them who will be glad to hear how we are faring in this the beginning of our year abroad'.[40] Like others, he described passing Sandy Hook as a signal of the departure from New York. His first morning was spent in the ecumenical company of Episcopalians at service, and the first days were passed in smooth seas and good weather.[41] Magill found himself transfixed by the sea on this, his fifth time crossing it, with its 'thousand changing hues and aspects', and marvelled that even in a day of modern communication, the vastness of the sea meant days could pass 'without the sight of single sail'.[42] In contrast to the monotony registered by other readers, he found amidst good conversation and brisk walks 'that inexpressible sense of perfect *rest* which comes from an ocean voyage'.[43]

Robert Dayton Williams's accounts of the travails of the sea crossing were especially evocative, but they were by no means unique, as these other accounts attest. Embodied discomfort, as well as new regimes of sociability and observational practices – during which fellow passengers were gazed upon and enumerated from a studied distance – were tropes in accounts of transoceanic journeys. The North Atlantic, with its chilly climate and churning seas, offered apt space to underscore the travails of the crossing. In an 1892 compilation of serial accounts published in 1890 in the Ontario newspaper the *Strathroy Age*, J. E. Wetherell, writer educator and sometime teacher of Canadian humourist Stephen Butler

39 Ibid., 264.

40 Edward H. Magill, 'Experiences at Sea: Letter from Edward H. Magill', *Friends' Intelligencer and Journal*, *Intelligencer*, 46/ 38, *Journal* 17/869 (21 September 1889), 595.

41 Magill, 'Experiences at Sea', 595.

42 Ibid.

43 Magill, 'Experiences at Sea', 596.

Leacock,[44] whose impetus to travel was to view 'scenes associated with the charms of history and poetry',[45] described a familiar, fraught seaborne journey beginning with 'bustle and confusion' on the Brooklyn Pier of the State-Line Steamship Company as passengers boarded the *Nevada*.[46] Wetherell recounted how 109 saloon-class passengers were seen off by at least twice or three times that number of people, some being 'mere idlers attracted hither by the curiosity of the moment', with others hawking wares to embarking passengers, and yet more being friends bidding farewell.[47]

As a panoramic view of New York left passengers beyond, Wetherell described an emotional response to the vastness of the sea that lay all around him: 'A strange sensation of solitariness takes possession of the traveller who leaves his native land for the first time to cross the broad ocean alone', he wrote (studiously avoiding in this printed account the first-person favoured by Williams in his manuscript account), 'and who, as he paces the deck while the distant hills are just receding from sight, sees no familiar face amid the groups that congregate here and there to take the last peering look at the vanishing continent that contains all that is dearest in life to them and to him'.[48] Comfort was offered in the 'fellowship of an exciting book, or still better, the cheering companionship of living men and women'.[49] Happily, he wrote, such companionship was in abundance. But like so much aboard the ship, social dynamics assumed an unfamiliar, if albeit welcoming, form: 'The ocean has a special code of its own. With the last sight of land all the supernumerary conventionalities of town and city, often stiff and formal as frowning peaks and rugged mountains, are thrown overboard'; within a short period of departure, every passenger would 'have a score of acquaintances, and two of three new friendships will be already in the bud'.[50] The alacrity with which social bonds developed was, to Wetherell, a unique feature of life at sea.

Wetherell's account, like E. A.'s briefer narrative, offered readers a cast of traveller 'types' – passengers often reduced to a descriptor by place of origin and trade

44 Cecilia Morgan, 'Wetherell, James Elgin', in *Dictionary of Canadian Biography*, vol. 16, University of Toronto/Université Laval, 2003–, accessed 3 December 2023, http://www.biographi.ca/en/bio/wetherell_james_elgin_16E.html.

45 J. E. Wetherell, *Over the Sea: A Summer Trip to Britain* (Strathroy, ON: Evans Brothers, 1892), preface, np.

46 As Douglas R. Burgess Jr. has written, these were no mere occasions for passenger embarkation, but spectacles in their own right. See Douglas R. Burgess Jr, *Engines of Empire* (Stanford University Press, Redwood City CA, 2016).

47 Wetherell, *Over the Sea*, 5.

48 Wetherell, *Over the Sea*, 6.

49 Ibid., 7.

50 Ibid., 7.

whose company would be intense but ephemeral – 'amiable and interesting people', but also 'odd specimens of humanity'. Amongst them Wetherell enumerated 'the Chicago merchant who, after the toil and moil of many busy years which have won him a substantial fortune, is going to Europe with his big and clever son, to visit places of which he knows as little as he does of the constellations in the heavens above him'.[51] There was also the 'dandy from the same western city whose assiduous efforts at subduing feminine hearts are as ludicrous as they are vain'; the 'glum and taciturn preacher from New York who frowns on harmless hilarity and grinds his teeth with fire-and-brimstone vigor at the sight of a game of cards'; the 'frisky middle-aged gentleman from Rochester whose constant antics are very diverting and who is the more interesting on account of the accomplishments and attractions of his lively wife';[52] 'the dyspeptic from the west who, instead of keeping his incurable ailment under cover, is constantly craving and asking for the sympathy of indifferent and disgusted fellow-voyagers'; the 'chronic grumbler from New England who hardly opens his lips except to cavil and censure'; the 'old Scottish lady who is crossing the sea with her dog "Bobby"'; the 'jolly fat bachelor from Toronto whose genial countenance, affable manners and delightful talk make him the most striking on board and "the observed of all observers"'.[53] In sum, Wetherell remarked later in the chapter, the only detraction to the romance of life at sea were fellow passengers.[54] For a passenger to be 'in touch with the spirits of the wave and wide and sea' required isolation not only from the grinding noises of the engines, but also the social world of the ship.[55] This observation and appraisal of fellow passengers was a central narrational conceit and supplied a way for writers to present distance from other passengers in the strange social realm of the ocean crossing. Intriguingly, it features less prominently in the manuscript accounts explored in this chapter, suggesting that it may have constituted a narrative strategy in published accounts of travel to establish an authorial persona, as well as to inject humour to appeal to a wide readership.

Landfall(s) on the Transatlantic Crossing

As we have seen, Robert Dayton Williams joined many other writers who recounted an unsettled journey from New York to Glasgow. There were real

51 Ibid., 7.
52 Ibid., 7–8.
53 Ibid., 8.
54 Ibid., 10.
55 Ibid., 22.

consequences for the planned arrival of Williams' ship: the captain proved fallible by a mistaken change of course, and thirteen days after departure land was reached in Moville, Co. Londonderry, where some steerage passengers disembarked, and the steamship continued to Glasgow. Within sight of land, on 1 October 1870, Williams rhapsodised about the sites he beheld from the vantage of the ship: the Giant's Causeway evoking the Hudson River Palisades (though the Irish site 'was more elevated and grander'); then, finally, the 'bold outlines of the Scottish mountains' came into view, albeit partly obscured by fog:

> But what we saw, in beauty and grandeur, is far beyond pen to describe – Soon we passed Dumbarton Castle – this is a natural fortification on the Clyde – Used in the early Scottish wars, as a stronghold for defence. It resembles in outlines an old time Castle with irregular formal towers.[56]

> The River CLYDE, properly speaking, is some 23 miles long – Some half century ago a person could wade, without fear of drowning up its entire length – Now vessels navigate it when drawing 25 foot of water – We pass immense ship yards with large numbers of iron hulls, in different stages of completion – this Clyde is a crooked narrow river. The turns are so short and abrupt that it is as much as (2) two tug boats – (one at bow – and stern) can to do keep the steamer from getting run aground.[57]

The relief that attended the first sight of land was a trope in travel accounts. J. E. Wetherell expressed the 'delightful throng of new sensations' on his first sight of Europe – Innistrahull, off the Donegal coast, where the ship touched before proceeding. Like Williams, he wrote of how passengers glimpsed 'green fields and rugged cliffs' along the Irish coast as the ship plied closer to its destination – Glasgow. 'The sail', he wrote, invoking locomotion of old, 'through the North Channel past the Mull of Cantire [sic], and up the Firth of Clyde past Arran and Bute prepare us by degrees for the "Land of brown heath and shaggy wood/Land of the mountain and the flood"'.[58] Soon the ships reached Greenock. Wetherell's narrative of a run up the tide invoked many elements of William's narrative:

> The principal object of interest to be seen as we move slowly up the river is Dumbarton Castle, – a ruin as old as the Scoto-Saxon monarchy, if not dating back to Roman times. The scenery of the Clyde is very pleasing. On one side of the river are the highlands and lochs and crags crowned with ancient castles, and on the other parks and farms and manor halls. Presently the river becomes little more than a large canal enclosed between the banks of pastoral meadows. As we approach the city we see the forests of tall masts and the skeletons of innumerable ships and are not surprised to learn that

56 Williams, Travel Journal 1870, np.
57 Ibid.
58 Wetherell, *Over the Sea*, p. 13.

> this Glasgow is perhaps the most famous city in the world for the building of sea-going vessels. We have now reached our port and the birth-place of the sturdy vessel that has carried us safely over three thousand miles of sea.[59]

As for the arrival of the unnamed author of the 1889 manuscript account, he recorded that when waking on 12 May 'the rough broken out-line of the North of Ireland it was a welcome sight after being out of sight of land for ten days' (though within two hours thick fog had obscured that welcome view).[60] While no stop in Ireland was recorded, the same day they 'came in sight of the main land of Scotland in the far distance'; as the fog lifted, the islands within view appeared, 'hilly and rough'; as the ship approached then, he remarked that they 'were beautiful to me to look upon. They were covered with smooth fields divided off into squares by green hedgerows with the little cottages of the farmers scattered about'.[61] The ship soon passed 'a point of land as beautiful as could be' belonging to the Duke of Hamilton, lighthouses and 'old ruined castles on some of the islands'.[62] By evening they entered the mouth of the Clyde. He declared this night on the ship to be his happiest, in comments pregnant with a level of emotion that was only matched by the feelings he had expressed on his departure:

> I will not attempt to put my feelings and emotions on paper, which I felt in my soul when I stood on deck and saw a low indistinct line in the horizon which was the North of Ireland. My first view of Scotland was above the clouds. I stood watching the heavy cloud of mist rolled away, revealing the tops of two mountains, standing clear-cut again the sky. They proved to be a large island off the coast of Scotland.[63]

By 9:30 pm the ship reached Greenock:

> ... the moon was shining clearly, and the lights of the city presented a fine picture, which we sat and watched for a long time. We passed Dumbarton Rock, and by the moonlight were able to distinguish old Dumbarton Castle very well indeed. As I thought of the old associations of Scottish history, and looked at the great rock, rising bold and grim out of the river, I began to realize that we were indeed nearing sacred historic ground![64]

So excited by the prospect of arrival, he awoke early at 5am, packed, ate his last meal onboard, and then gazed from the deck on the 'strange scene' of the

---

59 Ibid., 14.
60 Anonymous Travel Diary, 1889, Doc. 983, 21–22.
61 Ibid., 22.
62 Ibid., 23.
63 Anonymous Travel Diary, 1889, Doc. 983, pp. 23–24.
64 Ibid., 24.

expansive Clyde.[65] After customs inspection, the two men proceeded to the city's cathedral, 'the most interesting object in this city of 700,000 people'.[66] Deeply impressed, moved even, by that place, he dedicated several pages to it, before turning his attention to the '[s]igns of poverty' he glimpsed everywhere.[67] 'I have seen today more dirty, unkept, wretched women and children than I ever saw in any city of the United States', he averred.[68] Yet he also found the children 'chubby, rugged, sound, [and] healthy looking'. From the old Waverly Hotel, the two men set forth the next day to Edinburgh.

These accounts show how Ireland offered travellers their first sight of land and therefore mediated their encounter with Scottish landfall. Greenock also played a mediating role in the encounter with Glasgow, as did the Clyde, which offered (in clear weather) vistas of the shoreline. While Glasgow had, by this time, overtaken Greenock as a port in terms of tonnage as its docks developed, and drainage initiatives allowed larger ships to make their way farther up the Clyde, Greenock remained the point of arrival for passenger travellers in these accounts.[69]

The onward journey was one in which green banks gave way to shipyards, offering passengers an unfolding view of urban development. Martin S. Howard, for his part, having devoted much of his account of the passage to the topic of seasickness, recorded that the 'first view of land is hailed by the voyager with unalloyed delight'. As the hills of Ireland rose up into view, they failed to disappoint.[70] 'The northern coast of Ireland is hilly; at most mountainous resembling somewhat the Highlands of the Hudson, and to the ship which, on account of fog or false reckoning, makes acquaintance with one of those monstrous ledges which rise up in hideous proportions from that wild northern sea'.[71] Even as the journey ended, Howard, like others, narrated the risks that attended shoals. Having left on 14 May, on 27 May the traveller's ship entered the mouth of the Clyde:

> to our eyes unaccustomed so long to the green earth, everything was enchanting. Picturesque shores with mountains cloud capped rising beyond; pleasant fields running up through opening valleys; grounds and castles of noblemen; light-houses here and

---

65 Ibid., 25.
66 Ibid., 26.
67 Ibid., 30.
68 Ibid., 30.
69 John F. Riddell, 'Glasgow and the Clyde', in Peter Reed, ed., *Glasgow: The Forming of the City* (Edinburgh: Edinburgh University Press, 1993), 41–56; John F. Riddell, *Clyde Navigation: A History of the Development and Deepening of the River Clyde* (Edinburgh: John Donald Publishers, Inc., 1979), 3.
70 Travel journal, Martin S. Howard Papers, np.
71 Ibid.

> there along shore; the thick smoke of manufacturing towns; the quiet watering villages lose to the edge of the stream.[72]

Howard remarked on the expansive view as they arrived in sunshine. The indisputable signifier of their arrival escaped no one's attention: 'we passed Dumbarton Castle', which, Howard contended was 'in its day a stronghold which might well defy the strength of kings'. As the river narrowed, it presented views that 'seemed more beautiful than anything' Howard had ever beheld and then gave way to a bustling urban realm: 'We reached at last the great business city of Glasgow', he wrote, 'second only to Liverpool in the British Empire, thick with the smoke of its manufactories, a thoroughly busy city, full of enterprise and bustle, more like our American cities' than many which Howard subsequently visited. He hailed the remarkable cathedral, with windows more beautiful than any in Italy, in a church 'built by Roman Catholics' and now, to their grief, a place of Presbyterian worship. In 'Scotch drizzle', his party set out to find Glasgow's university; unable to locate it, they ended their first day on Scottish soil. The next day took them through Loch Lomond, Loch Katrine, and the Trossachs, to Edinburgh. The journey along the Clyde, then, brought all of these passengers into a connection with Scotland's wild, romantic history, epitomised by their views of its fertile banks, and by Dumbarton Castle, which soon gave way to a contrasting vista of busy manufacture.

In final remarks, Robert Dayton Williams declared that when his New York-to-Glasgow journey ended, he and Anna proceeded after customs examination to the 'unpretending Waverly House' hotel, where he planned to arrange a shave ahead of the Sabbath. With an account of the associated costs, his narrative abruptly ended. In contrast with this unfinished-seeming manuscript account, in James Wetherell's account Glasgow offered a gateway for travels that went on to encompass Scotland and England. Part II of his account begins within an observation common to many such accounts: 'Glasgow is not only the largest city in Scotland, but it is also the chief seat of manufactures and commerce'.[73] He also remarked that it offered comparatively few points of interest to recreational travellers: 'It is a city of smoke and turmoil, furnishing but few attractions to the tourist', amongst which he cited the expansive George Square, 'in the very heart of the great city', with its many public monuments; and the city's ancient cathedral.[74] 'Exhibition Week', he cautioned, revealed 'Old World life in some of

---

72 Ibid.

73 Williams, travel journal 1870, np.

74 Ibid.

its most sinister aspects' – 'horrible street brawls and harrowing scenes of poverty and sin glimpsed in twilight hours':

> Throngs of drunken men, hundreds of half-clad women hurrying over stones with bare and bleeding feet, scores of little children even at this late hour of the evening wandering aimlessly or crying in anxious quest, – these are the pitiable creatures that our boasted civilization has failed to civilize, – and that too in a land where religion and education and philanthropy have reached high-water mark.[75]

There ended Wetherell's short stay in Glasgow, before he set off to the 'Land of Burns', and many other Scottish sites in further instalments of his travel account. Upon their arrival, these passengers, journeying at different times over twenty-two years, proceeded on different paths of travel. But there are common touchstones in these accounts. It must be noted that these narratives of the New York-to-Glasgow crossing represent a narrow range of perspectives – five of six authors (excepting E. A., whose identity remains elusive) are male. All were travelling in comparatively comfortable classes of accommodation. Some narrational strategies – notably the distillation of fellow passengers into 'types' in published accounts – distinguish manuscript from printed narratives. But they shared many appraisals of the challenge of the New York-to-Glasgow crossing. Notwithstanding the comforts of their cabin class, seasickness often deprived them of comforts, recreations and delicacies available to them. The welcome sight of land – first Ireland, and then Scotland – signalled a return not only from the unsettled climatic, social and temporal regimes of the crossing, but the restoration of suspended geographic orientation, too.

A fictionalised account of travel, penned by 'An American Hobo' just before the outbreak of war, evinces many of these themes as well, even if the tone, contours and style diverge markedly from the nineteenth-century accounts reviewed here. One striking difference in 'Windy Bill's' account of travel (attributed to Ben Goodkind, and penned in the style of conventionalised 'vagabond writing'[76]) is that half of it is dedicated to the overland voyage to New York, underscoring that for many (indeed most) travellers, their 'departure' from the great American metropolis occurred long before they reached a New York Pier, and involved overland, and perhaps waterborne, travel of some kind. Windy Bill also recounts how he encountered an agent who sold him a $27 fare on the

---

[75] Ibid.

[76] Owen Clayton, *Vagabonds, Tramps, and Hobos: The Literature and Culture of U.S. Transiency, 1890–1940* (Cambridge: Cambridge University Press, 2023).

Anchor Line's *Furnessia* ('Steerage of course; I'm no Vanderbilt!').[77] Underlining how classes and spaces of travel produced different sensory responses amongst travellers, foul odour on his way down the stairway to steerage made him sick. Windy Bill's account included tropes such as passing Sandy Hook, the curse of seasickness, the visitation of blackening skies and stormy seas, and the travails of sea travel, which he recounted ironically: 'A life on the ocean is a gay thing. It is awful nice to be spun around like a cork and then see-sawed up and down with a possibility of touching bottom.'[78] The sight of land led Windy Bill to imagine how Columbus must have felt in a similar position:[79] 'The Irish passengers aboard', he wrote, 'and there were plenty of them, become frantic with joy. Ireland is such a beautiful country. Rocky headlands we saw, capes, bays, towering mountains in the background, green trees and farms'.[80] A tender steamed up and passenger alighted and discharged, and soon they were off again to Scotland which he described in a vein familiar to readers of other accounts.[81]

> Words are entirely inadequate to give one a proper idea of it. To be appreciated it must be seen and *felt*, for reading about it don't do much good.
>
> Here, right before us, were the Highlands of Scotland and many a place famous in song and story.[82]

The *Furnessia* anchored off Greenock, where '[w]e third-raters' were directed to the customs house. He then proceeded by rail for the 25-mile journey to Glasgow, passing fields on his right and the great shipyards on the banks of the Clyde to his left. The arrival at Glasgow proved disorienting: 'Everything was so different – the houses, the stores, the streets, the sidewalks, the driveways, the people, the vehicles, the dogs, the horses, the skies, the clouds, everything', Windy Bill wrote facetiously.[83] These unfamiliar elements included names of stores, the grey stone houses with mansard roofs, the tobacco brands, the bustling ethos of the Clyde, and then the Broomielaw and its vessels laden with people and

---

77 'Windy Bill', Ben Goodkind, *An American Hobo in Europe, by Windy Bill. A True Narrative of the Adventures of a Poor American at Home and in the Old Country* (San Francisco: Press of the Calkins Publishing House [c1907]), 151.

78 Ibid., 162.

79 Ibid., 163.

80 Ibid., 164.

81 Ibid., 166.

82 Ibid., 166.

83 Ibid., 167.

cattle from the Highlands.[84] Windy Bill's account of his efforts to seek lodgings and a visit to Glasgow Green provided more entertainment for the reader of this distinctive genre. For this 'hobo', travelling in steerage, professing deep poverty, and writing in a humorous tone and within a distinctive genre, Glasgow offered opportunities to explore his status as an outsider, and a man of limited means whose purpose was ill-defined. But other accounts of travel echo in his narrative of the contours of the crossing.

Conclusions

The narratives of travel explored in this chapter are a drop in the ocean of the varied experiences of millions of passengers who crossed the North Atlantic under steam before the First World War, each journey inflected by a passenger's own personal familiarity with, and relationship to, the places that began or ended their journey, by motivations for travel, by their gender, socio-economic, racial and religious identities – and even by their own bodily fortitude. Amid this vast expanse of travellers' stances and sensibilities, as wide as the ocean itself, some general comments can be drawn from these accounts: (1) New York was often represented not as a point of departure, but a point of arrival for people who had journeyed some distance to reach the city's piers; (2) New York's fading skyline inaugurated passengers' immersion in a new ocean realm, and the North Atlantic proved to be an unwelcome companion, as their bodies were left to the whims of the sea and sky; (3) many travel writers adopted a stance of detachment in evaluating fellow passengers, producing figures who were distilled into nameless caricatures, labelled by occupation and nationality; (4) the wider culture of shipboard sociability was shaped by a mixture of tedium and routine, sometimes punctuated by deep rumination inspired by the vastness of the ocean, in which even the comforts of cabin class could not always be fully enjoyed; and, finally (5), passing and stopping in Ireland, and then steaming up the Clyde, framed passengers' eventual landfall, with Greenock serving as the gateway to Glasgow in all of these accounts. Whether travellers stayed in the great Scottish city of manufacture and commerce, or departed to other destinations, arriving in Glasgow from New York signified the end of a journey whose contours echoed many tropes of transatlantic ocean travel generally, but also constituted a distinctive journey in its own right.

---

84 Ibid., 169.

'You Americans have the wrong impression of Great Britain': Glasgow, the Empire Exhibition of 1938 and Transatlantic Relations

Kieran Taylor

> A young lady dressed in a Royal Stewart tartan skirt and velvet doublet of dark green was received by the Lord Provost of Glasgow (Sir John Stewart) in the city chambers yesterday and given a batch of letters to be delivered to the mayors of cities throughout America and Canada during a coming visit.[1]

'The young lady', Marie Kane, was appointed Scotland's goodwill ambassador on behalf of the Scottish Development Council in 1937.[2] Kane's role was to 'sell Scotland', attracting visitors to the 1938 Empire Exhibition. She was to encourage prospective holiday makers and business people to visit the country, appreciate its traditions of hospitality, natural beauty and admire its expansive industrial infrastructure as a means to promote investment. In carrying out this important mission Kane was tasked with 'binding the natural affinities' of Scotland and America 'in a close bond of friendship'.[3]

This chapter discusses the Empire Exhibition, Kane's publicity tour of North America and Glasgow's relationship with the USA prior to and during the Second World War. The chapter asserts that the Empire Exhibition represented an attempt by Scottish industry and politics to drum up interest in the economy to stem the 'southward drift' of Scotland's industries.[4] The Empire Exhibition, although fundamentally an attempt to capitalise on the economic relationships with the Empire and Dominions, sought to bring Scottish products, services and the country itself as a destination, to a wider audience. In discussing the relationship of Glasgow to the USA in the interwar years, relevant global events preceding the Second World War are referred to. The chapter begins by providing an overview of the economic and political context in which the Exhibition took place. The chapter then discusses the way in which the Exhibition drew a global audience

---

1 'Boosting Exhibition in US & Canada', *Aberdeen Press & Journal* (23 December 1937), 5.

2 Ibid., 5.

3 'Selling Scotland', *The Scotsman* (3 May 1938), 11; 'Girl Artist for America', *The Scotsman* (23 December 1937).

4 'Southward Drift of Industry', *Dundee Courier* (27 December 1929), 3; 'The Southward Drift', *Aberdeen Press & Journal* (22 April 1936), 6; Angus MacKenzie 'Public-spirited men': Economic Unionist Nationalism in Inter-War Scotland', *Scottish Historical Review* 96/1 (2017).

through its diverse exhibits, in particular it discusses the subject of peace at the Exhibition. Finally, Kane and Lord Provost Patrick Dollan's work as cultural ambassadors for Glasgow is discussed, with particular reference to the New York World's Fair in 1939 and American concerns around the threat of war.

Through examination of the Empire Exhibition the chapter offers insight into Scotland's relationship with America through the mid-twentieth century. In doing this it makes reference to themes such as migration, empire, industrial decline and the risk of conflict. The paper argues that Kane's publicity tour of the USA and a subsequent visit to the World's Fair by Lord Provost Dollan contributed a Scottish influence on the transatlantic relationship at a time of uncertainty for Britain.[5] In representing Glasgow, Kane and Dollan played a small yet important role in reinforcing ties between the USA and Great Britain through the Second World War in their interactions with the media, the public and politicians.

A Transatlantic City Facing Decline

Glasgow's economy had historically been tied to transoceanic trade. As Munro and Slaven outline, Glasgow's shipping firms specialised in trade with two key areas which the west of Scotland had ties with North America and the Indian subcontinent.[6] Through the nineteenth century, Scottish identity had been primarily realised through a 'unionist-nationalism'.[7] Politicians and industrialists sought a stake for Scotland within the Empire and Scots were enthusiastic participants in the imperial project.[8] Scots provided both labour and capital to the Empire's colonies and dominions through emigration and investment.[9] By 1938 passenger and trading vessels registered in Glasgow reached a diverse array of

5 Kathleen Burk, *The Lion and the Eagle: The Interaction of the British and American Empires 1783–1972* (London: Bloomsbury Publishing Plc, 2019).

6 Forbes Munro and Tony Slaven, 'Networks and Markets in Clyde Shipping: The Donaldsons and the Hogarth, 1870–1939' *Business History* 43/2 (2001): 19–50. North America was the focus of the Allan, Anchor and Donaldson Lines whereas the City and Clan Lines focused on South Asia.

7 Graeme Morton, *Unionist Nationalism: Governing Urban Scotland 1830–1860* (Edinburgh: Tuckwell Press, 1999).

8 T. M. Devine and John M. MacKenzie, 'Scots in the Imperial Economy', in John M. MacKenzie, and T. M. Devine, eds, *Scotland and the British Empire, Oxford History of the British Empire Companion Series* (Oxford, Oxford University Press, 2011), 251. As Mackenzie and Devine outline, Scots supported the booming agricultural, engineering and mining industries in colonies such as Canada, Australia and South Africa.

9 Ibid., 251.

imperial destinations.[10] Despite cultural and economic relationships between Scotland and the Empire being interwoven through trade and migration, the USA was considered an attractive alternative to the colonies and dominions for Scots. By the early twentieth century tens of thousands of Scots were making their way to the USA, between 1921 and 1930 at least 64,000 Scots left for America on ships from Glasgow and Greenock.[11] Scots also invested heavily in American infrastructure and stock markets and while these ventures were sometimes riskier than imperial markets they were regarded as more profitable.[12]

Glasgow was therefore plugged into a maritime trade which was nurtured by and tied to the development of commercial ports, particularly those on America's Eastern seaboard. British shipping companies operated what Morton describes as a 'cartel' system with individual lines specialising in particular geographic routes.[13] In particular the Clyde-based Anchor, Allan and Donaldson Lines operated services between Glasgow and American ports such as: New York, Boston, Philadelphia.[14] Most prominent amongst these companies was Anchor Line, a principal sponsor of the Exhibition. In an exhibition pamphlet the company boasted that it 'held the foremost position in British shipping … with five passenger liners of 17,000 tons' operating regularly between 'Glasgow & New York'.[15]

Glasgow's transformation into the 'second city' of Empire was on account of the way in which the city had contributed to the economic opportunities

---

10 Glasgow City Archive (GCA), TD 329/20/5, Clyde Navigation Trust and Glasgow Chamber of Commerce, *True Reciprocity* (Glasgow: Clyde Navigation Trust and Glasgow Chamber of Commerce, 1939), 2. As the Clyde Navigation Trust Advertised: which included: Newfoundland, Montreal, Vancouver, Jamaica, Georgetown, Lagos, Egypt, Nairobi, Durban, Cape Town, Hong Kong, Colombo, Bombay, Calcutta, Rangoon, Singapore, New Guinea, Perth, Christchurch and Auckland.

11 Nicholas J. Evans, 'The Emigration of Skilled Male Workers from Clydeside during the Interwar Period', *International Journal of Maritime History* 18/1 (2006), 255–280.

12 T. M. Devine and John M. MacKenzie, 'Scots in the Imperial Economy', 247.

13 Fiona Scott Morton, 'Entry and Predation: British Shipping Cartels 1879–1929', *Journal of Economics and Management Strategy* 4/6 (1997), 680.

14 'Anchor Line', *The Scotsman*, (1 January 1910), 11. Halifax and Montreal were frequently destinations included on these journeys.

15 GCA, TD E38 The Empire Exhibition Official Guide, 'Anchor Line', (The Empire Exhibition, Glasgow, 1938). 'Empire Exhibition Boost', *Aberdeen Press and Journal* (5 January1938), 3. Anchor Line although renowned internationally, remained smaller than its rival Cunard-White Star Lines which operated throughout British ports, including Glasgow. Despite the endorsement of Anchor Line for the Exhibition it was a Cunard ship, the Scythia, that Marie Kane took to New York in January 1938.

and trading relationships facilitated by Empire.[16] By the middle of the 1930s however, trading links between Scotland and the colonies were increasingly less lucrative. Scottish manufacturers and exporters were replaced by competitors elsewhere. The Empire Exhibition aimed to reignite trade, as MacKenzie notes it renewed the focus on Scotland's place as a commercially important centre of Empire.[17] While Breitenbach shares this assessment, she notes that the 1938 Exhibition was 'less straightforwardly about Empire than its predecessors'.[18]

Exhibition publicity, however, put the benefits of imperial trade front and centre. As a publication informed readers 'The Empire's great necessity today is trade ... throughout Britain there is a growth in desire to support Empire products in preference to foreign'.[19] A strong emphasis was placed on the role of 'personal contacts' in facilitating trade.[20] Harold M Ford, a commercial manager for the Clyde Navigation Trust, argued that Scots would benefit by cutting out third parties based in London.[21]

The principal organiser of the Empire Exhibition was the Scottish Development Council (SDC). The SDC was a voluntary organisation which united industry and local government. It was established 1931 by the steel and shipping magnate Sir James Lithgowwith the aim of 'revitalising' Scotland's economy during the inter-war recession.[22] The SDC, although officially non-political, was mostly supported

---

16 Esther Breitenbach, 'Pro-Empire Sentiment in Twentieth Century Scotland Before Decolonisation', in Stephenie Barczewski and Martin Farr, eds, *The MacKenzie Moment and Imperial History* (Basingstoke, Palgrave MacMillan, 2019), 238. Breitenbach outlines that Scottish participation in the Empire was linked to a variety of industries but also emigration, church missions and the Scottish regiments.

17 Angus Mackenzie, 'Self Help and Propaganda: Scottish National Development Council, 1931–1939', *Journal of Scottish Historical Studies* 30/2 (2010), 124.

18 Breitenbach, 'Pro-Empire Sentiment in Twentieth Century Scotland Before Decolonisation', 253.

19 GCA, 2. TD 329/20/5, Clyde Navigation Trust and Glasgow Chamber of Commerce, *True Reciprocity*, (Glasgow: Clyde Navigation Trust and Glasgow Chamber of Commerce, 1939).

20 'Clyde Trade with Empire', *The Scotsman* (1July 1938), 8.

21 'Trade in the Empire', *Edinburgh Evening News* (8 October 1938), 11. Contemporary Scottish newspapers reported that networking had resulted in an increase of imported goods into the Clyde from Australia, New Zealand and South Africa. Vincent Massey, High Commissioner for Canada, celebrated the role that 'personal business contacts' could have in extending trade, in comments he made at the annual James Watt dinner at the Institution of Engineers and Shipbuilders in Glasgow.

22 Sarah Britton, 'Urban Futures/Rural Pasts', *Cultural and Social History* 8/2 (2011), 213–232.

by those involved in the Glasgow Progressive Party and received further financial support from industrialists such as Viscount Weir, a prominent unionist.[23]

The interwar period was marked by inflation, recession and unemployment for Great Britain, and urban Scotland suffered considerably.[24] Glasgow was particularly disadvantaged, following the return to the Gold Standard, as potential profits from exporting goods were greatly reduced.[25] The Wall Street Crash and subsequent Great Depression deepened economic concerns in Scotland, by 1938 some 82,000 people remained unemployed in Glasgow.[26] Further, the 'structural changes' beginning to take place in the British economy largely passed Scotland by.[27] The 'new industries' of electrical engineering, vehicle manufacturing and the production of consumer goods were concentrated in the Midlands and the South of England. Urban poverty prevented Scotland from becoming an attractive market to manufacture or sell these products.[28]

The competitiveness of Scotland's economy in the nineteenth century thus contributed to its deterioration in the twentieth, as low wages and cyclical employment prevented the development of local markets for consumer products.[29] The new industries were looked upon with alarm by Scotland's business community. Newspapers through the late 1930s reported on the internal migration of 'Scottish youth and brains' who were 'lured south'.[30] The board of the SDC was made up by those with significant financial investments in Scotland, such as industrialist

---

23 Mackenzie, 'Self Help and Propaganda,' 124; James Smyth, 'Resisting Labour: Unionists, Liberals and Moderates in Glasgow between the Wars,' *The Historical Journal* 46/2 (2003), 375–401, 395. The Progressive Party, an anti-Labour coalition of Unionists and Liberals dominated municipal politics through the 1920s to early 1930s in Glasgow.

24 Nicholas Crafts and Peter Fearon, 'Depression and Recovery in the 1930s: An Overview', in Nicholas Crafts, and Peter Fearon, *The Great Depression of the 1930s: Lessons for Today* (Oxford: Oxford University Press, 2013); Daniel K. Benjamin., and Levis A. Kochin, 'Searching for an Explanation of Unemployment in Interwar Britain', *Journal of Political Economy* 87/3 (1979), 441–78. The increase in employment in shipping, manufacturing and heavy industry associated with the First World War could not be sustained through the 1920s. As Benjamin and Kochin note Britain's unemployment rate between 1921 and 1938, averaged at 14 per cent.

25 Crafts and Fearon 'Depression and Recovery in the 1930s: An Overview', 289.

26 James Smyth, *Labour in Glasgow 1896–1936: Socialism, Suffrage and Sectarianism* (East Linton: Tuckwell Press: 2000), 66.

27 Neil K. Buxton, 'The Role of the 'New' Industries in Britain during the 1930s: A Reinterpretation', *The Business History Review* 49/2 (1975), 205–22.

28 Devine and MacKenzie, 'Scots in the Imperial Economy', 251.

29 Ibid., 251.

30 'The Drift South', *The Daily Record* (25 May1936), 14.

Steven Bilsland.[31] The 'drift South' was regarded by the SDC as an economic crisis with moral implications for the nation's youth. As the *Motherwell Times* reported, 'lads' of the mining and steel towns of Lanarkshire were 'solving their unemployment problem for themselves' departing for Corby and Coventry to find work.[32] The migration of young workers 'on transport lorries' from Scotland's industrial heartland deeply concerned Scottish employers.[33]

Dwindling economic prospects led Scots to pursue opportunities abroad. Glasgow built ocean liners were the primary vehicles of emigration for hundreds of thousands in the interwar period, with 110,000 Scots leaving for imperial colonies and dominions between 1921 and 1930.[34] Despite extensive promotion of Canada as an emigration destination and the introduction of the Empire Settlement Act 1922, America particularly New York and Philadelphia remained the preferred destination for migrant Scots.[35] Lewis born migrant Mary Anne Trump, (Nee MacLeod), the mother of President Donald Trump, was one of the thousands of Scots who departed from Glasgow to New York in November 1929 on the Anchor Line's SS *Transylvania*.[36] Almost 71 per cent of Scots emigrants departing Glasgow's surrounding counties would choose to make their new start in the USA in the 1920s.[37] Industrial workers from towns hard hit by the decline of steel and shipbuilding such as Clydebank and Motherwell in particular opted to emigrate. It was no coincidence that the largest shipping lines operating from the Clyde sailed directly to ports on the East coast of America.

The SDC hoped that the Empire Exhibition would reverse the trend of decline in Scotland.[38] The SDC set out to emulate earlier international exhibitions held

---

31 MacKenzie, 'Self-Help and Propaganda', 123. Bisland was the owner of the large Bisland Bakeries chain.

32 'The Drift South', *Motherwell Times* (23 October 1936), 7.

33 Ibid.

34 Evans, 'The Emigration of Skilled Male Workers from Clydeside during the Interwar Period', 267.

35 Marjory Harper and Nicholas J. Evans 'Socio-economic Dislocation and Inter-war Emigration to Canada and the United States: A Scottish Snapshot', *The Journal of Imperial and Commonwealth History* 34/4, (2006), 529–552.

36 Martin Hannan, 'The Mysterious Mary Trump', *The National* (21 May 2016); Mary Pilon, 'Donald Trump's Immigrant Mother', *The New Yorker* (24 June 2016). MacLeod would make several trips back and forth across the Atlantic in the 1930s. Residing with her sisters, already in New York Mary Anne worked as a 'maid' and 'domestic'.

37 The counties referred to are Lanarkshire, Renfrewshire, Dunbartonshire and Ayrshire. The looming introduction of immigration quotas in the USA in 1924 perhaps encouraged Scots to make it to America while they could.

38 Britton, 'Urban Futures/Rural Pasts', 214.

in Glasgow between 1888 and 1911 when the city was at its zenith.[39] Despite well-established trading relationships between Glasgow and the Empire, the Exhibition targeted new markets by attempting to draw investment and tourism from America.

The Exhibition, Empire and Peace

As MacKenzie assesses, the Empire Exhibition aimed to 'boost' the 'self-confidence of the Scottish people' at a time of uncertainty.[40] Scotland was therefore marketed as a place which embodied both modernity and tradition.[41] An extract from *Calling the World!* a magazine to accompany the Exhibition articulated this:

> Scotland presents the past and present face to face. One of her two pavilions deals with history, the other with the Scotland of today: on the one side the relics of the clans, the old wars, of life as it was lived hundreds of years ago, and on the other the living industries and culture of modern Scotland.[42]

It was hoped that in the mind of the visitor, Scotland would be seen as laying at the geographic, cultural and temporal crossroads of the world. In the months leading up to the exhibition there was speculation regarding the global attention that the city would receive through discussion of the numerous vessels that had been chartered by European travel agencies to visit. As the *Sunday Mail* reported, ships would arrive in Scotland directly from Antwerp, Rotterdam, Le Havre, Gothenburg and Hamburg.[43] Additionally the Exhibition was expected to be of 'great interest' to hundreds of 'American business men' who would attend.[44]

A pamphlet produced by the Clyde Navigation Trust and Glasgow Chamber of Commerce, proudly announced Scotland was a nation of '6 million consumers' with Glasgow the 'greatest' and 'most varied industrial areas of Britain' at its heart.[45] As the host nation Scotland had the spotlight and its pavilions would

---

39 The exhibitions of 1888, 1901 and 1911 would have been in the living memory of the industrialists and politicians on the board of the SDC.

40 Mackenzie, 'Self Help and Propaganda', 124.

41 Sarah Britton, 'Urban Futures/Rural Pasts', 215.

42 *Calling the World! Empire Exhibition 1938* (John Miller LTD, Glasgow, 1938), 2.

43 'All the World is Coming to the Empire Exhibition', *Sunday Mail* (6 February 1938), 12.

44 Ibid., 12.

45 Clyde Navigation Trust and The Glasgow Chamber of Commerce, 'True Reciprocity' (Clyde Navigation Trust and the Glasgow Chamber of Commerce, Glasgow: 1938) 2; Ronald Johnston, *Clydeside Capital, 1870–1920: A Social History of Employers* (East Linton: Tuckwell Press, 2000), 80. The Glasgow Chamber of Commerce was, as Johnston contends,

focus on the contrasting themes of innovation and tradition.[46] The Scottish Pavilion and the Palaces of Industry and Arts showcased the country's prowess in manufacturing as well as its rich history of artistic achievement.[47] Pavilions were also sponsored by an array of important Scottish companies and associated consortiums.[48] International firms such as Esso, Scottish Oils, Shell-Mex, Imperial Chemicals and Dunlop rubber were also present. Their pavilions outlined how these companies were at the cutting edge of design, production and price.

Anchor Line used the Exhibition as an opportunity to sell its services to a global audience. The shipping company took a novel approach to its own pavilion through construction of a boat shaped restaurant carved into a hillside in Bellahouston Park. The *Atlantic* offered customers a 'nautical atmosphere', and a luxurious taster of what embarking on a 'cosmopolitan' Anchor Line voyage was like.[49] Advertisements for the Anchor Line appeared regularly in urban American newspapers through late 1937 and early 1938. Publicity made regular references to the Exhibition at Bellahouston. Americans were invited to take the 'logical route' to Europe docking at Glasgow and visiting the Empire Exhibition in the process.[50] The marketing of both 'economy and luxury' options on Anchor Line boats ensured that travel would be accessible to a diverse range of passengers.[51]

Leading British newspapers and media outlets were also represented at the Exhibition. The *Times*, *Daily Express*, *Daily Mail* and Glasgow dailies the *Herald* and

---

one of the 'central cogs in the capitalist network' of Scottish industry. The Chamber of Commerce had long championed international and Imperial trade, publishing its listings in as many as four languages and lobbying Westminster to expand the construction of railways in India.

46 GCA, GC 606.4 'Plan of Exhibition', (Empire Exhibition, 1938) Those countries & regions represented were: Rhodesia & East Africa, West Africa, Malaya, the British West Indies, Burma, the Union of South Africa, Australia, New Zealand, Canada, Ireland and Northern Ireland. Ceylon and India refused to participate. Separate pavilions provided exhibits on a range of Imperial products including tea, rubber, timber, and coal.

47 Ibid.

48 Ibid. These included: Templeton Carpets, Beardmore and Colville Steel and Shipping, Sterne & Co Refrigeration, Union Bank of Scotland, the Scottish Motor Traction Company, Glenfield Engineering and the consortium of distillers.

49 'Empire Exhibition', *The Scotsman* (19 March 1938), 17. Arthur Giordano, a highly regarded restaurant manager from London, was appointed to the Atlantic.

50 'The Lucky Ones Go Anchor Line to Europe via Scotland and Ireland', *Evening Star* (6 March 1938), 21.

51 'Economy + Luxury = Anchor Line to Europe Via Scotland & Ireland', *Evening Star* (19 June 1938) 8.

the *Evening Times* all sponsored pavilions.[52] The BBC was also present and radio programming by the Corporation covered events at the Exhibition. Coverage was broadcast throughout the Empire, as radio was increasingly an important and accessible medium for entertainment.[53] The use of radio was significant in the advertisement of the exhibition in America.[54] Marie Kane used radio as one of the main sources of publicity during her tour of America and Canada. In six months, Kane spoke on the radio more than 60 times, estimating that she may have been heard by as many as 30 million Americans.[55]

Indeed, in promoting the exhibition Marie Kane remarked that, the Empire Exhibition was about more than just attracting investment and providing entertainment. Kane noted that the Exhibition also sought to educate. Profits derived from the exhibition, she argued, would be reinvested in other cultural and social endeavours.[56] Pavilions were sponsored by a broad range of social, ethical, religious and political groups. For instance, the Scottish Co-operative Wholesale Society (SCWS), the Trade Union Congress (TUC) and the National Fitness Movement all had pavilions.[57] Scotland's denominational churches were also present. The exhibition's role in promoting morality was a key consideration for these groups. Religious groups had been an important political lobby in influencing the type of exhibits offered. As an article in *Time* magazine remarked although 'straitlaced Scots' were unsuccessful in banning the sale of alcohol or censoring nude Art Deco statues, the exhibition remained closed on Sundays.[58]

Despite discussion of the way in which the profits would be reinvested in Scotland, the takings from the Exhibition were lower than expected, which lead to disputes between the SDC and Glasgow Corporation around the payment of

---

52 GCA, GC 606.4, 'Plan of Exhibition', (Empire Exhibition, 1938).

53 'Radio Programmes', *Civil and Military Gazette* (3 June 1938), 12.

54 'WATR Programms', *The Waterbury Democrat* (24 January 1938), 13.

55 'Selling Scotland', *The Scotsman* (3 May 1938), 11.

56 'Miss Marie Kane Brings Word of Constructive Deeds from Abroad', *Evening Star* (18 June1938). Kane added that the 'profits' would be turned to 'public use'.

57 GCA, GC 606.4 'Plan of Exhibition', (Empire Exhibition, 1938).

58 Callum G. Brown, 'Spectacle, Restraint and the Sabbath Wars: The Everyday Scottish Sunday', in Lynn Abrams and Callum G. Brown, eds, *History of Everyday Life in Twentieth-Century Scotland* (Edinburgh University Press, 2010), 153–180. 'Sunday Opening of Empire Exhibition', *Dundee Evening Telegraph* (25 April 1938), 6; 'Scotland: Symbol of Unity', *Time* (16 May 1938). Pavilions were sponsored by the Church of Scotland, the Episcopal Church, the Roman Catholic Church, the Church of Christian Science and the Christian Brethren

ratings.[59] The Exhibition was thus to be the 'last of its kind' in Scotland.[60] Perhaps anachronistic as a venture, 'times were not auspicious for this kind of event or for large expenditures', as the general economic context and a very wet summer impacted upon the overall profitability of the exhibition.[61] The sense of crisis which had influenced the Exhibition taking place would be further worsened by international conflict.[62]

Most important amongst the non-commercial exhibits was the Peace Pavilion. Erected by the League of Nations Union, an internationalist campaign group for the League of Nations, the pavilion was a temple like construction with a bell tower and a neon sign. The Union hoped that the Peace Pavilion 'would bring before everyone the question of peace'.[63] The presence of this pavilion served as a reminder of the uncertain international atmosphere that the Exhibition took place in. Exhibits inside the Peace Pavilion dealt with the work of the League and other intergovernmental organisations established during the period such as the International Labour Organisation (ILO) and the Permanent Court of International Justice (PCIJ).[64] The pavilion received official endorsement by the League of Nations when it was visited by its president, Aga Khan III, who reiterated the need for peace as he lay a symbolic stone in the pavilion's peace cairn.[65] The Aga Khan was accompanied by an entourage of high profile dignitaries from within the League of Nations and the All India Muslim League.[66] At a dinner held in the Aga Khan's honour by Glasgow's Lord Provost John Stewart, the

---

59 'Empire Exhibition Request to Government for £100,000 Proposed', *Scotsman* (3 March 1939), 7.

60 A. Peat. 'Scottish Internationalisms at the 1938 Empire Exhibition: Between Britain, Europe, and Empire', *Open Library of Humanities* 6/1 (2020), 21.

61 C. Montes Serrano, 'The Empire Exhibition of Scotland, 1938: the image and representation of an ephemeral modernity', *Expresión Gráfica Arquitectónica*, 25/39 (2020), 32–45, 35.

62 Peat, 'Scottish Internationalisms at the 1938 Empire Exhibition', 21. The aims of the SDC to strengthen links between Scotland and Empire were of limited benefit, by 1938 a number of colonies had popular anti-Imperial movements which exercised increasing political opposition. For example, political movements in India and Ceylon refused to formally participate in the Exhibition. Despite the participation of major leftwing organisations such as the TUC and the SCWS in the Exhibition, socialist opinion represented by the Independent Labour Party (ILP) opposed the exhibition.

63 'Peace Pavilion', *Arbroath Guide* (16 April 1938), 5.

64 GCA, TD E38, Empire *Exhibition Official Guide*, (1938).

65 'Aga Khan on Peace Ideals', *Civil and Military Gazette* (30 July 1938), 9; 'Indian Visitors to Empire Exhibition', *Civil & Military Gazette* (9 July 1938), 1.

66 The Aga Khan was accompanied by Muhammad Zafarullah Khan an Indian representative at the League of Nations who was later president of the United Nations and Feroz Khan Noon Indian High Commissioner and later a Prime Minister of Pakistan.

president appealed that the League remained valuable, but as nations left there were questions about whether it might be able to 'save mankind from another disaster'.[67]

The Peace Pavilion became a facet in the wider discussions around the threat of war in international media. The Garden of Good Neighbours, a representation of the border between America and Canada surrounding the Peace Pavilion, became the source of controversy in July 1938 following the removal of Japanese, Italian and German flags.[68] Italian newspapers claimed the removal of the Italian flag was a 'glaring outrage' and an insult to Italy's national honour.[69] The removal of the flags followed a protest from the socialist Glasgow Trades Council.[70] As the Californian *Santa Ana Journal* reported, 'The removal was made on the theory that Italy has been a poor neighbour to Abyssinia, Japan to China, and both Germany and Italy to Spain.'[71]

The subject of peace in Europe was of particular interest to many American visitors to the Exhibition. Comments from Robert F Peterson, a young Harvard Graduate, who spoke to the Women's Citizen Association and the National Council of Women at the Exhibition make this apparent. Peterson offered his British audience a domestic context for American isolationism:

> After 1920 America had moved farther and farther away from Europe. She had so much to do at home so she rolled up her sleeves and stopped thinking about the mess in Europe. First, prohibition came; then the big red scare; then the Ku Klux Klan against Jews, Catholics and Negroes. Next young people went wild and parents worried more about flaming youth than peace treaties or a league. But the greatest factor in their retreat from European troubles was prosperity ... I think we began to wake up in 1931 as Japan was stirring trouble at our back door.[72]

---

67 'Preservation of Ideal Advocated', *Civil & Military Gazette* (9 July 1938), 7.

68 GCA, TD E38, *Empire Exhibition Official Guide*, (1938).

69 'The Peace Pavilion', *Scotsman* (8 June 1938), 7; Peat, 'Scottish Internationalisms at the 1938 Empire Exhibition: Between Britain, Europe, and Empire', 21; Flavia Marcello, 'Mussolini and the idealisation of Empire: The Augustan Exhibition of Romanità', *Modern Italy* 16/3 (2011), 223–247; 'Il viaggio del Führer alla luce dell'accordo italo-inglese', *La Stampa*, (5 May 1938), 8. The Italian media was broadly critical of the Exhibition, as Glasgow competed with Rome's Mostra Augustea della Romanità a grand fascist celebration of Rome's ancient past held in the Palazzo delle Esposizioni. In May 1938 *La Stampa* mocked British newspapers for dedicating more coverage to Hitler's visit to Rome in May, than they had of the King's visit to Glasgow to open the exhibition.

70 'The Peace Pavilion', *Scotsman* (8 June 1938), 7.

71 'Good Neighbors', *Santa Ana Journal* (20 July 1938), 7.

72 'The Peace Mind', *Scotsman* (6 June 1938), 7.

Despite the turbulence of the USA's domestic politics in the interwar period, many Americans were ambivalent about assisting Europe. Although there was growing co-operation between the USA and Britain from the turn of the century, President Roosevelt was uncomfortable with Britain's desire to sustain its imperial territories.[73] Joseph Kennedy, ambassador to Britain from 1937 to 1940, was even less sympathetic toward Britain. Kennedy saw the risk of rising conflict as an opportunity for America to seize 'leadership of the English speaking world'.[74] As Burk argues, Britain appeared to be a world power that was increasingly less secure.[75]

Nevertheless, the Empire Exhibition sought to cultivate the extensive ties that existed between Scotland and the USA. An 'America Day' was even hosted by the organisers of the Exhibition on July 4th. This received official thanks from ambassador Kennedy by telegram. This cultural and public diplomacy reinforced transatlantic connections between Glasgow and New York and was continued by visits from those involved in the 1939 World's Fair.[76] The former executive of the *New York Times*, and progressive city politician, George McAneny was the guest of honour at 'America Day'. McAneny, who was chairmen of the board of directors for the World's Fair, used his visit to Glasgow to influence the planning of the expo.[77] This cultural exchange would be continued through Lord Provost Dollan's visit to the Fair and subsequent correspondence with New York Mayor La Guardia in the period that followed.[78]

Marie Kane and Attracting American Visitors

Marie Kane was dispatched to the USA to promote interest in the Exhibition. The SDC worked hard to draw American visitors and investors to the Empire Exhibition. As Peat remarks:

> There was an idealistic desire for a direct connection 'between foreigners and the people of Scotland', as Glasgow looked out at the globe and imagined the globe looking back.[79]

---

73 Burk, *The Lion and the Eagle*, 395; Stephen Bowman, *The Pilgrims Society and Public Diplomacy, 1895–1945* (Edinburgh: Edinburgh University Press, 2018). Regardless of the 'Great Rapprochement', there was lingering disapproval of British foreign policy within sections of American society on a range of issues.

74 David Mayers, *FDR's Ambassadors and the Diplomacy of Crisis: From the Rise of Hitler to the End of World War II* (Cambridge University Press, 2012), 176.

75 Burk, *The Lion and the Eagle*, 395.

76 'All the World is Coming to the Empire Exhibition', *Sunday Mail* (6 February1938), 12.

77 'America Day at Empire Exhibition', *Dundee Evening Telegraph* (11 July 1938), 6.

78 'First Impressions of New York and Mayor La Guardia', *Evening Times* (11 August 1939).

79 Peat, "Scottish Internationalisms at the 1938 Empire Exhibition', 21.

Kane, as a young, educated, stylish and cosmopolitan woman, was considered an ideal spokesperson. It was hoped that Kane's youth and familiarity with America would sell Scotland to potential visitors and investors. Following her arrival to New York on the *Scythia*, Kane embarked on a 12,000 mile air tour of America and Canada's forty-two largest cities.[80] Kane had been selected by the SDC and a consortium of British transport companies to serve as the Exhibition's cultural ambassador.[81] Kane first came to the United States as an art student and made subsequent trips back and forth across the Atlantic.[82]

Kane was in some ways an unusual figure to represent Glasgow. Born in Dundee to Jewish parents of Russian and Lithuanian descent, Kane's second name had been changed from Kahan to the more Celtic sounding Kane. She had initially worked at the *Dundee Courier* and then for a period as an artist.[83] Kane did not have strong social or political connections to Glasgow's elite. Rather the Kanes were part of a small but significant Scottish Jewish community who had arrived in the early twentieth century from Eastern Europe. As Jenkinson has identified, cities in Scotland served as a transit point for Eastern European, Italian and Jewish residents hoping to pass through Britain before making their way to the Americas in the early twentieth century.[84] Many of these families, however, remained in Scotland and by the 1930s had experienced some social mobility through involvement in small businesses, Kane's own family had become successful through their drapery shop in the middle of Dundee.[85]

It was Kane's knowledge of American culture and attitudes as well as her cosmopolitan identity, however, that made her a perfect goodwill ambassador. Goodman observes that in the United States during the Second World War, interest groups and charitable organisations tended to choose 'a feminine public

---

80 'Miss Marie Kane Brings Word of Constructive Deeds from Abroad', *Evening Star* (18 June 1938).

81 'Telling the World', *Scotsman* (18 February1938), 13.

82 'Miss Marie Kane Brings Word of Constructive Deeds from Abroad', *Evening Star* (18 June 1938); Hal Kalwasser, 'My Mother an Honorary Ambassador', *Four Corners* (2007), 14.

83 Kalwasser, 'My Mother an Honorary Ambassador', 14.

84 Jacqueline Jenkinson, 'The Impact of the First World War on Migrant Lithuanians in Scotland, c. 1917–1921', *Immigrants & Minorities* 31/2 (2013), 171–188, 175; Munro and Slaven, 'Networks and Markets in Clyde Shipping', 37. Populations of Eastern European Jews, Poles, Lithuanians, Scandinavians and Italians arrived in the East of Scotland and departed Glasgow and Liverpool.

85 Kalwasser, 'My Mother an Honorary Ambassador', 14. Kane's father had initially settled in Aberdeen prior to moving to Dundee to open a drapery shop.

face'.[86] It was felt that women might represent Britain in a favourable way, expressing themselves more freely around the risks posed to the USA from conflict with Axis powers.

By 1938 Kane had visited America thirteen times through her work as an artist and in her courtship with her fiancé and later husband, New York psychiatrist, Simon Kalwasser.[87] Kalwasser met Kane when he was a medical student at St Andrews in the early 1930s. Kane later emigrated to the USA, living the remainder of her life in the Jamaica Estate of Queens, New York. Kane's life in New York was very different from her upbringing in Scotland, moving from the small and closeknit Jewish community of Dundee to an area of New York with a mixed population of socially mobile Scots, Irish, Germans and a growing number of Jews.[88] Regardless of this transition, Kane was comfortable in her role as a spokeswoman for the Exhibition and Scotland more generally.[89]

Kane was treated by American media as something of a minor celebrity, attending numerous events held in her honour and was regularly photographed. In this regard Kane's appearance and her opinions featured as an adjunct to reports about the Exhibition in the press. Chauvinistic descriptions of Kane as a 'Scotch Treat' or a 'Good Will Gal' regularly accompanied media reports on the Exhibition.[90] Kane's thoughts on the gentlemanly quality of Boston's men even featured in one report.[91] Kane's glamour, modern sensibilities and humour, however, countered American stereotypes of Scotland. In the run-up to the exhibition Scottish media worried that America might be put off by unrealistic

---

86 David Goodman, 'Loving and Hating Britain: Rereading the Isolationist Debate in the USA', in Kate Darian-Smith, Patricia Grimshaw and Stuart Macintyre, eds, *Britishness Abroad Transnational Movements and Imperial Cultures* (Melbourn: Melbourne University Press, 2007), 198.

87 Kalwasser, 'My Mother an Honorary Ambassador', 14; 'KALWASSER--Marie Kane', *New York Times*, (29 January 2007); 'Dr. Simon Kwalwasser', *New York Times* (3 August 1971). Simon Kalwasser was important in pioneering controversial insulin and shock therapies for adolescents with psychiatric conditions.

88 Donald Trump was born in the Jamaica Estates. His father Fred Trump's construction company was involved in the area's development, Trump senior and Mary Anne MacLeod settled there in 1936.

89 Kalwasser, 'My Mother an Honorary Ambassador', 14. Kane later served as a brand ambassador for Imperial Airways, the forerunner of British Airways.

90 'Scotch Treat', *Daily Alaska Empire* (3 March 1938), 4; 'Good Will Gal', *Imperial Valley Press* (July 22 1938).

91 'Boston Men Win Praise of Envoy', *The Daily Alaska Empire* (21 June 1938).

representations of Scotland that pervaded media. An editorial in the *Dundee Courier & Advertiser* remarked that:

> The immense areas of the American continent whose inhabitants have derived from the films and otherwise a conception of the Scots as a race of drolls, who wear comic kilts and carry curly walking sticks and are always and everywhere 'pawky'.[92]

Scottish comedian and music hall star Harry Lauder and Glaswegian actress and singer Ella Logan had to some extent popularised this representation of Scotland in America. In spite of Scottish cynicism, concerns were raised that Americans might not attend the exhibition on account of 'Scottish modesty' in publicising the exhibition, as the nation 'had not always been happy in her advertising'.[93]

North American visitors to Glasgow were therefore invited to 'see Scotland', and in doing so 'see the world'.[94] Despite worries about misrepresentations of Scotland, exhibition programmes emphasised that the exhibition would fuse the historic and modern together, as 'shipyards and ancient castles' lay 'side by side'.[95] This was reflected in the design of the Exhibition itself as pavilions dedicated to new technologies and engineering were accompanied by *An Clachan*, a model Highland village populated by families from the Hebrides.[96] Visitors to Glasgow would also be charmed by Scotland's natural beauty, as the observation decks of the opulent Art Deco Tait Tower offered vistas of islands, mountains and lochs across the West.[97] Yet some American visitors were unimpressed by Glasgow. Miss Carpenter of Las Vegas described the Dear Green Place as a 'gloomy city' when discussing her visit to Great Britain with her local Rotary.[98]

---

92 'The Empire Exhibition', *Dundee Courier & Advertiser* (3 May 1938), 6.

93 'Empire Exhibition', *Edinburgh Evening News* (16 February 1938), 8.

94 'A Letter From Scotland', *The Winnipeg Evening Tribune* (11 June 1938), 7.

95 *Calling the World: Empire Exhibition 1938* (John Miller LTD, Glasgow, 1938), 2; Britton, 'Urban Futures/Rural Pasts', 215.

96 Serrano, 'The Empire Exhibition of Scotland, 1938: the image and representation of an ephemeral modernity', *Expresión Gráfica Arquitectónica* 25/39 (2020), 32–45, 35; Hayden Lorimer, 'Ways of seeing the Scottish Highlands: marginality, authenticity and the curious case of the Hebridean Blackhouse', *Journal of Historical Geography* 25/4 (1999), 517–533.

97 Jennifer Robinson, 'Johannesburg's 1936 Empire Exhibition: Interaction, Segregation and Modernity in a South African City', *Journal of Southern African Studies* 29/3 (2003), 759–789.

98 'Miss Carpenter in Travel Talk', *Las Vegas Age* (16 September 1938).

Nevertheless, Scotland's history and scenery were used to encourage its global diaspora and their offspring to return:

> The clans are scattered now to the dominions and colonies to London and the South to the United states. This year there will be many MacLeods of Toronto and MacDonalds of Boston returning to the glen of their fathers ... Scotland presents the past and the present, face to face.[99]

The Scots emigrant and their role in the New World was celebrated in much of the Exhibition. In an official Exhibition magazine, a former manager in the shipping industry discussed the contributions made by Scottish emigrants to American manufacturing:

> Thirty years ago many Scots were employed as managers in foreign shipyards and engine works and although national self-sufficiency does its best to exclude even that form of import they are still to be found. I met two this year at the launch of a ship in America. I think it is a mistake to imagine, as some speakers of Caledonian society meetings or Burns suppers seem to do that any Scotsman will be welcomed with open arms in foreign countries just because he is a Scotsman. The Scots who succeed abroad owe their success to their hard work.[100]

While the work ethic of Scots emigrants was praised, appeals were made to Caledonian migrants overseas. The wealthy emigrant would potentially boost the exhibition's attendance and income. Overt appeals were made to diaspora Scots and their offspring by the likes of Lord Provost Dollan. In a radio programme Dollan encouraged communities of Scots living abroad to send delegates: 'wherever there were a 100 Scots people it would be possible to for them to send a representative by paying £1 each toward such a trip.'[101]

The Exhibition's advertising campaign emulated familiar patterns in public diplomacy. Following the First World War efforts had been made in America by various cultural organisations to use public events to reinforce Anglo-American relations.[102] By the 1930s there was a growing understanding of the role that

---

99 *Calling the World: Empire Exhibition 1938* (John Miller LTD, Glasgow, 1938), 2.

100 Glasgow University Archive, UGD 212 9/1, WG Riddel, 'The Scot Who Succeeds Abroad owes it to Hardwork', *Scotland Empire Exhibition Magazine* 3/2 (1938).

101 'Scots Abroad', *Edinburgh Evening News*, (1 January 1938), 7.

102 Bowman, *The Pilgrims Society and Public Diplomacy, 136.* As Bowman notes 'Britain's Day' in December 1918, had seen groups host over 3000 events across American cities to celebrate the bonds of Anglo-American friendship following the Allies' victory. Bowman offers a detailed understanding of public diplomacy as a concept in *The Pilgrims Society*, in particular he outlines changing understandings of the term and its relationship to propaganda.

culture could play in conjuring sophisticated political messages in the minds of the public.[103] While public lectures, banquets and pageants had previously been used to articulate messages of transatlantic co-operation, Britain's ambassador to the USA, Sir Robert Lindsay 1930–1939, argued that the British government should harness new media forms to elicit positive emotional feeling for Britain.[104] Radio and film were to be used in particular to court an American public whose politicians favoured isolationism. Thus, Kane's public engagements, their broadcast and coverage in print and visual media would contribute a small part to Britain's wider cultural and public diplomacy through the interwar period.

Despite a strong publicity campaign, the Empire Exhibition had an image problem. The growing crisis in Europe and dissent in the colonies were seen to be deterring visitors and investors. American newspapers reported that Britain's colonies 'no longer cringed in fear' of the 'shaggy lion' as it predicted further dissent and conflict with the Axis powers.[105] In radio broadcasts, newspaper interviews and lectures Marie Kane worked hard to encourage Americans to reassess their perceptions regarding the threat of war.

> You Americans have the wrong impression of Great Britain now, you really do. Babies wearing gas masks, air demonstrations, construction of bomb proof structures, you think we are doing nothing but prepare for war. I think it is the result of the some what frenzied note of your newspapers ... Do you suppose that the quarter of the earth that composes the Empire could unite in such an exposition if they were not confident of peace?[106]

What Kane brushed off as alleged sensationalism in American press, contradicted the overt ways in which Great Britain had begun to prepare for war. As early as 1935 Glasgow had made arrangements for how civilians could be protected from air raids.[107] American newspapers covered the construction of coastal defences, the instalment of anti-aircraft weapons and the distribution of gas masks to civilians through 1938 with photographs making apparent the extent of preparations.[108]

---

103 Bowman, *The Pilgrims Society and Public Diplomacy*, 203. Bowman points to the establishment of the British Council in 1934 as indicative of this.

104 Michael Todd Bennet, 'Anglophilia on Film: Creating an Atmosphere for Alliance 1935–1941', *Film & History*, 27/1 (1997), 9. The popularity of British film stars, directors and American films that depicted British Imperialism favourably in part helped to reinforce Anglo-American cultural relations.

105 'British Empire, Beset by Woes, Faces Battle to Retain Position', *The Ely Miner* (15 December 1938), 11.

106 'Miss Marie Kane Brings Word of Constructive Deeds from Abroad', *Evening Star* (18 June 1938).

107 'Air Raid Drill', *Edinburgh Evening News* (2 August 1935), 2.

108 'Great Britain Plays Safe', *Frontier O'Neil Nebraska* (20 October 1938), 2.

Some coverage of the Exhibition even featured discussion of a blackout and a mock air raid held on the Clyde.[109] Despite overt signs that Britain would enter into a war, Marie Kane insisted that:

> Your press stresses the threat of War much more than ours. I do believe, its because yours prints everything you want to read. While ours considers itself the guardian of public opinion. Don't you think our calm way is best, humans are such irrational creatures.[110]

In selling the exhibition Kane dismissed discussion of war as a peculiar characteristic of American media. Prospective investment and cultural exchange at a time of economic recession and political uncertainty was seen as a lifeline. Kane's mission was therefore more than simply an advertising campaign as her work was seen as necessary to sell the exhibition to a sceptical American public.

The World's Fair and the Transatlantic Relationship

In spite of the spectre of conflict, a variety of American visitors were drawn to the Exhibition. For example, the Exhibition's seventh million visitor was Doretta Walsh, an adolescent from New Jersey visiting with her family.[111] American diplomatic staff in Glasgow were also invited to attend the exhibition and Leslie A. Davis, US Consul to Glasgow, was treated as a guest of honour at a variety of ceremonial events attached to the Exhibition.[112] Leslie celebrated the 'opportunity' the Exhibition provided for 'bringing people together' as '... nothing was more conductive to the ideals of peace'.[113]

The famous were also present and better-known visitors from America included actor Edward Everett Horton, violinist Fritz Kreisler, pianist Fats Waller and the singer and radical Paul Robeson.[114] Indeed Robeson's concert in May 1938 proved to be one of the exhibition's most popular shows, with Robeson selling out all

---

109 'A Letter From Scotland', *Winnipeg Evening Tribune* (7 January, 1938), 6.

110 'Miss Marie Kane Brings Word of Constructive Deeds from Abroad', *Evening Star* (18 June 1938).

111 'Empire Exhibition', *Linlithogowshire Gazette* (19 August 1938), 5.

112 'The Exhibition', *Edinburgh Evening News* (26 October 1938); Merril D. Peterson, *'Starving Armenians': American and the Armenian Genocide 1915–1930*, (Charlottesville: University of Virginia Press, 2004) 35. Davis was a former diplomat who had worked in Turkey and been a witness to Armenian deportations and the atrocities which followed. Davis' accounts were reported to the state department.

113 'Guests Piped in at Empire Ball', *Dundee Courier* (26 October1938), 3,

114 'Empire Exhibition', *Belfast News Letter* (2 August 1938), 8; 'Kreisler and Paul Robeson', *Edinburgh Evening News* (4 April 1938), 9; 'Fats Waller in Scotland', *The Pittsburgh Courier* (27 August 1938), 20.

the 1706 seats of the Exhibition's main concert hall.[115] Robeson's appeal was significant in Glasgow, partially on account of his support for trade unionism and Republican Spain.[116] Robeson had delighted Scottish fans by informing the press that he had made efforts to learn Gaelic so as to master 'the haunting melodies of the Hebrides'.[117]

As the Exhibition came to a close Scots looked toward the World's Fair in New York.[118] While the World's Fair had initially been considered a competitive threat to Glasgow, it was apparent that as the Empire Exhibition was wound down, that it might serve as an inspiration. For example, the World's Fair sought to build its own Highland Village and Scottish talent was recruited to assist. Donald Cameron, a Uistman who constructed *An Clachan*, was invited to design New York's own.[119] Visits from those involved in the World's Fair served to reinforce a shared desire to promote commerce, trade and cultural exchange across the Atlantic. For example George McAneny broadcast his impressions of Glasgow back to fellow New Yorkers.[120] McAneny was a veteran New York politician, reformer and former manager of the *New York Times* and his civic credentials matched that of Glasgow's own city fathers.[121] A steady stream of visitors from the organising committee of the World's Fair visited Bellahouston. In July 1938, a party of town planning experts came to Glasgow to inspect the housing pavilion and tour the municipal housing schemes of Knightswood and Pollok.[122] It seemed New York wished to learn from Glasgow's efforts at slum clearance, both cities held unenviable reputations for overcrowding. Lord Provost Dollan took a keen interest in New York's work to address its housing problems and was even sent copies of American exposes on the extent of overcrowding in its largest city.[123] While Dollan praised the new municipal housing he had seen in New York as

115 'Paul Robeson a Big Draw', *Edinburgh Evening News* (2 September 1938), 4; 'Paul Robeson's Contribution', *Edinburgh Evening News* (10 August 1938), 7; 'Exhibition's Celebrity Week', *Broughty Ferry Guide and Advertiser* (27 August 1938), 4. The queue to enter the hall was estimated to have been a quarter of a mile long.

116 'Paul Robeson a Big Draw', *Edinburgh Evening News* (2 September 1938), 4. Robeson used a later concert at the City Halls to raise money for the Scottish Trade Union Food Ship for Spain appeal.

117 'Exhibition's Celebrity Week', *Broughty Ferry Guide and Advertiser* (27 August 1938), 4.

118 'Empire Exhibition's After Thoughts', *Dundee Evening Telegraph* (31 October 1938), 3.

119 'New York World Fair', *Oban Times and Argyllshire Advertiser* (28 January 1939), 5.

120 'America Day at Bellahouston', *Scotsman* (7 July1938), 12.

121 'US Town Planning Expert', *Scotsman* (22 July 1938), 13.

122 Ibid., 13.

123 GCA, GA 432. Correspondence, Patrick Dollan to Ernest Kennedy (22 October 1939).

being equipped with 'superior' bathrooms and washing facilities, he commented that rents were 'three times as high' as those in Glasgow.[124]

Civic diplomacy between Glasgow and New York continued into 1939 as war grew closer. Duranti argues that the outbreak of war in Europe contrasted sharply with the utopian themes that were at the heart of the World's Fair.[125] It appeared, however, that the threat of war invigorated what Mayor La Guardia referred to as a 'fraternal' civic relationship between these two cities.[126] La Guardia and Dollan maintained a steady correspondence between the beginning of the World's Fair and the initial years of the war. A two week visit to New York by Lord Provost Dollan in July 1939 to see the World's Fair and to observe the work of the La Guardia administration in relation to housing and health received prominent coverage in both the American and Scottish press. Dollan's words of praise for social reform in New York and his credentials as Glasgow's first Roman Catholic Lord Provost, since the Reformation, received appreciation from newspapers in New York and the Tri-State Area.[127] Dollan's unassuming personality and humour made him a popular figure in American newspapers too. His notoriety in America continued when he made several public pronouncements in conflict with the British government regarding the motivation of Rudolph Hess's flight to Britain. Dollan even claimed to have spoken with the deputy *Fuhrer* following his capture on a Renfrewshire farm in 1941.[128]

Dollan was treated as an important diplomatic guest in New York when he visited the World's Fair in the summer of 1939. He, and the twenty members of the town council who also visited, were greeted after disembarking the Anchor Line's SS *Transylvania* by representatives from City Hall and a number of Scottish societies before being taxied by Rolls Royce in a police motorcade to the Waldorf Astoria.[129] Dollan's work on behalf of Glasgow's poor was lauded at a testimonial dinner and by the Magna Carta Day Association.[130] While officially on Corporation business Dollan consistently

124 Ibid.

125 Marco Duranti, 'Utopia, Nostalgia and World War at the 1939–40 New York World's Fair', *Journal of Contemporary History* 41/4 (2006), 595–787, 668.

126 GCA, GA 432. Correspondence, Mayor La Guardia to Patrick Dollan (13 May 1939).

127 'Mayor of Glasgow gets City Honors', *New York Times* (22 July 1939); 'Patrick Joseph Dollan', *Waterbury Democrat* (3 August 1939); 'It is of Interest', *Waterbury Democrat* (25 July1939).

128 'Foreign News', *Time* (23 June 1941).

129 GCA, GA 432 'Lord Provost of Glasgow', *Bulletin Federation of Scottish Societies of Greater New York*, 25 (August 1939) The *Transylvania* was later sunk by a U-Boat in 1940.

130 GCA, GA 432, Correspondence, JW Hamilton to Patrick Dollan (11 August 1939); 'Topic of the Times', *New York Times* (18 July 1939); Bowman, *The Pilgrims Society and*

underlined the economic, cultural and linguistic ties that existed between Great Britain and America and the importance of these in the face of 'war clouds'.[131] Correspondence between Dollan and La Guardia offers further insight into their shared beliefs in 'civic democracy' and progressive reform.[132] Newspapers in Britain had heaped praise on La Guardia and his administration.[133] In an article authored by Dollan for the *Evening Times* of his 'First Impressions of New York', he recounted the pride New Yorkers had for their civic government, the presence of many Scots in the La Guardia administration and the 'bewildering' contradiction that half a million unemployed lived in America's richest city.[134] Dollan commented that La Guardia and he 'became friends at first site' as they discussed local administration as well as international affairs.[135] In Dollan's words La Guardia had described him as a 'swell guy' who like him still occupied the same tenement house he had prior to his election.[136] Dollan went on to comment that La Guardia was happy as the pair preferred to 'study social services rather than patronise cabarets and nightclubs'.[137]

Returning to Glasgow Dollan lauded the ambitiousness of New York's civic administration arguing that Glasgow could learn lessons:

> Our people ... have got to stop lecturing the Americans when they go over there. They should go to learn. America is a young country, full of courage ... and wants to be taken seriously. After seeing public spaces equal to half the total acreage of Glasgow, and a community three times as healthy as Glasgow you get all the conceit knocked out of you.[138]

Dollan's honest reflections on his visit with the town council evidently left a lasting impression. Further, his camaraderie with La Guardia was continued through official civic gestures. Prior to the beginning of the Second World War

---

Public Diplomacy (Edinburgh: Edinburgh University Press, 2018). The Magna Carta Day Association represented a growing interest in the cultural heritage of Britain and America. Their work was typical of public diplomacy efforts carried out by groups interested in transatlantic co-operation.

131 GCA, GA 432 'Lord Provost of Glasgow', *Bulletin Federation of Scottish Societies of Greater New York*, 25, (August 1939). The Magna Carta Day Association set out to promote peace and interdependence between English speaking countries.

132 GCA, GA 432, Correspondence Patrick Dollan to Fiorello La Guardia, (6 April 1939).

133 'First Impressions of New York and Mayor La Guardia', *Evening Times* (11 August 1939).

134 Ibid.

135 Ibid.

136 Ibid.

137 Ibid.

138 'Dollan's Praise of America', *Dundee Evening Telegraph* (11 August 1939), 9.

La Guardia had intended to visit Glasgow to receive the Freedom of the City from Dollan. In thanking Dollan for his invitation La Guardia added that he hoped 'international conditions would be such' that he could 'avail himself'.[139]

Although La Guardia did not visit, events through the war strengthened ties between the two politicians and their respective cities and nations. This was apparent following the sinking of the Anchor Line's *Athenia* on the 3rd of September 1939 by U-boat. The sinking killed around 138 people, amongst this number were twenty-eight Americans.[140] La Guardia thanked Dollan for providing 'humane services' to the American survivors.[141] Many of the survivors were treated at Glasgow's Royal Infirmary and those who did not require medical attention were housed with Glaswegians, including Dollan himself.[142] In thanking Dollan, La Guardia went on to note that although New Yorkers were 'free' from 'the immediate and visual horrors of war', the threat of aerial bombardment was a terrifying prospect.[143]

The provision of humanitarian assistance by Glasgow Corporation to the victims and the creation of a charitable fund which raised £3,520 in the days following the attack was regarded highly by New York's Mayor.[144] In personal correspondence La Guardia thanked Dollan for providing 'humane services' to survivors.[145] Many of the survivors were treated at Glasgow's Royal Infirmary and those who did not require medical attention were housed with Glaswegians, including Dollan himself.[146] Glasgow further extended its hospitality to entertaining those survivors who had arrived in the city with a reception dinner featuring music from Glasgow Police Pipe Band and a performance by Sir Harry Lauder.[147]

---

139 'Mayor La Guardia Plans to Visit Britain' *Dundee Evening Telegraph* (5 August 1939), 8; 'Mayor La Guardia Greets Lord Provost', *Scotsman* (7 September 1939), 5. The former pilot planned a later visit to Britain in 1941 where Dollan again invited the Mayor of New York to visit Glasgow to receive honours.

140 'Athenia Survivors: U.S. Thanks Glasgow', *Daily Record and Mail* (9 September 1939), 3. The *Athenia* had departed Glasgow on the 1st of September and was intended for Montreal and had made stops in Belfast and Liverpool, before being sunk by U-Boat off the West Coast of Ireland.

141 GCA, GA 432, Correspondence Fiorello La Guardia to Patrick Dollan (24 November 1939).

142 'Athenia Survivors', *Scotsman* (7 September 1939), 11. The Lord Provost took in an American mother and her son.

143 GCA, GA 432, Correspondence Fiorello La Guardia to Patrick Dollan (24 November 1939); 'Invitation to New York Mayor', *Scotsman* (27 May 1941), 3. La Guardia's role as supervisor of air defence in America made him acutely interested in civilian defence procedures.

144 Ibid., 3.

145 GCA,, GA 432 Correspondence Fiorello La Guardia to Patrick Dollan (24 November 1939).

146 'Athenia Survivors', *Scotsman* (7 September 1939), 11.

147 'Civic Reception to Athenia Survivors', *Scotsman* (13 September 1939), 10.

This civic event again became a show of propaganda as the flags of those citizens killed in the sinking: British, Canadian, Polish and Czechoslovak, were draped from the balconies of the City Chambers. As Dollan remarked the *Athenia* was 'a veritable league of nations', which united citizens of democratic states.[148]

The notable loss of American life resulted in a diplomatic visit from the son of American Ambassador Joseph Kennedy. John F. Kennedy, then 19 years old, was dispatched to visit American survivors in Glasgow, with £10,000 at his disposal to assist survivors.[149] The young Kennedy praised the efforts taken by Glasgow Corporation and the Lord Provost in caring for Americans, remarking that 'I have never seen people more grateful for all that has been done for them by Glasgow than to those whom I spoke to today.'[150] Kennedy's attempts to reimburse Glasgow Corporation for the expense of the survivors' care was refused. His hosts 'insisted that Glasgow regards it as a privilege to undertake this responsibility'.[151]

While Kennedy was warmly received by his Scottish hosts, vocal protests were made by some of the 150 American survivors he met with at the Beresford Hotel.[152] The suggestion of American naval convoys to accompany passenger vessels was discounted by Kennedy, leading to angry outbursts from one gentleman who shouted 'you can't trust the goddamn German Navy', a group of female college students even informed Kennedy they would refuse to return without a convoy.[153] The quandary of how to transport the some 8000 Americans still in Britain back to America was a concern for Kennedy's father.[154] As the war in the Atlantic began it became apparent that convoys would be needed to protect civilian shipping.

Joseph Kennedy's hesitation toward increasing support for Britain eventually saw him replaced in 1941 by John Winant, a 'liberal internationalist' and former head of the ILO.[155] Winant, in his capacity as ambassador to Britain, visited Glasgow several times. Winant appeared a more popular figure than Kennedy senior and media covered his ambassadorial duties closely. His status as former head of the ILO and his frequent references to Christianity in speeches gave him broad appeal to the Scottish population and saw him honoured with awards,

---

148 Ibid. Dollan in particular noted the duel tragedy faced by the Polish and Czechoslovak victims who had 'lost' their countries too.

149 'Athenia Survivors: U.S. Thanks Glasgow', *Daily Record and Mail* (9 September 1939), 3.

150 Ibid., 3.

151 Ibid., 3.

152 'Athenia Survivors Demand Destroyer Escort', *Dundee Courier and Advertiser* (8 September 1939), 3.

153 'Athenia Americans demand a convoy', *Daily Record and Mail* (8 September 1939).

154 'Athenia Survivors: U.S. Thanks Glasgow', *Daily Record and Mail* (9 September 1939), 3.

155 Mayers, *FDR's Ambassadors and the Diplomacy of Crisis*, 194.

civic receptions, lunches, honorary degrees and ceremonial openings in Glasgow, Edinburgh, Aberdeen and Jedburgh.[156] In giving the Immortal Memory, at the victory dinner of the Scottish Burns Club in Glasgow during 1946, Winant looked forward to the role the United Nations would play in establishing peace, surmising that the end of the war had brought renewed importance to the core values that underpinned Burns. Winant stated that:

> Robert Burns believed in a world for all or he would have none of it. He was a man for our time. He understood the anguish of the homeless, the fear of want, he had a remorseless hate of persecution of man nor beast.[157]

In his address Winant went on to affirm his belief in the transatlantic relationship, hoping that 'the friendship between our countries will be never-ending.'[158]

As a frequent target of German bombardment Glasgow received financial assistance from American aid campaigns and charities such as the British War Relief Society (BWSR).[159] Dollan also continued to host prominent American visitors, furthering British and American strategic interests. Dollan provided a well-publicised civic reception for Prime Minister Winston Churchill and Harry Hopkins, President Roosevelt's personal envoy and when they visited Glasgow to inspect civil defences in January 1941.[160] Hopkins was regarded as Roosevelt's 'confidante', and was tasked with a responsibility for assessing the supply situation in Britain.[161]

Dollan boasted that he was one of the first people to know America would assist Britain in the war. At a party in Washington, DC, in 1950, the former Lord Provost recounted that he was instructed by Churchill to ascertain what FDR's position was. In a private conversation, at Glasgow's Central Station Hotel, Dollan claimed he asked Hopkins 'would America join the War?' and was directed by the diplomat to Ruth 1:16, 'Whither thou goest, I go.'[162] Dollan's retelling of his encounter with Hopkins was embellished to entertain his audience and to cast

---

156 'Mr Winant Looks at Britain', *Edinburgh Evening News* (9 July 1942), 2; 'Mr John G Winant', *Jedburgh Gazette* (16 February 1942), 3; 'Mr J. G. Winant American Ambassador in Edinburgh' *Edinburgh Evening News* (18 July 1941), 3; 'May Bring Winant to Aberdeen', *Aberdeen Press and Journal* (13 November 1941), 2; 'Glasgow Degree for Mrs Churchill', *Edinburgh Evening News* (24 May 1945), 2.

157 'Mr Winant on Burns', *Scotsman* (22 January 1946), 4.

158 'Mr Winant Too Late for the Haggis', *Aberdeen Press and Journal* (22 January 1946), 1.

159 'British War Relief Society', *Chapel Hill Weekly* (11 April 1941), 6. Dollan thanked the North Carolina chapter of the BWSR for their donation of £10,000 in April 1941.

160 'US Envoy Thanks Glasgow', *Edinburgh Evening News* (28 January 1941), 4.

161 Mayers, *FDR's Ambassadors and the Diplomacy of Crisis*, 194.

162 'Exclusively Yours', *Evening Star* (1 October 1950), 5.

himself as a leading figure in wartime diplomacy. Despite this exaggeration, however, the quip from scripture emphasised a continuing partnership between Britain and the US, a cause Dollan had certainly contributed to through his years of political work. Importantly, visits by such senior US diplomats provide evidence that Glasgow remained an important and strategic transatlantic urban centre through the war.

Conclusion

The Empire Exhibition thus took place at a time of transition for Scottish politics and industry. The Scottish economy had been badly affected by unemployment and the depression. This was reflected in severe economic decline and the significant migration of Scots in the years leading up to 1938. The Exhibition set out to help revive the Scottish economy by attracting tourism and investment. Although the promotion of trade with the colonies and dominions was fundamental to the Exhibition's purpose, the SDC set out to use the Exhibition as a means to capitalise on Glasgow's relationship with the United States. The SDC therefore dispatched Marie Kane to tempt American visitors to 'see Scotland'.[163] Kane was an ideal cultural ambassador on account of her familiarity with American culture. Her tour and radio broadcasts brought the Exhibition to audiences beyond the Empire. In her media campaign Kane downplayed the threat of war in Europe to allay the fears of potential American visitors. Nevertheless, the discussion of international conflict was inevitable as events in and out of the Exhibition made this apparent. While the presence of the Peace Pavilion and the Garden of Good Neighbours demonstrates that the Exhibition sought to promote international co-operation, the controversy surrounding these exhibits reflected the zeitgeist of political uncertainty.

In spite of this, the Empire Exhibition contributed to strengthening the relationship between Great Britain and the United States prior to the Second World War at a point where American attitudes toward Great Britain were increasingly ambivalent. Glasgow's status as an Atlantic city of international importance would be revived as influential and ordinary Americans visited the city. Events through the war such as the sinking of the *Athenia* meant that Glasgow would continue to receive the attention of the American public and their politicians. As the Empire Exhibition closed, interest moved toward the New York World's Fair of 1939 which Lord Provost Dollan was invited to visit. Despite being ostensibly in New York as a representative of Glasgow at the World Fair and studying the

[163] 'A Letter From Scotland', *The Winnipeg Evening Tribune* (11 June 1938), 7.

work of the La Guardia administration, Dollan acted as an eloquent propagandist on behalf of British interests in his dealings with the American public and media. Dollan was an effective diplomat, emphasising the extensive economic, cultural and personal links between Britain and the USA that were threatened by war. Dollan's correspondence with La Guardia further evidences the reciprocal efforts made by these two civic leaders to engage in civic diplomacy at a time of political uncertainty. Thus, although the Empire Exhibition did not receive the economic interest from America the SDC had hoped for, the event contributed in strengthening ties between Great Britain and the USA. The work of Kane, Dollan and others added a small but important Scottish dimension to the transatlantic relationship at a critical point for Great Britain.

Parallel Cities: Glasgow and New York

Stephen Bowman

What follows is a meditation on the processes involved in interpreting the history writing of nineteenth- and twentieth-century Glasgow in relation to New York and on writing modern Scottish urban history in relation to American. It is in part a comparison of two cities (and countries) and their historiographies but is in larger part an exploration of how these cities' history of transnational exchange actively shapes such a comparison in the first place. Simply, it explores how *historical* exchange and *historiographical* comparison are mutually constitutive.[1] Yet the decision to trace interconnections and draw historiographical parallels between these two ostensibly very different cities needs justifying. For one, the historical developments and associated academic responses explored here have been common to many large, (post-)industrialised cities since the second half of the twentieth century. At the same time, with New York, is it not the case that everyone wants 'to be a part of it'?[1] In other words, the act of comparing and connecting Glasgow and New York could be dismissed as a reflex caused by the ubiquity of US culture during and since the 'American Century', a century Martin Shefter crowns New York the 'capital' of.[2] As S. G. Checkland wrote in the 1970s, however, Glasgow's experience of depopulation and deindustrialisation was the 'most dramatic case among the British provincial cities'.[3] Its example is therefore impossible to ignore. At the same time, John Hull Mollenkopf is right to say that, for all its fame and infamy, New York is 'more archetypical than atypical' and that '[b]y concentrating extremes, it reveals forces, trends, and conflicts latent elsewhere.'[4] Glasgow is one such 'elsewhere', and an important one at that, with very real linkages with New York.

---

1 John Kander and Fred Ebb, 'Theme from *New York, New York*', 1977.

2 Martin Shefter, 'New York's National and International Influence', in Shefter, ed., *Capital of the American Century: The National and International Influence of New York City* (New York: Russell Sage Foundation, 1993), 1; the cultural, social, and economic significance of New York to what later become known as the 'American Century' was also expressed at the beginning of the twentieth century by German philosopher Georg Simmel in terms of the 'Amerikanismus', the influence of which European cities were seen as increasingly coming under. See Nick Yablon, *Untimely Ruins: An Archaeology of American Urban Modernity, 1819–1919* (Chicago: University of Chicago Press, 2009), 15.

3 S. G. Checkland, *The Upas Tree: Glasgow, 1875–1975* (Glasgow: University of Glasgow Press, 1976), 97.

4 John Hull Mollenkopf, 'Introduction', in Mollenkopf, ed., *Power, Culture, and Place: Essays on New York City* (New York: Russell Sage Foundation, 1988), xvii.

Nicolas Kenny and Rebecca Madgin have written persuasively about how researching the historical city 'involves not just accounting for its various manifestations, but more probingly, requires us to think of cities as plural, in relation to one another, both comparatively and transnationally'.[5] This chapter's contention is that we may also think of what initially seem distinct historiographies as plural and in parallel. It identifies key discourses that, like those emphasising the 'light and darkness' or 'pleasure and pain' of city life, the historiographies of both cities have developed *within*.[6] These discourses are about 'transnationalism' and being

---

5 Kenny and Madgin, 'Urban History as Comparative and Transnational Practice', 4; There is no shortage of publications examining the connections and comparisons between cities (significantly, many of these incorporate New York). Examples include T. Bender and C. Schorske, *Budapest and New York: Studies in Metropolitan Transformations, 1870–1930* (New York: Russell Sage Foundation, 1994); Susan S. Fainstein, Ian Gordon, and Michael Harloe, *Divided Cities: New York and London in the Contemporary World* (Oxford: Wiley-Blackwell, 1992); Joachim Schlor, *Nights in the Big City: Paris, Berlin, London, 1840–1930* (London: Reaktion Books, 1998); very recently on Manchester and Chicago, Tom Hulme, *After the Shock City: Urban Culture and the Making of Modern Citizenship* (Woodbridge: Royal Historical Society, 2019); Bill Marshall, *Montreal-Glasgow* (Glasgow: University of Glasgow French & German Publications, 2005). None, however, have examined Glasgow and New York in tandem; Shane Ewen, *What is Urban History?* (Cambridge: Polity, 2016), 11; On debates within urban studies about the relationship between the particular and the universal see Keith Kintrea and Rebecca Madgin 'Conclusion: beyond the post-industrial: narratives of time and place', in Kintrea and Madgin, eds, *Transforming Glasgow: Beyond the Post-Industrial City* (Bristol: Policy Press, 2020), 283.

6 Commentators have long pondered the apparently dichotomous and contradictory nature of the modern city. This characterisation of city life was partly shaped by Charles Baudelaire's depictions of nineteenth-century Paris but a similar picture of 'the city' as a place of hitherto unknown danger and pleasure is also made explicit in the various 'urban sketches' of the period, such as *Lights and Shadows of New York Life* and, for Glasgow, 'Shadow's' *Midnight Scenes and Social Photographs*. The complexities of such urban imaginaries have been examined most forcefully by Judith Walkowitz's cultural history of Victorian London and were grounded in contemporary middle-class anxieties about poverty, capitalism, class, and gender. See Mark D. Steinberg, *Petersburg Fin de Siècle: The Darkening Landscape of Modern Times, 1905–1917* (New Haven: Yale University Press, 2011), 6; James D. McCabe, *Lights and Shadows of New York Life* (Philadelphia, 1872) and Eugène Sue, *Les* Mystères de Paris (Paris, 1842/43) referenced in Angela M. Blake, *How New York Became American, 1890–1924* (Baltimore: Johns Hopkins University Press, 2006); *Midnight Scenes and Social Photographs Being Sketches of Life in the Streets, Wynds, and Dens of the City, By Shadow* (Glasgow, 1858: reprint 1976); Judith Walkowitz, *City of Dreadful Delight: Narratives of Sexual Danger in Late-Victorian London* (Chicago: University of Chicago Press, 1992), 17; Other examples of studies of the contested nature of the historical city include Joan Neuberger, *Crime, Culture, and Power in St Petersburg, 1900–1914* (Berkeley: University of California Press, 1993); Daniel R. Brower, *The Russian City between Tradition and Modernity, 1850–1900* (Berkeley: University of California Press, 1990).

'not of the nation' (interwoven with notions of 'translocalism'), and about 'decay' and 'rebirth'. They are scholarly and popular discourses that are instructive both about the past and about why writers have chosen to analyse it in the ways they have often done.[7] Each is also a dialectical puzzle and a contradiction existing in discursive relation with the other, encapsulated by Marx's dictums about a modern world where 'everything seems pregnant with its contrary' and where 'all that is solid melts into air.' They are yet further evidence that the identification, perception, and experience of contradiction is a defining characteristic of urban modernity and modernist writing.[8] Moreover, the discourses identified in this chapter are indicative of how an intricate web of place-based interconnections can shape historiographical comparison, requiring 'comparative judgements' of 'historical reconstructions' and also of 'the – historiographical – reconstructions of those historical reconstructions'.[9]

The chapter seeks to maintain a focus on the historiography but its interest in changing historical and cultural contexts means that it necessarily adopts a fluid approach to chronology; its structure is thematic rather than linear. Nevertheless, the narrative of the visit to New York by Patrick Dollan, Glasgow's Lord Provost between 1938 and 1941, provides a central conceit that will help readers orientate themselves in time and space. As Kieran Taylor established in the previous chapter, Dollan – cast now in the role of Baudelairean flâneur – visited New York in July 1939 to attend the city's World Fair as the guest of its mayor Fiorello La Guardia and was himself struck by the parallels between Glasgow and New York. With the outbreak of the Second World War shortly thereafter, Dollan's written account of his trip across the Atlantic was entitled *A Tale of Two Cities, Glasgow-New York* and was sold to help raise funds for the Glasgow Central War Relief Fund. Importantly for the purposes of this chapter, Dollan's writing shows that there

---

7 The identification and labelling of these discourses raise questions of reflexivity and also of how such discourses may be compared across different local, national, and transnational contexts. The notion of 'crossed histories' provides one possible approach to these problems. See Michael Werner and Bénédicte Zimmerman, 'Beyond Comparison: Histoire Croisée and the Challenge of Reflexivity', *History and Theory* 45/1 (2006), 30–50.

8 Marshall Berman, *All That Is Solid Melts Into Air: The Experience of Modernity* (London: Verso, 1982), 20.

9 Chris Lorenz, 'Comparative Historiography: Problems and Perspectives', *History & Theory* 38/ 1 (1999), 29; Fiona Paisley and Pamela Scully, *Writing Transnational History* (London: Bloomsbury Academic, 2019), 84; For definitions of the 'translocal' see Clemens Greiner and Patrick Sakdapolrak, 'Translocality: Concepts, Applications and Emerging Research Perspectives', *Geography Compass* 7/5 (2013), 373–384, in particular 376: Translocality can include the 'visualisation and imagining of linkages between places', or what some scholars call 'translocal imagination'.

is historical precedent for taking Glasgow and New York as a parallel study. In *A Tale of Two Cities* Dollan highlighted what he regarded as the many similarities between the two cities, including in their architecture and in the temperament of their people. He felt that '[l]ooking down upon New York from the heights of any of its great buildings made me think I was viewing an enlarged Glasgow' and commented that 'Glasgow and New York are complementary communities. It is difficult to view the one without thinking of the other.'[10] In making these comments, Dollan was thinking about the views from the top of buildings on Glasgow's Bothwell Street but may equally have had in mind nearby buildings such as the Union Bank of Scotland on St Vincent Street. Completed in 1927 the building was designed by James Miller, who was inspired by the Guaranty Trust building in New York. It remains a strikingly American feature of Glasgow's built environment [see the photographs on p. xiv and p. 15].[11] The translocalist sentiment expressed by Dollan that it is 'difficult to view the one without thinking of the other' further emerges from this chapter's examination of what has been written about Glasgow and New York by urban historians in the years since.

Transnationalism/Not of the Nation

Dollan sailed to New York from Glasgow on the Anchor Line ship the *Transylvania*. The Second World War resulted in the permanent end of the regular passenger services between Glasgow and New York that Kevin James so evocatively described in his earlier chapter; Dollan's trip in 1939 was therefore one of the last such return voyages.[12] It is stretching credibility to say that the end of regular steamer services between Glasgow and New York severed the two cities' transatlantic connections but it remains the case that very few writers since have made an attempt to study or compare them in a sustained or scholarly fashion. Yet both have been

---

10 Patrick Dollan, *A Tale of Two Cities, Glasgow-New York* (Glasgow, 1940), 26–28.

11 Neil Baxter and Fiona Sinclair, eds, *Scotstyle: 100 Years of Scottish Architecture, 1916–2015* (Edinburgh: the Royal Incorporation of Architects in Scotland, 2016), 34. This was a built environment that utilised steel frame technologies around the same time as did Chicago (a city which competes with New York and Minneapolis for the honour of having first developed the means to build the skyscraper in the 1880s and 1890s). See Christoph Lindner, *Imagining New York City: Literature, Urbanism, and the Visual Arts, 1890–1940* (Oxford: Oxford University Press, 2015), 29–31 and John M. MacKenzie, '"The Second City of the Empire": Glasgow – imperial municipality', in Felix Driver and David Gilbert, eds, *Imperial Cities: Landscape, Display and Identity* (Manchester: Manchester University Press, 1999), 225.

12 Dollan, *Two Cities*, 11; David Daiches, *Glasgow* (London: Grafton, 1982), 224–225; Indeed, the *Transylvania* itself was sunk by a German submarine in 1940.

written as 'transnational' and 'transatlantic' cities. Such interpretations rely on New York's real and imagined connections with Europe and Glasgow's real and imagined connections with North America. Evidently Bernard Aspinwall's 1984 *Portable Utopia* remains the most important publication tracing the transatlantic connection between Glasgow and the United States. His basic premise was that between 1820 and 1920 Glasgow acted as a clearing house for distinctly Scottish contributions to American society, particularly in the realms of religion, democracy, and social reform. According to Aspinwall, this 'Atlantic community' was enhanced by Glasgow's own 'American' characteristics, including a 'self-made' optimistic confidence.[13] This was a sentiment that had been articulated by the Glasgow journalist Charles Oakley in 1946, when he wrote that 'democracy has evolved in Glasgow along the same lines as in New York, rather than along those to be observed in London.' According to Oakley, Glasgow and New York were together 'more individualistic, less well-mannered places' where '[a]uthority is not so readily accepted'.[14] Oakley's comments are perhaps unverifiable but, as with Dollan's observations seven years previously, they provide clear evidence of a perception in the Scottish city of a joint Glasgow-New York worldview. They also raise questions about what such perceptions mean for Glasgow's Scottishness and New York's American-ness. As will become apparent, the place of each city within and outwith the 'nation' is a recurring theme in the historiography.

With the exception of the antiquarian histories of the pre-modern burgh published by the likes of the Scottish Burgh Records Society urban history was a relative latecomer to Scottish historiography. While H. J. Dyos' work at the University of Leicester helped encourage the growth of the field of urban history in Britain from the 1960s, this too often focused on London at the expense of what Dyos referred to as the 'provincial towns' and the 'Celtic fringes', whose nineteenth-century urban history he considered largely in relation to the British capital.[15] Ian H. Adams' 1978 *Making of Urban Scotland* was a major contributor

[13] Bernard Aspinwall, *Portable Utopia: Glasgow and the United States, 1820–1920* (Aberdeen: Aberdeen University Press, 1984).

[14] C. A. Oakley, *The Second City* (Glasgow, 1946), 337–338.

[15] H. J. Dyos, 'Greater and greater London: metropolis and provinces in the nineteenth and twentieth centuries', in David Cannadine and David Reeder, eds, *Exploring the Urban Past: Essays in Urban History by H. J. Dyos* (Cambridge: Cambridge University Press, 1982), 37–55; Geoffrey Best – an English historian working in Scotland – provided an early historiographical challenge to British neglect of Scottish urban history. See Best, 'The Scottish Victorian City', *Victorian Studies* 11/3 (1968), 329–358. It is also worth noting that Best also writes that to 'anyone who knows the remarkable place held by Chicago in the cultural and political history of the United States, it is an interesting possibility, that Glasgow may

to the development of Scottish urban studies, motivated in part by Adams' frustration at the 'distortions' caused by an 'historical preoccupation with Mary Queen of Scots and Bonnie Prince Charlie, and the geographical preoccupation with the Highlands'. For Adams, Scots since the industrial revolution had been an 'urban people' and their history had yet to be written. As such, the dominance of the rural in the Scottish historical imagination had hitherto implied that what was urban was not Scottish.[16] Something similar may also be said of American historiography, itself torn between the competing influences of Frederick Jackson Turner's frontier thesis, which presents US national history as a unique evolutionary tale of westward expansion of which the city was the natural endpoint, and Charles A. Beard's alternative view that the American past was shaped not by settlement of the West but instead by the shift from a pre-modern agrarian society to a modern industrial and urban one, apparently mirroring historical economic developments in other capitalist countries. In the view of Kenneth Jackson and Stanley Schultz, whose 1972 *Cities in American History* remains a very useful resource on American urban history, Beard and Turner 'cast such long shadows over American scholarship' that the 'role of the city in the United States' was then still 'little understood'.[17]

That is not to say that authors had not been trying to understand the American city. Writing in 1996, Carl Abbott identified four distinct phases or 'generations' in US urban history. The first of these generations typically include statistical accounts and 'booster' histories produced by local elites in the period 1840–75.

---

be best placed as the Chicago of Victorian Britain'; On Glasgow in the context of British urban history, see also C. M. Allan, 'The Genesis of British Urban Redevelopment with Special Reference to Glasgow', *The Economic History Review* 18/3 (1965), 598–613.

16 G. Gordon and B. Dicks, 'Prolegomena', in Gordon and Dicks, eds, *Scottish Urban History* (Aberdeen: Aberdeen University Press, 1983), 1–2; I. H. Adams, *The Making of Urban Scotland* (London: Croom Helm Ltd, 1978), 9; Robert D. Mitchell, 'Reviews: *The Making of Urban Scotland*, by Ian H. Adams; *A Geography of Scotland*, by K. J. Kea', *Geographical Review*, 69/3 (1979), 368–370; Ewen, *What is Urban History?*, 16–17; Glasgow's 1938 Empire Exhibition revealed in stark terms the contradictions between Scottishness, progress, and the rural and the urban. Whilst some exhibits were designed to showcase Scotland's industrial prowess, others focused on the sorts of historical tropes identified here by Adams. See Sarah Britton, 'Urban futures/rural pasts: representing Scotland in the 1938 Glasgow Empire Exhibition', *Cultural and Social History* 8/2 (2011), 213–232.

17 Richard C. Wade, 'Urbanization' in C. Vann Woodward, ed., *The Comparative Approach to American History* (Oxford: Oxford University Press, 1997), 188–189; Kenneth T. Jackson and Stanley K. Schultz, 'The City in American History', in Jackson and Shultz (eds), *Cities in American History* (New York: Knopf, 1972), 1; Turner himself admitted in 1925 that American historians would need to devote more attention to American urban history. See Arthur M. Schlesinger, 'The City in American History', *Mississippi Valley Historical Review* 27/1 (1940), 43.

The second generation was characterised by more substantial histories written in the period 1875–1930, though these were no less concerned with accounting for the progress of both the American city and the American nation than were the first-generation histories. Urban history in this period was in part imagined as a national undertaking, with the US Congress encouraging the writing of local histories as part of the nation's centennial celebrations in 1876. The third generation, meanwhile, was influenced by the 'Chicago School' of sociologists at the University of Chicago from the 1920s onwards. For scholars like Robert Park, the city could serve as a 'laboratory to explore the changing patterns and experiences of human society and culture'.[18] These approaches fostered linkages between history and the social sciences in the US, as shown by the work of Bayrd Still.[19] Of this 'third generation' of American urban historians, Arthur Schlesinger Snr was probably the most consequential. Schlesinger's 1933 *The Rise of the City, 1878–1898* argued for the centrality of the city (implicitly contrary to Turner) in American history and, in the view of one scholar, 'marks the invention of American urban history'. Despite the fact he was writing during the Great Depression, or perhaps because of it, Schlesinger regarded the city as a locus for hope, improvement, and progress. For that reason, his book 'merits attention for what it says about American civilization in the 1930s – it is a liberal, democratic, pluralistic, and curiously optimistic look at the past and the future of American cities and civilization'.[20] For Abbott, a fourth generation of urban historians emerged in the 1950s and 1960s under the influence of one of Schlesinger's students, Richard Wade, who – like Asa Briggs in England (for Briggs' seminal 1963 book *Victorian Cities* makes scant reference to Glasgow) – adopted more comparative approaches to the study of cities.[21]

What Scottish urban history writing there was by the second half of the twentieth century, meanwhile, often tended towards the social or economic, or indeed the geographical as in the case of Adams and others, implicitly concurring with Sidney Pollard that there are no other ways to study city life: 'modern British social history *is* urban history.'[22] There are, however, some important exceptions to what Cameron and Reeder regard as the dominant empiricism of Scottish and

---

18 Carl Abbott, 'Thinking about Cities: The Central Tradition in US history', *Journal of Urban History* 22/6 (1996), 687–701; Ewen, *What is Urban History?*,16; Robert E. Park, Ernest W. Burgess, and Roderick D. McKenzie, *The City* (Chicago, 1925).

19 Ewen, *What is Urban History?*, 16–20.

20 Andrea Tuttle Kornbluh, 'Introduction' in Arthur Meir Schlesinger', *The Rise of the City, 1878–1898* (Columbus: Ohio State University Press, 1999), xi and xxvi.

21 Carl Abbott, 'Thinking about Cities', 687–701.

22 Ewen, *What is Urban History?*, 11.

British urban history. An early outlier from empirical Glasgow history writing is Ian Spring's 1990 *Phantom Village: The Myth of the New Glasgow*, which explores the multiple and contradictory versions of the city that he regarded as existing in tension between the 'traditional' and the mythical new.[23] Spring's work appeared at a particular point in Glasgow's past, specifically after it had been named 1990 European City of Culture and when a range of cultural initiatives appeared to reinvent the city for the postmodern age at the expense of dealing with its existing social and economic inequalities. Meanwhile, Glasgow has featured in the recent work of some Scottish-based cultural historians, most notably Tanya Cheadle, Jeff Meek, and Angela Bartie and Alistair Fraser, all of whom are interested in the city as gendered and/or sexualised spaces.[24] These texts, however, are not urban histories in the strictest sense and do not exist within the historiographical tradition of urban biography in which the city itself is the focus of study. More relevant is MacKenzie's 1999 work on the role nineteenth-century imperialism played in helping construct Glasgow's sense of self in that period, while questions of urban identity form the basis of Craig Lamont's 2021 monograph on the ways in which Victorian Glasgow has overshadowed Georgian Glasgow in the historical imagination.[25] Meanwhile Michael Fry's history of Glasgow, published

---

23 Ian Spring, *Phantom Village: The Myth of the New Glasgow* (Edinburgh: Polygon, 1990), passim; Ewen A. Cameron, 'Glasgow's going round and round: some recent Scottish urban history', *Urban History* 30/2 (2003), 287; D. Reeder, 'The industrial city in Britain: urban biography in the modern style', *Urban History*, 25/3 (1998), 368–378; Gerard Carruthers and Catriona M. M. MacDonald, 'Fictive Pasts and Past Fictions', *The Scottish Historical Review* XCII, Supplement: No. 234 (April 2013), 137–166.

24 Tanya Cheadle, 'Music Hall, "Mashers" and the "Unco Guid": Competing Masculinities in Victorian Glasgow', in Lynn Abrams and Elizabeth Ewan (eds), *Nine Centuries of Manhood: Manhood and Masculinities in Scottish History* (Edinburgh: Edinburgh University Press, 2017); Jeff Meek, 'Risk! Pleasure! Affirmation! Navigating Queer Urban Spaces in Twentieth-Century Scotland', in Deborah Simonton (ed.), *The Routledge History Handbook of Gender and the Urban Experience* (London, 2017); Angela Bartie and Alistair Fraser, 'Speaking to the "Hard Men": Masculinities, Violence and Youth Gangs in Glasgow, c. 1965–75', in Lynn Abrams and Elizabeth Ewan (eds), *Nine Centuries of Manhood: Manhood and Masculinities in Scottish History* (Edinburgh: Edinburgh University Press, 2017): See also Eleanor Gordon and Gwyneth Nair, *Public Lives: Women, Family and Society in Victorian Britain* (New Haven: Yale University Press, 2003).

25 MacKenzie, '"The Second City of the Empire"', 215–237; Craig Lamont, 'Georgian Glasgow: the city remembered through literature, objects, and cultural memory theory', University of Glasgow PhD thesis (2015); Lamont, *The Cultural Memory of Georgian Glasgow* (Edinburgh: Edinburgh University Press, 2021); Abrams and others in 2020 examines how the city's post-war high-rise flats shaped the identities of the people who lived in them. See Lynn Abrams, Ade Kearns, Barry Hazley, and Valerie Wright, *Glasgow: High-Rise Homes, Estates and Communities in the Post-War Period* (Oxon: Routledge, 2020).

in 2017 for a non-scholarly audience, also attempts a more cultural approach, though his methods have been criticised for showing 'no real engagement with the well-established methodological toolbox provided by cultural theory' and for accepting 'influential city mythologies at face value and consequently regurgitating rather than interrogating discourses'.[26] In general, though, Scottish historiography has proven reticent to engage with the conceptual work of the likes of Henri Lefebvre and Edward Soja, with only cultural heritage scholar Rebecca Madgin – principally through her work on the role emotions play in understanding Glasgow's historical built environment – really developing a conceptually sensitive urban history.[27] By contrast to Glasgow and Scotland, scholars of other historical cities – including New York – have increasingly studied the 'urban imaginary', with Andreas Huyssen and Christoph Lindner exploring the idea that cities are 'palimpsests' or loci of forever changing meaning and contested realities (scholarship in part interested in the apparent decline of the modern city in the face of globalised, neoliberal post-modernity). There is, for example, no Scottish equivalent of Patrice Higonnet's work on Paris.[28] In light of this, it is perhaps unsurprising that urban historians based in France – specifically the authors of the Groupe de Recherches Anglo-Américaines de Tours conference publication *Towns and Town Life in Scotland* from 2005 – have been among the

---

26 For Michael Fry, cultural and political histories of Scotland are a necessary corrective to unionist-dominated economic and social histories. See his *Glasgow: A History of the City* (London: Head of Zeus, 2017), viii; Charlie Lynch, 'Review: *Glasgow: A History of the City*', *Scottish Historical Review*, 98/2 (2019), 302–303.

27 Rebecca Madgin, 'Recognising Emotions within Urban Development', in Katie Barclay and Jade Riddle, eds, *Urban Emotions and the Making of the City: Interdisciplinary Perspectives* (New York: Routledge, 2001), 143–163.

28 Lindner, *Imagining New York City*, 6–9 and 12–14; Andreas Huyssen, *Present Pasts: Urban Palimpsests and the Politics of Memory* (Stanford: Stanford University Press, 2003); Huyssen, ed., *Other Cities, Other Worlds: Urban Imaginaries in a Globalizing Age* (Durham, NC: Duke University Press 2008); a British example of what is lacking in Glasgow's historiography is Jonathan Schneer's *London 1900: The Imperial Metropolis* (New Haven: Yale University Press, 1999); Patrice Higonnet, *Paris: Capital of the World* (Cambridge, MA: Belknap Press of Harvard University Press, 2002); it is perhaps worth acknowledging that the dominance of cities like New York and Los Angeles in conceptual 'global' urban history may simply be a product of being the professional home of writers such as Soja. In other words, scholars have written about where they know. Liam Kennedy, for instance, questions 'why it was that a select number of academics in a handful of New York and Los Angeles universities came to script the meanings of global urbanism and its postmodern forms'. See Liam Kennedy, 'How American Is It? Transnational Urbanism and the Cultural Politics of Place-Making, *49th Parallel* 8 (2001), np.

few scholars to write about Glasgow and other Scottish towns and cities in more conceptual and comparative terms.[29]

It is, of course, deeply challenging to firmly grasp the essence of a city and its history. Writing about St Petersburg, W. Bruce Lincoln has written that the city 'is a blend of conflicting and contrasting images that must be distilled with caution if its inner nature is not to evaporate' and the same caution should be applied to many other places too.[30] Attempts by historians and others to access the 'inner nature' of Glasgow are trapped within discourses about the city, the nation, and the transnation. Glasgow's transnationalism and the discourses that scaffold its imagining as such revolve around three apparently different, though in truth interlinked, aspects of its past: its position in the transatlantic trade and slave triangle, its reputation as a reforming municipality, and its status as an imperial city. The first of these – Glasgow's connection to slavery – remains a contentious issue and received greater public scrutiny amidst global campaigns for Black rights in 2020. A popular belief exists that the city has failed to sufficiently incorporate this past into the historical imagination; reading Patrick Dollan's explanation in his *Tale of Two Cities* that Glasgow's American street names were simply evidence of 'the affection our people had for the land of Columbus' would do nothing to challenge that belief.[31] Dollan's failure to explain that many of Glasgow's street names are rooted in their connections to slave-run cotton and tobacco plantations is, however, not necessarily a result of simple racism or wilful ignorance. Lamont, for example, argues that the narrative of Glasgow's involvement with slave economies has been overshadowed by more positive narratives about its nineteenth-century industrial heritage (itself transnational and transatlantic in nature, especially in shipping and shipbuilding). This in turn has meant that Enlightenment-era criticisms of slavery from figures within the city such as Adam Smith have also largely been forgotten. In Lamont's words, to 'perceive Glasgow now as a city built on slavery-implicated trading such as tobacco, sugar and cotton, is to ignore the "theoretical" condemnations of the trade itself'. This means that 'the city essentially lost a tangible connection to slavery discourse' as the 'fame of the Tobacco Lords has outweighed the fame of Smith in Glasgow just as the fame of the Clyde's shipbuilding scene has outweighed the same river's

29 Rosie Findlay, Tri Tran, and William Findlay, eds, *Towns and Town Life in Scotland* (Presses universitaires François-Rabelais, 2005), GRAAT, 32, https://books.openedition.org/pufr/4562, accessed 1 July 2022.

30 W. Bruce Lincoln, *Sunlight at Midnight: St Petersburg and the Rise of Modern Russia* (New York: Basic Books, 2000), 4.

31 Dollan, *Two Cities*, 25.

implications with transatlantic slavery.'[32] In sum, slavery is 'but one of the many factors discoloured by time in Glasgow; not by any scandalous cover-up, but rather by the major influences of its historiography and the gradual inheritance of aggressively dominant narratives'.[33] This suggests that it is too simplistic to argue, as the *Daily Record* did in June 2020, that Glasgow's historical associations with slavery are a 'little known fact'.[34] In any event, the nature and importance of the city's (and Scotland's more generally) involvement with the West Indies and North American plantations in the eighteenth century is not a new field of historical inquiry even if it is a growing one. Writers such as Tom Devine and Stephen Mullen have published specifically on Glasgow's role in slavery and its place in the 'Scottish Atlantic' and have done so against the backdrop of scholarship interested in exploring the role plantation-derived capital had in Britain's industrialisation into the nineteenth century and with the aim of complicating exceptionalist Scottish myths of egalitarianism. Mullen in particular has developed this strand of Glaswegian historiography which, among other important contributions, problematises the ways in which Glasgow's late twentieth-century regeneration downplayed wealth derived from slave economies, including the anodyne rebranding of the 'Merchant City'.[35]

---

[32] Lamont, *Georgian Glasgow*, 98; See also Alexander Murdoch, *Scotland and America, c. 1600–c.1800* (Basingstoke: Palgrave Macmillan, 2010), 93–105 for more on Scotland's transatlantic anti-slavery movement.

[33] Lamont, 'Georgian Glasgow', 173.

[34] 'Scotland's murky and shameful slave trade history', *Daily Record* (5 June 2020).

[35] Stephen Mullen, 'A Glasgow-West India Merchant House and the Imperial Dividend', *Journal of Scottish Historical Studies* 33/2 (2013), 196–233; T. M. Devine, 'An Eighteenth-Century Business Elite: Glasgow-West India merchants, 1750–1815', *Scottish Historical Review* 57/1 (1978), 40–67; T. M. Devine, 'Did Slavery Make Scotia Great?' *Britain and the World* 4/1 (2011), 40–64; Douglas Hamilton, *Scotland, the Caribbean and the Atlantic World, 1750–1820* (Manchester: Manchester University Press, 2005); debates about the relationship between slavery and British industrialisation centre around Eric Williams, *Capitalism and Slavery* (1944); Such histories may also be understood using Paul Gilroy's framework of the 'Black Atlantic'. In this model, the very idea of Atlantic history becomes something 'forced on black historiography and intellectual history by the economic and historical matrix in which plantation slavery … was one special moment'. It is for that reason that Joseph Roach prefers the term 'circum-Atlantic' to the term transatlantic. For him, the former 'insists on the centrality of the diasporic and genocidal histories of Africa and the Americas … in the creation of the culture of modernity'. Paul Gilroy, 'The Black Atlantic as a counterculture in modernity', in Susan Manning and Andrew Taylor, eds, *Transatlantic Literary Studies: A Reader* (Edinburgh: Edinburgh University Press, 2007), 146; Joseph Roach, 'Introduction: History, Memory and Performance', in Manning and Taylor, eds, *Transatlantic Literary Studies*, 236; Few, if any, urban histories have placed Glasgow and New York in the context of the Black Atlantic, though important work by Jacqueline Jenkinson has analysed the

The second feature of Glasgow's transnationalism centres on analysis of it as a reforming municipality. This line of analysis has been pursued most comprehensively by Aspinwall's *Portable Utopia*, which presents a compelling argument about the ways in which American Progressive reformers were inspired by Glasgow's (and other British and European cities') municipal socialism at the turn of the twentieth century, including in relation to its publicly run tram system and utilities. Glasgow in this period was known internationally for its advances in these areas, in part through the writings of US Democratic politician William Jennings Bryan and New York-based journalist Albert Shaw. By 1939, Dollan wrote that while Glaswegians remained 'inclined to regard Glasgow as the first and last word in civic administration' much could be learned from La Guardia's New York. Nevertheless, he felt that residents of Glasgow and New York shared a similar wish to keep their cities at the 'forefront of municipal progress'.[36] Certainly Glasgow's municipal socialism was a central feature of the city's transnational and transatlantic status in 1890's and 1900's and has rightfully figured as such in the historiography, including in American publications such as Daniel Rodgers' *Atlantic Crossings*. Rodgers' central argument – motivated by a desire to challenge Louis Hartz's notion of American liberal exceptionalism, a desire shared by writers such as Ian Tyrell and Thomas Bender – is that from the late nineteenth century until the Second World War 'American social politics was of a part with movements of politics and ideas throughout the North Atlantic world that trade and capitalism had tied together.' As Rodgers argues, '[u]nlike the nation, the city was small enough, and tangible enough, to carry' programmes and ideas of social reform. It might similarly be argued that cities provide a small and tangible enough (that is to say, 'translocal') framework of analysis for transnational historians, hence the approaches taken by Rodgers and the urban historians examined here.[37] It is important, however, to acknowledge

transatlantic nature of the 1919 race riots in Glasgow and other British cities. See Jacqueline Jenkinson, *Black 1919: Riots, Racism, and Resistance in Imperial Britain* (Liverpool: Liverpool University Press, 2009); Madgin, 'Recognising Emotions, 158.

36 Dollan, *Two Cities*, 17 and 27.

37 Daniel T. Rodgers, *Atlantic Crossings: Social Politics in a Progressive Age* (Cambridge, MA: Belknap Press of Harvard University Press, 1998), 3 and 143; Ian Tyrell, *Transnational Nation: United States History in Global Perspective since 1789* (London: Palgrave Macmillan, 2015); Thomas Bender, 'The Boundaries and Constituencies of History', *American Literary History*, 18/2 (2006), 267–282, and *A Nation Among Nations: America's Place in World History* (New York, 2006); Peter Baldwin has questioned whether Rodgers' aim is really as important as it would first appear. In Baldwin's view, the existence of transnational connections are not in doubt but they are only part of the story. For him, Rodgers' lengthy championing of transatlantic exchange was a 'classic case of killing the proverbial gnat' of American

that Glasgow's positive historical reputation as a reforming municipality is part construction, part reality. The American socialist and birth control advocate Margaret Sanger first visited the city in 1913 and found it wanting. Sanger identified 'flaws in the vaunted civic enterprises', including the ways in which regulations designed to prevent overcrowding in the tenements in effect meant that larger families were forced out into alternative substandard housing distant from the city centre. She criticised the paternalism of the municipal authorities, later contrasting their 'stingy, tight-fisted, middle-class stereotype' with the 'hospitable, generous, mentally alert' members of the working classes she met. In sum, however, Sanger found Glasgow 'infinitely cold, dreary, and disappointing'.[38]

The third feature of Glasgow's transnationalism – that is to say the third feature of discourses about Glasgow's place in the world as mediated through the Scottish nation and beyond – comes through its association with British imperialism. For some writers, Scotland's place in the British Empire is Glasgow's place in the British Empire writ large. Charles Oakley's 1946 book was called *The Second City* even though he acknowledged the city could probably no longer claim that title come the middle of the twentieth century (it had in any event long had competition from places such as Liverpool, Birmingham, and Calcutta). Nevertheless, in an effort to dispel some of the more negative portrayals of the city as a crime-ridden and poverty-stricken backwater – which for Oakley included its 'Red Clydeside' reputation and followed William Bolitho's 1924 depiction of the city as the *Cancer of Empire* – he insisted that Glasgow was 'one of the most important places in the world' and argued that by the 1900s it had become the 'Sixth City of Europe'.[39] Many of these aspects of Glasgow's identity – tempered by an acknowledgement of increasing competition from American heavy industries – are summed up in James Hamilton Muir's *Glasgow in 1901*, a short illustrated book published as a guide and introduction to the city for visitors to the 1901 International Exhibition. For example, Muir wrote that Glasgow:

> ... claims to be the Second City of the Empire, as she is undoubtedly the first in Scotland for population, trade, industries, and wealth. She is not merely a home of manufactures ... but a seaport and a centre of trade. Her river and her railways, giving access

isolationism with an historiographical "howitzer".' See Peter Baldwin, 'Review: Daniel T. Rodgers, Atlantic Crossings: Social Politics in a Progressive Age', *International Review of Social History* 45/2 (2000), 316.

38 Margaret Sanger, *An Autobiography* (New York, 1938), 97–99 and 274.

39 According to Oakley, by the 1890s Glasgow was behind only London, Paris, Berlin, Vienna, and St Petersburg in terms of population. See Oakley, *The Second City*, 149, and 314–16; Irene Maver, *Glasgow* (Edinburgh: Edinburgh University Press, 2000), 253.

> the one to the ocean, the other to every British town, have made her the main centre of distribution north of the Tweed. Moreover, she is the Model Municipality …[40]

This quotation, including its reminder of the pride felt by what was an international interest in its municipal socialism, can be taken as evidence of the way in which understandings of Glasgow's place in the world have been grounded by a sense of the city's Scottishness. Indeed, another section of *Glasgow in 1901* describes the city as the 'heart of Scotland' and portrays it as the nation's source of 'employment and energy'. This is contrasted with Edinburgh, a 'town so purely Scottish as to seem cut off entirely from the world at large'. In this interpretation, Glasgow's Scottishness is modern and outward looking while Edinburgh's is about 'tradition … on a "Hogmanay" night with old Scots drink and currant buns'.[41] As such, Glasgow provides meaning and significance to Scotland's position in the British Empire and the modern world. This notion is explored most fully by MacKenzie, who argues that Glasgow's international exhibitions in 1888, 1901, 1911, and 1938 were each 'concerned to explore Scottishness'. Importantly, this was 'not a remote Scottishness, uninformed and unreformed by modernity, but a Scottishness that gave a distinct meaning to Glasgow's industry and place in the modern world'.[42] MacKenzie's article is one of the relatively few examples from the scholarship on Glasgow that examines the city as an 'imagined community' and does so by exploring the ways in which the 'Second City of the Empire' concept was not simply a 'statistical point' but was instead a 'distinct municipal identity, a means whereby a complex and potentially explosive mix could manufacture … an imagined community which defined itself in relation to Scotland, England, the United Kingdom and empire'.[43] It is clear that the boundaries between nation

---

40 J. H. Muir, *Glasgow in 1901* (Glasgow, 1901), 43–44. James Hamilton Muir is a pseudonym of James Bone, A. H. Charteris, and Muirhead Bone. See Lamont, 'Georgian Glasgow', 232.

41 Muir, *Glasgow in 1901*, 26–27.

42 MacKenzie, '"The Second City of the Empire"', 227.

43 MacKenzie, '"The Second City of the Empire"', 232; This is a slightly different argument to that made by Lamont, who pursues the notion that nineteenth-century Glasgow – cosmopolitan, imperial, and industrial – was characterised by an 'unquestioned Britishness', depictions of which have further served to obscure an apparently more authentic Scottish Georgian past (itself imperial and transnational) to which Glasgow has as much claim as Edinburgh. Indeed, a recent article by Miel Groten focusing on the architecture of Glasgow's nineteenth-century City Chambers building highlights the same elements of Glasgow's identity as does Mackenzie though, like Lamont, he emphasises the greater pull of Britishness over Scottishness; for Groten (referencing Richard Finlay) Scotland only became 'nationalist' in its understanding of its place in the British Empire once it was faced with the question of how to respond to demands for Irish home rule as they developed after 1886. See Lamont, 'Georgian Glasgow', 177; Miel Groten, 'Glasgow's new town hall:

and the transnational are blurred and that Glasgow's later nineteenth-century transnationalism was as much rooted in Scottishness as not.

A transnational approach is an evidently necessary component of urban history (and indeed of national histories).[44] Pursuing this line of inquiry reveals that Glasgow and New York occupy an uncertain position in their respective country's histories and historiographies. This has meant the 'nation' has been decentred in the historiographies of Glasgow and New York not only by an active outward-facing transnationalism and translocalism but also by a rejection of – and by – the nations in which the two cities are physically located. Glasgow and New York have at times been presented as entities that have existed apart from their respective national cultures and, as a result, are not only 'transnational' but are also 'not of the nation'. In MacKenzie's words, 'Glasgow seemed to be in Scotland, but not wholly of Scotland. Its river was indeed a highway to empire, with the first stop North America.'[45] Likewise, Edwin Burrows and Mike Wallace constructed their Pulitzer-winning *Gotham* around the central themes of New York's relationship with the global economy, including via the British Empire, and its relationship with the rest of the US. Importantly, many in the US had long been suspicious of the city's links with Europe and its appearance as an 'agent of imperial powers and host to an "alien" population that spawned political machines, organized crime, labor unions, anarchists, socialists, Communists and birth controllers'.[46] In this analysis it is no coincidence that both Glasgow and

imperialism, nationalism and civic pride, 1877–1889', *Journal of Urban History*, First View (2020), 1–19; without undermining the transatlantic premise of this chapter, it is worth noting that Glasgow's nineteenth-century architecture, including the City Chambers, is notable for its international influences, including Italian and Greek and, in the case of the Art Noveau 'Glasgow Style', Africa and Japan. See also MacKenzie, 'The Second City of the Empire', 225.

44 Ewen, *What is Urban History?*, 116; See also Werner and Zimmerman, 'Beyond Comparison', 43, for more on the relationship between the local, the national, and the transnational.

45 MacKenzie, '"The Second City of the Empire", 221; See also Lamont, 'Georgian Glasgow', 177, and *Georgian Glasgow*, 114–138. For additional commentary on Glasgow's non-Scottishness. For Lamont, Glasgow's identity as a nineteenth-century British city has obscured its connections to an apparently more 'authentic' Scottish Georgian past with which Enlightenment Edinburgh is more commonly associated.

46 After passing from Dutch to English control in 1664, New York became the principal transatlantic gateway for supplies to Britain's imperial possessions in the sugar-producing Caribbean. Then, after the Revolution, the city – the United States' first capital – was the main link between the industrialising British economy and America's rural and slave economy in the South and the agricultural Midwest. See Edwin G. Burrows and Mike Wallace, *Gotham: A History of New York City to 1898* (Oxford: Oxford University Press, 1999), xix & 122. See also Wallace, *Greater Gotham: A History of New York City from 1898 to 1919* (Oxford: Oxford University Press, 2017).

New York are 'second cities' and are not (or, with New York, did not remain) their nation's political capital. In Glasgow's case, its second city status has been not only in relation to London as part of the British Empire but also in relation to Edinburgh, a city which, in addition to its dominance in the historical imagination of the Scottish Enlightenment, has since the re-establishment of the Scottish Parliament in 1999 secured its role as the capital of a devolved Scottish nation. Within Scotland, Edinburgh has of course long been Glasgow's 'other'. Indeed, Robert Crawford has suggested that the prodigious amount of writing about Glasgow through the centuries – by his estimate upwards of '10,000 works have been published with the word "Glasgow" in their title' – has in part been the result of a literary arms race between the two cities. In the view of Andrew Wallace, the late nineteenth-century author of one of those 10,000 publications, Edinburgh may have been Scotland's 'Metropolitan City' but its role had been in 'recording history, and in enjoying the blessings of civilisation' whereas Glasgow had '*made* [original emphasis] history, and been the originator of the means of advancing civilization and the amenities of modern life'.[47] This quotation could be dismissed as an instance of civic chauvinism but it can also be read in a way that emphasises other elements behind perceptions of Glasgow's significance. In this view, Glasgow's importance indeed transcends the nation: just as imaginings of Scotland were couched by a pre-modern rural idyll here the City of Glasgow stands as a cypher for urban modernity and progress. This is a theme echoed in John Wilson's paper for the Old Glasgow Club in 1906 – when city authorities had greater say over the lives of its citizens, for example in the realms of public health, than they perhaps do today – in which he argued that it 'was really on cities and not nations that the welfare of many races depended'.[48] Yet this is also the basis for Glasgow's apparent ejection from the Scottish nation, just as it provides a rationale for a translocal outlook. Even in the early nineteenth century, Scottishness had become increasingly identified with what Devine has called 'Highlandism'. It is no coincidence that this took place alongside the rapid and often alarming changes wrought by industrialisation and urbanisation,

---

47 Robert Crawford, *On Glasgow and Edinburgh* (Cambridge, MA: Harvard University Press 2013), 9; Andrew Wallace, *A Popular Sketch of the History of Glasgow from the Earliest to the Present Time* (Glasgow, 1882), iv; Lamont, *Georgian Glasgow*, 1–10 & 'Georgian Glasgow', 22–28.

48 John Wilson, 'Civic Patriotism', 23 April 1906, Paper No. 7, Session 1905–1906, *Old Glasgow Club Transactions Vol 1, Sessions 1900–08* (Glasgow, 1908), 113; In 1906, Glasgow's then Medical Officer of Health A. K. Chalmers similarly wrote that it was 'Local Authorities who are responsible for the nation's health'. See A. K. Chalmers, *Infant Mortality* (Glasgow, 1906), 3.

a process through which Scotland was divided by the mid-nineteenth century along a Highland versus Lowland, or rural versus urban, fault line. More than that though, and to return to Devine's interpretation, this was a process through which an 'urban society had adopted a rural face'.[49]

Perhaps Glasgow has been too large an urban area for a country the size of Scotland, especially if some conceptions of the nation and its history indeed rely on a rural idyll. The big city infringed on the big country: there was nowhere else in Scotland as large as Glasgow and by the second half of the nineteenth century the city had, in MacKenzie's words, 'outgrown its immediate context'.[50] Yet such a perspective brings to mind William Cronon's environmental history of nineteenth-century Chicago, which serves as a reminder to consider the 'boundary between the abstraction called the city and the abstraction called country' as more apparent than real.[51] Just as industrial Chicago relied on livestock and labour from the prairies and grain grown by immigrant farmers, so Glasgow's growth was in large part a result of migration from the rural hinterland itself. In fact, immigration provides another of the reasons supporting a reading of the city as 'not of the nation'. Nineteenth-century immigration by Catholic Irish brought to the city a very sizeable population perceived as religiously and racially different to native Scots.[52] Scottish discrimination against the Catholic Irish reached a peak in the xenophobic years of anxiety following the First World War. It is perhaps for all of these reasons that just over twenty years later Oakley could still observe that there 'is no subject on which writers and speakers about Glasgow are less willing to dwell than that of the Irish in Scotland'.[53]

---

49 Devine, *Clanship to Crofters' War: Social Transformation of the Highlands* (Manchester: Manchester University Press, 1994), 84.

50 For MacKenzie, it is this reality that explains Oakley's interest in comparing the size of Glasgow with other world cities. See MacKenzie, '"The Second City of the Empire"', 218; Novelist George Blake wrote in similar terms in 1934: 'Glasgow is big – really much too big for Scotland. It sprawls. It has grown almost anyhow, without plan and without regard for tradition ... It is a city so chaotic that one despairs of discovering a generalisation to come within measurable distance of describing its quality.' Blake quoted in Peter Reed, 'The Forming of the City', in Reed, ed., *Glasgow: The Forming of the City* (Edinburgh: Edinburgh University Press, 1999), 1.

51 William Cronon, *Nature's Metropolis: Chicago and the Great West* (New York: W. W. Norton, 1991), 19.

52 Charles Withers, 'The demographic history of the city, 1831–1911', in W. Hamish Fraser and Irene Maver, eds, *Glasgow, Volume II: 1830–1912* (Manchester: Manchester University Press, 1996), 150. It is worth noting that migrants from Ireland often came from urban and not rural areas, despite popular myths to the contrary.

53 Stewart J. Brown, '"Outside the Covenant": The Scottish Presbyterian Churches and Irish Immigration, 1922–1938', *Innes Review* 42/1 (1991), 19–45; Oakley, *Second City*, 70.

It is clear that Glasgow has been a city where national and religious identities – Scottish, British, Irish, Catholic, and Protestant – have both overlapped and been contested in ways that have rendered the identity of the city and its place in the nation unstable. This has been reflected in historiographical debates, for example the controversy between Gerry Finn and Bill Murray on the reasons for, and the nature of, religious sectarianism in west central Scotland, particularly in relation to the Old Firm rivalry between Glasgow's two biggest football clubs, Rangers and Celtic. This disagreement centres on Murray's 1984 social history of these clubs, a publication that remains the only scholarly book-length study on the topic. In an argument that further complicates the question of the extent to which Glasgow's history is 'Scottish' or 'not of the nation', Finn criticises Murray for presenting sectarian division in Glasgow as the fault of the Catholic Irish for not assimilating into an apparently Protestant Scottish society, a product of which was the establishment of Celtic Football Club. In Finn's view, Murray is guilty of national essentialism and uncritically accepting the myth of Scottish egalitarianism, leading Murray to the view that the racial and religious tension centred on the Catholic Irish in Glasgow was somehow not Scottish. Tom Gallagher adopts a more nuanced position by arguing that the tensions transplanted from Ireland by both Catholic and Protestant migrants in the nineteenth century (albeit tensions created as a result of Scottish and English Protestant migration to Ulster in the seventeenth century) were mediated and ultimately eased by Scottish particularities, though this necessarily involved Protestant Scots and Irish initially making 'common cause against the Catholic immigrant Irish'.[54]

By the second half of the nineteenth century, migration from Eastern and Central Europe became increasingly important. It is for that reason that in 1934 Lewis Grassic Gibbon described the Gorbals area of the city as 'lovably and abominably and delightfully and hideously un-Scottish' and a place where somebody may visit to remember that 'there were really and actually other races on the earth apart from the Scots.'[55] There has therefore long been a tension between Glasgow's status as a Scottish city, its status as a transnational city, and its status as a city existing apart from the nation. This is perhaps best summed up by what appear contradictory sentiments in Archie Hind's 1966 novel *The Dear*

---

[54] Gerry P. T. Finn, 'Scottish myopia and global prejudices', *Culture, Sport, Society* 2/3 (1999), 54–99; Bill Murray, *The Old Firm: Sectarianism, Sport and Society in Scotland* (Edinburgh: John Donald, 1984); Tom Gallagher, *Glasgow: The Uneasy Peace* (Manchester: Manchester University Press, 1987), 2.

[55] Withers, 'Demographic history', 150; Lewis Grassic Gibbon, 'Scottish Scene or The Intelligent Man's Guide to Albyn', in *Smeddum: A Lewis Grassic Gibbon Anthology* (Edinburgh: Canongate Books, 2001), 106.

Green Place. In it, the novel's central character Mat Craig – a working-class man struggling to establish himself as a writer – describes Glasgow as a 'Calvinist, Protestant city' that the 'influx of Roman Catholic Irish and Continental Jews had done nothing to change' yet also admits that he 'loved the journey home from his work which took him through the Gorbals with all its movement and excitement' and where he could purchase 'Jewish bread and properly roasted coffee and exotic fruits from the Jewish and Indian shops'.[56]

Writing on New York – a city that is not even fully on the United States mainland – has similarly had to engage with themes of migration and the extent to which the city is, or is not, of the nation. Echoing Gibbon's comments on the un-Scottishness of Glasgow, *New Yorker* journalist A. J. Liebling wrote in 1938 that 'New York, of course, just isn't America.' For Liebling this was manifest in the accents of many of the city's population, which he perceived as the 'common speech of early nineteenth century Cork'.[57] As Bayrd Still wrote, by the later nineteenth century and beginning of the twentieth, the city was indeed regarded by many commentators as much as 'New Cork' or 'New Naples' as New York. Patrick Dollan himself described it in 1939 as a 'municipal League of Nations'. This was a point of direct comparison with Glasgow for Dollan: 'We are used to hearing strange languages and dialects, just as New York; the Broomielaw and its environs are not unmindful of what one sees on the New York waterfront.'[58] New York's 'not of the nation' status has been explored most recently and fully by two scholars: Angela Blake and Thomas Bender. In her 2006 book *How New York Became American* (based on her PhD thesis), Blake argues that between the 1890s and the 1920s commercial interests in the city successfully rebranded New York as an attractive tourist destination. Importantly, this necessitated the obscuring

56 Archie Hind, *The Dear Green Place & Fur Sadie* (Edinburgh: Polygon, 2008), 63 and 129; For work on the Jewish community in Gorbals see the work of Avram Taylor, including Taylor '"In Glasgow but not quite of it"? Eastern European Jewish immigrants in a provincial Jewish community from c. 1890 to c. 1945', *Continuity and Change* 28/3 (2013), 451–477.

57 A. J. Liebling, *Back Where I Came From* (San Francisco: North Point Press, 1990), 13 and 16–17; New Yorker Liebling wrote in acerbic terms about Chicago, publishing a collection of his works on the city in the book *Chicago: The Second City* (New York: Knopf, 1952). For Liebling, Chicago was the US's second city after New York. He observes that 'Los Angeles is now a serious threat to its hold on even second place. The hopes for all-round pre-eminence, to come as an automatic bonus for being the biggest, have faded too. Still, the habit of purely quantitative thinking persists. The city consequently has the personality of a man brought up in the expectation of a legacy who has learned in middle age that it will never be his.' See Liebling, *Chicago*, 44.

58 Bayrd Still, 'The Essence of New York City', *New-York Historical Society Quarterly* 43/4 (October 1959), 416; Dollan, *Two Cities*, 19 and 26.

of previously dominant images of the city as poverty-stricken, corrupted, and populated by foreign migrants; all images that had served to differentiate the city in pejorative ways from WASP America even while also forming an important aspect of the activism of well-meaning social reformers. In part, New York became increasingly American by guidebooks, leaflets, cartoons, and photographs relating its canyon-like skyline to apparently quintessentially American frontier landscapes. The city could never sell itself entirely as American, however, and by the later 1920s its travel guides presented its immigrant districts as 'a miniature Europe, or China, or Middle East conveniently located in America'. In turn, the city's Midtown (probably the part of the city still most familiar to tourists today) became 'New York's brand image, its avowedly American heart'. Blake further argues that New York became more lastingly acceptable as an American city when in time America itself became more pluralistic.[59] Similarly, Bender argues that the multicultural cosmopolitanism of the city has at times sat uneasily alongside the 'most influential myths of America', referring especially to New England Puritanism and Virginian Jeffersonianism (though these regions' contributions to American identity differ yet further from the contribution of the Midwest). While New York appears as the very quintessence of Americanism to foreigners, to Americans the city seems anything but.[60]

Here the parallels between New York's place in US historiography and Glasgow's place in Scottish historiography become clearer. Just as Glasgow exists uneasily alongside the Scottish rural idyll and the dominance of 'Highlandism' in perceptions of Scottishness, so has New York contended with 'the study of the communitarian myth of the American town and the agrarian myth of the American frontier'. For Bender, the 'myth of rural and small town America' are predicated on the exclusion of difference whereas New York culture is predicated on the inclusion and celebration of difference. John Winthrop's 'Citty upon a Hill' from the 1630s was open only to those who subscribed to the puritan ideal, just as Thomas Jefferson's late eighteenth-century conception of an egalitarian society of yeoman farmers relied upon homogeneity achieved through restrictions on immigration.[61] Acts of inclusion can also foster simultaneous acts of exclusion and, for Bender, it is the latter that has characterised the main foundation myths of American identity. Gotham therefore sits very much outside of the American

---

59 Angela M. Blake, *How New York Became American, 1890–1924* (Baltimore: Johns Hopkins University Press, 2006), 110 and 138; Thomas Bender, *The Unfinished City: New York and the Metropolitan Idea* (New York: The New Press, 2002).

60 Bender, *Unfinished City*, 185.

61 Bender, *Unfinished City*, 185–190.

nation. Of course, Bender's point can only be taken so far. As Bayrd Still wrote in 1959, New York commercialism was anything but 'un-American': it 'symbolized the achievement of the American economy'.[62] Indeed, Bender's argument is shaped in response not to the achievements of American capitalism but instead in response to its failings and excesses in the final decades of the twentieth century. For Bender, US identity by the early twenty-first century was increasingly characterised by the homogeneity of globalised consumerism, conceived of as the pejorative transnationalism of the global city.[63] Bender was concerned with the New York that emerged from the 1970s and 1980s and argues that 'consumerist definitions of the US (and perhaps the world) threaten both the peculiarity of place, the recognition of difference, and the significance of politics'.[64] In other words, cosmopolitan New York was the solution to the problems caused by capitalist globalised New York. Some of this is examined in more depth in the second section of the chapter.

As with Glasgow, imaginings of New York are intrinsically connected to the nation, the transnation, and the places in between. This suggests commonalities not only between these two cities but also hints at similarities in how 'second cities' are imagined and conceptualised more generally. Indeed, Bender himself notes how New York and Shanghai both became major cities without being their nations' capitals.[65] Yet the uneasy and fluid position of Glasgow and New York in their respective national histories and historiographies is paralleled even more strikingly by St Petersburg. The Russian city grew from the site of a fort on the Neva River built by Tsar Peter the Great in 1703 and quickly became Russia's new capital and 'window on the West'. Its status as Russia's gateway to Europe and the aping of European tastes, fashions, and styles particularly by empresses Anna and Elizabeth from the 1730s meant that St Petersburg was 'too foreign' for many Russians and too familiar for many European visitors. St Petersburg's position in imaginings of the Russian nation fluctuated with debates about, and developments in, the empire's relationships with Europe and Asia. Renamed Leningrad, it finally became Russia's 'second city' once Moscow became the Soviet capital in 1918. Just as transnational Glasgow invites comparisons with 'Scottish' Edinburgh, Westernising St Petersburg invites comparisons with Slavic Moscow. Yury Arabov

62 Still, 'Essence of New York City', 416.

63 Bender, *Unfinished City*, 191.

64 Bender, *Unfinished City*, 196; Kenneth T. Jackson, 'Review: *The Unfinished City: New York and the Metropolitan Idea*, by Thomas Bender', *Journal of American History* 90/4 (2004), 1472–1473; David C. Hammack, Review: '*The Unfinished City: New York and the Metropolitan Idea*, by Thomas Bender', *American Historical Review* 108/5 (2003), 1459–1460.

65 Jackson, '*Unfinished City*, by Thomas Bender', 1472.

describes elements of the St Petersburg-Moscow divide as myths rooted partly in nineteenth-century liberal critiques of 'patriot-Slavophile[s]' and despotism and is 'sadly contradicted by the realities of life in the twenty-first [century]', but it is nevertheless indicative of how certain discourses inform how cities are imagined within or outside the nations in which they are physically located.[66] It is, meanwhile, no coincidence that New York's most prominent theorist of modernity and its contradictions – Marshall Berman – devotes an entire chapter of his 1982 book *All That is Solid Melts Into Air* to St Petersburg. Berman does not so much focus on St Petersburg's status within the Russian nation, instead examining the paradoxes of a city built as a symbol of Russian might and modernity but whose existence came at great cost to its people. As Berman argues, this paradox was most compellingly articulated in Alexander Pushkin's 1833 poem *The Bronze Horseman*, in which a statue of Peter the Great comes alive and chases down the poem's protagonist during the major flood that devastated the city in 1824. For all of these reasons, and in distinctive if not necessarily unique ways given the evidence from the other cities examined here, Russia's sometimes-second-city has been a 'symbol of warped and weird modernity'.[67]

Decay/Rebirth

Efforts to grasp the inner essence of Glasgow have been bounded also by discourses about the decayed city and its opposite, the reborn or regenerated city. These discourses exist in discursive formation with those about the nation and the transnation, as is suggested by Bender's examination of the tensions between cosmopolitanism and globalised capitalism. They are also particularly evocative of Huyssen's 'urban palimpsests' as they necessarily imply the overlap of real and imagined change. From this emerge parallels with how writers on New York – but also other 'second cities' whose culture, identity, and prosperity are not necessarily tied to their status as national capitals – have grappled with questions of social, economic, and cultural continuity and change. Certainly, when Patrick Dollan

---

66 Bruce Lincoln, *Sunlight at Midnight*, 346–361; Yury Arabov, 'The Petersburger's Psychology: A Moscow View', in Frank Althaus and Mark Sutcliffe, eds, *Petersburg Perspectives* (London: Booth Clibborn Editions, 2003), 41.

67 Berman, *All That Is Solid Melts Into Air*, 181; For more on Berman see Eric Homberger, 'Marshall Berman Obituary', *Guardian* (27 September 2013), https://www.theguardian.com/books/2013/sep/27/marshall-berman, accessed 29 July 2022, and Owen Hatherley, 'How Marshall Berman reclaimed modernity for Marxists', *Guardian* (17 September 2013), https://www.theguardian.com/commentisfree/2013/sep/17/marshall-berman-modernity-marxists, accessed 29 July 2022.

visited New York in 1939 he would have been acutely cognisant that Glasgow had suffered not just from the Depression of the 1930s but also from the economic decline of the early 1920s. Though a model for municipal government at the turn of the nineteenth and twentieth centuries, home to important developments in art nouveau, and an internationally renowned centre for heavy industries like shipbuilding, Glasgow's own *belle époque* had ended by the beginning of the First World War.[68] When Dollan was writing, employment in key industries had only recently improved as a result of Britain arming itself in preparation for another war. The year before the New York World's Fair, Glasgow's Empire Exhibition in 1938 was the city's own public relations effort to improve its economic and cultural confidence following the decline of the interwar years.[69]

This section of the chapter contends that many urban histories have necessarily operated within discourses of 'decay' and 'rebirth' and that analysing them has been an integral, if not always explicitly acknowledged, element of efforts to account for historical continuity and change in the city. Burrows and Morgan presented their history of New York to 1898 as one of 'remakings' but it is a theme in need of further conceptualisation and comparison.[70] Indeed, in his very stimulating 2009 book *Untimely Ruins*, which argues against the historiographical orthodoxy that the United States has always been too 'new' a country to share European aesthetic tastes in ruined buildings, Nick Yablon shows how some nineteenth and early twentieth-century writers gave expression to a cultural preoccupation with the ruined modern city. They did this in a variety of ways, including by the

68 The argument that Glasgow had a *belle époque* is made explicit by Peter Hall's chapter on the city in his book *Cities in Civilization*. For Hall, a happy mixture of cultural and geographical circumstance, together with the networks of key people and business that underpinned the growth of shipbuilding in the city, meant that Glasgow experienced a 'golden age' in the second half of the nineteenth century. He presents Glasgow in this period as an 'innovative milieu' in the service of his wider argument that cities are intrinsically centres of creation, be it technological or cultural. Glasgow is one of Hall's examples. Other cities' whose 'golden ages' Hall examines include Ancient Athens and nineteenth-century Paris. See Hall, *Cities in Civilization: Culture, Innovation, and Urban Order* (London: Weidenfeld and Nicolson, 1998), 348–376; Robert Fishman, Review: '*Cities in Civilization* by Sir Peter Hall', *Harvard Design Magazine – Constructions of Memory: On Monuments Old and* New 9 (1999), np; Maver, *Glasgow*, 182–185 and 203–210.

69 Maver, *Glasgow*, 252–286; Marco Duranti, 'Utopia, Nostalgia and World War at the 1939–40 New York World's Fair', *Journal of Contemporary History* 41/4 (2006), 663–683; Joanne Reitano, *The Restless City: A Short History of New York from Colonial Times to the Present* (New York: Routledge, 2018), 155; Britton writes that the 'conceptual keystones of the Glasgow Empire Exhibition' were '[r]ebirth and regeneration'. See Britton, 'Urban Futures/Rural Pasts', 215.

70 Burrows and Wallace, *Gotham*, xix–xx.

publication of future fictional historical narratives about American cities each reflecting the contemporary concerns of their Gilded Age authors (the dangers of foreign migration or the conflicts between trade unionists and monopolistic capitalists), many of whom utilised the language and framework of Edward Gibbon's 1776 *History of the Decline and Fall of the Roman Empire*.[71] As a result, discourses of decay, ruin, and decline have long been 'baked in' to writing on cities. Similarly, for Marshall Berman – invoking Marx and Nietzsche – progress and decay were an intrinsic element of industrialised modernity. In Nietzsche's words, there exists a 'fateful simultaneity of spring and autumn'.[72]

Concluding an introductory chapter on the 'progress of Glasgow' in the 1884 edition of *Glasgow: Past and Present* (a three-volume collection of 'reminiscences' and collected source material about the city), John Carrick writes of his wish to 'indulge the hope that the day is still far distant when the New Zealander, standing on Glasgow Bridge, shall see any symptom of decay'. This was a paraphrasing of Thomas Babington Macaulay's 1840 description of 'some traveller from New Zealand' sitting 'on a broken arch of London Bridge to sketch the ruins of St Paul's', an image recreated in visual form in Gustave Doré's 1872 illustration and later a common trope among nineteenth and early twenty-first-century writers – including in the US, as explored by Yablon – concerned with what they saw as the various possibilities for decline and degeneration inherent to modern urban life. That he felt the need to make this reference suggests that Carrick, despite in the preceding pages having gone into great detail about the benefits brought to Glasgow by then recent developments such as the Loch Katrine reservoir, felt some anxiety about the city's future.[73] Nevertheless, it was not until later that decay and decline became more characteristic of Glasgow's reputation. For Irene Maver, the 1920s and 1930s were decades when 'a negative image of the city began to overwhelm the popular consciousness'.[74] This is reflected in fictional depictions of the city, which stood in contrast to those which preoccupied nineteenth-century

---

71 Yablon, *Untimely Ruins*, 147–189.

72 Friedrich Nietzsche, *Beyond Good and Evil* (1882), quoted in Berman, *All That Is Solid Melts Into Air*, 22.

73 John Carrick, 'Introductory Chapter on the Progress of Glasgow', *Glasgow Past and Present, Illustrated in Dean of Guild Reports and in the Reminiscences and Communications of Senex, Aliquis, J. B., Etc* (Glasgow, 1884), lx; Macaulay's words were taken out of context and were in fact written in an article about the history of the Catholic Church. Nevertheless, Macaulay – perhaps counterintuitively for the chief Whig historian – had become pessimistic about societal progress, often citing what he saw as the dangers of mass democracy. See Yablon, *Untimely Ruins*, 154.

74 Maver, *Glasgow*, 252.

Scottish literature. With the partial exception of John Gault, nineteenth-century Scottish writers have a reputation for having proved squeamish about incorporating depictions of modern industrialisation into a literature otherwise preoccupied by a comforting rural idyll.[75] As it emerged in the 1930s, however, the 'Glasgow novel' (of which the oft-referenced 1935 *No Mean City* is only the most famous and sensationalist example) depicted the city via a conglomeration of metropolitan stereotypes: poor, crime-ridden, and in industrial decline. Alasdair Gray's 1981 *Lanark* provided a corrective to the earlier inward-looking nature of Glasgow's literary canon through its self-conscious undercutting of its own realist tale about Duncan Thaw by the post-modernist and more universal narrative of the novel's eponymous protagonist. Indeed, Gray's work, alongside that of James Kelman, reflected what Robert Crawford has described as a 're-energised cosmopolitan sophistication in west-coast Scottish writing' in part influenced again by American literary traditions.[76] Until then, however, authors had adopted a deliberately realist approach to their fiction, with the author of the 1936 *The Shipbuilders* George Blake going so far as to describe his and his fellow novelists' role as being the 'reporters and colourists of history'. Motivated by the laudable aim of highlighting the very real hardship caused by the economic decline of the interwar years, this nevertheless entailed an essentially one-dimensional way of looking at the city, grounded in an exceptionalist narrative highlighting the apparent uniqueness of the experience of Glasgow's urban poor. Paradoxically, Michael Fry (borrowing the phrase the 'urban kailyard' from Moira Burgess, the authority on Glasgow fiction) has described Blake as having 'almost transferred the kailyard to the shipyard', especially with his romanticised notion of the relationship between industrial employer and working man. This argument chimes with Spring's contention that 1930s depictions of the city as a hellish place – for example in the writing of Edwin Muir – were 'based on the mythology of a lost Golden Age'.[77]

75 Andrew Noble argues that Scottish fiction writing since Walter Scott had displayed a 'sorry failure of nerve'. See Noble, 'Urbane Silence: Scottish writing and the nineteenth-century city', in George Gordon, ed., *Perspectives of the Scottish City* (Aberdeen: Aberdeen University Press, 1985), 64–90; Beat Witschi, *Glasgow Urban Writing and Postmodernism* (Frankfurt: Peter Lang, 1991), 30–31 and 59–81; literary engagement with the Glasgow's industrial-era overcrowding was perhaps initially limited to the sentimental flourishes of Chief Medical Officer James Burn Russell's 1888 pamphlet and lecture *Life in One Room*. See James J. Smyth, 'The Power of Pathos: James Burn Russell's *Life in One Room* and the Creation of Council Housing', *The Scottish Historical Review* XCVIII/1/246 (2019), 103–127.

76 Crawford, *On Glasgow and Edinburgh*, 36.

77 Witschi, *Glasgow Urban Writing*, 40–55; Crawford, *On Glasgow and Edinburgh*, 36; Fry, *Glasgow*, 334; Spring, *Phantom Village*, 69; In Burgess's words, Scottish kailyard fiction

Writing in the *Guardian* in 1962 following a recent and rare visit to Scotland, Glasgow-born Cambridge Americanist Denis Brogan identified various ongoing social and economic changes happening not just to his home city but also to towns and villages across the Scottish Central Belt. For Brogan, there was 'something paradoxical about the changes ... For many of these little towns are in danger of death. Their basic industries – above all, coal – are threatened with extinction; local industries are threatened with concentration and automation. But there are new houses, new shops'. In Glasgow itself, Brogan contrasted '[d]ecaying' areas such as the Gorbals ('half ruin, half modernity') and Dennistoun with the 'new skyscraper housing blocks' then being built across the city. Tellingly, and indicating how transatlantic connections and transatlantic comparison are constitutive of each other, he concluded that the whole 'combination of decay and renewal is very American'.[78] These painful changes and their lasting legacy preoccupied Adams in his conclusion to *The Making of Urban Scotland* in 1978, in which he expressed the fear that Glasgow would become 'a sad city with an ageing, under skilled workforce, an obsolete industrial structure, a housing stock unattractive to incomers, much of the inner city lying as urban fallow, and human problems such as vandalism, all fostered by the crash programmes of the 1950s and 60s'.[79] By the time Adams published his book, Glasgow's economic fortunes had been further shaken by the 1973 oil crisis and the painful process of continued deindustrialisation. Inflation reached over 25 per cent in the UK in 1975, the same year that New York experienced its infamous major fiscal crisis and came close to bankruptcy. In New York's case, city authorities deprived of federal support applied drastic cuts to a range of public services prompting protests and strikes by teachers, police, and sanitation workers. This is remembered as a period of poverty, crime, and anxiety barely obscured by its 'I♥NY' public relations campaign and which reached a violent crescendo with the 1977 'blackout riots'. From this emerged the New York of the neoliberal 1980s. Under Mayor Edward Koch a place previously labelled 'Fear City' by its own embattled police officers became an increasingly gentrified city dominated by business and real estate interests.[80]

---

refers to a 'body of work characterised by sentimentality, narrowness of vision, and the acceptance of a code of unshakeable assumptions regarding conventional conduct and belief'. Kailyard fiction was typically set in rural Scotland, but Burgess identifies some urban novels – though not necessarily Blake's – as displaying similar characteristics. See Moira Burgess, *Imagine a City: Glasgow in Fiction* (Glendaruel: Argyll Publishing, 1998), 68.

78 Denis Brogan Papers, University of Glasgow Archives and Special Collections, GB 247 MS Gen 1581/157, 'The return of a native Scot', *The Guardian* (27 August 1962).

79 Adams, *Urban Scotland*, 276.

80 Reitano, *Restless City*, 210–226; Maver, *Glasgow*, 214–216.

For more recent audiences in Glasgow, the city's apparent decay in this period is perhaps most evocatively portrayed in Raymond Depardon's photographs, taken across 1980 and 1982 for the *Sunday Times*, depicting a grey, dirty, and poverty-stricken city not unlike the popular image of New York in the same period. Depardon's photographs remained unseen by the public until 2013 and unpublished until 2016, in Ian Jack's view because such a grim depiction of the city was unremarkable and too self-evident to be of interest to anyone in the 1980s.[81] Not coincidentally, 1980s Glasgow is the setting for Glasgow-born, New York-based author Douglas Stuart's 2020 Booker Prize-winning *Shuggie Bain*, the most significant Glasgow novel of recent years and an unflinching – perhaps even excessively grim – portrayal of abuse, addiction, and poverty in the city during the period.[82]

The seemingly drastic changes in the fortunes of Glasgow and New York across the twentieth century have influenced their historiographies and helped shape popular perceptions of the cities. In 1993, journalist, academic, and activist Robert Fitch published *The Assassination of New York*, a biting critique of the city's reliance on the finance, insurance, and real estate sectors in the years since the 1975 fiscal crisis (but with precedents in the 1920s), including the speculative office building of the 1980s and concomitant attempts to make New York the 'world capital'. Fitch's work traces New York's transformation into a post-industrial city and examines how bad debts accrued by the municipal authorities created the crisis in 1975. These circumstances paved the way for further economic instability, not least the downturn and high unemployment of when Fitch was writing in the early 1990s.[83] Other journalistic accounts emerged from, and analysed the legacy of, the fiscal crisis, including Ken Auletta's 1979 *The Streets were Paved with Gold*. For Auletta, New York's excessive borrowing was the result of the city authorities' attempts to fund public services in support of what he problematically calls the 'flood of poor people' who had increasingly replaced higher wage-earning – and therefore more taxable – residents who had moved to the suburbs. In Auletta's words, the home of Franklin Roosevelt and progenitor of New Deal America 'was not compelled to create a vast municipal hospital or City University system, to continue free tuition … ignore budget limitations, impose the steepest taxes

---

81 Raymond Depardon, *Glasgow* (Seuil: Paris, 2016); 'Picturing Glasgow: Raymond Depardon in Conversation', University of Glasgow (5 November 2020), https://www.gla.ac.uk/events/raymonddepardon/, accessed 8 February 2021; Steven Brocklehurst, 'How a Frenchman captured the "exotic" Glasgow in 1980', BBC News Scotland (8 November 2020], https://www.bbc.co.uk/news/uk-scotland-54800689, accessed 8 February 2021.

82 Douglas Stuart, *Shuggie Bain* (London: Picador, 2020).

83 Robert Fitch, *The Assassination of New York* (London: Verso, 1993).

in the nation, borrow beyond its means, subsidize middle-income housing, continue rigid rent control, reward municipal workers with lush pension, pay, and fringe benefits'. In his view, '[L]iberal politics dominated sound economics' and the fiscal crisis would be 'liberalism's Vietnam'. In making this argument, Auletta was seeking to challenge the view that the crisis was caused by what he regarded as a misconception in New York that the US government was to blame for not supporting the city with federal aid, something that further emphasises narratives of the city's apparent detachment from the nation.[84] More scholarly analyses of New York's economic and social changes in this period were produced by academics involved with the Committee on New York City, created in 1985 in association with the Social Science Research Council and spearheaded by John H. Mollenkopf, Thomas Bender, and Herbert Gutman. Combining social science and cultural approaches, a 1988 collection of essays edited by Mollenkopf was an important initial output produced at a time when the city had 'experienced a qualitative and not simply quantitative change' from an industrial city to a service-based economy. More publications followed, including the 1991 *Dual City: Restructuring New York*, the 1992 *Landscape of Modernity*, and the previously referenced *Capital of the American Century.*[85]

To those familiar with Glasgow's historiography, perhaps the best-known text dealing with the city's rise and fall to have emerged during the period of its transition to a post-industrial economy is Sidney Checkland's 1976 *The Upas Tree, 1875–1975: A Study in Growth and Contraction*. Checkland used the metaphor of the upas tree to explain how Glasgow's historical reliance on declining heavy industry had prevented the growth of a more sustainable mixed economy. He identified three main phases in Glasgow's modern economic history: massive growth before 1914; 'decline' since 1945; and 'controlled contraction' as a potential response to that decline. It was not clear at the point when Checkland was writing what the final outcome of these developments would be, though he was concerned that Glasgow had become a 'deficit city to an extent greater

84 Ken Auletta, *The Streets were Paved with Gold: The Decline of New York – an American Tragedy* (New York: Random House, 1979), 38, 253, 123–144; See also Martin Shefter, *Political Crisis/ Fiscal Crisis: The Collapse and Revival of New York City* (New York: Basic Books, 1985).

85 Mollenkopf, 'The post-industrial transformation of the political order in New York City', in Mollenkopf, ed., *Power, Culture, and Place*, 223; George J. Lankevich, 'Review: *Power, Culture, and Place: Essays on New York City*', *New York History* 71/2 (1990), 241–243; Mollenkopf and Manuel Castells, eds, *Dual City: Restructuring New York* (New York: Russell Sage Foundation, 1992); David Ward and Olivier Zunz, eds, *Landscape of Modernity: Essays on New York City, 1900–1940* (New York: Russell Sage Foundation, 1992); Shefter, ed., *Capital of the American Century.*

than most' and that it would need 'taken into wardship' and supported by UK and European funding.[86] The work of other scholars was necessarily shaped by contemporary events in this period. Seán Damer's sociology-influenced work on the history of Glasgow's housing, focusing on the Moorepark housing scheme from the 1930s to when he was writing in the 1980s (though based on research, including oral interviews, started in the 1970s), was a Marxist critique of the city's 'problem' reputation and a product of the author's distaste for Margaret Thatcher-era stigmatisation of the working classes.[87] Meanwhile, in his preface to the 1976 University of Glasgow press reprint of the 1858 *Midnight Scenes and Social Photographs Being Sketches of Life in the Streets, Wynds and Dens of the City* John F. McCaffrey wrote that the book – which provides written descriptions, or 'social photographs', of scenes from nineteenth-century Glasgow – deserved 'to be better known' in 1976 because of 'its relevance to contemporary interest in urban blight'. He hoped that knowledge of the squalor of Victorian Glasgow would 'place the present problems of the city in perspective by providing a measure which will show how relative are our conceptions of urban deprivation'.[88] These points may serve as a reminder that perceptions of the city's fortunes are indeed tied to its Victorian past or, more accurately, that writing on the city has found it difficult to see beyond the lasting negative and positive material and cultural legacies of modern industrial capitalism and its aftermath. It was for that reason that Tom Hart felt that by the 1980s Glasgow's late nineteenth and early twentieth-century economic strength and importance as a reforming municipality had been 'forgotten by modern commentators pre-occupied with the city's contracting role in a national economy itself of much reduced international status'.[89] Much more recent work by Chick Collins and Ian Levitt has complicated the narrative of Glasgow's decline by arguing that it was not simply the result of the 'force of economic circumstance' common to other deindustrialising British, European, and American cities in the age of globalisation but was instead caused by UK Government policies encouraging investment and population movement away

86 Checkland, *The Upas Tree*, 48 and 97–99; Stuart Patrick, Gordon Kennedy, and David Macleod, 'Escaping the Shadow of the Upas Tree', in Kintrea and Madgin, eds, *Transforming Glasgow*, 39–60.

87 Seán Damer, *From Moorepark to 'Wine Alley': the rise and fall of a Glasgow Housing Scheme* (Edinburgh: Edinburgh University Press, 1989).

88 John F. McCaffrey, 'Introduction', *Midnight Scenes and Social Photographs Being Sketches of Life in the Streets, Wynds, and Dens of the City, By Shadow* (Glasgow, 1858: reprint 1976), 6.

89 Damer, *Glasgow: Going for a song* (London: Lawrence & Wishart, 1990), 12; Tom Hart, 'Urban Growth and Municipal Government: Glasgow in a Comparative Context, 1846–1914', in Anthony Slaven and Derek H. Aldcroft, eds, *Business, Banking and Urban History: Essays in honour of S. G. Checkland* (Edinburgh: Donald, 1982), 194.

from the city.[90] Such questions about how best to explain decline echo the debates about the causes of New York's 1975 fiscal crisis.

Discourses about Glasgow's decline are bookended by the convenient end-point of the city's apparent rebirth in 1990 through its status as European City of Culture, an event that motivated Ian Spring to write that he doubted whether the 'New Glasgow has made any more than the most superficial difference to the economic and social reality of the lives of the poor or unemployed'. This was a sentiment shared by many of the city's intellectuals and cultural figures.[91] Discourses of decline and decay necessarily therefore have their opposite, namely what Colta and Vélez-Serna have called the 'miracle narrative' of Glasgow's culture-led regeneration. As such, the currency of narratives about Glasgow's decay in the 1970s and 1980s relies upon the city's post-modernist repacking in the 1980s

---

90 Chick Collins and Ian Levitt, 'The policy discourses that shaped the "transformation" of Glasgow in the later 20th century: "overspill", "redeployment", and the "culture of enterprise"', in Kintrea and Madgin, eds, *Transforming Glasgow*, 21.

91 Spring, *Phantom Village*, 3; Damer was similarly critical and felt motivated by Glasgow's gentrification to write what was an occasionally polemical 'people's history' of the city. Damer did, however, feel more positively about some aspects of the City of Culture nomenclature. See Damer, *Glasgow*, 5–20; The obvious comparison with Glasgow's attempts to improve its public image is Barcelona, the European city probably best known for post-industrial culture-led regeneration initiatives. The so-called 'Barcelona Model' of urban planning promotes the service and tourist sectors as replacements for a city's declining industrial base. In Barcelona's case, this is associated in particular with the 1992 Olympic Games. Yet for James Amelang, in an important article which argues convincingly for the benefits of comparing city histories, Barcelona's natural comparator is Edinburgh. While the national contexts may be different, Amelang contends that Edinburgh and Barcelona's similarities are rooted in the fact that they both lost their statuses as national capitals at the beginning of the eighteenth century (1707 for Edinburgh and 1714 for Barcelona) previously also having lost their royal courts. As such, Edinburgh and Barcelona are joined by their 'ex-capitality' and the concomitant flowering of urban civil society. From the perspective of Scottish historiography, however, it makes little sense to consider Edinburgh a 'second city' in the way that we may consider Barcelona, Glasgow, New York (itself an ex-capital) or St Petersburg 'second cities'. When Amelang goes on, therefore, to argue that Barcelona's self-image necessitates viewing capital city status as a 'demeaning role rejected on grounds of greater urban authenticity' in contrast to its own 'unquestionable superiority in regard to "artificial", "parasitic" centres such as state capitals' it is Glasgow and not Edinburgh that should come to mind. Moreover, unlike Edinburgh, Glasgow and Barcelona similarly have an uneasy and ambivalent relationship with 'national' historical and historiographical traditions. The Barcelona-Glasgow comparison is even more compelling once their apparent qualities as 'comeback cities' navigating decline and rebirth is taken into account. Nor does Amelang sufficiently acknowledge the differing national contexts: whilst he analyses the question of Barcelona's relationships with Catalonia and Spain, he does not consider the relative Scottishness or Britishness of Edinburgh; See James Amelang, 'Comparing cities: a Barcelona model?', *Urban History* 34/2 (2007), 173–189.

and 1990s; a repacking that involved the I♥NY-inspired public relations campaign proclaiming 'Glasgow's Miles Better', the 1988 Garden Festival, together with the 1990 City of Culture.[92] The years around 1990 saw the publication of a number of important books critiquing Glasgow's postmodern repackaging. Spring's 1990 *Phantom Village* adopted a cultural approach to this critique, Damer's 1990 *Glasgow: Going for a Song* a more sociological and anthropological approach, and Keating's 1988 *The City that Refused to Die* a political science approach.[93] This was also a time when some commentators identified similarities between Glasgow and New York, for example Jonathan Glancey's 1999 *Guardian* article which described Glasgow as the 'New York of the North'. This was not just because the Scottish city felt 'big' in the same ways that 'Chicago, London, and New York feel big' but also because it was, for Glancey, 'a city united in a razzle-dazzle attempt to be the smartest, hippest, coolest'.[94] These were not just surface-level comparisons, but were characteristic of the city's transatlanticism. From this 'razzle-dazzle' milieu emerged scholarly titles including Maver's *Glasgow* (2000) and a 1993 collection edited by Peter Reed entitled *Glasgow: The Forming of the City* (republished in 1999 to coincide with Glasgow's status as UK City of Architecture and Design that year). Maver's excellent, if rather conventional, book was both a child of post-industrial Glasgow and the first publication to locate the repackaging of the city in the 1980s and 1990s in the broad sweep of historical change. It also builds on her and others' work on the important Manchester University Press histories of Glasgow published in 1995 and 1996, together dealing very comprehensively with the social, political, and economic history of the city to

---

92 Maver, *Glasgow*, 220; Alexandra-Maria Colta and María A. Vélez-Serna, 'Between scenes: Glasgow's alternative film spaces in the 1990s', *NECSUS* [European Network for Cinema and Media Studies], (Spring, 2019), https://necsus-ejms.org/about-necsus/, accessed 22 February 2021; See also Mark Livingston, Chapter 5: 'Living in the urban renaissance? Opportunity and challenge for 21st-century Glasgow', and Venda Louise Pollock, 'Revisiting the creative city: culture and regeneration in post-industrial Glasgow', in Kintrea and Madgin, eds, *Transforming Glasgow*. The issue of culture-led regeneration raises a number of questions about whose culture is being represented and the extent to which it is a top-down or bottom-up process. Pollock engages with many of these issues, including with reference to more recent events such as the 2014 Commonwealth Games; For primary source material on cultural developments in Glasgow from the 1970s, specifically the Third Eye Centre and the Centre for Contemporary Arts, see 'The Glasgow Miracle: Materials for Alternative Histories', https://www.glasgowmiraclearchives.org/, accessed 28 June 2021.

93 Michael Keating, *The City That Refused to Die: Glasgow: The Politics of Urban Regeneration* (Aberdeen: Aberdeen University Press, 1988).

94 Ian Spring, *Phantom Village*, 4; Jonathan Glancey, 'New York of the North', *The Guardian* (18 January 1999), https://www.theguardian.com/theguardian/1999/jan/18/features11.g23, accessed 15 June 2020; Glancey also quoted in Maver, *Glasgow*, 284.

1912. Meantime, the economic and cultural legacy of post-industrial Glasgow's repackaging has been explored most recently and most comprehensively in the 2020 essay collection *Transforming Glasgow: Beyond the Post-Industrial City* edited by Rebecca Madgin and Keith Kintrea. In their introductory chapter Madgin and Kintrea present many of the contradictions between decay and rebirth examined here in terms of the city's 'epic' history (for example the scale of its nineteenth-century industrial economy) and its 'toxic' history (the poverty and hardship associated with that economy and the difficulties in mitigating it) and agree with Checkland that Glasgow's story, in a British context, 'stands out'. In their words, 'epic and toxic elements were often combined in one domain'.[95] In contrast to the likes of Checkland and Damer, *Transforming Glasgow* surveys the city's late twentieth-century changes with the benefit of hindsight and questions whether it is now moving 'beyond' the processes these historians were attempting to come to terms with in the 1970s and 1980s. They conclude that while Glasgow 'still contains many elements that are attributable to the twentieth century' it is 'not just a hollowed-out relic of industrialism'. As a result, descriptions of the city as 'post-industrial' themselves provide an unhelpful and outdated lens through which to study the city in the twenty first century.[96]

Analysis of the 'decline' of a city necessarily involves engaging with perceptions of its criminality and violence. Such perceptions are ambiguous and are rendered neither entirely positively nor negatively, as is encapsulated by the concept of cities as places of 'dreadful delight'. As Rosemary Wakeman has observed of 1930s Barcelona, its reputation as the 'capital of anarchist terrorism, of vice and crime' attracted visitors and writers alike. As such, it was a 'place of otherness, of libertine pleasure punctuated by working-class protest and violence'.[97] Much the same could be said of Glasgow, whose apparent decay has often been analysed in ways that have served to underline the non-Scottishness of the city but also in ways that sensationalise its darker side and make it more exciting and appealing. As a result, discourses of transnationalism/not of the nation overlap with discourses of decay/rebirth. For example, the English journalist George Gale described Glasgow in 1973 as 'the most foreign town in Britain'. He readily drew comparisons with

---

[95] Stana Nenadic, 'Review: Maver, *Glasgow*', *English Historical Review* 117/471 (2002), 436; R. J. Morris, 'Urban biography: Scotland, 1700–2000', *Urban History* 29/2 (2002), 276–283; Kintrea and Madgin 'Introduction: transforming post-industrial Glasgow – moving beyond the epic and the toxic', in Kintrea and Madgin, eds, *Transforming Glasgow*, 5.

[96] Kintrea and Madgin, 'Conclusion: beyond the post-industrial: narratives of time and place', in Kintrea and Madgin, eds, *Transforming Glasgow*, 279.

[97] Rosemary Wakeman, *A Modern History of European Cities, 1815 to the Present* (London: Bloomsbury Academic, 2020), 247.

New York and Chicago. Focusing on these cities' perceived propensity for violence, Gale wrote that Glasgow was 'a place I could imagine becoming dangerous, like the Chicago I imagine, or the New York which I know and liked. It is Glasgow's capacity to produce such imaginings that makes it the most foreign of towns I feel not lost and abroad in'.[98] Here it is precisely Glasgow's Americanisms that meant that it was 'not of the nation', further emphasising how historical connection underpins superficial comparison. This was not a new development in the 1970s with fears about gang-related crime in the 1930s resulting in the description of Glasgow as the 'Scottish Chicago'.[99] Andrew Davies has explored this aspect of Glasgow's history and argues that there were three ways in which Glasgow and Chicago were interlinked in the 1930s press:

> This rhetorical twinning of Glasgow with Chicago took three forms: firstly, warnings that Glasgow was turning into Chicago; secondly, claims that Chicago-style 'gangsterdom' was already rife in the city; and thirdly, attempts to deny the validity of the Glasgow-Chicago parallel, thus reasserting the conventional view that the violent ways of the American underworld could never take root in Britain.[100]

Here there is an implication – in the first and second of Davies's examples – that there is something about Glasgow that is 'not Scottish' (or British). In this case that something was 'violence'. It is striking that a similar – and probably more pronounced – phenomenon was happening in Barcelona, itself labelled the 'Catalan Chicago' and Marseilles, France's 'Chicago' and second city, both cities with which Glasgow was also compared in this period.[101] Yet in Glasgow the comparison with Chicago perhaps has particular resonance, not because of any violent reality, but instead because of the city's historical connections with

---

98 George Gale quoted in Alan Taylor, ed., *Glasgow: The Autobiography* (Edinburgh: Birlinn, 2016), 216.

99 Andrew Davies, 'The Scottish Chicago? From "Hooligans" to "Gangsters" in Inter-War Glasgow', *Cultural and Social History* 4/4 (2007), 511–527; See also Avram Taylor, '"Are you a Billy, or a Dan, or an old tin can?": street violence and relations between Catholics, Jews, and Protestants in the Gorbals during the inter-war years', *Urban History* 41/1 (2014), 124–140.

100 Davies, 'Scottish Chicago', 517.

101 See Davies, 'Scottish Chicago', 523. Davies quotes from Oakley, *Second City*, 313; Christopher Ealham, 'Anarchism and Illegality in Barcelona, 1931–1937', *Contemporary European History* 4/2 (1995), 133–151; Laurence Montel, 'Le Chicago français? Marseille dans *Détective* (1928–1939) in Christian Amalvi, Alexandre Lafon, Céline Piot (dir.), *Le Midi, les Midis dans la IIIe République (1870–1940)*, Actes du colloque de Nérac (13 mai 2011), éditions d'Albret, Amis du Vieux Nérac (2012), 173–188.

the United States and the wider parallels between its historiography and that of Chicago's American neighbour, New York.

Davies and earlier writers, including Oakley, are right to point out that Glasgow's propensity for violence has been both exaggerated and sensationalised. Yet a comparison between Oakley's writings from the 1940s and more recent attitudes to the topic demonstrate the changeable and contested nature of Glasgow's reputation for radicalism and violence. Whereas the 'Red Clyde' has in more recent years been incorporated into the wider mythos of Scottish egalitarianism (especially for supporters of Scottish independence), for Oakley the city's association with trade union and anti-war activities during and immediately after the First World War was deeply problematical and a risk to its prosperity. He raises the question of whether Glasgow's reputation had dissuaded businesses from investing or establishing new factories in the city and writes that:

> In the confused public mind gangsters and labour malcontents have been identified, and some people assume that the occasional Glasgow man, who is said to thrust razor blades or broken bottles in front of pedestrians' faces, is the same man as the one who goes ca' canny and has sit-down strikes in his factory during the day.[102]

We might further add that the activists of 'Red Clydeside' were also frequently associated with 'foreign Bolshevism' and that by 1918 opponents of Labour in Glasgow, including the *Glasgow Herald*, chose to draw insidious conclusions from the involvement of Irish nationalists in the local party, for example by suggesting political corruption was sure to follow. Such views should of course be placed against the backdrop of wider anti-Irish and anti-Catholic sentiment in Scottish society. The overlap between anti-Irish xenophobia, opposition to the left, and concern about the city's declining prosperity lay behind MP for Hillhead Sir Robert Horne's statement in 1931 that there 'were very few people who wanted to come to the Clydeside to establish industries unless they could demonstrate that they were not being over-ridden by the Irish revolutionaries in their midst'.[103]

---

102 Oakley, *Second City*, 314; Gordon J. Barclay has in recent years attempted to challenge what he regards as problematic mythmaking about some of the events of Red Clydeside, specifically the 'Battle of George Square' See Barclay, '"Churchill rolled the tanks into the crowd": mythology and reality in the military deployment to Glasgow in 1919', *Scottish Affairs* 28/1 (2019), 32–62. For more substantive analysis of Red Clydeside see John Foster, 'Red Clyde, Red Scotland', in Ian Donnachie and Christopher Whatley, eds, *The Manufacture of Scottish History* (Edinburgh: Polygon, 1992), or Joseph Melling, 'Whatever happened to Red Clydeside?: industrial conflict and the politics of skill in the First World War', *International Review of Social History* 35/1 (1990), 3–32.

103 Significant historiographical debate exists in relation to the role of the Irish vote in explanations of support for Labour in Glasgow. The orthodox view is that Labour only

The historical experience of capitalism has therefore provided the basis of opposing views about what constitutes 'decay' and 'rebirth' in Glasgow and New York. This point is emphasised by depictions of the material-built environment. For Lindner, the themes of decay and rebirth are manifest in perceptions of Manhattan's skyline, which he describes as 'capitalist modernity's most emblematic and volatile urban texts'.[104] Lindner – influenced in part by the likes of Bender and Blake – demonstrates that some early twentieth-century writers' depictions of New York's increasing penchant for building upwards reflected a deep anxiety about modern urban capitalism's threat to Old World America. Examples of such writers include Henry James, who returned to New York in 1904 having spent two decades in Europe, and Willa Cather, who in 1912 published a fictional story about a lethal fire in a New York skyscraper. Yet, as Lindner argues, the skyscraper has also stood as a 'space of liberation and renewal'. This was demonstrated by architect Daniel Libeskind's intentions for the original designs for the One World Trade Centre (on the site of the destroyed Twin Towers), which reflected his background as a Polish immigrant to America and his belief that the New York skyscraper symbolised New World inclusivity and opportunity. Here, New York is perceived as the quintessence of Americanism, though importantly this is the perspective not of the rest of America but instead of European migrants to the city. Lindner may use the words 'estrangement' and 'liberation' to describe the contradictory feelings aroused by New York's cityscape, but these personal reactions can equally by mapped onto the complementary concepts of the city's own 'decay' and 'rebirth' as they have appeared in the historiography.[105]

Themes of decay and rebirth exist symbiotically. This much is shown by the oft-repeated notion of New York's apparent 'restlessness'. As Bayrd Still wrote in 1959, a 'persistent feature of New York's personality' was its 'restlessness' and

succeeded once home rule was achieved for Ireland in 1922 and Irish Catholics finally moved away from the Liberals. Smyth challenges this essentially one-dimensional view and argues that Irish Catholic support for Labour was dependent on many of the same fluctuations (including those caused by the changing franchise) as other elements of the working class vote. Labour was indeed the natural home for Irish Catholics – most of whom were working class – but there was no Irish voting bloc or 'machine'. See James J. Smyth, *Labour in Glasgow, 1896–1936: Socialism, Suffrage, Sectarianism* (East Linton: Tuckwell, 2000), 125–154. For Horne quote, see 153.

104 Lindner, *Imagining New York City*, 62; For Nick Yablon, New York's built environment can be read longitudinally – 'delineating the length of an ostensibly representative avenue or boulevard' – and not only vertically or horizontally. See Yablon, '"A Curious Epitome if the Life of the City": New York, Broadway, and the Evolution of the Longitudinal View', *Journal of Urban History* 44/5 (2018), 155.

105 Lindner, *Imagining New York City*, 44–58, quote 53.

the 'transient, ever-changing character of the physical scene'.[106] According to Reitano in her book *The Restless City: A Short History of New York from Colonial Times to the Present*, New York's restlessness was already evident to observers in the mid-nineteenth century, with the city's former mayor Philip Hone writing in 1845 that 'Overturn, overturn, overturn! is the maxim of New York', a place he regarded as moved by the 'spirit of pulling down and building up'.[107] Reitano's central conceit is that the history of the city is characterised by conflict and change. This analysis had previously been made explicit by Bender's presentation of New York as an 'unfinished city', but Reitano's approach was in part shaped by events contemporaneous to the writing and publication of the text, in particular its second and third editions in 2010 and 2018 which include the story of political and economic change in the years around the Great Recession of 2008. More obviously, the terrorist attacks on the World Trade Centre in 2001 have left their mark on the city's historiography, including in the work of Steven Jaffe and Michael Sorkin and Sharon Zukin. For Birgit Däwes (in part following the work of Huyssen) some New York literary fiction has responded to the devastation of 9/11 by seeking 'creative re-assemblies, re-combinations and palimpsestic readings of familiar topographies' and by representing the diverse multiculturalism of the city. In that way post-9/11 writing has imagined New York as a 'four-dimensional space of convergence, in which dimensions of time and historicity, of transnational connection and of global political responsibilities overlap'.[108]

All of this points to the existence of influential discourses binding much historical and literary writing on the urban past. For instance, Bryan Waterman has identified in twentieth-century New York literature a reaction against the processes through which the 'modern city threatened repeatedly to eclipse its previous incarnations'.[109] As Max Page explains in his rebuttal of what he regards as some writers' habit of presenting Manhattan's history 'as something akin to a flowering plant', the 'crucial dynamic of urban life', especially in the period 1900

106 Still, 'The Essence of New York City', 416–417.

107 Reitano, *Restless City*, 1.

108 Reitano, *Restless City*, 244–276; Nick Juravic, 'Back to the Future: New Histories of New York in a New Age of Inequality', *Journal of Urban History* 41/5 (2015), 943–950; Steven Jaffe, *New York at War: Four Centuries of Combat, Fear and Intrigue in Gotham* (New York: Basic Books, 2012); Michael Sorkin and Sharon Zukin, eds, *After the World Trade Center: Rethinking New York City* (New York: Routledge, 2002); Birgit Däwes, '"The Sixth Borough": Imagining New York after 9/11', in Ross Wilson. ed., *New York: A Literary History* (Cambridge: Cambridge University Press, 2020), 252–264.

109 Bryan Waterman, 'Epilogue: Nostalgia and counter-nostalgia in New York City Writing', in Cyrus R. K. Patell and Waterman, eds, *The Cambridge Companion to the Literature of New York* (Cambridge: Cambridge University Press, 2010), 232–233.

to 1940, has in reality been the 'intentional destruction and rebuilding of the city'. This is the physical manifestation of what the economist Joseph Schumpeter regarded as the 'creative destruction' inherent to capitalism.[110] The archetype for creative destruction in the modern city, of course, is Baron Haussmann's restructuring of Paris during the 1850s, something Glasgow's councillors looked to for inspiration in the 1860s when they established their City Improvement Trust, the first municipal urban renewal body in Britain.[111] The emphasis on violent renewal remained a feature of analysis of Glasgow into the late-twentieth century, as shown by the words of Lord Esher in 1971, whose report into the city's built heritage highlighted city planners' apparent predisposition to 'destroy and build better'.[112] Similarly, Spring – who, to borrow Lindner's words, was himself feeling 'estranged' by the New Glasgow – commented that the city since the 1960s had been characterised by 'an undue regard for the new' and that it had 'suffered from a tendency to continually start afresh, forsake the past, and follow, blindly, the particular architectural fancy of the time'.[113] More in hope, David Daiches noted in the late-1970s that Glasgow 'has been re-made more than once, and it will be re-made again'.[114]

Recalling Brogan's article in the *Guardian* from 1962, what really joins modern Glasgow and New York in discourses of decay and rebirth, then, are the controversies surrounding twentieth-century rather than nineteenth-century urban planning, in particular in relation to the building of new roads through old residential areas and the creation of new housing. In New York's case, this is a history dominated by the figure of Robert Moses. From the mid-1920s until the late-1960s, Moses shaped practically all development programmes in New York via his control over a conglomeration of municipal agencies under the auspices of the Triborough Bridge and Tunnel Authority. In his capacity as Park Commissioner, Construction Coordinator, member of the City Planning Commission, and a number of other unelected posts, Moses oversaw the construction of all of New York's parkways, all except one of its expressways, and iconic buildings such as the United Nations headquarters and the Lincoln Centre. His legacy is a controversial one, however, and his biographer Robert Caro shows in the pointedly titled *The Power Broker: Robert Moses and the Fall of New York* how Moses's urban

110 Max Page, *The Creative Destruction of Manhattan, 1900–1940* (Chicago: Chicago University Press, 1999), 2.

111 David Harvey, *Paris: Capital of Modernity* (New York: Routledge, 2006), 1–20; Hamish Fraser and Maver, 'Tackling the Problems', 415.

112 Madgin, 'Recognising Emotions', in Barclay and Riddle, eds, *Urban Emotions*, 152.

113 Spring, *Phantom Village*, 26–27

114 Daiches, *Glasgow*, 245–255.

renewal efforts came at the expense of the hundreds of thousands of poorer New Yorkers – many of whom were from ethnic minorities – displaced to make way for many of his various developments. The result was the creation of new ghettos of substandard public housing while his highways 'flooded the city with cars ... to city-destroying dimensions'. In Moses's view, he was renewing and improving the city. To his opponents, who included urbanists Lewis Mumford and Jane Jacobs, he was destroying its social fabric. In turn, Moses would shape the intellectual outlook of the Bronx-born Marshall Berman as much as he shaped the landscape of Berman's local neighbourhood. For Berman, Moses himself personified the contradictions of modernity as experienced in New York: 'Moses struck a chord that for more than a century has been vital to the sensibility of New Yorkers: our identification with progress, with renewal and reform' and though he 'was destroying our world ... he seemed to be working in the name of values that we ourselves embraced'.[115] The New York that Patrick Dollan surveyed in 1939 was beginning to feel Moses's influence, for example through the construction of some of its parkways and the Triborough Bridge (a bridge Dollan felt 'surpassed in glory and strength' Scotland's – or perhaps Edinburgh's – Forth Bridge). Indeed Moses, in his capacity as Parks Commissioner, had overseen the clearing of the land on which the World's Fair was being held, just as the Fair's General

---

115 Caro presents Moses as power hungry, unaccountable to anybody but himself, and dangerous to those who stood in his way. *Power Broker* was published in 1974 and was the winner of the 1975 Pulitzer Prize in Biography, immediately after the Watergate Scandal and subsequent resignation of President Richard Nixon when biographies of over-powerful public figures would have held particular resonance. It was, however, only recently published in the UK, in 2015. Robert A. Caro, *The Power Broker: Robert Moses and the Fall of New York* (London: Bodley Head, 2019), 19; Oliver Burkeman, 'The Power Broker: Robert Moses and the Fall of New York by Robert Caro review – a landmark study', *The Guardian* (23 October 2015), https://www.theguardian.com/books/2015/oct/23/the-power-broker-robert-moses-and-the-fall-of-new-york-robert-caro-review, accessed 16 February 2021; For Fitch, Moses deserves less criticism than the Rockefellers, who he argues had the economic and political power to shape the development of New York in ways that suited their interests. See Fitch, *Assassination of New York*, xvi–xvii and 149; Berman, *All That Is Solid Melts Into Air*, 294–295; See also Samuel Zipp, *Manhattan Projects: The Rise and Fall of Urban Renewal in New York* (London: Oxford University Press, 2010). Zipp (29) argues that " ... the lens of urban renewal helps us to see how these two seemingly disparate developments – the rise of a world city and the decline into urban crisis – were coterminous and mutually dependent. Together they worked to create the distinct profile of modern, late twentieth-century Manhattan, with its bifurcated landscape of shimmering towers and stark ghettos.' In the context of the Cold War, 'urban renewal' post-1945 contributed to notions of American soft power. See also Marcio Siwi, 'The Making of New York's Avenue of the Americas: Transnational Circuits of Urban Renewal', *Journal of Urban History* 47/1, (2019), 1–26.

Motors-sponsored 'Futurama' exhibit of Moses-esque urban highways was one of its most popular.[116]

Glasgow historiography lacks a Robert Caro, presumably because no single figure dominated the city's urban planning the way his subject did New York. Nevertheless, urban planning in Glasgow in the second half of the twentieth century, including City Engineer Robert Bruce's influential though ultimately unrealised reports of 1945 and 1946, was shaped by American ideas. This is most obviously the case with Glasgow's network of motorways and flyovers, including the M8 and Kingston Bridge (the principal completed sections of Bruce's plans for an inner ring road), the creation of which fundamentally altered much of the city's built environment. Concomitant concerns about Moses-esque damage to the social fabric were encapsulated by Billy Connolly's mournful folk song 'I Wish I Was in Glasgow', with the lyrics 'Oh I was born in Glasgow, Near the centre of the town, I would take you there and show you, But they've torn the building down, And when I think about it, It always makes me frown; They bulldozed it all to make a road.'[117] In the years after the Second World War Glasgow sought radical solutions to its long-standing housing problems, including the creation of new estates, new towns, and high-rise flats in place of demolished Victorian tenements. Douglas Robertson has identified three principal 'narratives' that have been constructed around the history of Glasgow's housing. The first narrative focuses on the city's 'brutal slums', of which the Gorbals is taken as the archetype. The second narrative centres on the city's 'mitigation' of these slums, for example through the creation of council house estates and new towns after the Second World War. The third narrative focuses on Glasgow as a 'housing renewal innovator', for example the creation of community housing associations in the deindustrialised city. As Robertson acknowledges, each of these narratives 'fits a distinct chronology' that reinforces a sense of decay and rebirth. For Robertson, the narratives have 'framed Glasgow, in housing terms, as being highly problematic and somewhat unique – both epic and toxic – in terms of scale and intensity'. They have also crowded out other less dominant narratives, including histories focusing on Glasgow's owner occupiers, detailed studies of particular

116 Dollan, *Two Cities*, 27; Berman, *All That Is Solid Melts Into Air*, 303.

117 Maver, Glasgow, 261; Glasgow's motorways have lately enjoyed something of an historical renaissance and now have their own online archive. Indeed, this is a valuable resource for students and academics. See Glasgow Motorway Archive, https://www.glasgowmotorwayarchive.org/, accessed 22 February 2021; Madgin, 'Recognising Emotions', in Barclay and Riddle, eds, *Urban Emotions*, 149.

housing estates building on Damer's work on Moorepark, and 'neighbourhood testimonies' from residents of now demolished 1950s and 1960s high-rise flats.[118]

There has, however, been some new research undertaken on residents' experiences of Glasgow's high-rise flats. In their 2020 book, Lynn Abrams, Ade Kearns, Barry Hazley, and Valerie Wright, argue that this form of housing has been studied 'almost solely … in terms of … decline and failure'. Abrams et al. criticise social historians for focusing too much on the design failures of modernist housing and for not addressing more intangible questions about everyday life. In particular, they suggest that the 'narrative' of decline 'rests almost entirely upon a perspective that gives greater weight to the form of this kind of housing and to external policy decisions than to the experience of those who lived in the high flats'. In their 2020 book, Abrams and her collaborators utilise new oral testimony and evidence first gathered in the 1960s by social scientist Pearl Jephcott to present a more nuanced – if not always positive – history of life in Glasgow's post-war modernist housing.[119] Abrams et al. demonstrate how many residents of the flats appreciated their modern amenities and the opportunity they provided to create a new domestic life, while also acknowledging their shortcomings and challenges. They also identify feelings of nostalgia for now demolished buildings.[120] The ways in which discourses of decay and rebirth intersect with considerations of the built environment and peoples' physical and temporal relationship to it are further demonstrated by Colson Whitehead's 2003 literary ode *The Colossus of New York*. The coexistence of the old and the new at the centre of urban identity creates a conflict between feelings of forward-looking modernity on the one hand and of loss shaped by memory on the other.[121] For Tamar Katz, Whitehead articulates a form of urban identity located within the very bricks and mortar of the built environment. When Whitehead writes that '[w]hen the buildings fall, we topple, too' he is indeed suggesting 'less that New Yorkers *imagine* things are as they used to be than that seeing and then remembering a vanished city actually constructs this city'.[122] In other words, decay and rebirth – together with a

---

118 Douglas Robertson, 'Dynamic housing transformations: following the money', in Kintrea and Madgin, eds, *Transforming Glasgow*, 139–157.

119 Abrams et al., *High-Rise Homes*, 4 and 28–29.

120 Ibid., 69.

121 Tamar Katz, 'City Memory, City History: Urban Nostalgia, *The Colossus of New York*, and Late-Twentieth-Century Historical Fiction', *Contemporary Literature* 51/4 (2010), 811.

122 Colson Whitehead, *The Colossus of New York* (New York: Doubleday, 2003), 9; Katz, 'Urban Nostalgia', 826 and 848; Craig Taylor noted the strong feelings of nostalgia and loss among the people he interviewed for his 2022 popular oral history of New York: 'Many of them told me I'd missed the real New York – by a couple years, or by a decade, or by

complex nostalgia – are unavoidable features of any attempt to experience cities or to pinpoint their essence.

The present's relationship to the past is therefore characterised not by a straightforward nostalgia for a factual, communal former reality. Instead, the 'imagined community' of New York – and indeed of any city, not least Glasgow – is constructed by the individual's engagement both with that which is forever lost in time and that which remains, namely the very physical and extant traces of the past in the ever-changing built environment. This is the underlying premise of Madgin's 2021 exploration of emotional attachment to Glasgow's historic buildings. Madgin identifies three stages in Glasgow's post-Second World War development, each characterised by contrasting emotions towards urban planning proposals in the city. In the 1940s and the 1960s the Bruce Plan was indicative of feelings of 'shame and disdain' towards the city's nineteenth-century buildings and a preference for Le Corbusier-inspired modernism; the 1960s and the 1970s then witnessed a reaction against such modernism, with feelings of 'pride and anger' about what Wordsall called 'the city that disappeared' motivating heritage groups such as the New Glasgow Society to campaign to protect the city's older architecture; then the period since the 1980s has seen the city's historic buildings being co-opted as part of efforts to rebrand the city.[123]

Conclusion

An obvious criticism of this chapter's argument is that its entire approach has been influenced by the ubiquity of American culture in Western society and New York's status as a global city. In other words, given New York is probably the most famous modern city in the world is it really surprising that it comes to mind when writing about other cities? This, however, is itself one of the conundrums examined here. As Angela Blake explains in her book on New York's 'Americanness', the discipline of American Studies has long grappled with questions of what is and what is not American. Such questions were particularly pertinent in the twentieth century, which was 'defined by the globalization of American culture

several decades. "New York was better before", they'd say, or "You should have known Avenue C when it was ... " (and he'd waggle his hand), or "You should have known Jackson Heights when it was ... " (and he'd give the thumbs up). "This is good," one woman said and gestured to the noodles spread on her plate, "but Flushing isn't what Flushing was." The place with the good pupusas in the Bronx? Of course it was gone by the time I arrived; it's always gone.' See Craig Taylor, *New Yorkers* (London: John Murray, 2022), xxi.

123 Madgin, 'Recognising Emotions', in Barclay and Riddle, eds, *Urban Emotions*, 143–163; Frank Wordsall, *The City that Disappeared* (Glasgow: Richard Drew Publishing, 1981).

and military power'.[124] Yet if such questions needed to be asked of a US city by American Studies scholarship, then similar ones should also be asked by – and of – scholars studying those other places in the world that have most directly experienced the American Century. Counter-intuitively, this is an act of decentring American Studies away from America and is fundamentally about how the local and the transnational interact.[125] Cities are where such an interaction is at its most obvious. In this light, it is important that Scots-born Cambridge don (and expert in American history and politics) Denis Brogan chose to describe what he saw as the 'combination of decay and renewal' taking place across urban Scotland in the 1960s as altogether 'very American'.[126]

This chapter's exploration of the historiographies of Glasgow and New York brings into sharper relief what is distinctive about writing on these two cities, what is underpinned by historical transatlantic exchange, and also which areas of analysis can be applied more universally. Its basic contention is that historiography and other writing on Glasgow parallels New York's in important ways and occupies a space within a discursive formation of ideas about nationhood, transnationalism, decay, and rebirth. This is indeed true of much of what Glasgow's Lord Provost Patrick Dollan expressed in 1939 after his visit to the World's Fair, and his interpretation of New York was shaped both through the act of comparison with Glasgow and with reference to the two cities' historical linkages. The historiographical parallels between Glasgow and New York are grounded in similarities between the particularities of how each city has navigated historical phenomena including imperialism, migration, economic change, and political and social tension. They are also cities with very real historical entanglements, be it via long-standing transatlantic shipping routes, municipal politics, shared architectural and planning influences, or urban rebranding campaigns.

Dollan was reminded of many of Glasgow and New York's entanglements and similarities in 1939. He made the journey home with the additional impression that the American city was one of 'paradox and bewildering contrasts'.[127] This element of New York has also been recognised by historians since and is the assumption underpinning Reitano's presentation of it as a 'restless city'. Yet the idea of paradox and contradiction emerges too in the analysis of Glasgow, described by Daiches as a city characterised by a 'combination of nobility and

---

124 Blake, *How New York Became American*, 2–3.

125 Kennedy, 'How American Is It?', np.

126 Brogan Papers, University of Glasgow Archives and Special Collections, GB 247 MS Gen 1581/157, 'The return of a native Scot', *The Guardian* (27 August 1962).

127 Dollan, *Two Cities*, 11.

vulgarity, of friendliness and roughness, of Highland prudence and Lowland recklessness', and cities like St Petersburg, whose '[w]ealth, poverty, despotism, servitude, palaces, hovels, clear vistas, fog-clogged streets ... seemed to generate an opposite'.[128] Ironically, comparison exists alongside a sense of exceptionalism that seems implied by Daiches on Glasgow, Reitano on New York, and Bruce Lincoln on St Petersburg. As Alan Taylor explains, residents of Glasgow can hold the belief that the city is 'without doubt the greatest city in the universe'.[129] Such exceptionalism is common to many large and historically significant cities, not least New York, which *Charlotte's Web* author E. B. White described in 1949 as incomparable to anywhere else and second to none: 'New York is nothing like Paris, it is nothing like London ... It is by all the odds the loftiest of cities.'[130] This chapter challenges such pretensions to incomparability. While Glasgow, New York, and other cities indeed possess their own particularities, this study of their historiographies suggests that none is truly exceptional. The most compelling conclusion to draw is that it is pointless to isolate how any one city is thought about.

---

128 Daiches, *Glasgow*, 254–255; Bruce Lincoln, *Sunlight at Midnight*, 358.
129 Alan Taylor, ed., *Glasgow: The Autobiography* (Edinburgh, 2017), 1.
130 E. B. White, *Here is New York* (New York, 1949), 22.

PART II

Experiences

Americans in Glasgow, 1850–1900

Tahitia McCabe

> Monday October 20, 1862 –
>
> Got appartment in West Regent Street, [Glasgow]. I spent the day looking out the window hoping first impressions might not be lasting and wondering what the people of Britain would think if the sun should accidentally peep thru the mist the rain and this everlasting fog. I am perfectly disgusted with this climate. Rain, rain, rain ... [1]

While Glasgow's visitors may have found the weather challenging, the city still attracted many thousands of American tourists and immigrants from 1850 through the early years of the 1900s. This chapter provides demographic information on those found in the five decennial census returns of that period and adds a deeper look at the lives and relationships of certain individuals. These are preliminary research results and more remains to be discovered about these people, their time in Glasgow and their social networks. Several questions are considered including: what type of migrants were these Americans? What kind of occupations did they have? Did they have long-standing family ties to Scotland and thus were coming to a place which was not totally foreign? Some were the children of return migrants and were moving along with their families. What was their experience of being American in Scotland and did local and familial connections provide support for their transition to a new place?

Americans have been present in Britain since the colonial period, visiting for a variety of reasons and lengths of time or settling permanently. Before the Revolutionary War passage between the two was merely travel from one part of the British Empire to another with no legal barriers. Though differences between those in the colonies and those located in Great Britain were certainly present, family ties and cultural bonds facilitated a continuing Anglo-American relationship.[2] After independence, a long process of separation ensued with Americans getting to grips with their separate identity and Britain reluctantly letting go. The impact of Scotland upon America and vice-versa and the relationship

---

1 Quote is from the diary of Josie Underwood, the twenty-two-year-old daughter of the American Consul to Glasgow from 1862–1864. The family arrived in October and Josie wrote often of the wet and cold weather as so different to her native Kentucky. Nancy D. Baird, 'Josie Underwood's Civil War Diary, Part Two', *The Register of the Kentucky Historical Society* 112/3 (2014), 359.

2 Kathleen Burk, *Old World, New World: The Story of Britain and America* (London: Abacus, 2007), 101.

between the two countries have been explored by authors who have focused on social reform, cultural exchange, return migration and commercial and foreign relationships, though most have focused on earlier time periods.[3] Works on the relationship between Glasgow and America consider the effects of the American Civil War and the ties between religion, the anti-slavery movement, temperance and other social reform.[4] Bernard Aspinwall's *Portable Utopia: Glasgow and the United States, 1820–1920,* is the work which inspired this consideration of Americans in Glasgow.[5] Unsurprisingly, given the wealth of material available for them, he focused on the influences and experiences of better-known individuals who gave lectures, published books, had articles written about them in newspapers and/or created organisations. In contrast, this chapter will provide a broad demographic overview of Americans in Glasgow evidenced in census records and is an exploration of a variety of Americans residing in or visiting the city. These, for the most part, are not well-known individuals and were woven into the fabric of the city in a number of ways.

This chapter's main source material comes from the Scottish decennial census for the years 1851 through 1901. Americans were identified by searching the Ancestry database of transcribed census records by birthplace and using terms such as 'America' and 'United States'. Other sources used include US consular records, birth, marriage and death records, newspapers, passenger lists and many other primary sources typically used in genealogical research. Case study individuals and families were chosen to represent different aspects of the American-born population and in-depth genealogical research was done to trace their lives, family connections and experiences in Glasgow and beyond. The geographical area covered by the research matches the current Glasgow city limits and thus

3 For example: Jenni Calder, *Scots in the USA,* (Edinburgh: Luath Press, 2006); Andrew Hook, *Scotland and America: A study of cultural relations, 1750–1835* (Glasgow: Blackie, 1975); Alexander Murdoch, *Scotland and America, c. 1600-c. 1800* (Basingstoke: Palgrave, 2010); Mario Varricchio, ed., *Back to Caledonia: Scottish Homecomings from the seventeenth century to the present,* (Edinburgh: John Donald, 2012); John Clive and Bernard Bailyn, 'England's Cultural Provinces: Scotland and America', *The William and Mary Quarterly* 11/2 (1954), 200–213.

4 See Rachael Jezierski, 'The Glasgow Emancipation Society and the American Anti-Slavery Movement', PhD Thesis, University of Glasgow, Glasgow, 2010; George Shepperson, 'The Free Church and American Slavery', *The Scottish Historical Review,* 30/110 (1951), 126–143; and Bernard Aspinwall, 'The Scottish Religious Identity in the Atlantic World, 1880–1914', in Stuart Mew, ed., *Religion and National Identity* (Studies in Church History, 18) (Cambridge: Cambridge University Press, 1982).

5 Bernard Aspinwall, *Portable Utopia: Glasgow and the United States, 1820–1920,* (Aberdeen: Aberdeen University Press, 1984).

does not include outlying suburbs such as Rutherglen and Paisley which historically have their own identity. The research cohort includes American-born children of return migrants and adult migrants or visitors to Scotland. There are challenges in using data from the census as information may be unreliable arising from confusion or deliberate obfuscation by those reporting the data, census enumerators not recording data correctly or the mis-transcribing of data when added to online databases. However, reassuringly small rates of discrepancy in birthplace accuracy of between 4 and 8 per cent have been identified for this crucial piece of information.[6] It has been found through corroborating research that some people initially identified as American on the census records were born in Canada or countries in South America. These have been removed from the research cohort however it is likely that some remain.

Foreign relations between Britain and the United States were distinctly mixed post-American Revolution with tensions arising from the War of 1812 and the vision of American 'Manifest Destiny' conflicting with British interest in the Oregon Territory.[7] Along with frosty official relations came often scathing reviews of America and Americans in published travel narratives and articles in newspapers and magazines.[8] Of course there were more balanced considerations as well with magazines such as the *Edinburgh Review* noting, 'Why the Americans are disliked in this country, we have never been able to understand ... they are brave, and boastful, and national and factious like ourselves'.[9] Importantly, however, the American Civil War (1861–1865) had a huge impact on relations between Scotland and the United States. Americans in Glasgow included those from both sides of the conflict; some would have had family members fighting and being in a county which vacillated between condemnation and support of the combating parties surely must have been difficult at times. The influence of the war on industry is dealt with later in this chapter but anti-slavery organisations had been active for years in Glasgow petitioning parliament, raising money for publications and hosting American speakers such as Frederick Douglass, the campaigner, who lectured numerous times in Glasgow and Harriet Beecher Stowe,

6 Audrey Perkyns, 'Birthplace accuracy in the censuses of six Kentish parishes, 1851–1881', in Dennis Mills and Kevin Schurer, eds., *Local communities in the Victorian Enumerators' Books* (Oxford: Leopard's Head Press, 1996), 229–245.

7 For more on these tensions see Burk, *Old World, New World: The Story of Britain and America*, and Walter LaFeber, *The American Age: U.S. Foreign Policy at Home and Abroad, 1750 to the Present* (New York: W. W. Norton, 1994).

8 Among these are Frances Trollope's *Domestic Manners of the Americans*, (London, 1832) and Charles' Dickens' *American Notes* (London, 1842).

9 'The War in America', *Edinburgh Review*, XXIV (November 1814), 264.

the author of *Uncle Tom's Cabin* who visited in 1853.[10] However, the reliance of Glasgow's textile industry on American cotton and other slave-produced goods and the sale of Clyde built ships to the Confederacy meant that support for the Union was certainly not unanimous.[11] Warner Underwood, Glasgow's US consul from 1862 to 1864, paid agents to report on ships under construction and worked with pro-Union and abolitionist societies. His daughter, Josie, kept a diary of her time in Glasgow and this mentions her father's frequent meetings with local industry and business leaders.[12] From the 1870s relations between the countries became better with economic ties growing steadily as British (including many Scottish) investors poured money into American railways, agriculture and other industries and with the United States exporting food to Britain in vast amounts (including 70 per cent of Britain's grain imports by 1890) along with increasing amounts of manufactured goods.[13] Glasgow's transatlantic trade ties were strong with a third to half of its shipping tonnage being North American-focused in the last half of the nineteenth century.[14]

Aspects of diplomatic and industrial relations in this period were funnelled through the American consulates in Britain. American consular officers were present in Scotland within twenty years of the American Revolution with the first consulate opening in Leith in 1798 and then in Glasgow in 1801. Initially, the main duties of consuls were to support shipping and seamen and to help with the estates of Americans dying abroad. As American foreign commercial expansion developed after the Napoleonic war, the number of consulates and consular agencies increased, with eight across Scotland by 1891. These slowly decreased from 1909 with Glasgow's consulate closing in 1965 leaving only

10 Jezierski, 'The Glasgow Emancipation Society and the American Anti-Slavery Movement', 182. For more on these visits, see Alasdair Pettinger, 'Douglass in Scotland' (2018), https://www.bulldozia.com/douglass-in-scotland/, accessed 11 February 2024; George Shepperson, 'Harriet Beecher Stowe and Scotland, 1852–3', *The Scottish Historical Review* 32/113 (1953), 40–46.

11 Much has been written about foreign relations during and the British reaction to the Civil War. These have been particularly helpful: Robert Botsford, 'Scotland and the American Civil War', PhD Thesis, University of Edinburgh, Edinburgh, 1955; Peter O'Connor, *American Sectionalism in the British Mind, 1832–1863* (Baton Rouge: Louisiana State University Press, 2017); Lorraine Peters, 'The Impact of the American Civil War on the Local Communities of Southern Scotland', *Civil War History* 49/2 (2003), 133–152.

12 Nancy D. Baird, 'Josie Underwood's Civil War Diary, An Introduction and Part Two', *The Register of the Kentucky Historical Society* 112/3 (2014), 335–493.

13 James Belich, *Replenishing the Earth: The Settler Revolution and the Rise of the Anglo-World, 1783–1939,* (Oxford: Oxford University Press, 2009), 479–480.

14 Gordon Jackson and Charles Munn, 'Trade, Commerce and Finance', in W. Hamish Fraser and Irene Mavor, eds., *Glasgow, volume II: 1830–1912,* (Manchester: Manchester University Press, 1996), 65.

Edinburgh's remaining to the present day.[15] Consular duties changed over time to include the promotion of commerce and the support of Americans abroad with the emphasis very much on the former throughout the nineteenth century.[16] Most of the twelve consuls and vice-consuls that served in Glasgow between 1850 and 1906 were American citizens.

Given the level of migration to the United States from Scotland during the nineteenth and twentieth centuries with more than half of emigrating Scots going to the USA between 1853 and 1914 with a total of around 726,000 immigrants from 1820 to 1930, most Glaswegians must have known someone living in America.[17] Letters, visits from family and discussion with return migrants would have provided a sense of what life was like beyond the reporting in newspapers or by emigration promoters. For those travelling the other way, tourism was being promoted with the Allan Line offering package tours to Americans from 1872 but information about living in Scotland would have been harder to come by. Glasgow and Scotland were described in various travel narratives published in the United States throughout the century and while some came away horrified by living conditions in the urban areas, the overall impression was of a place where picturesque vistas loomed around every corner. The popularity of Scottish authors and poets including Robert Burns and James Macpherson but especially Sir Walter Scott, whose *Waverley* novels were a publishing phenomenon in America, served to promote the idea of Scotland as wild, remote and above all, romantic.[18] How well these tropes served to help those moving to Scotland, particularly to Glasgow, is questionable. However, those involved in the Scottish

---

[15] By the end of the 1960s, most of the sixty American consulates in the United Kingdom had closed with services being run out of Belfast, Edinburgh and the American Embassy in London. This appears to have been a cost-savings rationalisation as better and easier communication developed. See the Department of State's Office of the Historian's *Guide to Consular Relations: The United Kingdom*, https://history.state.gov/countries/united-kingdom, accessed 20 January 2024.

[16] Charles Kennedy, *The American Consul: A History of the United States Consular Service, 1776–1924* (Washington, D.C.: Bloomsbury Academic, 2015), 101–102.

[17] Tom M. Devine, *To the Ends of the Earth, Scotland's Global Diaspora, 1750–2010*, (London: Allen Lane, 2011), 125 and 142.

[18] Margaret Fuller visited Glasgow in 1846 and felt, 'the place … more resembles an *Inferno* than any other we have yet visited. The people are more crowded together and the stamp of squalid, stolid misery and degradation more obvious and appalling.' Margaret Fuller Ossoli, *At Home and Abroad, or, Things and Thoughts in America and Europe*, (Boston: Brown, Taggard and Chase, 1860), 159. See Andrew Hook, *From Goosecreek to Gandercleugh: Studies in Scottish-American Literary and Cultural History*, (East Linton: Tuckwell Press, 1999) for an engaging consideration of the effect of literature on America's view of Scotland in the nineteenth century.

American community would have had access to first-hand information and some of the Americans looked at in this study did have these familial links.

A Growing and Changing Population

Glasgow's population quadrupled between 1831 and 1911, from 202,426 to 784,496 persons.[19] This boom reflected many processes which fluctuated over the period including natural increase, annexation of outlying areas and in-migration from Scotland, Ireland and to a much lesser extent, from England and outside Britain. The city's industrialisation attracted workers and entrepreneurs, and the growth provided opportunities for the development of service businesses, entertainment, education and religion. The mid-nineteenth-century population was broadly 'divided into five equal parts: native inhabitants, Lowlanders (two-fifths), Highlanders, and Irish-born'.[20] Foreign-born migrants made up only a fragment of Glasgow's population and while the percentage did grow over time, the number remained small.

Table 1: The birthplace of migrants to Glasgow as a per cent of the city's population[21]

Birthplace	1851	1861	1871	1881	1891	1901	1911
Scotland	34.68	30.04	34.52	31.56	29.89	27.00	26.18
Ireland	18.17	15.69	14.32	13.12	10.57	8.87	6.73
England/Wales	2.51	2.63	3.06	3.16	3.36	3.72	3.81
Other	0.53	0.86	0.67	0.85	0.96	1.67	1.74
Total	55.89	49.22	52.57	48.69	44.78	41.26	38.46
[Glasgow]	[44.11]	[50.78]	[47.43]	[51.31]	[55.22]	[58.74]	[61.54]

Americans were part of the 'other' group, which was primarily made up of Italians and those from Eastern Europe, many of whom were Jewish. These migrants were part of a great expansion of globalisation during the mid-to-late nineteenth century which saw the flow of trade, capital and migration increase substantially between Europe and the rest of the world. Rising fertility, support from friends and family who had previously emigrated and falling transport

[19] Charles Withers, 'The Demographic History of the City, 1831–1911', in W. Hamish Fraser and Irene Mavor, eds., *Glasgow, volume II: 1830–1912*, (Manchester: Manchester University Press, 1996), 142.

[20] Withers, 'The Demographic History of the City, 1831–1911', 149.

[21] Withers, 'The Demographic History of the City, 1831–1911', 149.

costs all increased emigration rates.[22] Some of Glasgow's migrant groups may have intended to continue travelling to the Americas or elsewhere but ended up staying due to lack of money or having found local opportunities.

In a city thronged with people from elsewhere, did overseas immigrants feel more at home and fit in more easily or did they retain a sense of otherness? Often anti-immigrant feeling stems from challenges to employment, safety or health and while there were some issues with the Italians and the Jewish during this period, overall, the people of Glasgow did not seem to see them as a serious threat. Italians, who began showing up in the city from the 1870s largely supported themselves by setting up food related businesses and thus did not pose a challenge to local jobs. They dispersed broadly across the city but had small concentrations in the city centre's Garnethill area and in Govan located on the cheaper south bank of the River Clyde.[23] Meanwhile, Jewish immigrants had been in Glasgow in small numbers from the early 1800s, rising precipitously from 1881 when Jews were expelled from Russia having been blamed for the assassination of Tsar Alexander II. The Jewish population in 1881 was 1,061 growing to 8,928 by 1911 with many of these people moving into the Gorbals district and by 1885 half of the children at the Gorbals Primary School were Jewish.[24] This neighbourhood, on the southside of the River Clyde, hosted waves of immigrants who later moved on as they found better jobs and integrated.

The lack of strong anti-immigrant feeling in Glasgow against these groups did not mean that there was no discrimination or challenges. Around the turn of the century, there was grumbling about Italian-owned ice-cream shops, which opened on Sundays and were seen to encourage young people to 'hang about and loaf'.[25] Deterioration in working-class housing was also blamed on foreigners with Jewish immigrants being noted as being particularly problematic.[26]

---

22 Guillaume Daudin, Matthias Morys and Kevin H. O'Rourke, 'Globalization, 1870–1914', in Stephen Broadberry and Kevin O'Roarke, eds., *The Cambridge Economic History of Modern Europe: Volume 2: 1870 to the Present* (Cambridge: Cambridge University Press, 2010), 6, 16.

23 Terri Colpi, *Italian's Count in Scotland, the 1933 Census Recording History* (London: The St James Press, 2015), 111–15.

24 Kenneth Collins, et al., '"Two Hundred Year of Scottish Jewry": Towards a new Historical Narrative', in Kenneth Collins, et al., eds., *Two Hundred Years of Scottish Jewry*, (Glasgow: Scottish Jewish Archives Centre, 2018), 39; Mary Edward, *Who belongs to Glasgow?* (Edinburgh, 1993), 62.

25 Edward, *Who belongs to Glasgow?*, 84.

26 Linda Fleming, 'Garnethill Ladies and Gorbals Women: Gender, Class and Ethnicity in the Story of Glasgow Jewry', in Kenneth Collins, et al., eds., *Two Hundred Years of Scottish Jewry*, 224.

Second-generation Italians reported daily antagonism pre-World War One from customers and school-mates based on differences of appearance, religion and language.[27] The 1871 official census report for Scotland has a section discussing the 'races in Scotland' which shows clear alarm over the 'invasion or immigration of the Irish race … which slowly increased till it attained enormous dimensions after 1840'.[28] While any large group of immigrants who suddenly descend into a country might elicit alarm from the residents, Bradley says, in relation to ill-feeling towards the Irish in Scotland, that it is the 'relationship between Scottishness and Protestantism on the one hand, and the anti-Catholic dimensions of Presbyterianism on the other that have had a significant impact on relations between Protestants and Catholics in Scotland'.[29] Unlike the Italians, Catholic Irish and Jewish immigrants who were noticeable due to language, religion or large numbers, Americans seem to have melted seamlessly into Glasgow's population. In some cases, this was helped by being a return to an ancestral homeland. They may also have benefitted from the popularity of Anglo-Saxonism which led to the 'great rapprochement' between the United Kingdom and the United States during the late nineteenth and early twentieth centuries.[30] Americans and the people of Britain were thought to hold similar traits such as a common religious background, culture and work ethic as well as a shared language, which led to a superior civilisation.[31] In 1898, Samuel M. Taylor, US Consul in Glasgow, spoke about 'an alliance between the United States and Great Britain based on a similarity of business practice and moral aims', which was well received by the Glaswegian audience.[32] Other less noticeable immigrant groups included Germans and the Protestant Irish. Before the First World War, German immigrants in Scotland were well respected, working in industry, retail and food and drink with perhaps their most influential contribution being an entire brewery and its brewers being shipped in from Augsburg by J. & R.

27 Wendy Ugolini, '"Spaghetti Lengths in a Bowl?" Recovering Narratives of Not "Belonging" Amongst the Italian Scots', *Immigrants and Minorities* 31/2 (2013), 220–21.

28 Registrar General of Scotland. *Census of Scotland, 1871 – report: races of men in Scotland* (Edinburgh, 1871), xix.

29 J. M. Bradley, 'The Irish diaspora in the west of Scotland: famine, religion, racism, sport and identity', in *The individual and community life: Scottish Life and Society: A Compendium of Scottish Ethnology* (Edinburgh: John Donald, 2005), 560.

30 Stephen Bowman, 'The Scottish-American Association, 1919–1923: A Study in Failure', *Journal of Scottish Historical Society* 39/2 (2019), 21.

31 The Scottish census did not record a person's religion or ethnicity at this time. A few non-Anglo/Celtic-Americans have been identified in the cohort.

32 'British-American Alliance', *Daily Record* (22 October 1898).

Tennent to produce lager.[33] Around a third of the Irish migrating to Scotland in the second half of the nineteenth century are thought to have been Protestant and these blended more easily, as did the Americans, becoming effectively an 'invisible community' of immigrants.[34]

As can be seen in Chart 1, the number of Americans who were foreign subjects, as noted in the official census reports, is quite small across the latter half of the nineteenth century at 1,196 individuals.[35] Figures are not available for 1851 from the census reports as statistics broken out by specific areas/countries by birth were not provided. Overall, these figures broadly agree with the number of Americans who were not British subjects identified in individual census records for this study, at 1,282 individuals.

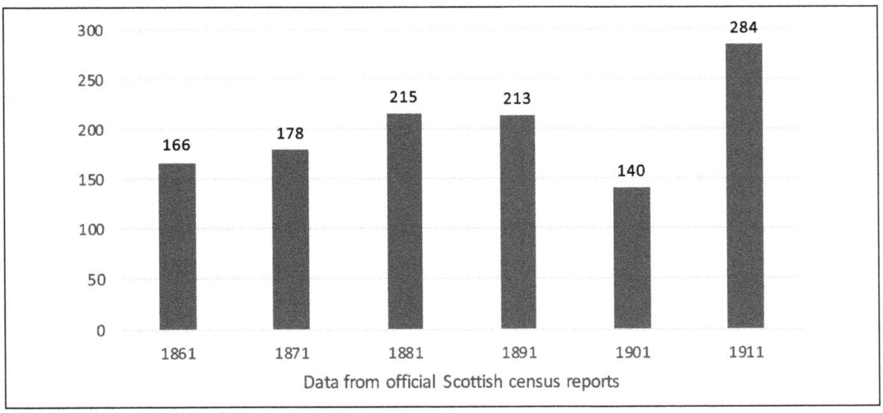

Chart 1: Number of foreigners in Glasgow born in the United States

However, there are two census years where the figures are a bit different, that of 1861 where fewer numbers of Americans were found (ninety-six as opposed to the official figure of 166) and that of 1901 where current research shows 289 as opposed to the official figure of 140. The reduced number in 1901 is possibly due

[33] Ben Braber, 'Immigrants', in T. M. Devine and Jenny Wormald, eds., *The Oxford Handbook of Modern Scottish History* (Oxford: Oxford University Press, 2014), 502.

[34] Geraldine Vaughan, 'Irish Protestants in the West of Scotland (1851–1914): An "Invisible" Community?', *Études Irlandaises* 30/1 (2005), 179; Also see: Graham Walker, 'The Protestant Irish in Scotland', in Thomas Devine, ed., *Irish Immigrants and Scottish Society in the Nineteenth and Twentieth Centuries* (Edinburgh: John Donald, 1991), 44–66.

[35] Registrar General of Scotland, *Census of Scotland 1861–1901 Reports: Birth-places of the People of Scotland: Tables on Birth-places of Foreigners Present in the Principal Burghs of Scotland.* http://www.histpop.org/, accessed 06 May 2023.

to a change in data collection which was to include information on whether a person was a foreign national. However, census records for individuals in 1901 *do* show many who are clearly American foreign nationals but not are indicated as foreign citizens, thus these official statistics are suspect.[36] For example, the eleven members of the American choral ensemble specialising in Negro spirituals, the Fisk Jubilee Singers, all had places of birth in the USA but none were identified as American citizens.[37] The Singers spent the first two weeks in April staying at the Waverley Temperance Hotel and performing at the St Andrew's Hall in Glasgow on a return visit to sell-out crowds and rave reviews.[38]

American-Born Children of Return Migrants

The majority of the Americans found in the census records were adult British subjects or the children of return migrants (67 per cent). Most of the children were living with both parents or in a one-parent household but some were with extended family, primarily grandparents but also with aunts or uncles. They were mainly Scottish but Irish, English and other nationalities were represented.

Table 2: Number of American-born children of return migrants in Glasgow

Children of Return Migrants	1851	1861	1871	1881	1891	1901	Total
Female	40	81	83	144	196	446	990
Male	33	87	88	175	237	451	1071
Total	73	168	171	319	433	897	2061

There were a further 512 American-born British subjects not living with parents. Most of these were adults in households of their own or living as servants, lodgers

[36] Data in the census was provided by the head of household and we are reliant upon their knowledge of the individuals within the household and compliance with census instructions. These regarding birth-places for the 1901 census state, 'If [born] in a foreign country, [provide] the name of the country and whether the person be a *"British Subject,"* a *"Naturalized British Subject,"* or a *"Foreign Subject,"* specifying nationality such as *French, German, etc.*' This information was then used to create the statistics found in the census reports; if the data was not provided, then it could not be captured. Research is needed to assess the provision of nationality data.

[37] See for example: Census records, Scotland. Blythswood, Glasgow. 31 March 1901. LOUDIN, Frederick (Fisk Jubilee Singer manager). 644/7 45/ 3.

[38] 'Fisk Jubilee Singers', *North British Daily Mail* (08 April 1901).

or boarders. It is probable that they were the children of return migrants and further research into their childhoods would provide some clarity.

Table 3: Number of American-born British subjects in Glasgow

British Subjects	1851	1861	1871	1881	1891	1901	Total
Female	30	25	15	34	48	88	240
Male	16	19	18	27	59	133	272
Total	46	44	33	61	107	221	512

'Generation 0.5', foreign-born children of return migrants, have not been researched by many scholars but recent studies of American-born children moving to Mexico with their return-migrant families indicate that many do so due to the desire for family reunification, legal status or a regular pattern of circular migration. Interviews show that these children were aware of the reasons for return and struggle with feelings of societal limbo or not fitting in anywhere.[39] A study working with Polish born children residing in Glasgow found that family was crucial in their construction of home and belonging and having a density of local connections; social, familial and environmental, helped them adjust to their new home. They retained a sense of the importance of their place of origin and searched out similarities between their Polish and Glaswegian places of residence to feel at home.[40] Current day migrants between the United States and Mexico or Poland and Scotland have more substantial legal, cultural and language barriers than Victorian era Scots would have experienced, but feelings of dislocation and limbo and the value of family and local connections are likely to have been familiar for American-born children arriving in Glasgow.

Jane Walker was at least six when she immigrated to Scotland with her Glaswegian parents. She was born in New York City in May 1844, a few years after her parents married in Glasgow in 1841. Her father worked as a dyer in the

39 Victor Zúñiga and Edmund T. Hamann, 'Children's Voices about 'Return' Migration from the United States to Mexico: the 0.5 Generation', *Children's Geographies*, 19/1 (2021), 88–101 and Victor Zúñiga and Silvia E. Giorguli, *The 0.5 Generation* (Oakland: University of California Press, 2024).

40 Marta Moskal, 'When I think home I think family here and there': Translocal and Social Ideas of Home in Narratives of Migrant Children and Young People', *Geoforum*, 58 (2015), 143–152.

textile industry and the family spent around four years in New York before moving north to the city of Waterbury, Connecticut where her brother John Alexander was born in July 1846 and sister Marion was born in 1848. Waterbury at this time was particularly known for manufacturing items made from brass but there were also factories dealing with cloth and it is likely that their father Andrew worked in one of these. The city was flourishing and doing so well that public education was made free to its residents. However, at some point after 1850, the family moved to Glasgow where they can be found living in Hutchesontown, a better working-class area on the southside of the River Clyde in 1861. Jane, now aged sixteen, was working as a power loom cotton weaver, her father continued in the cotton wool dying trade and her fourteen-year-old brother had started employment as a tin smith. The change from leafy and bucolic, though still industrial, City of Waterford to the tightly packed neighbourhoods of Glasgow, must have been striking. Having extended family nearby, including maternal McLean relatives, must have helped with their adjustment to a new community. The family support included taking in Jane's younger sister Marion in the 1861 census and this relationship continued as family members served as witnesses to marriages and deaths. Jane went on to have a long life, marrying an umbrella manufacturer who was prosperous enough for the family to have a live-in servant and to retire on private means.[41] Marion spent twenty years living with her grandmother in the suburbs of Glasgow before marrying and in the 1891 census she and her husband have McLean relatives living with them thus helping keep the local family connections ongoing.[42]

Spouses

The census records relationships based on a person's connection to the head of the household and categories were used such as wife, son, daughter, servant, lodger, boarder and visitor.[43] Heads of households were male, unless there was

41 Baptisms, NYC, USA. 13 September 1844. WALKER, Jane; Marriages, Scotland. Glasgow, 25 January 1841, WALKER, Andrew and McNEIL, Agnes; Census records, USA. Waterbury, Connecticut. 1850. WALKER, Andrew; Thomas Baldwin and J. Thomas, *A New and Complete Gazetteer of the United States: Waterbury, Connecticut* (Philadelphia: Lippincott, 1854); Census records, Scotland. Hutchesontown, Glasgow. 7 April 1861. WALKER, Andrew. 644/10; Census records, Scotland. Hutchesontown, Glasgow. 7 April 1861. REED, Kenedy. 644/10; Deaths, Scotland. Glasgow, 17 February 1880. WALKER, John. 644/12 144; Census records, Scotland. Tradeston, Glasgow. 5 April 1891. McGREGOR, Jane. 644/13.

42 Census records, Scotland. Anderston, Glasgow. 5 April 1891. MOFFAT, Marion. 644/10.

43 A census household does not correspond with a biological family unit and is an administrative construct consisting of those present in a residence (houses, hotels, institutions,

no man present who had 'general control or dominion over the whole house' in which case a female having that power would be listed as the head.[44] There were 449 male and ninety-seven female head of households across all of the census years. None of the female-headed households had a spouse present but most of the men (407) had spouses listed.[45] Only twelve couples in the cohort were both born in the USA, 279 women were married to non-American men and 357 men were married to non-American women.[46] To assess the nationality of the non-American spouses, 10 per cent of each census year's cohort of married persons was randomly selected and the birthplace of their spouse ascertained. Most were born in Scotland (fifty-one out of seventy-four) with a number from Ireland (nineteen) and a few from England (four). Of those born in Scotland, half were from Glasgow and aside from a few born in far flung places such as Orkney and Aberdeenshire, the rest were from the central belt. Further research would help our understanding of where and how couples met, particularly for Americans migrating to Scotland as adults, and whether the American-born spouse had Scottish, Irish or English family links.

Occupations

An adapted version of the HISCO (Historical International Classification of Occupations) system was applied to occupations noted in the census and other records.[47] This system has its difficulties but using it allows for easier comparison with other research projects.[48] HISCO categorises occupations broadly into 9 groups, for example Groups 0/1 Professional, Technical and Related Workers or Groups 7/8/9 Production and Related Workers, Transport Equipment Operators

etc.) on the night of the census. This means that those temporarily absent should not be listed in a household though sometimes householders did include family members sleeping elsewhere.

44 Edward Higgs, *Making Sense of the Census, Revisited.* (London: Institute of Historical Research and The National Archives, 2005), 72.

45 A small number of female heads of households were noted in the occupation field as a wife; two as soldier's wives and one as a manufacturer's wife.

46 These numbers represent the total across all census years. Individuals appearing in more than one census may have been counted more than once, however, where possible, these have been accounted for.

47 'History of Work – HISCO', nd, *International Institute of Social History*, https://iisg.amsterdam/en/data/data-websites/history-of-work, accessed 19 Oct 2023.

48 Difficulties with using HISCO are shared with other occupational classification systems such as terms found in records not appearing in the classification system. However, some difficulties are caused by the quality of the data as a description of an occupation may be too vague to allow for easy classification.

and Labourers. Four groups were created for this study so that students, those living off private means, vagrants and the unemployed and 'others' could be captured. The 'other' category was created for the retired and manufacturers.[49] Table 4 represents all Americans with occupations stated in the census records. Of these, 1812 were in paid occupations and the rest were students, living on private means, unemployed or retired.[50] Not surprisingly occupations involved in production and transport are most prevalent. Early on Glasgow flourished through trading tobacco with the American colonies and began to develop a textile industry. The damp, cool climate was favourable to the spinning and weaving of cotton goods and by the early nineteenth century, over 109 steam-driven cotton mills were operating. This trade was severely impacted by the American Civil War and the resulting restriction of raw cotton from the Confederate south, but woollen manufacturing was boosted by the war.[51]

By the 1860s, a wide range of other industries were present including locomotive engineering, machine tools and consumer goods such as sewing machines along with ship building and its ancillary businesses.[52] Indeed Glasgow's pre-eminence in ship building and its prowess in creating the fastest steamers in the world led to it producing more than a third of the 300 or so iron-clad ships which attempted to break the Union blockade of Confederate ports.[53] Industry continued to thrive throughout the nineteenth century and the resulting need for employees meant that, as noted previously, the city was a magnet for migrants both from within Scotland, the rest of Britain and from overseas.

---

49 These manufacturers were owners of companies creating steel, china, sewing machines, food, chemicals, etc. They do not fall into the various categories within HISCO groups 7, 8 and 9 which deal with workers, not management. It was felt that being able to easily identify heads of industry was useful.

50 This number includes the eleven merchants found in HISCO group 13.

51 Botsford, 'Scotland and the American Civil War'; Peters, 'The Impact of the American Civil War on the Local Communities of Southern Scotland', 133–152.

52 John Loudon, et al., 'Formative Influences', in *The Third Statistical Account of Scotland: Glasgow* (Glasgow: Collins, 1958), 141–142.

53 Eric J. Graham, *Clyde Built: Blockade Runners, Cruisers and Armoured Rams of the American Civil War.* (Edinburgh: Birlinn Limited, 2006), 2.

Table 4: Number of Americans in all HISCO Groups

HISCO Groups	1851	1861	1871	1881	1891	1901	Total
GROUPS 0/1 – Professional, Technical & Related Workers	4	7	15	21	37	111	195
GROUP 2 – Administrative & Managerial Workers	4	3	2	8	4	19	40
GROUP 3 – Clerical & Related Workers	4	9	8	21	37	51	130
GROUP 4 – Sales Workers	4	9	18	17	45	79	172
GROUP 5 – Service Workers	15	15	12	21	43	57	163
GROUP 6 – Agricultural, Animal Husbandry & Forestry workers, Fisherman & Hunters	2	0	1	3	4	7	17
GROUPS 7/8/9 – Production & Related workers, Transport Equipment Operators & Labourers	58	89	127	164	253	378	1069
GROUP 10 – Living Off Private Means	2	5	3	4	10	13	37
GROUP 11 – Students	39	64	52	182	118	506	961
GROUP 12 – Vagrants/ Unemployed	0	0	0	2	9	3	14
GROUP 13 – Others	1	0	3	2	6	12	24
Total	133	205	243	446	567	1243	2837

American women in Glasgow were found in a diverse set of occupations but overall followed the general trends of female employment in the city with concentrations in textile and dress manufacturing and service workers, primarily servants. However, women also had professional roles such as teachers, nurses, performing artists and worked in shops or as typists, telegraph operators and clerks. Most of the females with occupations listed (not counting students) were single and 218 of these were daughters (42 per cent), 128 were boarders, lodgers or servants (24 per cent) and the rest were extended family or visitors. One of

Table 5: Number of Female Americans in all HISCO Groups

HISCO Groups	1851	1861	1871	1881	1891	1901	Total
GROUPS 0/1 – Professional, Technical & Related Workers	1	0	1	7	10	29	48
GROUP 2 – Administrative & Managerial Workers	3	0	2	6	3	10	24
GROUP 3 – Clerical & Related Workers	0	0	0	4	4	8	16
GROUP 4 – Sales Workers	0	3	4	2	12	16	37
GROUP 5 – Service Workers	13	14	10	13	22	34	106
GROUP 6 – Agricultural, Animal Husbandry & Forestry workers, Fisherman & Hunters	1	0	0	0	0	0	1
GROUPS 7/8/9 – Production & Related workers, Transport Equipment Operators & Labourers	24	31	39	44	79	84	301
GROUP 10 – Living Off Private Means	1	4	3	2	7	8	25
GROUP 11 – Students	22	26	25	85	49	247	454
GROUP 12 – Vagrants/ Unemployed	0	0	0	0	2	1	3
GROUP 13 – Others	1	0	0	0	2	1	4
Total	66	79	85	163	193	440	1023

these daughters was Margaret McWilliams, born in Pittsburgh, Ohio in 1842 to Scottish parents, who started working as a robe maker by the age of 19. She continued in this trade for at least the next twenty years while living with her mother and Scottish born brothers and sisters in the St Rollox area of Glasgow.[54]

[54] Census records. Scotland. St Rollox, Glasgow. 05 April 1861–03 April 1881. McWILLIAMS, Margaret. 644/1.

Also in this neighbourhood, in 1901, American-born thirty-eight-year-old Ellen Young, was the female turn-key, or warden, at the police station on Tennant Street in the shadow of the huge St Rollox chemical plant. She looked after twelve female prisoners resident at the station on the night of the census.[55]

Out of the 343 women listed as wives in the censuses, only thirty-seven of them had occupations related to paid employment. Agnes Calder, in 1891 living with her Glasgow-born husband, Alex at 6 King Street in the east end of Glasgow, is one of seven wives involved in the weaving trade. She was a power loom weaver and by the 1901 census, now living with her sister, was working as a coloured work weaver in the Bridgeton area of Glasgow which was known for its factories specialising in dye and cotton spinning.[56] Mary Woods, in 1891 living with her Irish-born husband William at 16 Charlotte Street in the St Rollox area of Glasgow, is one of seven wives shown as a 'housekeeper'.[57] This was the most frequent occupation shown for wives and arguably may indicate that a woman kept house for her own household and did not work outside the home for pay. Other married women with occupations included four dressmakers, several performing artists, nurses or midwives and a few working in shops.

Manufacturing and Industry

The paid occupations that the American-born held reflect Glasgow's strength in industry and trade with 54 per cent working in HISCO groupings 7, 8 and 9; those related to production, transport or labouring. Americans worked across the industries and trades in positions from labourers to owners of major manufacturing companies. Chart 2 shows the breadth of occupations undertaken by men and women.

---

55 Census records. Scotland. St Rollox, Glasgow. 31 March 1901. YOUNG, Ellen. 644/1.

56 Census records. Scotland. Camlachie & Bridgeton Parishes, Glasgow. 05 April 1891–31 March 1901. CALDER, Agnes. 644/1.

57 Census records. Scotland. St Rollox, Glasgow. 05 April 1891. WOODS, Mary. 644/6.

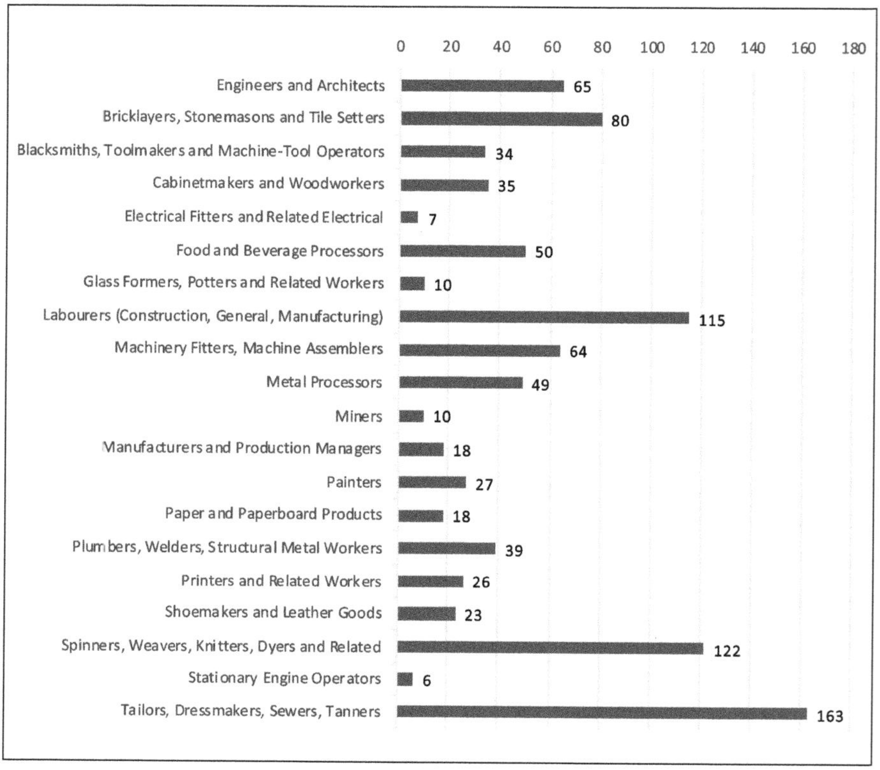

Chart 2: Number of Americans occupied in manufacturing or industry (All census years)

Women are most heavily concentrated in two areas, working in the textile industry as spinners, weavers and knitters with 100 women out of 122 in total and as dressmakers, sewers and related roles with 126 out of 163 total in that area. However, females did work in other fields such as Mary King aged sixteen and her fourteen-year-old sister Lottie, who were both book binders living in the Calton district of Glasgow in 1901. Their mother and father, a night watchman, were born in Ireland and had moved to the United States in the early 1880s where they had at least six children and then moved back to Ireland by 1895 where their daughter Annie was born. They were new arrivals into Glasgow with their youngest son's birth in Ireland in 1898 showing a move within the previous three years.[58] It's impossible to know where the King sisters worked but a number of the more than 100 bookbinders in Glasgow at this time were within easy walking distance of their home, including the 'American

58 Census records. Scotland. Calton, Glasgow. 31 March 1901. KING, John (head). 644/4, 47, 116.

Printing and Stationary Co'.[59] Relative to the national picture at the time, Glasgow women were more than twice as heavily concentrated, compared to female employees elsewhere, in surprising areas such as brewing, leather goods manufacture, pottery metal working and printing and Americans can be found employed in all of these.[60]

One of the twenty-six men working in the Printers and Related Workers category, Gavin Connell was born in New York around 1843 to Glaswegian parents and the family returned by the mid-1850s.[61] After a short interlude in Liverpool during the mid-1860s where Gavin married his Welsh wife, Hannah, he returned to Glasgow to work fairly steadily as a newspaper or letterpress printer for the rest of his life.[62] Glasgow had a number of newspapers at this time including the *Glasgow Citizen*, the *Glasgow Herald* and the *Glasgow Sentinel* however there is no indication where he worked. In December of 1882, Gavin spent three nights in the Greenock Prison for a breach of the peace and drunkenness. It is noted that he could read and write well and 'has had education superior to merely being able to read and write', which is not surprising given his skilled trade. Unfortunately, in 1891 both he and his daughter Mary, a twenty-four-year-old saleswoman for a jeweller, were unemployed but by 1901 he was again working as a newspaper printer.[63]

Professional and Clerical Workers

There were 212 Americans working in professional and clerical jobs (12 per cent of those with paid occupations).[64] Engineers and architects have been counted previously in the manufacturing and industrial section. Whereas one in twenty male Glaswegians were in professional and clerical roles, one in twelve American men (154 in total) were so employed.[65]

---

59 *Post Office Annual Directory, Glasgow: Bookbinders*, (Glasgow, 1900–1901), 999.

60 Richard Roger, 'The Labour Force', in W. Hamish Fraser and Irene Mavor, eds., *Glasgow, volume II: 1830–1912*, (Manchester: Manchester University Press, 1996), 171.

61 Census records. Scotland. Calton, Glasgow. 07 April 1861. CONNELL, Gavin. 644/4, 73, 51.

62 Marriages, England. Liverpool, Lancaster. 17 October 1864. CONNELL, Gavin and VALENTINE, Hannah.

63 Prison Register, Greenock. 04 December 1882. CONNELL, Gavin. HH21/033/011; Census records. Scotland. Barony & St Luke Parishes, Glasgow. 05 April 1891–31 March 1901. CONNELL, Gavin. 644/4.

64 These represent HISCO groups G0/1 – professional, technical and related workers and group G3 – clerical and related workers.

65 Roger, 'The Labour Force', 167.

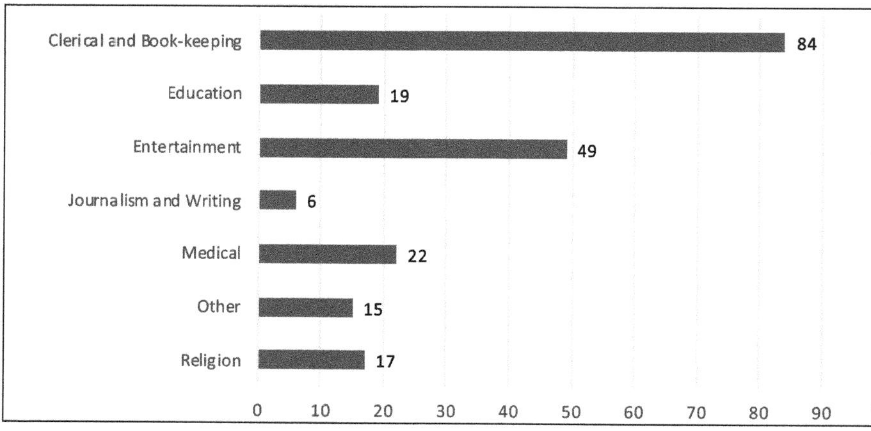

Chart 3: Number of Americans working in the professions and clerical employment (All census years)[66]

Clerks and book-keepers appear in all of the census years with four in 1851 but there is a steady rise, partly due to the overall growth in the number of Americans, but also to a 'general proliferation of clerks and inspectors and of office workers' towards the end of the Victorian era.[67] By 1901, thirty-two men and women worked as clerks, typists or book-keepers in a number of settings from legal offices to sewing machine factories. Margaret and Mary Jane Oliphant, sisters born in New Jersey, aged nineteen and seventeen, were both typists in 1901, one working in a warehouse and the other in a commercial setting.[68] Their parents had returned to Glasgow around 1898 and lived in the Partick neighbourhood but emigrated again in 1905, this time to Alberta, Canada with their seven children.[69] Families such as the Oliphants may have created a concept of 'home' distinct from their physical location and centred it around routine social and familial interactions.

The forty-nine people involved in entertainment were bolstered by the eleven members of the Fisk Jubilee Singers mentioned previously and the city clearly attracted American entertainers. Included in these numbers are thirteen actors and actresses, three theatrical producers, twenty singers and six theatrical producers. The best known of these producers was Hubert Thomas Rossborough,

66 The 'Other' category includes four telegraphers, three chemists and two veterinarians.

67 Roger, 'The Labour Force', 173.

68 Census records. Scotland. Partick, Glasgow. 31 March 1901. OLIPHANT, Margaret and Mary Jane.646/4, 46, 3.

69 Census records, Canada. Edmonton, Alberta. 1906. OLIPHANT, Wm. 27D.

born in New York around 1838, who was the proprietor of the Britannia Music Hall in the Trongate, now known as the Britannia Panopticon and the world's oldest surviving music hall.[70] He managed the Britannia for at least twenty years from the mid-1860s until his death in 1887.[71]

Sales and Service Workers

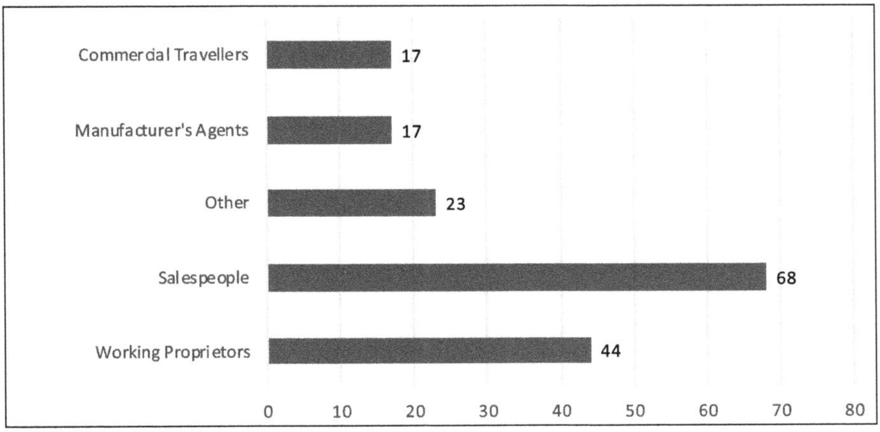

Chart 4: Number of Americans working in sales (All census years)

Note: This represents HISCO group G4 – sales workers. The 'Other' category includes seven insurance salesmen, three shipbrokers, three pawnbrokers and five hawkers and pedlars.

Stana Nenadic suggests that 'in the second half of the nineteenth century [in Glasgow], 75 per cent of middle-class families were headed by business owners, of whom about two-thirds could be classed as petty entrepreneurs, either shopkeepers or tradesmen.'[72] Many of the 169 Americans involved in retail or sales would have been part of Glasgow's middle class. As can be seen in Chart 4, forty-four were working proprietors in the retail or wholesale trade. These thirty-eight men and six women either sold groceries, draperies, tea, oil or wine and spirits directly to the public while some imported goods

---

70 Census records. Scotland. Milton, Glasgow. 07 April 1861. ROSBOROUGH, H.T. 644/7, 2, 12.

71 'Britannia Music Hall, 113 Trongate', *Glasgow Evening Citizen* (09 October 1867); Deaths, Scotland. Luss, Dumbarton. 28 March 1887. ROSSBOROUGH, Hubert Thomas. 499/4.

72 Stana Nenadic, 'The Victorian Middle Classes', in W. Hamish Fraser and Irene Mavor, eds, *Glasgow, volume II: 1830–1912*, (Manchester, 1996), 267.

from North or South America to sell to other traders. Both men and women in Glasgow were more likely to be employed in commerce compared to the rest of Scotland by 1911; men were twice as likely and women 1.75 times as likely and the relatively high number of American salespeople in this field reflects these trends.[73]

Of course, people did not necessarily stay in the same occupational category throughout their lives. Alonzo Kimball started out in sales, immigrating to Glasgow in 1859 as the local agent for the Singer Sewing Machine Company, founded in New York City. He was thirty-three years old and his wife of two years, Laura moved with him after their marriage in Massachusetts. For eight years he represented Singer, working out of their office on Buchanan Street in the heart of the city centre, selling sewing machines across the west of Scotland. However, he had greater ambitions and set up Kimball & Morton in 1867, a sewing machine manufacturing company with a factory in the Anderston area of Glasgow. His partner, John Morton, had also been an agent for Singer and they used their experience to create industrial sewing machines as well as the famous 'Lion' sewing machine for home use. In 1874, Alonzo left the company and returned to the United States where he set up a company manufacturing pin tickets, cardboard tags which identified items of clothing in retail stores, a forerunner of punch cards. He lived on Park Avenue in New York City with his Glasgow-born daughter, Mary and her husband, where he died in 1916.[74] His life shows an entrepreneurial man ready to take advantage of transnational opportunities and contacts begun during his time in Glasgow to enrich himself and his family.

---

73 Roger, 'The Labour Force', 171–2.

74 *Post Office Annual Glasgow Directory* (Glasgow: John Graham & Co., 1859), 151; Marriages, USA. Prescott, Massachusetts. 06 January 1857. KIMBALL, Alonzo and CROSETT, Laura; *Post Office Annual Glasgow Directory* (Glasgow: John Graham & Co., 1868), xvi; David G. Best, 'Kimball & Morton Ltd', http://www.sewmuse.co.uk/Kimball%20&%20Morton.htm, accessed 15 January 2024; Deaths, USA. Manhattan, New York. 12 February 1894. KIMBALL, Laura. 5552; Census, USA. Manhattan, New York. 1900. KIMBALL, Alonzo. 17/727/234; 'Alonzo Kimball', *Brooklyn Daily Eagle* (03 December 1916).

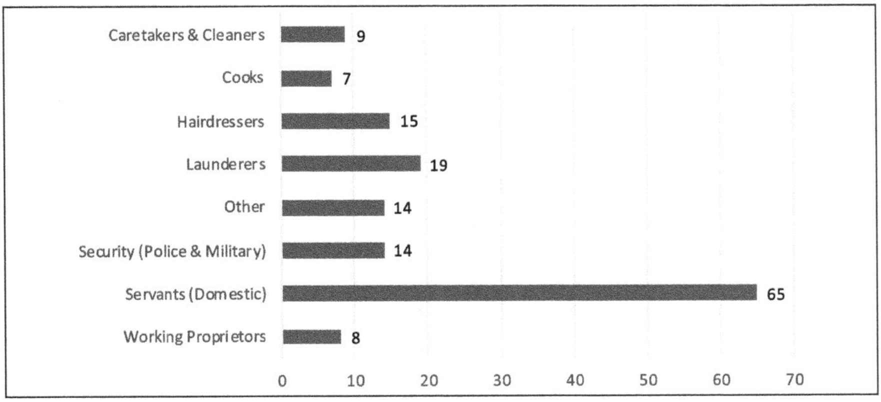

Chart 5: Number of Americans working in service (All census years)[75]

Most of the 151 Americans working in what HISCO classifies as service occupations were female (106). Of the forty-five men, fourteen were serving in the military, working for the police or as watchmen and, as was found in the general population of Glasgow where male domestic servants were outnumbered 25:1 by female domestic servants, the same was true of the Americans where only two domestic servants were male.[76] Sixty-nine per cent of the domestic servants (45) were 'living-in' on the night of the census with the rest primarily found staying with their parents. In 1901, Elizabeth Sproat, a general servant born in America, was living at 146 Park Road, just around the corner from Kelvingrove Park in the west end of Glasgow, with James Newall, a plumber from Glasgow, his wife and their four young children. Elizabeth was twelve years old and legally allowed to work half-time if she had reached 'Standard III' in writing, arithmetic and reading or full time by reaching 'Standard V'.[77] She was not the only twelve year old American-born servant in the cohort, Elizabeth Kingham was living with the Marwell family in the Anderston area of Glasgow in the 1871 census, but most servants were in their late teens or twenties.[78]

---

75 This represents HISCO group G5 – service workers. The 'Other' category includes five nursemaids, a man-servant, a lamplighter and a student's assistant. The working proprietors noted here were running guest or lodging houses, restaurants and pubs.

76 Roger, 'The Labour Force', 170.

77 T. C. Smout, *A Century of the Scottish People, 1830–1950* (London: Fontana Press, 1997), 96.

78 Census records. Scotland. Kelvin, Glasgow. 31 March 1901. SPROAT, Elizabeth H. 644/9, 46, 19; Anderston, Glasgow. 02 April 1871. KINGHAM, Elizabeth. 644/8, 11, 11.

Being American in Glasgow

Who were these Americans coming to Glasgow when most migrants were moving the other way across the Atlantic? The majority were generation 0.5, children born in the United States to Scottish immigrants who then returned to Glasgow. They would have had little choice but to migrate to Scotland with their families; those who moved at an early age would have had little memory of their American origins, but older migrants may have struggled with feelings of being different and not fitting in. Local family networks could have helped with integration, and many children were found living with Scottish extended family members. However, the study found 1,282 people on the five decennial censuses between 1851 and 1901 who came to Glasgow for other reasons. Most, such as Alonzo Kimball, the Singer Sewing Machine Company representative, were involved in business, trade and industry; others were here for education including William B. Gregory, an American citizen living in the Gorbals area and studying medicine in 1851.[79] There were American-born wives and husbands, who immigrated to start a new life in their Scottish spouse's home. Visitors, including entertainers on tour, missionaries and tourists experiencing Glasgow's sights and weather are all represented. Many were only found in one census, showing a high level of transience. Presumably, many would have returned home again but others, such as the Humphries family, moved on to other countries. Forbes and Eugenia Humphries, came to Glasgow from Albany, New York. Forbes, a foreman tailor, was born in Charleston, South Carolina and the family moved frequently within the United States, living in Philadelphia in 1847 and then in Albany in 1850. They were in Glasgow by 1859, living in the Anderston district but had moved by early 1865 to a flat closer to the city centre and the family emigrated to Australia later that year. The family may have decided to move further afield rather than return to the USA during the American Civil War as they were Black, but their true motivation for continued migration is unknown.[80]

What was the physical experience of being in Glasgow for these Americans? Horace Greeley, the editor of the *New York Tribune*, said that Glasgow 'Looks more American than any other city I have seen in Europe. Half of Pittsburgh spliced on to half of Philadelphia would make a city very like Glasgow'.[81] Indeed,

---

79 Census records, Scotland. Gorbals, Glasgow. 30 March 1851, GREGORY, William. 644/2. 12B, 31.

80 Census records, USA (African American). Philadelphia, Pennsylvania. 1847. HUMPHREYS, Forbes; Census records, USA. Albany, New York, 1850. HUMPRHEY, Forbes. 19/596; Electoral register, Glasgow. 1859; Valuation roll, Glasgow. 1865; Passenger list, *Chariot of Fame*, Liverpool, England to Melbourne, Australia. 2 December 1865.

81 Horace Greeley, *Glances at Europe: in a Series of Letters* (New York: Dewitt and Davenport, 1851), 306.

its broad streets laid out in a grid pattern would have made many feel at home but some would have come from farms or small towns and the streets teeming with people, horses and carriages and eventually omnibuses and tramways, must have been overwhelming.[82] Noise and odours from the numerous workshops and factories located side by side with residential housing would have also posed a challenge. Diaries and travel logs reflect different and, at times, contradictory opinions. Some praise the popularity of attending church and how Glasgow was the 'first place in Europe where we have found what may properly be called an American Sabbath'.[83] While others complained about the quality of services, 'Sunday – Went to hear a very poor sermon. How I wish I could hear some plain good preaching like we have at home'.[84] One visitor mentioned the 'exceedingly beautiful' streets with their 'lofty stone houses' and how the factory chimneys gave the city 'a sort of towering appearance'.[85] However, reactions clearly depended on what parts of the city were visited as many found the dirt and squalor of the slums and deep poverty of their inhabitants distressing.[86] No evidence of clubs or groups specifically for Americans in Glasgow during this time have been found. However, Josie Underwood's diary makes it clear that some did socialise with one another. She mentions dining and visiting with the Merrow and the Stoddard families, American steamship-line managers and carpet manufacturers, respectively.[87] The US consulate would be a natural hub for migrants and visitors and was a focus for Independence Day celebrations and important national events. Evidence of this includes a meeting held after President Lincoln's assassination of 'native-born Americans, convened at the United States Consulate in Glasgow, for the purpose of expressing their feelings with respect to the late distressing news from the United States'.[88] American government ministers also regularly gave addresses to city council members and to public meetings. In 1867, Mr Reverdy Johnson, the United States ambassador to the United Kingdom, spoke at a crowd at the Glasgow City Hall and praised the welcome he received which 'satisfied me that Scotland of all her Majesty's possessions, was true in her wish to preserve friendship to the United States'.[89] Though no specific American church has been identified, ministers from the United States did lead churches in Glasgow during

[82] James Schmiechen, 'Glasgow of the Imagination: Architecture, Townscape and Society', in W. Hamish Fraser and Irene Mavor, eds., *Glasgow, volume II: 1830–1912*, (Manchester, 1996), 493.

[83] Erastus Benedict, *A Run Through Europe* (New York: D. Appleton & Co, 1860), 527.

[84] Baird, 'Josie Underwood's Civil War Diary, Part Two', 374.

[85] Benedict, *A Run Through Europe*, 528.

[86] Aspinwall, *Portable Utopia*, 8–9.

[87] Baird, 'Josie Underwood's Civil War Diary, Part Two', 371, 374.

[88] 'Americans in Glasgow', *Glasgow Herald* (1 May 1865).

[89] 'Public Meeting in the City Hall', *Glasgow Evening Citizen* (10 February 1869).

this time including the Wellpark Free Church in Dennistoun, the New Jerusalem Church, also known as the Swedenborgian Church which had at least three American ministers, and the St Paul's Universalist Church in Pitt Street led by Caroline A. Soule, who in 1880 became the first woman ordained in the United Kingdom. US born missionaries from the Church of Jesus Christ of Latter-day Saints were also present with seven noted on the 1901 census.[90]

Keeping in touch with news and trends from the United States would have been facilitated by coffee houses which provided US publications and the popularity of lectures and sermons given by visiting Americans. These ranged from the leader of the American women's suffrage movement, Elizabeth Cady Stanton who spoke at St Andrew's Halls in November 1882, to the evangelists Dwight L. Moody and Ira Sankey, who brought religious revivalism to the masses in the 1870s and 80s.[91] Newspapers in Glasgow also provided information on American politics, trade and finance including regular correspondence on market prices for goods.[92]

As noted earlier, many Americans blended easily due to shared language, religion and cultural background in a way that other immigrants would not. But that does not mean they felt totally at home or were lacking challenges. Travel journals and a few diaries provide limited insight into the experiences of these individuals but interviews with modern migrants give a sense of the realities of day-to-day life in a foreign country. American expatriate spouses in the Netherlands describe having 'Dutch Days' when small problems that would be easy to resolve at home, spiral into overwhelming difficulties due to cultural differences.[93] Considerations of acculturation and identity are also present, with some feeling like they are 'neither fish nor fowl ... and [you] never become totally integrated' with others reconfiguring their identity to acknowledge their new home while maintaining elements of their previous life.[94] While some may have struggled at times with life in Glasgow, local family ties and business relationships would have helped most adjust over time. These Americans contributed to the city during the nineteenth century through their creativity, business acumen, government connections and family relationships, enriching themselves as well as the community around them.

---

90 The Scottish census records these ministers and missionaries, most of whom were male but along with Caroline A. Soule in 1891, there were two female assistants at the Little Sisters of St. Joseph's Home for the Aged in Dennistoun and in 1901 two female Church of Jesus Christ of Latter-day Saints missionaries.

91 Aspinwall, *Portable Utopia*, 95.

92 For example, see 'American Trade Notes', *Glasgow Herald* (21 June 1886).

93 Jennifer Jones-Corley, '"Just one of those Dutch days": American Expatriate Spouses in The Netherlands: Towards an Expatriate Frame Management Theory of Acculturation', PhD Thesis, Pennsylvania State University, University Park, 2002, 71.

94 Marjory Harper, *Testimonies of Transition: Twentieth Century Migrants, Settlers and Returners* (Edinburgh: Luath Press, 2018), 156.

'Man, we fear, is naturally a dirty animal and so is woman': Keeping Clean in the City, c. 1870s–1950s

James Smyth

In autumn 1912 the recently retired Master of Works of the Corporation of Glasgow, Frank I. Cohen, visited New York as a first stop on an intended world tour. The attraction lay in the opportunity to learn lessons 'in good government' from the 'leading metropolis in the world'. Rather than a fortnight, Cohen stayed for months but was surprised and astonished to discover that New York was actually, the 'Worst Governed City in the World', the title of the article he published in the *Sun* newspaper on 4 May 1913. Whether the tone of the piece was fuelled by tabloid exaggeration, Cohen did not spare the feelings of his hosts, making it clear that New York had more or less everything to learn from 'the marvellous municipal achievements … [of] the finest and best governed city in the world'. He was of course referring to Glasgow.

Questioning America's supposedly more egalitarian and democratic ethos, Cohen eulogised Glasgow's tramways, telephone service, its Common Good Fund, but, more than anything, he contrasted the virtue of Glasgow's public wash-houses, with New York's 'primitive' back yard washing lines, the like of which could be seen 'nowhere in Glasgow. … It seems incredible that in the year 1913 A. D. people should still hang out their linen in a contaminated atmosphere, there to gather disease and make the eyes of a sensitive man smart with pain'. In contrast, at any municipal wash-house in Glasgow:

> A woman brings the family wash, pays a penny and is assigned a compartment which she occupies alone until she is through. Her linen is thrown into a basin, she turns on an electric switch and in a few minutes her soiled articles are delivered to her immaculately clean.[1]

Such Glasgow chauvinism appears almost embarrassing, but it did have some basis in a (comparative) reality. Glasgow was one of the pioneers of municipal socialism and on the cusp of the First World War could genuinely claim to be the exemplar of the provision of public services. The purpose of this chapter is to examine why wash-houses, with the usual attached baths and swimming pools, played such an

---

1 *Sun* (4 May 1913). He added, 'Our public baths are models for the entire world.' Cohen had been the sub-convenor of Glasgow Corporation's 'Committee on Public Baths and Wash-houses', *Glasgow Post Office Directory 1911/12*, 1708.

important role within public health in Glasgow and why the steamie (Glasgow's popular term for a municipal wash-house) became such an iconic, if sentimentalised feature within the modern history of the city. In so doing it will comment also on New York's own struggle in keeping clean, and consider why, despite the apparent need and much greater population, it did not go down the wash-house route. We shall have cause also to query Cohen's utopian view of the apparent lack of effort the electric powered wash-house afforded the women who used it.

Much of the appreciation and affection felt for the steamie is due to Tony Roper's eponymous play, perhaps the most popular and most-often revived theatrical production in Scotland in recent times. First performed live in 1987 to instant acclaim, a more or less immediately filmed version broadcast on Scottish Television (STV) on Hogmanay 1988 (regularly repeated since) broadened its appeal across the whole population. A product of the 1980s, but located in the 1950s, 'The Steamie' was 'revolutionary for its day', its author has argued, because of the dominance of women in the story and cast; reversing the usual structure, 'This was all women with a token man'.[2] The wash-house was a female space where women gathered to do a woman's task; the weekly wash for her family. With the only males in evidence likely being the superintendent or the boilerman, it was almost perfect as a stage for women to express themselves freely about their lives, families and men. A native Glaswegian and a comic actor, Roper gives the cast a superbly funny script to perform. While often wistful and at times verging on bathos, it is the humour of the play that lies behind its enduring appeal; it 'has a kind of hilarious perfection', said the *Scotsman*.[3] And as the humour rings true both to the location and subject matter, so The Steamie somehow has become synonymous with Glasgow, even though other towns and cities in Scotland and the UK had their own public wash-houses.

The genesis of the play is itself significant. The idea, oddly enough, first came to Roper when he was selling his flat in Edinburgh. The main attraction to the woman who bought it was that there was 'a decent-sized laundry round the corner and I can go there and meet up wi' my pals'.[4] When, in 1984, Borderline Theatre Company offered him a commission to write a play Roper recalled the woman's remark and went back to Glasgow to research the subject matter at the Mitchell Library in Anderston, the area he grew up in, where his

---

2 NLS, 'The Steamie'. https://digital.nls.uk/, accessed 26 October 2023.https://digital.nls.uk/scottish-theatre/steamie/index.html Where 'The Steamie' is used in the text it refers to the play, where 'steamie' is used it refers to the municipal wash-houses.

3 NLS, 'The Steamie'.

4 Tony Roper, *I'll No Tell Ye Again: My Autobiography* (Edinburgh, Black and White Publishing, 2014), 214

mother still lived and where he first experienced a 'steamie'. Borderline never performed the play but a few years later Elaine C. Smith of Wildcat Stage Productions approached him. Wildcat had been offered a grant from the trade union NALGO 'for a play about communities' but did not have one on their stocks. Roper offered The Steamie, to which Wildcat added music and an overnight sensation was born.[5]

The play, therefore, looks back from the 1980s – a time when working-class communities were under the threat of deindustrialisation – to an apparently more stable era – the 1950s when working-class solidarity was expressed as much by the natural companionship of housewives as by the masculine trade unions of heavy industry. At the same time the awareness of the passing of that way of life gives The Steamie its elegiac more than simply nostalgic quality. Witnessing the blows of 'Thatcherism' and the accelerated decline of manufacturing, many other Scottish artists were grappling with this sense of loss; it is hardly coincidental that 1987 was the same year of the Proclaimers' anthemic 'Letter from America', and when Deacon Blue released 'Raintown', aka Glasgow, the album cover depicting a rainy and windswept city with the giant Finnieston Crane in the background, symbolic of the city's past industrial glory.

The Struggle to Keep Clean

It was not until late in the nineteenth century that the provision of water closets and clean water in most homes started to become the norm. Even then, the difficulty in heating water and the lack of dedicated space for washing and drying clothes, and bodies, made keeping clean a more or less permanent effort. It was a struggle in which the odds were stacked heavily against the working-class housewife, perhaps nowhere more so than in Glasgow, infamous for its small houses. As enlightenment thought on the physical and moral properties of cleanliness trickled down the social hierarchy, it reached an apparent dead end with the poor. Castigated and feared as the 'Dangerous Classes' and as the 'Great Unwashed', the working classes had to be educated, as Wear has put it, 'in an almost coercive sense'.[6] In one of the periodic paeans of praise to its own sagacity, the authors of *Glasgow: its Municipal Organisation and Administration*, wrote in 1896:

> Man, we fear, is naturally a dirty animal, and so is woman, and the almost godly virtue of cleanliness requires to be encouraged and oft inculcated. For this cause, and as a part

5 Roper, *I'll No Tell Ye Again*, 218–27.

6 Andrew Wear, 'The History of Personal Hygiene', in W. F. Bynum and Roy Porter, eds, *Companion Encyclopaedia of the History of Medicine* (London: Taylor & Francis, 1993), 1298.

> of their great sanitary scheme, the Police Department have erected and equipped in various districts of the City the Corporation Baths and Wash-houses, specially for the benefit of the poorer classes. They are valuable institutions which deserve to be better known and more fully appreciated by the class in whose interest they are maintained.[7]

The first public wash-house in the city can be traced back to 1732 when the town council established one on Glasgow Green.[8] Dorothy Wordsworth has left a vivid description from 1803 of this 'bleaching ground' which:

> the whole summer through is covered with women of all ages, children and young girls spreading out their linen. [In the middle of the Green was] a wash-house, whither the inhabitants of this large town, rich and poor, send or carry their linen to be washed. There are two very large rooms, with each a cistern in the middle for hot water; and all round the rooms are benches for the women to set their tubs upon. Both the rooms were crowded with washers; there might be a hundred, or two or even three; ... It was amusing to see so many women, arms, head, and face all in motion, all busy in an ordinary household employment, in which we are accustomed to see, at the most, only three or four women employed in one place. The women were very civil.[9]

Here Wordsworth captured the essence of the wash-house as a communal space, and the activity of the women which would remain unchanged in the later 'steamies'. It was not until the 1870s, however that the modern City began to renew and expand the provision. In 1876, a full decade after gaining the powers to provide wash-houses and baths, the Corporation took over the old Glasgow Green wash-house and two years later re-opened it as the Greenhead Baths and Wash-house. Two privately owned bath houses were bought over by the Corporation in 1874 then leased to a tenant, though both closed in 1883. By 1885, however, four more municipal baths and wash-houses had been opened in Woodside, Cranstonhill, Townhead and Gorbals. The era of the 'steamie' had arrived.[10]

In their first full year of operation (1886), the five establishments attracted 386,570 bathers, and there were 76,718 washings. By 1895 these numbers had increased to 527,313 and 197,035 respectively. Proud as they were with their achievement in providing these buildings, the authors of the 1896 account were

---

[7] James (Sir) Bell and James Paton, *Glasgow: its Municipal Organisation and Administration* (Glasgow, 1896), 174. Paton was curator of Glasgow's museums and galleries, while Bell was the Lord Provost.

[8] 'Ask the Archivist – Baths and wash-houses', www.glasgowlife.org.uk, accessed 26 October 2023.

[9] Dorothy Wordsworth, 'Recollections of a Tour Made in Scotland (A.D. 1803)', in *Journals of Dorothy Wordsworth, Vol 1*, edited by William Knight (London, MacMillan & Co, 1897), 209–10.

[10] Bell and Paton, *Glasgow*, 176.

less than impressed with the response of the poorer citizenry. They calculated that the total number of actual bathers had grown from 15,000 to 20,000 and that the number of women or households using the wash-houses from 1200 to 4,000. Given that in Glasgow in 1901 there were 163,416 'separate families' and 155,414 'inhabited' houses, their disappointment appears merited.[11] Moreover, recognising it was likely that many of the customers 'do not strictly speaking belong to the industrial classes', their analysis of the figures led to the conclusion that, 'It must be confessed that washing and cleaning are not popular operations with a large mass of the poorer among the industrial population'.[12]

Such a perspective was based on the continuing view that the industrial poor were ignorant and in need of education, if not compulsion. Yet, at the same time the authors provided an alternative explanation for the disappointing response to the services offered. They recognised that in such a large place as Glasgow, advertising the benefits of the wash-houses and baths to the public was 'difficult', and it was just as 'difficult to change the habits of certain classes'. While this sounds disparaging, what they were referring to was the effect of distance between home and the wash-house. Those who lived nearby were more likely to be aware of the wash-house in the first place, and more likely to use it given its proximity. In the case of the Gorbals, a mapping exercise had been conducted in 1892; the customers were asked their names and addresses which were then plotted on a map. This revealed that women who lived within a quarter of a mile comprised more than two-thirds of its clientele, those living between a quarter of a mile to a half a mile away comprised around twenty per cent, while those who lived more than half a mile away accounted for only one tenth.[13]

While there remained the nagging doubt that the public wash-houses were not as popular as they ought to be, nonetheless the Corporation was convinced that providing them created its own demand, 'even in localities where every tenement has its own wash-house and drying court'. This belief was based on the use made of the steamies and 'from interviewing many of the women who use them'. The attractions of the steamie were numerous; women did not have to wait on the rota within the tenement so they could choose their own times; there was no delay as the water slowly reached boiling point, and the coal needed to operate the boiler 'costs almost as much as all the conveniences at a public establishment'. Additionally, the tenement wash-houses could only cope with smaller loads, were most likely 'draughty and dingy' and kitchens had to be utilised as

---

11 Census of Scotland 1911, *Report*, Volume 1, Part 2, 'The City of Glasgow', 51.

12 Bell and Paton, *Glasgow*, 178.

13 Glasgow Department of Baths and Wash-Houses, *Annual Report* (1892), 8; *Glasgow*, 178.

'drying stoves'. This latter point was critical in 'forcing their husbands and sons to dislike their homes'.[14] The message was clear; housewives washing clothes at the steamie helped ensure cleanliness and domestic harmony.

As most customers of the steamies did a single wash each week, the loads would have been substantial and heavy (usually carried in prams) and women did not like transporting their 'bundle of clothes, dirty or clean, a great distance through the streets of the City'.[15] Moreover, Bell and Paton also recognised that the need for such facilities was rooted in the domestic situation faced by most of the population, 'The luxury of a bath is not to be thought of in connection with houses of one or two apartments, and in such the washing of clothes can only be done at the cost of much domestic discomfort.'[16]

Such observations open up an alternative, more generous perspective on the difficulties if not impossibilities facing working-class families and the particular strains placed on women. This was most famously expressed by Glasgow's Medical Officer of Health Dr James Burn Russell in his seminal publication, *Life in one Room* (1888), where he condemned Social Darwinism and appealed to the middle class to imagine how they would live their lives within the confines of a single apartment.[17] While Russell was not opposed to compulsion, for instance in trying to reduce overcrowding, nonetheless it is important to recognise that more humane attitudes existed or rather co-existed alongside the declamatory and the judgemental. Such can be found even earlier, as in Chadwick's *Sanitary Report* of 1842. Discussing the supply of water to working-class homes, Chadwick stressed the practical difficulty, and effort, in obtaining water from wells that may be some distance away. Compounded by the long hours in hard work and faced by darkness in winter and the vagaries of the weather it was perfectly understandable that all this, 'acts as an obstacle to the formation of better habits'. Logically, it followed that those 'better habits' would be inculcated by the direct provision of clean water to every house, preferably through the agency of 'the most eligible local administrative body' rather than by private enterprise. In making his argument on the forming of 'habits' Chadwick stressed that when middle-class households experienced an interruption in their water supply, for instance due to frozen pipes, so the cleanliness of their homes suffered. Furthermore, he argued

---

14 Baths and Wash-Houses, *Annual Report* (1892), 6–7.

15 Bell and Paton, *Glasgow*, 178.

16 Bell and Paton, *Glasgow*, 173–4.

17 James B. Russell, *Life in One Room* (1888). For the long-term impact of this text see James J. Smyth, 'The Power of Pathos: James Burn Russell's Life in One Room and the creation of council housing', *Scottish Historical Review* 98/ 1 (April 2019), 103–127.

that if the middle class had to obtain their water from a distance and collect it 'in all weathers, their habits of household cleanliness would be deteriorated'.[18]

Almost sixty years later Peter Fyfe, the Chief Sanitary Inspector of Glasgow was making the same argument. In a talk given to the Association of House Factors and Property Agents in Glasgow, subsequently printed as a pamphlet, Fyfe challenged the slum landlord that

> ... he ought to understand the meaning of the unwholesome and insanitary conditions under which his tenants have to live. I do not think it is necessary for me to go into nauseating details in order to exemplify, within the homes of the poor, the practical import of the want of 'suitable and convenient water-closet accommodation', or the want of sink and water supply for each family. Each can imagine for himself what would happen in his house at times if these all-important adjuncts to a clean family life were absent or difficult of access. You all may see the results I refer to by visiting the homes of the poor *at night*, or, if you cannot see it, *you can smell it*.[19]

Fyfe was an acolyte of Dr Russell (to whom he dedicated this pamphlet), and like his mentor, he condemned the 'myth' that, regardless of the state of the houses of the poor this 'should in no way prevent inner sweetness and scrupulous cleanliness', stating 'You do not look for grapes in a land where there is no sunshine.' In this piece Fyfe was specifically arguing against the common view that the inhabitants of the 'Back Lands', that is those tenements built on the back courts of existing tenements and notorious for lack of space and poor ventilation, were 'on a distinctly lower plane socially than their front-land neighbours'. Employing the lady sanitary inspectors of his department with their intimate knowledge of the lives of the poor, Fyfe conducted a survey of 5,505 one and two apartment ticketed houses in front-facing tenements and in back lands and concluded there was no social or economic dividing line between the populations. The survey also included a calculation on tenants' 'respectability' and found a clear majority of all satisfied that designation, ranging from 76 per cent in the one apartment back lands to 88.6 per cent in the two apartment front lands, regardless of place of birth or religion.[20] How these figures were arrived at was hardly a scientific process given that they were partly reliant upon the 'undefinable something' that the experienced sanitary visitor learned to employ. What is significant though is

[18] M. W. Flinn, ed, *Report on The Sanitary Condition of the Labouring Population of Great Britain by Edwin Chadwick 1842* (Edinburgh, Edinburgh University Press, 1965) 141, 151.

[19] Peter Fyfe, *Back Lands and their Inhabitants* (Glasgow, Robert Anderson, 1901), 32.

[20] Fyfe, *Back Lands*, 14–17.

that Fyfe sought to defend the slum dwellers from condemnation and vilification, stating his belief that '50 per cent of the poor ... wish to be clean.'[21]

This strikes a more consistently optimistic tone than that of Bell and Paton from five years earlier yet suggests that those champions of the wash-houses were right in believing that the public demand was there. While Sheard has commented on Glasgow, like Liverpool, losing interest in baths and wash-houses 'towards the end of the nineteenth century', this seems to have been a temporary decline only.[22] Indeed, increasing use, allied to the expansion of Glasgow's physical boundaries, led to more municipal provision. In 1902, with the opening of Whitevale Baths and Wash-house, the number of establishments reached twelve, not all of which provided swimming and private bath facilities, but all did have wash-houses. By 1914 eight more baths and wash-houses were opened, with two more in construction and, due to the 1912 City Boundaries Act, it was understood that more would 'have to be erected'.[23] Bell and Paton calculated their figure of 4,000 households using the steamies in 1895 from a total 197,035 individual 'washings'. In 1913 the attendance figures for all the city's wash-houses stood at 821,329. Without knowledge of Bell and Paton's conversion formula, it nonetheless seems fair to state that the use of the steamies had increased exponentially. In addition, there were recorded for 1913 almost half a million 'attendances' at the city's regular 'swimming ponds', just under 300,000 'hot baths' were taken, and almost another 200,000 attended as members of swimming clubs or enjoyed free admission as schoolchildren. Across all the facilities offered the total attendance for the year was 1,790,189.[24] While we cannot provide the exact number of individual users, there certainly seems to have been many Glasgow citizens who wanted to keep themselves clean and healthy. Given that the growth in numbers followed the expansion of the facilities one is tempted to say, 'Build it and they will come'.

On the eve of the First World War, of these twenty municipal establishments, only six (the original five opened before 1896 plus Whitevale) provided the full range of facilities: wash-house, separate swimming ponds for men and women, and separate 'private baths' for men and women. Only three – Kennedy Street, Stobcross and Bain Square – operated solely as steamies. Seven of the twenty lacked any swimming pool but did have private baths as well as wash-houses. Ten had men-only swimming pools, while seven of these had female-only pools as

---

21 Fyfe, *Back Lands*, 32.

22 Sally Sheard, 'Profit is a Dirty Word: The Development of Public Baths and Wash-houses in Britain 1847–1915', *Social History of Medicine* 13/1 (2000), 77.

23 *Municipal Glasgow, its evolution and enterprises.* With a preface by Sir Daniel M. Stevenson, Issued by the corporation of the city of Glasgow (Glasgow, 1914), 97.

24 *Municipal Glasgow*, 98.

well, and all, with one exception, Govan, had a wash-house attached. Pollokshaws offered the fewest facilities, only six private baths for men and two for women, but it was the least 'industrial' of the localities. The eighteen establishments that were also wash-houses provided between them 979 separate 'washing stalls'.[25]

The gendered nature of the facilities is striking. The women's swimming pools were noticeably smaller than the men's; a typical men's pool would be 75ft by 40ft, whereas for women 40ft by 24ft would be more likely. Interestingly though, Govan had exactly the same dimensions for both, 75ft by 35ft. All the establishments with baths provided for both men and women but all had more for men, and often by a significant margin; by a factor of six in Cranstonhill and Maryhill. Across the city there were 102 private baths for women compared to 373 for men. Since none of the accounts provide a rationale for the difference, was this simply patriarchy in practice, male needs somehow being obviously greater than female and needing no explanation? On the other side of the coin were women assumed to be more modest about revealing their bodies, even if in a 'private bath'? There could, however, be a more practical if partial reason; simply that male bodies, due to the jobs they undertook, were that much dirtier. It was a wash-house rule (and a sub-plot in Roper's play) that men's overalls were not to be included in a wash, the dirt on them was simply too oily for the machines. The challenge that women faced when trying to clean that particular item was vividly recalled by Morry Weir, 'At the word "dungarees" the women would groan in sympathy. Washing dungarees was a job they all hated.'[26] If that dirt was on their clothes it was certainly on parts of their bodies also and likely demanded the soap and unlimited hot water provided at the baths.

If not all steamies had baths and swimming pools attached, the association between the facilities became a permanent feature of Glasgow life: well into the twentieth century anyone (adult or child) who was going for a swim would say they were going to 'the baths'. The buildings were often ornate, designed to exhibit the prestige of the Corporation; whatever could be provided by the private baths for the middle classes could be more than met by the public baths for all citizens. The commemorative brochure produced to celebrate the opening of 'Whitevale Baths' in 1902 displayed both the range of services provided and the municipal ambition and pride encapsulated by the building.

Covering 2,765 square yards and costing £37,000, Whitevale comprised male and female 'swimming ponds', 12 first-class and 16 second class 'slipper baths'

[25] *Municipal Glasgow*, 99.

[26] Molly Weir, *Shoes Were for Sunday*, in *Molly Weir's Trilogy of Scottish Childhood* (Edinburgh: Lomond Books, 2000), 112.

for men, as well as 12 'spray baths' ('as in vogue on the continent'). For women, however, there were only eight slipper baths. The addition of a 'suite of Turkish baths' and a gymnasium differentiated Whitevale from every other existing establishment. Another new feature was that the swimming pool galleries were designed so that in winter (when attendance fell) they could be utilised as public halls seating 1500 and 750 people. Swimming galas were encouraged with the galleries and platforms around the pools accommodating some hundreds of spectators. While the gym adjoined the men's swimming pool nevertheless it could be separated and made available to women exclusively on certain days. While clearly there was greater provision for males, it is not the case that women were excluded. For instance, while the Turkish bath, a collective experience accommodating up to eight people at a time, may have been used mostly by men, Tuesdays were women-only.[27] This seems to have been common practice across the city, as Molly Weir recalled that Springburn swimming pond had a women-only day on a Tuesday.[28]

New York and the Absence of Wash-Houses

In 1918 the *New York Tribune* ran an article arguing that 'There is probably no city in the world that has greater need of a public laundry than New York'. While a relatively late comer to the movement, the city did happily build public baths and indeed became famous for these. What it did not do, however, was to build on the European model, where baths (including swimming pools) and wash-houses were located within a single building; 'siamese twins' as the *Tribune* put it, which allowed 'economy of maintenance, heating, water supply and so on'. Why New York did not follow this approach is unclear though one argument made in 1918 was that since the baths had been built already it would be too expensive to retrofit a wash-house into any of them.[29]

It would appear that the US in general did not have the need for public wash-houses that European cities did. By 1918 there were perhaps only 15 or 16 operating in a handful of places: Cincinnati, Philadelphia, and especially Baltimore. These followed the model of baths and wash-houses and provided similar services at a similar cost to the Glasgow steamie though without creches. This element, 'deemed essential in European cities', was held responsible for the

---

[27] Corporation of Glasgow, *Baths and Wash-Houses: Souvenir of the Opening of Whitevale Baths* (1902).

[28] Weir, *Shoes Were For Sunday*, 113–4.

[29] *New York Tribune* (30 June 1918), 4.

'limited use' made by 'women from the congested districts', yet the biggest group of customers in Baltimore were the 'colored women who live in the alleys and crowded tenement districts'.[30] If there was an association between wash-houses and tenements then New York would appear to have been the obvious location, with its more European pattern of urban housing.

While other American cities had tenements nowhere had them to the extent that New York did. In 1865 the Council of Hygiene and Public Health estimated that of a population of 700,000 (not including Brooklyn) 480,368 persons 'lived in 15,309 tenement houses with sub-standard conditions'.[31] Thereafter matters accelerated; by the end of the century greater New York had 80,000 tenements (three-quarters of which had been built in the previous twenty years) housing 2.3 million citizens out of a total population of c. 3.4 million.[32] They were hardly salubrious. New York's grid plan of development whereby the city was divided into lots of 25 by 100 feet led to similar problems as Glasgow's 'back-lands'; the plots were so small that 'back' tenements were often squeezed in right up against the rear of the 'front' tenement meaning many rooms had no natural light at all.

As in Glasgow and elsewhere the 1860s saw the beginnings of efforts directed to improve housing conditions in New York. The Tenement House Act of 1867 stipulated that there had to be one water closet for every twenty tenants. However, the powers in the Act and the subsequent one of 1879 were discretionary and were in the main disregarded. In 1884 it was reported that only 30 per cent of tenements had any water closets and there was almost no provision of running water above the first floor.[33] It seems clear, therefore, that New York, just like any other rapidly growing city (and New York was expanding faster than anywhere else), was in need of public bathing and laundry facilities. Sanitary pioneers, philanthropists and concerned journalists and academics certainly believed so and in looking for municipal examples to follow, most often referenced Glasgow.

In 1894 New York State established the Tenement House Committee, the remit of which was to 'inquire into the "so-called tenement-house question" and to provide "such recommendations as it deems wise to enable the best and

30 *New York Tribune* (30 June 1918), 4.

31 Quoted in Richard Plunz, *A History of Housing in New York City* (New York: Columbia University Press, 2016), 22.

32 Plunz, *Housing in New York City*, 30. 'Greater New York' was created in 1898 when the process of 'consolidation' saw the City of Brooklyn along with part of Queen's Count and Staten Island amalgamate with the City of New York.

33 Plunz, *Housing in New York City*, 33.

highest possible condition for tenement-house life"'.[34] Among the witnesses was Adah S. Woolfolk of the College Settlement who had investigated the difficulties faced by the inhabitants of the tenements 'in their attempts to live in a sanitary fashion'. Woolfolk supported the proposal that New York should establish public laundries, 'because, in all the ordinary tenements, there are no laundries and the washing must be done in the room, and when there is only a single living room, this results in many inconveniences'. She added that washing in such small houses was injurious to children's health particularly due to the damp. When the weather permitted, the tenement housewife dried her clothes on the roof if they lived to the front of the building, while those at the back of the tenement used pulley lines across the court, the sight of which so upset Frank Cohen.[35]

Another witness was Albert Shaw, a prominent figure in the study of urbanism and municipal reform who had given up a scholarly career for campaigning journalism.[36] His most significant works were two volumes on municipal government in Britain and Europe both of which were at press when he gave his evidence in late 1894 and were published the following year.[37] While also enthusiastic about public laundries Shaw's evidence was slightly contradictory. He strongly recommended that New York should build public baths 'with or without the attachment of laundries' though he considered the latter to be hugely beneficial and referenced Glasgow in particular where, 'the attachment of municipal laundries has proved a very fortunate thing for the improvement of the social condition of the poorest tenement districts'. At the same time, however, he recognised that the laundries were not as well patronised as had been hoped and in 'one or two English cities' the wash-houses had been abandoned due to 'poor women' preferring 'to do their washing at home'. In Glasgow the laundries had been operating for some years, and even though the customer base had been growing he expressed his 'surprise' that demand was not greater. This perception was similar to that within Glasgow, but Shaw's explanation focused exclusively on the failings of the slum dwellers themselves:

> ... it is a well-known fact that improved facilities for the benefit of the poorest classes in city slums are seldom very eagerly appreciated at first; If the people had enterprise enough to show quick appreciation there would be less necessity for considering their unfortunate condition.

---

34 State of New York, *Report of the Tenement House Committee of 1894* (Albany: James B, Lyon, 1895), 4, 9.

35 *Report of the Tenement House Committee*, 433–6.

36 Lloyd J. Graybar, 'Albert Shaw's Search for the Ideal City', *The Historian* 34/ 3 (May 1972), 421–436.

37 Albert Shaw, *Municipal Government in Great Britain* and *Municipal Government in Continental Europe* (New York: The MacMillan Company, 1895).

Nonetheless Shaw's advice to the committee was that the city should build public baths on the lines of the best that were found in Liverpool and Glasgow and, additionally, it should also build one or two establishments that incorporated baths and a laundry within the same building, 'the experiment would not be very costly for so rich a city as New York, and it could certainly do no harm; its success would point the way to a gradual development of the system.'[38] Although the Sub-Committee on Baths and Lavatories supported this approach, the full Tenement House Committee did not, restricting itself to baths only. Construction of the first public bath on Rivington Street began in late 1897 but the opening was delayed until 1901. From then until 1915, however, was the heyday of New York's public baths with a series being built across the city, more incorporating swimming pools, and becoming more expensive and 'elaborate'. Only at the end of this period was there a public bath built on the European model; the West 28th St Bath was equipped with showers, a swimming pool, a gymnasium with indoor track, a roof garden, playground and 'public laundry facilities'.[39] It would appear, however, that the experiment did not thrive, the *Tribune* article of 1918 commenting that, 'even this feeble little idea died in its infancy'.[40]

It is likely that for the full committee the most significant element of Shaw's testimony was the comment on the laundries not being used extensively. Regardless of what conclusions were come to, however, it is noticeable how often Glasgow was referenced by the committee and within the witness testimonies; apart from London, Glasgow was the most cited city, far surpassing Manchester, Liverpool, Berlin or Paris. In Shaw's book on municipal Britain Glasgow provides the longest single chapter; its seventy-five pages being significantly more than the twenty-two pages given to both Manchester and Birmingham.[41] If, for New York Glasgow represented the best that could be done by a progressive municipality, the 'steamie' was clearly one reform that did not migrate across the Atlantic.

In New York, unlike Glasgow, there was no common wash-house for each close, so women either washed within their own kitchen or had to use the communal sink on each landing or 'hall', a source of great antagonism among the tenants.[42] Given the similarities in tenement life between the two cities, and the positive example that Glasgow seemed to provide, it is not clear why New York never developed wash-houses of its own. One possible explanation may be that, as bad as

---

38 *Report of the Tenement House Committee of 1894*, 375.

39 M. T. Williams, 'New York City's Baths: A Case Study in Urban Progressive Reform', *Journal of Urban History* 7 (1980), 70–1.

40 *New York Tribune* (30 June 1918).

41 Shaw, *Municipal Government in Great Britain*. London is given two chapters which together comprise 102 pages.

42 Robert W. deForest and Lawrene Veiller, eds, *The Tenement House Problem Vol 1* (New York: The MacMillan Company, 1902), 'Tenement Evils as Seen by the Tenants', 383–417.

its tenements were, they were never quite as bad as Glasgow's. Crucially perhaps, they were not so small. Even as late as 1911, two-thirds of Glasgow's families lived in a house of two rooms or less; from 34 per cent in 1861 the proportion living in a one-roomed house had fallen to 20 per cent but that still represented over 100,000 of the city's almost 800,000 inhabitants.[43]

It was, as Dr Russell pointed out in 1888, these 'small houses which produce the high death-rate of Glasgow' and we might add, so much else.[44] Overcrowding was the major problem within Glasgow, and indeed across Scotland, whereas in New York, despite its massive density of population, actual overcrowding within houses was less of an issue. In his evidence to the Tenement House Committee in 1894, Elgin R.L. Gould of John Hopkins University and ex-statistician in the Department of Labour, made this distinction, 'there is more overcrowding on space in New York than in any foreign city; there is not as much overcrowding within the rooms as is found in some European cities, notably in Glasgow'.[45] His interviewers could hardly believe the reality of Glasgow's single room houses:

> Q. These are tenements in which it is intended to have one family in a room?
> A. Yes; practically one room; one room with a screen.
>
> Q. That is a condition that does not exist to any appreciable extent in this city or in this country?
> A. Not to my knowledge.
>
> Q. There are very few cases, comparatively speaking, of a family being obliged to live in one room in this country?
> A. Comparatively speaking.[46]

Of course, there were such houses in New York, as Woolfolk's evidence indicated, just not to the extent as in Glasgow. The tenement houses may have been small but as the average was three rooms this was, possibly, sufficient to permit the washing of clothes in the home. Furthermore, with the passing of the Act of 1901 genuine improvements in tenement building and facilities became a reality. The 'New Law' as it became known (and which still regulates low-rise housing in New York) 'radically improved the quality of tenement housing'. Ventilation

---

43 John Butt, 'Working Class Housing in Glasgow, 1851–1914', in Stanley D. Chapman, ed, *The History of Working Class Housing: A Symposium* (Newton Abbot: David and Charles, 1971), 61, 80.

44 Russell, *Life in One Room*.

45 *Report of the Tenement House Committee of 1894*, 350.

46 *Report of the Tenement House Committee of 1894*, 355.

and light were improved, and the stipulation that every room had to have an external window did away with the problem created by the 'back' tenements. Of most concern here was the rule that, 'Every apartment had to have running water and a water closet.'[47] In addition, the owners of existing tenements began to retrofit taps and toilets which, it could be argued, made domestic washing, of clothes and bodies, easier and lessened any demand for public laundries. Opened in 1914 the West 28th Street Baths (including laundry) was the last such municipal enterprise, with the exception of the West 134th Street Bath built in the late 1920s for the Black population of Harlem.[48]

Wash Day

Without the steamie women could either send their clothes to a commercial laundry, including those run by the Co-op, employ another woman to do their washing, or use the common wash-house located in the back court.[49] Not all tenements had these though they became increasingly common in the later nineteenth century, more so in Glasgow than in Edinburgh.[50] Women working casually as cleaners or 'taking in washing' was a common way of making an income, and in The Steamie, the oldest member of the group, Mrs Culfeathers, essentially works at the laundry. Nonetheless, it seems that most women did their own washing while often helping out family and neighbours.

Washing clothes in a one or two roomed home with no running hot water was a near impossible task. Water would have to be boiled on the stove and then transferred into a tub and the clothes hand-scrubbed. Drying facilities indoors were minimal with, at best, a 'pulley' – a simple device for holding clothes on a series of wooden poles which would be pulled up to the ceiling by a rope. Pulleys were ubiquitous and even provided in later council houses, usually in the kitchen or scullery. Otherwise, clothes were hung over the fireplace or wherever. Outside drying was preferable, though given Glasgow's propensity for precipitation, this could hardly be relied upon. However, each close would have a drying 'green', essentially part of the back court, shared among the tenants with each having their own space or washing line, a rope on which they could 'peg' their clothes and which was held up by a long wooden pole. The wash-houses, also located in

47 Plunz, *A History of Housing in New York City*, 47–9.
48 Williams, 'New York City's Baths', 73.
49 Sheard, 'Profit is a Dirty Word', 78-9.
50 Helen Clark and Elizabeth Carnegie, *She Was Aye Workin', Memories of Tenement Women in Edinburgh and Glasgow* (Oxford: White Cockade, 2003), 14; Frank Worsdall, *The Glasgow Tenement: A Way of Life* (Edinburgh: Chambers, 1989), 34–6.

the court, allowed women to do large loads which was almost a necessity given there was a strict rota which every tenant had to adhere to. The term 'wash day' referred to this arrangement and to the fact that doing a full family wash took up most of a day. Sam Watt, born in 1919, describes his mother's routine:

> she was generally on a wash day up about half past five in the morning an' got the boiler started down in the back. The old wash-house. An' then came up and made the breakfast, and got us all tae school. And then went back down, finished her washin', then came up and did the rest of the cooking.[51]

The tenement wash-house could be both a source of mutual support and of tension. Someone might not need her 'turn' and offer it to a neighbour, or the hot soapy water would be left for the next user to steep her clothes in.[52] Women might congregate at the wash-house, often with children, to 'blether' and offer encouragement, especially to young women, as Molly Weir recounts, 'They were all experts. This was their world. And the young washerwoman would listen to them all, glad of their company and of their advice.' Potential disaster, however, was never far away; an overloaded washing line might collapse into the dirt.[53] Even worse, a bad neighbour, careless with how they lit the boiler so that it produced black smoke or how they disposed of ashes at the bins, could ruin a whole wash.[54] Faced with such calamities, going to the public wash-house would seem the obvious choice, but there was still a charge and, as Sheard has argued, in Glasgow as in Liverpool, 'the pricing system … kept away the poorest poor'.[55]

The practical difficulties of simply getting to and from the steamie pushing a heavy load and having to go up and down tenement stairs were a further disincentive. There was also the matter of personal preference. In her memoirs Molly Weir joyfully recounts going to the Springburn baths, both to enjoy the swimming pond with her friends and, when a bit older, to take an actual bath. The other aspect of 'the baths', however, the wash-house, remained a mystery to her:

> Another glimpse of the world of washing-day could be caught at the 'steamy', when we went to the baths. These were tubs and apparatus hired by women who had no proper wash-house in their tenement back courts, or who preferred the community atmosphere of the 'steamy' to a solitary session in their own wash-house. I used to pause in the open doorway, on my way out to the street, and watch the women at their work. It was like a scene from a play. … I had a great longing to penetrate these mysteries and take part

---

51 J. Faley, *Up oor close: Memoirs of Domestic Life in Glasgow, 1910–1945* (Oxford, White Cockade Publishing, 2008), 106.

52 Faley, *Up oor close*, 106–8; Clark and Carnegie, *She Was Aye Workin'*, 119; Weir, *Shoes Were For Sunday*, 111–13.

53 Weir, *Shoes Were for Sunday*, 112–13.

54 Faley, *Up Oor Close*, 110–12.

55 Sheard, 'Profit is a Dirty Word', 79.

> in the ritual myself, but I never did so, and these tantalizing glimpses were all I ever knew of this enchanting side of the baths.[56]

Weir never explains why her family did not use the steamie; since she lived with her mother and grandmother perhaps the two women felt capable of doing the washing at home, and their tenement wash-house does seem to have been a good one.

Frank Cohen's cheery description of how effortless washing was at the public laundry may have fooled some gullible New Yorkers but would not have been given the time of day by Glasgow housewives. Far from flicking a switch and waiting a few minutes for their linen to be delivered 'immaculately clean', washing in the steamie demanded considerable physical effort. Oral testimonies by women who used the steamies are consistently positive, but they also remembered the labour involved. Agnes Muirhead, born in Glasgow in 1918 recalled the Springburn steamie:

> Ye could go to the wash-house in Kay Street, but it was just the same, 'hand-washin''. I mean no machinery then, it was all done with a washin' board. The only thing was when ye wrung your clothes out, ye put them on tae these, what they termed 'drying-horses'. An' they were put in an' it half-dried your clothes. Ye were only allowed in for so long.[57]

Elizabeth Dawn, from south of the Clyde, was younger but her memory confirms what was demanded, while providing some more detail:

> It was tubs with a boiler beside them. You just pulled a big wooden crate up to your waist. You would wheel it up and put your washing in and you'd put your coloured washing somewhere and put your whites in first and then throw in the coloured and then put them in the trolley soaking wet and let them drip. After that you took them to a drier and hung them out for the air. It was a lot of work then.[58]

Washing at the steamie, as in the back court, could produce similar instances of co-operation and conflict. Typical of the positive memories of the friendliness and camaraderie, are oral testimonies such as Margaret Thomson's from Glasgow, 'The steamie was great, you had as much hot water as you needed. You got two hours to do the washing in that time. It was a great way to see your friends'. This sociability was not confined to Glasgow. Dodo Keenan recalled her days at Abbeyhill wash-house in Edinburgh after the Second World War, 'You got a good washing done there. It was a hot place! You were usually there two or three hours. You'd get a rare blether and hear all the local gossip. You knew everybody

---

56 Weir, *Shoes Were for Sunday*, 113.

57 Quoted in *Up Oor Close*, 108.

58 Quoted in *She Was Aye Working*, 121.

that went at that time. It was like going to a club really.'[59] Disagreements and disputes, however, could arise.

In Zola's novel of 1877, *L'Assommoir*, laundries play a central role, and his description of how the women worked and talked there would have been recognised in any Glasgow steamie. Early on there is an extended account of a very violent fight between Gervaise (the central character) and her love rival Virginie which takes place in the public wash-house.[60] In Glasgow it would appear quarrels were focused more prosaically on the actual operation of the laundry, with a particular source of tension being access to the 'wringer'. In 1915, Mr Williamson, the Superintendent of the Parkhead wash-house wrote to Mr Thomson, the General Manager of the Baths Department, about the regular flare-ups, 'I have been greatly vexed to witness women engaged – not only in verbal combat but using actual physical violence to each other, because of disagreements regarding a turn at the wringer.' He went on to make this observation, 'These women, on the whole, are self-respecting and well-doing women – who after being tempted into a violent quarrel by reason of some alleged injustice on the part of another washer, – keenly feel the humiliation of it all.'[61]

The fact that this was happening in the early days of the war may have lowered people's tolerance, though other accounts at other times do make references to friction among the steamie's customers.[62] Williamson thought the solution to the problem was to introduce precise instructions and regulations 'to clearly define the rights of each washer regarding her turn' and even drew up a draft of 'such a rule'. Whether this rule was ever implemented is not certain, but it appears Williamson might have had a predilection for rules and regulations. Some years earlier, in 1908, he sent another memo to Thomson about young girls using the steamie to do their families' washing and requested a legal age limit, suggesting 16, for those using the wash-house. Williamson argued that young girls were in danger in using the stalls and even more using the wringer and raised the issue of whether the Baths Department would be legally liable for any injury. He referred to 'mere children' of twelve or thirteen being sent to the wash-house and the indignation of mothers when their daughters were refused entry. The first response of the Department was to take no notice of Williamson's memo, but he refused to let it lie and requested an official response. Thomson then took the matter in hand, and his judgement is worth some attention. The practice

59 Both quotes from *She Was Aye Workin'*, 119–21.

60 Emile Zola, *L'Assommoir* (Oxford: Oxford University Press, 2009), 25–31.

61 GA D-BW3/1 Letter, Parkhead Baths, to W. Thomson, 30 January 1915.

62 See *The Sunday Post* (7 September 2018), 'Remembering the Scottish steamie: Glasgow exhibition revives wash house culture', www.sundaypost.com, accessed 26 October 2023.

in all public wash-houses was to admit any girl regardless of age so long as she had the means to pay. But more than simply a financial concern, his reasoning shows a sympathetic understanding of the lives of housewives and the mutual support within the steamie:

> Very seldom does a girl enter who seems to be too young, but when a very young girl is seen in a stall the washers, themselves, help her with the work, and our attendants in the office, and at the extractors, give her special attention, in order to guard against an accident. The washhouse boilers too seem to me to be less dangerous than a large pot placed on a kitchen fire, or boiler in a back court washhouse; and doubtless the mothers are the best judges as to how, and where, certain things are to be washed by their children.[63]

Privacy in a Public Space

Despite the popularity of wash-houses in Glasgow and other towns and cities such as Edinburgh, Liverpool and Manchester, it was the public baths that were most numerous. By 1915 more or less all towns in Britain with a population above 50,000 had a public bathing facility; while there were 69 wash-houses, there were fully 343 public baths.[64] Making direct comparisons is difficult as Agnes Campbell pointed out in 1918. For instance, in places where employers provided baths at the workplace or where local authorities had made 'substantial provision for school baths', as in the case of Glasgow and Liverpool, the public's use of the baths could appear less than it actually was.[65] And, as already indicated, of Glasgow's twenty public baths fully eighteen also operated as steamies. The 300,000 hot baths that were taken by Glasgow citizens in 1913 would increase significantly after the war.

The difficulty of washing clothes in very small houses was replicated for washing bodies. Just as the one and two roomed flats had no private water closets, neither did they have bathrooms; with often no internal water supply and certainly no running hot water, having an actual bath was hardly an option for many, as Bell and Paton recognised in 1896. Even if a zinc tub could be filled with water heated on the stove and used as a bath, there was the issue of privacy; children would be kept out of the kitchen while an adult or older sibling washed, but even

---

63 D/BW/3/1, Letter, 13 November 1908. from W. Williamson (Parkhead Baths) to Mr Thomson, General manager Baths Dept re age of girls attending wash-house, plus typed memo in response, 17 November 1908.

64 Sheard, 'Profit is a Dirty Word', 68; Agnes Campbell BA, *Report on Public Baths and Wash-houses in the United Kingdom* (Edinburgh, for the Carnegie United Kingdom Trust, 1918), 8.

65 Campbell, *Report*, 8.

that would have been impossible in a single end. Oral testimonies make it clear that most people did wash regularly even if a 'bath' might be a weekly event. The only members of the family likely to be bathed regularly would be babies and young children; they could easily be washed in the kitchen sink or the tub (needing less water) or even plunged into the wash-house boiler.[66]

When, however, the younger members of the family reached puberty, the issue of privacy became critical and, perhaps ironically, that was provided by the public baths. This was not a practice confined to Scotland but was common across urban Britain.[67] It was, perhaps more usual in Scottish towns and cities where tenements and very small houses predominated. Marion Smith, born in 1906, recalled the distinct stages of bathing in Glasgow:

> The small children were bathed in a huge zinc bath, the very tiny ones in the sink. We older ones went to Kay Street to the Public Baths, a weekly ritual, purchasing Radox bath cubes at the wee shop in Springburn Road, so you would come out smelling of rose or lavender.[68]

Friday was the favourite night for most people to go for a bath with many coming straight from their work, as recalled by Betty Knox, born 1922 in the same location,

> Right up to I was thirty-six years old, I had to go to the public baths to get a hot bath. It was next to the steamie. They had these hot baths for the men and the women beside the pool. There were two different doors. You were segregated, naturally, an' ye had to pay fourpence in they days for a hot bath. When ye were a bit older ye had tae graduate tae the hot baths. There wernae any privacy![69]

Molly Weir, also of Springburn. provides a more detailed account of the whole baths experience starting with early morning visits to the swimming pond in summer as girls, then slightly older when taken for afternoon swimming lessons by their school, and later again as young women going in the evening. It was then,

> that we penetrated the mystery of the other side of the bath building. We were getting too big now for the zinc bath at home, and were given fourpence on Fridays to have a hot bath. This was indeed a luxury.

---

66 Faley, *Up Oor Close*, 46–8.

67 Victoria Kelley, *Soap and Water: Cleanliness, Dirt and the Working Classes in Victorian and Edwardian Britain* (London: I. B. Tauris, 2020), 85.

68 quoted in Faley, *Up Oor Close*, 47.

69 quoted in Faley, *Up Oor Close*, 48.

She goes on to recount the less than appealing aspects of the baths, such as having no control over the water supply or its temperature, having to rely on the female attendant to provide both, and being aware of those eagerly queuing for the next slot. For all the inconveniences however, the fourpence was well spent:

> The soap was coarse and yellow, the floor was stone, and the towel was hard, but what a luxury it seemed to be able to wallow in a long 'wally' bath, and feel a gentle sleepiness steal over one as familiar voices rose and fell on every side, and chums called to each other through partitions. There were squeals of mock terror when the final cold spray was applied to keep one from catching cold on the way home, and beatific smiles on our pink steamy faces when we at last emerged, scrubbed, rinsed and dried, and more than ready for a pennyworth of chips to eat as we walked home.[70]

The Steamies Post-First World War

During the War the Carnegie Trust produced a *Report on Public Baths and Wash-Houses in the United Kingdom*, compiled and written by Agnes Campbell which provides a record of the provision of such establishments around 1915. Pointing out that Scotland came somewhat later to the baths movement than England, and that 'the rigorous climate makes a regular bathing habit more difficult to establish', nonetheless Campbell concluded that Scottish burghs compared favourably with English towns in terms of provision and use.[71] She did, however, indicate one significant difference, 'The provision of public wash-houses in proportion to the population is more extensive in Scotland.'[72] While not offering any substantial analysis why this was so – the prevalence of tenements and one and two roomed houses was not examined – Campbell did suggest it was 'due in part to different housing conditions' and that in Scotland 'respectable women often appear to prefer the Public Wash-house'.[73] Her report enumerated 39 wash-houses in nine Scottish towns which accounted for more than half the total of 69 across the whole of Britain. In proportion to population Glasgow and Edinburgh provided more 'washing stalls' than London and moreover they were 'better used'.[74] Boasting 20 wash-houses compared to Edinburgh's six and London's 36, it seems clear that Glasgow's association with the steamie was already firmly established.

---

70 Weir, *Shoes Were for Sunday*, 114–7.
71 Campbell, *Report*, 27.
72 Campbell, *Report*, 14.
73 Campbell, *Report*, 50.
74 Campbell, *Report*, 8, 50; Sheard, 'Profit is a Dirty Word', 68.

Post war, with the expansion of the electorate and the increase in labour representation, the steamies became more politicised. For instance, in April 1922 Agnes Dollan, recently returned for Springburn as one of the first labour women councillors, took up the issue of the lack of tubs in each stall of the wash-house. She visited the Kay Street steamie with the ward's other two councillors where she interviewed 'nearly all the women' who 'without exception ... all had the same complaint'. Writing to Thomson, still in charge of Baths and Wash-Houses, Dollan pointed out the same issue had been raised 'and remedied' elsewhere, and she expected the same for her constituents.[75]

The City Council did not rest on its laurels but built more establishments and provided more services. By 1934 the total number of municipal baths stood at 28 with all bar one (Ibrox) operating also as steamies. As indicated by the Lord Provost before the war, Glasgow intended building more facilities; Garngad and Partick Baths had opened in early 1914 with Kingston and Govanhill actually being built during the war. Thereafter, seven new baths and wash-houses were opened by the Council between 1925 and 1933 with, according to the Department's Annual Report for 1934, three more in the process of construction, including a wash-house to adjoin Ibrox baths, and a further three planned. Compared with 1913's total of 821,329 who attended the eighteen public wash-houses, in 1934 the twenty-seven operating steamies attracted almost half a million more; 1,309,669 separate 'washers' in total, 30,760 more than the previous year. While the single use of the wash tub remained the most popular with women, fourteen of the steamies now had 'washing-machines' as well and customers could choose either to use a washing machine on its own or in conjunction with a stall. Opening and closing times remained the same, from 7 a.m. to 6 p.m. Monday to Friday with early closing at 2 p.m. on Saturday. Charges, however, had increased from 2d. per hour pre-war to 3d. with washing machines costing considerably more at 9d. per load which, presumably, explains their limited use.[76]

The popularity of exercise and cleaning the body showed a similar increase; attendance at the swimming ponds in 1913 was 667,502 and in 1934 it stood at 1,850,263.[77] As with New York, it was swimming that proved the most popular attraction of the baths and their opening times were longer; 7 a.m. to 9 p.m. Monday to Friday in the summer months and 10 a.m. to 9 p.m. in winter. On Saturdays the pools were open from 7 a.m. to 6 p.m. all year round and even,

---

75 D/BW/3/1, Letter, handwritten on City Chamber notepaper, from Agnes Dollan, April 8th, 1922, To, Mr Thomson, Spt. Of Baths and Wash-houses.

76 Glasgow, Department of Baths and Wash-Houses, *Annual Report* (1934), 15–16, 19–20.

77 *Municipal Glasgow*, 98; Baths *Annual Report* (1934), 16.

in a partial challenge to Scottish sabbatarianism, opened on Sunday mornings; 7 to 10 a.m. in summer but only 8 to 10 a.m. in winter.[78] Among the categories of customer was the 'unemployed', of whom 121,855 used the swimming ponds in 1934. Until October 1932 they had enjoyed free admission but thereafter at a reduced rate of one penny (as opposed to the regular adult charge of 4d.) and this was available on 'Wednesdays only (during certain hours)'.[79] The same restricted access was applied to the 'Hot Private Baths' where the unemployed were charged one penny rather than the normal 4½ d. for a 'third class slipper bath', and 168,918 such baths were purchased over the year. Overall, use of the private baths more than doubled, from 301,126 in 1913 to 645,473, with the expansion of 'luxury' provisions such as Turkish baths now being offered in Govanhill, Whiteinch, Pollokshaws, and Shettleston, as well as Whitevale. Glasgow's determination that it should match the best of the best was evidenced in the introduction of Foam baths, Seawood baths, Zotofoam baths, a 'Stimulator', and Sun-Ray baths.

The gender difference remained but subtle changes were taking place; there was now 'mixed bathing' offered at four new establishments: Pollokshaws, Shettleston, Whiteinch and Govan Central. This was only permissible, however, from 2 to 8 p.m. on certain days at each, though on a Sunday at all four. Although nine 'baths' had male and female ponds, only Govanhill and Whiteinch offered constant access for women, the others offering perhaps four days as at Govan Ibrox or only two, as at Springburn. The latter at least was an improvement on the Tuesday only rule that Molly Weir experienced as a child. In winter, however, a couple of baths operated only one pond, and this led to women being restricted to a single day.

Of the total number of attendances at the swimming ponds 1,333,049 (72 per cent) were men and 517,314 (28 per cent) were women, while of the 645,473 who took a private bath, 403,838 (62.4 per cent) were men and 241,635 (37.5 per cent were women). When, however, we look closely at the classifications of the those using the services more interesting patterns emerge. Of the 'unemployed' using the swimming ponds only 7 per cent were female, while of the unemployed taking a bath, 17.5 per cent were women. Swimming was clearly a popular form of exercise and among adults it was predominantly a male pastime; 76 per cent against 24 per cent female. Amongst 'juveniles' the proportions were a little less extreme: 72 per cent to 28 per cent, while for schoolchildren the differential was significantly smaller: 58 per cent male and 42 per cent female. For those (37,226) who had achieved the Certificate of the Royal Life-Saving Society, and hence

---

78 Baths, *Annual Report* (1934), 19; Williams, 'New York City's Baths', 73.

79 Baths, *Annual Report* (1934), 18, 20; Baths, *Annual Report* (1933), 14.

secured free admission, the sex differential was huge; 88 per cent male against 12 per cent female. Yet, for those attending as members of swimming clubs (215,847) the differential was much less: 61 per cent male against 39 per cent female.

Glasgow's twenty-five public baths offered 606 baths for men and only 210 for women whose 'share' had increased marginally; 26 per cent as against 21.5 per cent in 1913. The 'unemployed' bathers were overwhelmingly male; 168,918 or 82.5 per cent of the total, though this differential may simply indicate that many more men were officially recognised as unemployed. The share of baths taken by regular customers was 55.5 per cent male and 44.5 per cent female. With 1,137 bathers per female 'bath room' compared with 664 bathers per male bath room, it would appear women were making greater use of the smaller number of rooms available to them. While in every single location there were more baths provided for men the use of baths varied quite widely. For instance, at North Woodside, Cranstonhill and Whitevale men represented fully 63 per cent of patrons, while in Parkhead and Govan Central there was little difference, only 256 and 86 more men than women using the baths. More intriguing were the locations where female users outnumbered males; Hutchesontown, Springbank, Cowcaddens, Pollokshaws, Shettleston, Plantation and Oatlands. I have no clear explanation for this as there were quite sharp differences between the locations; Cowcaddens being one of the worst slum areas of the city and Pollokshaws one of the most respectable. One possible indication might be that apart from Hutchesontown and Springbank the other five were the newest public baths, having been opened between 1927 and 1933. It might be that they were designed to be more attractive to women, and they did have a (slightly) higher proportion of female baths, 29.5 per cent, than the city average. Whatever the reasons, clearly large numbers of women were using the facilities for health and cleanliness.[80]

Conclusion: 'In a Few Years the Old 'Steamie' Image Will Be Forgotten'

Glasgow and New York were both 'tenement cities' facing similar issues over housing and health problems. Both were very familiar with each other's municipal provision, yet their responses to how to keep clean differed. Neither city's history can be contained within the boundaries of a 'national' history, and it is their distinctiveness which interests us here. This reflects the concern that this volume has with translocality and its emphasis on place and the movement of

[80] All data extracted from the 1934 *Annual Report*; analysis of male and female use of the baths above is limited to regular users only and does not include the unemployed.

ideas as much as of people.[81] Similarities in experience, however, do not necessarily translate into common solutions. While in some respects New York could be seen as primed to copy Glasgow, it never constructed wash-houses (apart from one quickly aborted effort), its building programme of public baths ended with the First World War, and after 1945 these were either demolished or turned into other uses.[82] Had New York built wash-houses in the 1890s it may be that they would have become more popular as they became more familiar to the population, as in Glasgow. And it may be that attaching wash-houses to the public baths was simply too expensive. But the main explanation for the different paths taken surely was the housing in both. New York tenement apartments may have been small, but they were rarely as small as in Glasgow. Having more space to begin with it was easier to introduce taps and water closets to existing properties as well new-builds, making it possible to wash bodies and clothes in the home. For most of Glasgow's huge number of small houses, this was simply not possible; the origin and sustained popularity of its wash-houses were based on their necessity.

While The Steamie has imprinted the municipal wash-house in the public's consciousness, it has also stamped it with the image of a certain period; post-war Glasgow just before the construction of the huge new housing schemes. The planned council houses would provide thousands of families with their own front door, indoor toilets, separate kitchens with space for a washing machine, and surprisingly large gardens where clothes could be hung out to dry. In the play the youngest of the four main characters Doreen has her eyes on 'A House in Drumchapel' and the 'luxury' items that would be part of a new lifestyle. She gets ribbed by her older friends for such ambitions though much of the humour for the audience lay, even in 1987, with their knowledge of the reputation that Drumchapel then had. The play shows both that the promised land of post-war reconstruction was not so promising after all and that something of value of the old inner-city slum communities had been lost. However, in so doing the steamie is preserved in aspic – the steamie of a Hogmanay at some point in the early 1950s would have been much the same as in the 1930s or even the 1890s.

Deliberately or inadvertently, presented in this way it is hard not to regard the public wash-houses as totems of the past and their disappearance as inevitable as the single end. Municipal services, however, in the shape of Glasgow Corporation Baths and Wash-Houses Department was more ambitious than that. As detailed above the Department extended the number of baths and wash-houses after 1918

[81] Clemens Greiner and Patrick Sakdapolrak, 'Translocality: Concepts, Applications and Emerging Research Perspectives, *Geography Compass* 7/5 (2013), 373–384.

[82] Williams, 'New York City's Baths', 75.

both in terms of actual numbers and the services offered. Post 1945 the steamies did not go into some sort of slow and irreversible decline. While there was no repeat of the ambitious building programme of the pre-1914 and interwar years, two new steamies were constructed, Kingston in 1957, and Calton as late as 1960.[83] There was limited need for new steamies given, 'the continuous movement of the population from the centre of the City to outlying districts'. Recognising this in its *Report* for 1961 the Department was particularly pleased that revenue was more or less the same as for the previous year; at £229,034 it was only down by £772.[84]

The focus of the Department's work was not just maintenance but improvements in both the machines used by its customers and the engines that powered the laundries. For instance, in 1958 it was delighted to report on 'the installation of the new washing machines, hydro-extractors and drying chambers at Maryhill and Springbank', especially as this was completed while keeping the wash-house open. The change for the women at the steamie was that where previously in their cubicle they had a wash tub, a rinsing tub, a boiler and a drying horse, now they had access to a washing machine and a single tub for 'the odd woollen or coloured article' with 'access to the hydro-extractors immediately her machine is finished'. After this a drying horse was also available with the option of booking more. Since in winter the 'vapour' from the boilers and tubs 'accumulated in the wash house', the health benefits of the new system were apparent. In words that echoed those of Frank Cohen of 45 years ago, but with perhaps more justification, 'Wash day has now become a pleasure and no longer does the washer have the laborious task of hand washing.'[85] Such conversions from wash stalls to washing machines continued as at Partick and Pollokshaws in 1961. With Partick no longer needing its (earlier improved) electric hydro pump, which was now transferred to Whitevale to replace its 'obsolete steam driven pump', resulting in cheaper fuel costs and the elimination of the 'black smoke' belched out by the old machinery.[86]

Other improvements were also made, such as at Parkhead with the installation of additional baths for women which were 'a great boon to the … district'. The total number of slipper baths did fall over time, but not dramatically. Across all the corporation's facilities the total of 816 in 1934 had reduced to 762 by 1972. The gender divide continued to narrow; in 1972 female baths accounted for 37 per cent of the total. While no establishment provided more women-only baths,

---

83 Baths, *Annual Report* (1972), 7, plus Osborne Street was reconstructed in 1954.
84 Baths, *Annual Report* (1961), 3.
85 Baths, *Annual Report* (1958), 3.
86 Baths, *Annual Report* (1961), 3.

a number now had equal numbers for each sex: in Parkhead where there had been twenty-three male and only six female baths, there were now fourteen of both. The terminology had changed with 'gents' and 'ladies' replacing 'male' and 'female'. While I am hesitant to argue this represented a more progressive attitude it is interesting that there was now less gender classification of the use of both the baths and the swimming ponds.

While it seems safe to assume that those who used the wash-houses remained female (I have yet to come across any reference to a man using the steamie), the categorisation of bathers and swimmers was becoming more neutral. Not completely, as although the number of 'private baths' available were still enumerated by sex, the numbers of those using the baths were now identified only as 'adults', 'juveniles' or 'old age pensioners'. Some other gender categorisation remained: no longer three classes of bath for men, there was now just the single 'bath' for 'gents' and 'ladies', but since the charge for both was the same (10p.) there was no practical distinction. Turkish and Sun-Ray baths were still available in the five establishments listed above (plus Ibrox offering Sun-Ray only) and in each different days were restricted to men or women. While each provided for both sexes it would appear there were more opportunities for men; all five provided Turkish baths for men on a Saturday, but there was no provision at any for women and only one (Govanhill) did so on a Sunday. As for swimming there were two (Gorbals and Whitevale) where the larger ponds remained exclusive to gents, and there were five (Gorbals, Whitevale, Govanhhill, Townhead and North Woodside) where the smaller ponds were for ladies only. In all the other fourteen, however, mixed bathing was now the norm.[87]

The popularity of the baths remained even though attendances were down in 1972 due to the miners' strike. The Department kept the steamies open and most of the swimming pools but closed the 'premises during the hours of darkness in case of a failure in the electricity supply'.[88] Nonetheless there were still 1,795,176 attendances at the swimming ponds, over one million of whom were 'juveniles' or 'school classes' while only 492 were pensioners. There were 440,577 users of the 'slipper baths', 17,953 of whom were juveniles while pensioners, who had free access to both ponds and baths, accounted for 82,948. The Turkish baths were enjoyed by 54,561 persons and the Sun-Ray baths by 29,984, giving a grand total of 2,320,298. Attendances at the wash-houses were given by 'hours' spent at 'washing machines' and 'total washing hours', which were effectively the same thing, the former totalling 442,377 and the latter 469,216. The shortfall in washing

87 Baths, *Annual Report* (1972), 17–19.
88 Baths, *Annual Report* (1972), 3.

machine hours was due to the two steamies which still operated washing stalls, Rutherglen Rd and Townhead, whose combined total of 26,839 hours at the stalls accounted for the difference. None of the other steamies now had stalls, all provided washing machines only.

The high point of the steamie was 1957 when attendances reached 2,341,548, a ratio of 2,158 users per 1,000 of the population. Thereafter the numbers fell consistently and by 1965 there were fewer than one million, a figure last recorded in 1915. In 1966 there was a revision of how attendance was calculated which exaggerated the subsequent decline but still by 1972 there were fewer than half a million users, representing 525 per 1,000 of population, a ratio surpassed as early as 1903.[89] Yet the Department still had ambitious plans. A step into the future had been taken with the opening between 1968 and 1971 of the new 'swimming pools' (note the terminology) in the massive council estates of Drumchapel, Easterhouse and Castlemilk. These pools, at 110' by 42', far surpassed all existing ponds, and they were purely for recreation, containing no slipper baths, Turkish baths, and certainly no wash-houses. Open for men and women equally with no separate times or restrictions, they also contained that symbol of modernity, cafés.[90] The wash-houses were not neglected; the programme of replacing old plant and machinery was complete and the parallel programme of modernisation was continuing. All this led the Baths convener, Constance Methven, to confidently declare, 'In a few years the old "steamie" image will be forgotten.'[91]

Such optimism was badly misplaced; ten years later there were no steamies left in Glasgow. The last one, Partick, closed in 1982, the same year Edinburgh closed its remaining wash-houses.[92] Faced with declining attendances, rising fuel prices, the expansion of white goods, and the end of the old City Corporations through local government reorganisation in 1974 their end can seem predetermined. It needs to be noted, however, that every closure took place in the teeth of local opposition.[93] That story, however, is for another time. This collection of essays is being written during a cost-of-living crisis that shows little signs of abating. Rising prices and sustained inflation have resulted in a historic fall in real incomes,

---

89 Baths, *Annual Report* (1972), 13; Baths, *Annual Report* (1934), 17.

90 Baths, *Annual Report* (1972), 7–8, 11; the cafés contributed £35,000 to the Department's revenue.

91 Baths, *Annual Report* (1972), 3.

92 'All change at the steamie', Glasgow Times, (26 May 2008) www://glasgowtimes.co.uk/news/12801823.all-change-at-the-steamie/, accessed 26 October 2023. Stephen Robb, 'The Public Washhouses of Edinburgh', *Book of the Old Edinburgh Club*, New Series Vol. 10 (2014), 146.

93 Clark and Carnegie, *She Was Aye Workin'*, 122.

with millions going hungry while struggling to heat their homes.[94] In Scotland during the winter of 2022/23 over 200 'warm banks' were established alongside a similar number of 'food banks', with local authorities utilising libraries and community centres alongside churches.[95] No one is recommending a return to public wash-houses, but the collective provision of basic necessities such as food and warmth (and one needs heat to keep clean) no longer seems so distanced from our current situation. Memories of the good old bad old days can encourage a warm glow of nostalgia while being thankful that things are now so much better. Yet surely Glasgow and the other municipalities that built and operated public baths and wash-houses deserve credit for their determination to provide such a valuable public service for so long.

Constance Methven was wrong also about the image of the steamie being forgotten because it is that 'old' image that remains, largely due it has to be said to Tony Roper's play. The modern, cleaner, less exhausting steamie of the later 1950s and 1960s, more akin to a launderette, has not impinged on the public memory. The Steamie has embedded the municipal wash-house into modern Scottish folklore, a depiction of women washing in a steamie is part of the Great Tapestry of Scotland.[96] There have been numerous revivals of the play, two in 2022 alone, including a drag version. But however it might be re-imagined it cannot be relocated geographically; the play and the actual steamies remain forever associated with Glasgow.

---

94 www.resolutionfoundation.org, 'UK households just halfway through two-year cost-of-living crisis with incomes set to fall by £2,100', 9 January 1923, accessed 26 October 2023; *The Guardian*, 'Cost of living leaves 1m UK children destitute', 24 October 2023.

95 https://news.stv.tv/, How to find a 'warm bank' in your local area as fuel poverty increases', 28 October 2022, accessed 26 October 2023.

96 Inspired by Alexander McCall Smith, with the episodes from Scotland's history chosen by Alistair Moffat, and stitched by 1,000 volunteers, the Great Tapestry of Scotland was first unveiled in 2013 at the Scottish Parliament. It is now permanently housed in Galashiels, www.greattapestryofscotland.com, accessed 26 October 2023.

Health and Wealth in Glasgow and New York, 1900–1939

Graham MacSporran

A recent study has shown that life expectancy in Glasgow is falling for the first time since the mid-1870s and that this reduction is most marked in the most deprived sections of the community. This has been attributed to government austerity measures which have reduced their standard of living.[1] Mortality rates in New York have been in decline since the 1850s but this improvement has stalled since 2010 with only modest improvements in life expectancy between 2010 and 2018, with non-Hispanic Blacks having the lowest life expectancy among ethnic groups.[2] These changes have led to renewed debate on the relationship between living standards and health. This chapter explores the relationship between health and wealth in Glasgow and New York between 1900 and 1939 by identifying the extent to which health varied with changes in living standards or whether other factors such as public health initiatives, medical advances, welfare assistance or differing cultural norms between communities had a more significant influence.[3] Ill health in both cities was concentrated in the poorer districts so this is primarily a study of those who lived near, or below, the poverty line and were most vulnerable to changes in economic conditions. This period has been chosen since both cities experienced benign and quite challenging economic conditions over these years. Did health improve during the years of plenty and deteriorate during the years of want?

Glasgow and New York had common histories. Both were immigrant cities and had absorbed adjacent neighbourhoods to create larger metropolitan entities. Wealth was the preserve of the few and there was widespread urban

1 Glasgow Centre for Population Health (hereinafter 'GCPH') (2021) *A Study of Changes in Health, Demographics, Socioeconomic and Environmental Factors in Glasgow over the last 20 Years*. Glasgow: GCPH, accessed from http://www.gcph.co.uk, on 13 September 2023, 80–81, 109–111. See figure 28, 81, for graph of life expectancy since 1870.

2 New York City Department of Health and Mental Hygiene (2020) *Summary of Vital Statistics 2018, The City of New York*. New York: Bureau of Vital Statistics, accessed from http://nyc.gov on 4 September 2023. For mortality rates see 'The Conquest of Pestilence in New York City' in the frontispiece; for life expectancy see 9.

3 Health will be primarily measured by mortality rates since morbidity was not well-documented in this period.

poverty, overcrowded slum housing and high mortality rates in the poorer districts. Glasgow had expanded rapidly during the second half of the nineteenth-century and enjoyed its final period of pre-eminence as the 'Second City of the Empire' between 1900 and 1914 with an economy based on staple shipbuilding and heavy engineering industries with international market positions. During this period, New York enjoyed a period of expansion in population and economic activity, particularly in the garment industries. The second period from 1914 to 1919 was one of profound change in Glasgow as the industrial base was re-directed towards the manufacture of war materials which created opportunities for some and hardship for others. New York did not enter the war until 1917, but the war had consequences before this not the least of which was relations between immigrant groups on both sides of the conflict. The third period from 1920 to 1938 included periods of economic depression and high levels of unemployment. Glasgow's staple industries collapsed shortly after the war with high levels of unemployment throughout most of the interwar years. New York enjoyed a buoyant economy in the 1920s but also lapsed into depression after the 'Great Crash' of 1929 which continued throughout the 1930s.

Although Glasgow and New York shared common histories there were differences in timing and circumstances particular to each city: for example, immigration profoundly affected New York in this period, less so, in Glasgow. Also, the onset of industrial decline and high levels of unemployment preceded New York by some 10 years. Both cities, however, experienced significant changes in living standards between 1900 and 1939 such that a comparison of the effect of these changes on public health between two cities with different economies and ethnic communities would inform the debate on the extent to which changing living standards impacted public health. This will entail determining whether the effect of rising living standards had beneficial consequences for public health and whether any improvements were reversed during periods of economic hardship leading to poorer health outcomes.

It is proposed to concentrate on three areas of research. Between 1900 and 1914, child mortality in New York will be studied since it was regarded as the time as the major public health issue of these years and child health is regarded as being indicative of the overall health of the population. The urban poor in Glasgow will be the focus for the second period, from 1914 to 1919, with reference to the dramatic changes in their circumstances due to the war conditions. The final period from 1920 onwards will consider how the economic depression in both cities affected public health and whether the measures introduced to alleviate distress were effective.

City of Dreams? New York 1900–1914[4]

New York consisted of two boroughs in 1897, Manhattan and The Bronx, with a combined population of two million. In the following year, the nearby boroughs of Brooklyn, Queens and Richmond were absorbed into New York increasing the population to 3.4 million.[5] Manhattan was the most densely populated borough and the destination for most immigrants.[6] The less fortunate found themselves in a penitentiary, mental asylum or hospital for the poor on one of the small islands within the metropolitan boundary.[7] New York had an influx of some 700,000 immigrants between 1900 and 1914, mainly Eastern European Jews escaping persecution, and Italians escaping poverty. They had been preceded by 1 million immigrants in the latter half of the nineteenth century from Germany, Eastern Europe, Italy, and Ireland. By 1910, immigrants accounted for 40 per cent of the population and their experience of the 'City of Dreams' is central to this study since they were the poorest in New York, living in overcrowded districts, with the lowest life expectancies.[8]

The Board of Health Report for 1900 highlights the high incidence of child mortality with 25,836 children under five years of age dying in the year, 36 per cent of all deaths.[9] In its review of the period, *Protecting Public Health in New York City*, the Department of Health noted that the two key public health issues for the period from 1900 to 1913 were child mortality and tuberculosis with much of the work of the Department in this period being focused on reducing child mortality.[10] Child health is a key social indicator. Richard Arthur Bolt, General

---

4 For clarity and to avoid repetition, all references to New York will relate to New York City, not New York State unless stated otherwise.

5 Department of Health of the City of New York (hereinafter 'DHCNY'), *Annual Report of the Board of Health for the Year ending December 31, 1900*, accessed from http://hathitrust.org on 5 September 2023, 7. For an account of the amalgamation, or 'Consolidation' as known at the time, see Mike Wallace, *Greater Gotham; A History of New York City from 1989 to 1919* (New York: Oxford University Press, 2017), 49–60.

6 DHCNY, *Annual Report of the Board of Health, 1901*, 104–108.

7 For example, Randall's Island had a hospital for sick and destitute immigrants and a mental asylum. Roosevelt Island had a penitentiary and the Metropolitan Hospital, which was its principal use after 1921. Rikers Island was used for landfill then a penitentiary to take the overflow from Welfare Island. See Wallace, *Greater Gotham*, 215, 587. Also, 'The History of Rikers Island' accessed from http:/www.classicnewyorkhistory.com on 17 December 2023.

8 DHCNY, *Annual Report of the Board of Health, 1914*, 126; Tyler Anbinder, *City of Dreams* (New York: Mariner Books, 2017), 572–575.

9 DHCNY, *Annual Report of the Board of Health, 1900*, 12.

10 New York City Department of Health and Mental Hygiene (hereinafter 'NYDHMH'), (2005) *Protecting Public Health in New York City: 200 Years of Leadership, 1805–2005*. New York: Bureau of Communications, NYDHMH, http://www.nyc.gov, accessed on 18 April 2023,

Director of the American Child Hygiene Association, commented in 1921 that infant mortality should be regarded as the 'most sensitive index that we have of social and sanitary progress'.[11]

Children in New York faced many challenges. Compromised maternal health, due to malnourishment or arduous work during pregnancy, often led to a premature birth which was particularly hazardous with some 40 per cent of infants who died in their first year doing so in the first few weeks after birth.[12] Home would have been a maelstrom of humanity in a small badly ventilated space where cleanliness was almost impossible. Many homes, particularly in the Jewish districts, would also have been a workshop filled with clothing offcuts, dust and fibres. Infants needed to survive the cold winters, without succumbing to pneumonia, and the hot summers, without contracting dysentery or typhoid fever which claimed the lives of 1,500 infants each week during hot weather.[13] Having navigated the perils of infancy, measles, diphtheria, whooping cough and scarlet fever lay in wait for young children with high infection rates in crowded neighbourhoods. In 1900, these infectious diseases claimed the lives of 4,000 children.[14] There was little sympathy for these children. In the early 1900s, 'respectable' society, held the view that poverty, and associated poor health, was the inevitable consequence of laziness, dishonesty, dirtiness, and spendthrift ways.[15] Dr S. Josephine Baker thought otherwise and worked in the poorest communities to improve public maternal and child health care as did Lillian D. Wald who campaigned for the introduction of community nursing care.[16]

Politics determined whether there would be an improvement in the provision of public health services. The Tammany administrations had a reputation for corruption rather than the reform of public health services.[17] Baker was appointed as a medical inspector in schools in 1901 and found that the perfunctory inspections were a 'pathetic farce' which simply excluded infectious children from school with no attempt at treatment. Her colleagues were 'negligent political

---

20–23. The New York Department of Health changed its name to the Department of Health and Mental Hygiene after the consolidation with the Department of Mental Health in 2002.

11 Richard A. Bolt, 'Fundamental Factors in Infant Mortality', *Child Welfare* (1921), 98, 9.

12 Bolt, 'Fundamental Factors in Infant Mortality', 10, 12.

13 Sara Josephine Baker *Fighting for Life* (New York: New York Review of Books, 2013; Original text, 1939), 58; Wallace, *Greater Gotham*, 544.

14 DHCNY, *Annual Report of the Board of Health, 1900, 56–57.*

15 John Duffy, *A History of Public Health in New York City, 1866–1966* (New York: Russell Sage, 1974), 220.

16 See Baker *Fighting for Life* (1939) and Lillian D. Wald (1938) *The House on Henry Street* (New York: Henry Holt, 1938).

17 Wallace, *Greater Gotham*, 107–109; Baker, *Fighting for Life*, 55.

hangers-on firmly attached to the public payroll'.[18] Tammany were replaced in 1902 with Mayor Seth Low who started a process of reform. Lillian Wald, who promoted community nursing care from the Henry Street Settlement charity in the Jewish quarter of Lower East Manhattan, became involved in an initiative which led to nurses being appointed in schools throughout New York.[19] At this time, Baker was given a broader remit to improve child health in Hell's Kitchen, an Irish immigrant neighbourhood, where she 'climbed stair after stair, knocked on door after door, met drunk after drunk, filthy mother after filthy mother and dying baby after dying baby'.[20] Tammany came back into power in 1903 with Thomas Darlington, the new Commissioner for Health, being given full support to improve public health provision.[21] Baker's successful trial in 1908 in reducing chid mortality through encouraging breast feeding and improving home cleanliness led to her being appointed the first Director of the Division of Child Hygiene later that year.[22] Much of Baker's work was in the poorer and overcrowded immigrant communities in Manhattan. In 1910, 80 per cent of all births in New York were to immigrants with Italian and Eastern European parents accounting for one in every two births in the city.[23] Baker's pioneering work is credited with saving the lives of 90,000 children in her period in office up to 1923.[24] Politics had eventually allowed humanitarian principle to prevail.

There was a significant improvement in adult and child health in New York between 1900 and 1914 with a 35 per cent reduction in the overall mortality rate.[25] Most diseases showed a similar reduction which suggests a general improvement in public health rather than a significant advance in the treatment of any one disease. Within the overall 35 per cent reduction of mortality for all ages in New York was a more striking figure: child mortality for under five years old had reduced by 48 per cent in Manhattan. This dramatic improvement compares to a more modest improvement of 17 per cent for the remainder of the population in Manhattan over five years old.[26] The population of Manhattan had increased by 480,000 persons between 1900 and 1914 yet there were 3,500 fewer deaths

18 Baker, *Fighting for Life*, 56.
19 Baker, *Fighting for Life*, 80–81; Wald, *The House on Henry Street* (1938), 49–53.
20 Baker, *Fighting for Life*, 58.
21 Duffy, *History of Public Health*, 257.
22 Baker, *Fighting for Life*, 85–87.
23 DHCNY, *Annual Report of the Board of Health 1910*, 189.
24 Baker, *Fighting for Life*, editorial comment on the end page.
25 DHCNY, *Annual Report of the Board of Health, 1900*, 8; DHCNY, *Annual Report of the Board of Health, 1914*, 116.
26 DHCNY, *Annual Report of the Board of Health, 1900*, 61; DHCNY, *Annual Report of the Board of Health, 1914*, 150–151.

of children under five years old. The improvement in child health was not the preserve of the affluent wards; most wards with a poor health record reduced at a similar, or higher, rate to the Manhattan average. For example, the child mortality rates in Wards 4 and 14, mainly Irish, reduced by 48 and 45 per cent respectively and Ward 11, mainly Jewish, by 58 per cent.[27] The Department of Health attributed this city-wide improvement in child mortality to the pioneering work of Dr Baker.[28] Bolt, General Director of the American Child Hygiene Association, commented in 1921 that the reduction in infant mortality was 'one of the outstanding phenomena of the new public health movement'.[29] However, child mortality had already been reducing before the inception of the Division of Child Hygiene so this was not the sole reason for the improvement. There may have been other influences on child health, such as ethnicity.

Contemporary health professionals considered ethnicity as a factor in determining child health as well as large families and crowded living conditions. Bolt despaired of the 'native American stocks which are rapidly dying out and being replaced by races or mixtures of races which do not refuse to bear children' citing Russian and Polish Jews.[30] There was not a simple correlation between high population density and poor health. For example, in 1901, Ward 11, a Jewish district, had an overall death rate which was a third of the rate in Ward 4, an Irish community, despite being twice as densely populated as Ward 4.[31] Baker, who was from an affluent Quaker family, regarded ethnicity as a significant determinant of child health.[32] The homes of German immigrants were regarded by Baker as being the cleanest, Italians as moderately clean, having made some effort to create a brighter home, and that the houses of the 'colored' population were also clean in a sad poverty-stricken fashion, as were their children. However, Baker was much less complementary about other communities stating that 'the Irish and the Russian Jews vied for the distinction of living in the most lurid squalor'.[33] The Irish did so, according to Baker, out of a mixture of discouragement and apparent shiftlessness. The four wards with the highest mortality rates in 1901

27 DHNYC, *Annual Report of the Board of Health, 1901*, pp. 104–105; DHNYC, *Annual Report of the Board of Health, 1914*, 150–151.

28 NYDHMH (2005) *Protecting Public Health in New York City*, 23–24.

29 Bolt, 'Fundamental Factors in Infant Mortality', 9.

30 Bolt, 'Fundamental Factors in Infant Mortality', 13–14.

31 DHCNY, *Annual Report of the Board of Health, 1901,* 104–105.

32 See Baker (1939) *Fighting for Life*, 2–13, for an account of her early life and Chloe Zelenitz, 'Sara Josephine Baker', accessed from http://www.iFeminist.org on 2 December 2023, for her Quaker background.

33 Baker, *Fighting for Life*, 70–72.

for children under five years old had significant Irish populations; however, these four wards accounted for only seven percent of the Irish population in Manhattan. The other wards with significant Irish populations had mortality rates close to the Manhattan average.[34] Baker portrayed the Russian Jews as thrifty, to the point of meanness, with every penny being put towards the advancement of one son who would, in time, support the whole family, and to this end they 'worked like mad under sweat-shop conditions and skimped incredibly on food, clothes and rent, not to mention soap and sunlight'.[35] Baker's views may seem racist or anti-Semitic but it should be recognised that she devoted her life to improving the health of children in these poorer Irish and Jewish communities. Health professionals regarded ethnicity as having a significant influence on health. In doing so, they reflected popular opinion which reserved the harshest judgements for the most 'alien' of the ethnic groups. The health statistics provide a more objective perspective on the influence of ethnicity on health with particular regard to the Jewish and Irish communities.

The predominately Jewish wards, in fact, had a lower mortality rate in 1901 for children under five years of age than the Manhattan average with Ward 11, the largest of the Jewish wards, having the lowest mortality rate for under-fives in 1914.[36] Deborah Dwork notes that Jewish communities in Europe also had a better health record than non-Jewish communities and suggests that the lower child mortality rates in New York was due to the Jewish social customs of personal hygiene, home cleanliness and wholesome meals eaten at least once a week.[37] Mortality rates, for all ages, tend to support the impact of ethnic differences with the rates in 1900 for German immigrants, and their descendants, being marginally lower than the overall New York average, Russian and Polish Jews being 40 per cent lower, and Irish 37 per cent higher.[38] While politics, ethnicity and population density had an influence on child health, this does not account for the steady improvement in child health between 1900 and 1914 which was most marked in the poorest and most overcrowded districts. Rising living standards in this period may have been the most important factor in the improvement in

---

34 DHCNY, *Annual Report of the Board of Health, 1901,* 104–5; Table A.6, 558, Appendix 1. Statistical tables.

35 Baker, *Fighting for Life*, 70–71.

36 DHCNY, *Annual Report of the Board of Health, 1901,* 104–5.

37 Deborah Dwork, 'Health Conditions of Immigrant Jews on the Lower East Side of New York, 1880–1914', *Medical History*, 25, (1981), 28–29.

38 Ira Rosenwaike, *Population History of New York City* (Syracuse: Syracuse University Press, 1972), 80, Table 32.

health and this will be considered in more detail with regard to the Irish and Jewish communities.

Irish emigration to New York had started before the failure of the potato crops between 1845 and 1849.[39] The resulting famine led to a large influx of immigrants which was repeated in the 1890s due to further crop failures. By 1900, the Irish community was the second largest ethnicity after German immigrants with most Irish having moved into the southern tip of Manhattan.[40] Irish immigrants, in this period, were ill-equipped for an urban environment with few having skilled trades or commercial skills.[41] Men found casual and poorly paid work as day labourers on the docks, railways and building sites which was menial, poorly paid, often hazardous and with no security of earnings. Work was seasonal and not always easy to secure.[42] Twice as many Irish women worked compared to other immigrant groups – mainly as domestic servants which entailed long hours, hard work and little free time for $4 to $8 a month plus room and board.[43] By 1900, half of Irish-born men were still working as unskilled labourers and three-quarters of women were servants.[44] There was widespread discrimination against the Catholic Irish. Jobs would be advertised for someone of 'any country or color ... except the Irish' or employers would ask for applications from 'Protestants' or 'Americans'.[45] Irish immigrants, and their children, found it more difficult to obtain a white-collar position than the children of native-born Americans.[46]

However, the arrival of some 200,000 Italian and 300,000 Russian immigrants between 1900 and 1910 was a turning point.[47] Native-born Americans

---

39 The ships carrying early immigrants to America returned in late 1844 with a cargoes of seed potatoes which carried a fungus originating from Peruvian guano which had been used as a fertiliser on American farms. The fungus did not thrive in hot, dry summers in America but did so in the cool and damp conditions in Ireland with devastating effect. Some 1.1 million died in Ireland in the ensuing famine. See Tyler Anbinder, *City of Dreams, The 400-Year Epic History of Immigrant New York* (New York: Mariner, 2017), 127.

40 Anbinder, *The City of Dreams*, Appendix, 572–573; Irish immigrants settled in the 1st Ward on the southern tip of Manhattan, 4th Ward on the East River waterfront and the adjacent 6th Ward in the centre of Southern Manhattan which was known as Five Points.

41 Lawrence J. McCaffrey, 'Forging Forward and Looking Back', in Ronald H. Bayor and Timothy J. Meagher eds, *The New York Irish* (Baltimore: John Hopkins University Press, 1996), 214.

42 Anbinder, *The City of Dreams*, 158–159.

43 Anbinder, *The City of Dreams*, 165–166.

44 Anbinder, *The City of Dreams*, 158, 165, 293.

45 Anbinder, *The City of Dreams*, 165–166.

46 Anbinder, *The City of Dreams*, 293–295.

47 Anbinder, *The City of Dreams*, Appendix, 572–573.

now found Irish workers less 'alien' than the Italians and the Jewish Russians.[48] Daughters of Irish mothers who had been servants became teachers and nurses. Sons of Irish day labourers became skilled workers and staffed the police and fire departments, post office and local government offices and there was an increase in Irish-owned small businesses. As incomes improved, Irish families started to move to the more affluent Upper East and West Sides of Manhattan, The Bronx and Brooklyn and their children were sent to Jesuit and Franciscan Colleges.[49] More recent Irish immigrants lagged behind their predecessors and remained in the working-class enclaves, such as Hell's Kitchen, which was one of New York's poorest and roughest neighbourhoods. The Irish had become one of the most economically and occupationally diverse ethnic groups in New York in the early twentieth century.[50]

The Jewish community was highly dependent on the garment industry. Some 1.35 million Jewish immigrants arrived in the United States between 1881 and 1914 with most finding work in the 'needle' industries in the Lower East Side of Manhattan which was the most densely populated district in New York.[51] For example, in Ward 10, a six-storey block of tenements accommodated 2,781 persons with 28 per cent of the rooms having no daylight and 40 per cent only ventilated by narrow air shafts.[52] Home was also their workplace. Two teams of workers could be working in a twelve-foot by twelve-foot tenement room with fabric strips, coarsely torn strips of cloth, and bits of thread piled high on the floor.[53] The hours were long with low earnings; a male could earn just under $4 per week, a female $1 per week.[54] Work was seasonal since most clothing was bought in spring and autumn.[55]

The garment trade, which was New York's largest industry, expanded rapidly in the 1900s as it changed from home and tailor-made to ready-to-wear clothing.[56] Demand in America for ready-to-wear tripled every year and the industry in New York doubled its labour force and, by 1919, provided three-quarters of the national output of clothing.[57] Outwork in homes was taken over by Italian

48 Anbinder, *The City of Dreams*, 295.

49 McCaffrey, 'Forging Forward and Looking Back', 229–231; Wallace, *Greater Gotham*, 269.

50 John R. McKivigan and Thomas J. Robertson, 'The Irish American Worker in Transition, 1877–1914', in Bayor and Meagher, eds, *The New York* Irish, 312.

51 Dwork, 'Health Conditions of Immigrant Jews', 1–6.

52 Dwork, 'Health Conditions of Immigrant Jews', 8.

53 Anbinder, *The City of Dreams*, 371.

54 Dwork, 'Health Conditions of Immigrant Jews', 18.

55 Anbinder, *The City of Dreams*, 372.

56 Wallace, *Greater Gotham*, 307.

57 Wallace, *Greater Gotham*, 317.

immigrants with Jewish labour moving into more productive purpose-built workshops. This freed the home environment from soot, tiny shreds of fabric, and millions of specks of dust which had been the cause of respiratory problems, such as bronchitis and asthma.[58] Signs of growing affluence emerged. Every year, growing numbers of Jewish textile workers became small shopkeepers, insurance agents and clerks.[59] Jewish families in Lower East Manhattan started to migrate north to better districts, such as East Harlem and later to Brownsville in Brooklyn. Between 1905 and 1915, over 60 per cent of the East Side's Jews had left to better districts.[60] In these new districts, immigrant Jews began to replace Anglo, Irish and German contractors in the booming property markets having better access to capital and cheaper non-unionised Jewish labour.[61]

Living standards in the Irish and Jewish communities improved as the second and third generations prospered due to the buoyant economic conditions in New York. It is not possible to prove a direct causal link between rising living standards and improved public health; however, the evidence is compelling. There were no major medical advances in the period and the public health initiatives, while commendable, were still at an early stage of implementation. It would be reasonable to conclude that higher earnings lifted many immigrants out of poverty with a consequent improvement in their health.

Employment Was Available for All, Glasgow: 1914–1919[62]

Glasgow Corporation published *Municipal Glasgow* in 1914 as a response to the 'daily' requests for information on its highly regarded municipal initiatives. American correspondents were seemingly particularly interested in the provision of public utilities, such water supply, electricity, tramways and housing, which the Corporation regarded themselves as 'long having taken a foremost place'. Glasgow is presented in the publication as a progressive and prosperous industrial city with a working class imbued with civic pride; perhaps this was, indeed, the 'City of Dreams' rather than New York. Glasgow had increased its population to one

---

58 Anbinder, *The City of Dreams*, 373.
59 Anbinder, *The City of Dreams*, 374.
60 Wallace, *Greater Gotham*, 273, footnote 9.
61 Wallace, *Greater Gotham*, 270.
62 Quote on the war years in Glasgow; 'Money was plentiful with employment available for all' from W. R. Scott & J. Cunnison, *The Industries of the Clyde Valley During the War* (Oxford: Humphrey Milford, 1924), 171.

million in 1912 by absorbing Govan, Partick and other burghs.[63] Its successful staple export industries held world positions; for example, the Clyde launched 21 per cent of the world's shipbuilding output in the years leading up to 1914 and North British Locomotive became the largest locomotive manufacturer outside the United States.[64] Utopia in the west of Scotland.

However, buried in the text there is information on public health which challenges this utopian view. Infants were twice as likely to die in one-roomed houses, which were more prevalent in the poorer districts, than in the larger houses in the more affluent areas; children between one and five years old in one-roomed houses, four times more likely to die with similar health inequalities evident in older age groups. These differences were attributed to 'economic conditions' without further comment.[65] Utopia did not extend to the urban poor who accounted for 30 per cent of the population who subsisted on earnings too low and erratic to rescue a family from real need.[66] These were unskilled labourers, and their families, many of Irish birth or descent, who provided a large reservoir of cheap labour, as did the Irish in New York.[67] An unskilled labourer earned between 20 and 25 shillings per week for a full week's work during the immediate pre-war period but many were employed on a casual basis or had seasonal work shortages. A quarter of all skilled and unskilled male workers in Glasgow in 1911 experienced irregular employment; the proportion within the unskilled would have been higher.[68] Women who supplemented their family income in the clothing industry also suffered irregularity in work due to the seasonality in the demand for clothing.[69]

---

63 J. Cunnison, and J. B. S. Gilfillan, eds, *The Third Statistical Account of Scotland: Glasgow* (Glasgow: Collins 1958), 789, 799.

64 A. Slaven, *Development of the West of Scotland: 1750–1960* (London: Routledge, 1975), 9–10; I. Maver, *Glasgow* (Edinburgh: Edinburgh University Press, 2000), 122.

65 Corporation of the City of Glasgow, *Municipal Glasgow; Its Evolution and Enterprises* (Glasgow: Robert Gibson, 1915), 208.

66 S. Checkland, 'British Urban Health in General and in a Single City', in O. Checkland and M. Lamb, eds, *Health Care as Social History: The Glasgow Case* (Aberdeen: Aberdeen University Press, 1982), 173; W. H. Fraser and I. Maver *Glasgow Volume 2, 1830–1914* (Manchester: Manchester University Press, 1996), 382.

67 J. J. Smyth, *Labour in Glasgow, 1896–1936: Socialism, Suffrage, Sectarianism* (East Linton: Tuckwell Press, 2000), 21.

68 R. Rodger, 'Employment, Wages and Poverty in the Scottish Cities, 1841–1914'. In G. Gordon (ed.) *Perspectives of the Scottish City* (Aberdeen: Aberdeen University Press, 1985), 47.

69 J. H. Treble *Urban Poverty in Britain 1830–1914* (London: Batsford Academic, 1979), 16, 22, 60–79: J. H. Treble, 'The Seasonal Demand for Adult Labour in Glasgow, 1890–1914', *Social History*, 3 (1978), 60, Appendix 1.

The unskilled labourer could not afford a balanced diet so bread, tea and potatoes were staple foods with insufficient fat and proteins.[70] Food and rent absorbed between 83 and 92 per cent of their income with little or no surplus for other expenses such as heat or clothing.[71] Dorothy Lindsay's survey in 1911/12 showed that where income was below 20 shillings per week that the diet was 'quite inadequate for the proper development and growth of the body or for the maintenance of a capacity for active work' with 70 per cent of the families surveyed having an inadequate diet.[72] Glasgow School Board found that 30 per cent of children examined were malnourished and showed signs of rickets, a deficiency disease, with children in the poorer areas being markedly shorter and lighter than in the more affluent districts.[73]

Poverty did not always engender compassion. James Ferguson, Indoor Inspector of the Poor for Glasgow Parish Council, commentated to the Royal Commission on the Poor Laws in 1906 that poverty was due to immorality, improvidence and indolence deploring that the upkeep of 'these people' should fall on the respectable and industrious ratepayer.[74] Richard Tawney, economist and social reformer, suggested to the Royal Commission that poverty was due to a structural problem in the labour market with a permanent over-supply of low-skilled labour that led to a large mass of chronically unemployed or half employed low-skilled labourers who were continually on the verge of distress. Tawney disagreed with the view that 'any man can get work if he wants it' and stated that low-skilled workers were the victims of a system over which they had no control.[75] It was difficult for the low-skilled to escape poverty. In New York, immigrant families had been able to progress, in time, away from day labouring or contract needlework to skilled work or white-collar positions. This migration was less evident in Glasgow with successive generations perpetuating the cycle of casual work, erratic and low wages and poor health. New York experienced an improvement in living standards and health between 1900 and 1914 but there was little change in the circumstances of the labouring poor in Glasgow. For example, mortality rates of young children in New York reduced by forty per cent but there was little

[70] Fraser and Maver, *Glasgow Volume 2*, 362; I. Levitt, *Poverty and Welfare in Scotland, 1890–1948* (Edinburgh: Edinburgh University Press, 1988), 37.

[71] D. E. Lindsay, *Report upon a Study of the Diet of the Labouring Classes in the City of Glasgow carried out during 1911–12* Glasgow: Corporation of Glasgow (1913), 32–33.

[72] Lindsay, *Report upon a Study of the Diet of the Labouring Classes*, 6, 17–19.

[73] Fraser and Maver, *Glasgow Volume 2*, 362.

[74] Royal Commission on the Poor Laws and Relief of Distress (1910) Cd 5068, Appendix Volume III and IX, Minutes of Evidence, *Parliamentary Papers*, pp. 49–50.

[75] Royal Commission on the Poor Laws (1910) Minutes of Evidence, 329–330, 335.

improvement in infant mortality rates in the poorer districts in Glasgow in the lead up to the outbreak of the war.[76]

The war provided an escape from poverty – but only for some. Glasgow became a major munitions centre working at maximum capacity to satisfy the insatiable demand for war materials which led to full employment and high earnings for unskilled men, women and youths.[77] The differential between skilled and unskilled workers narrowed with unskilled workers receiving proportionally higher increases.[78] Dilution provided opportunities for labourers to become semi-skilled and earn significantly more; for example, a shipyard fitter's helper could earn between 60 and 80 shillings per week.[79] Unskilled labourers could earn an additional 20 shillings per week working overtime or an additional shift premium of 10 shillings a week on night shifts.[80] Before the war, women had worked in a narrow range of low-paid occupations, such as domestic service, cleaning or sewing outwork.[81] The munitions factories provided a well-paid alternative with earnings which exceeded the pre-war earnings of a skilled man.[82] Shop girls could now earn 14 shillings a week, compared to 7 shillings a week before the war and a tailoress 14 shillings a week in 1918 compared to 4 to 6 shillings a week in 1914.[83] Boys who earned 7 shillings a week before the war as a delivery boy could now earn 12 shillings a week as a mess boy or 28 shillings a

76 Fraser and Maver, *Glasgow Volume 2*, 353, 358–360.

77 Scott and Cunnison, *The Industries of the Clyde Valley*, 93–100, 155–159.

78 A. L. Bowley, *Prices and Wages in the United Kingdom, 1914–1920* (Oxford: Humphrey Milford, 1921), 43 Table XVI, 96, 98, 105, 107.

79 Glasgow City Archives (hereinafter 'GCA'), Govan Parish, Applications for Relief, D-HEW 17/811, 189586, 8 April 1918. 'Applications for Relief' refers to requests from individuals for Parish Poor Relief. The reference numbers, such as 189586, are the sequential numbers given to individual applications.

80 GCA, Govan Parish, Applications for Relief, D-HEW 17/812, 190041, 11 May 1918; D-HEW 17/811, 189744, 19 April 1918; D-HEW 17/811, 189434, 26 March 1918; D-HEW 17/804, 186738, 11 October 1917.

81 J. H. Treble, 'The Characteristics of the Female Unskilled Labour Market and the Formation of the Female Casual Labour Market in Glasgow, 1891–1914', *Scottish Economic and Social History*, VI (1986), 33–35; Appendix 1, 45.

82 M. Baillie, 'The Women of Red Clydeside: Women Munitions Workers in the West of Scotland during the First World War' (PhD thesis, McMaster University, Hamilton, Ontario, 2002), 26, 28, 34, 36; GCA, Govan Parish, Applications for Relief, D-HEW 17/807, 188320, 22 January 1918.

83 GCA, Govan Parish, Applications for Relief, D-HEW 17/808, 188394, 26 January 1918; D-HEW 17/754, 164729, 21 September 1914; D-HEW 17/807, 188045, 7 January 1918; D-HEW 17/753, 164526, 14 September 1914.

week as a clerk.[84] Consequently, the household income of an unskilled labourer with three children in work could have increased from 43 shillings per week to 145 shillings per week.[85] Circumstances would vary dependent on the number and the age of children; however, even the supplemented war wages for the main wage earner and one child at work would have been transformative and have lifted the family out of poverty.

There was a negative consequence of the war: price inflation. In the first four months of the war, retail prices increased more than in the previous 40 years and continued to increase thereafter and had doubled by the end of the war.[86] An engineering labourer would have needed to earn an additional 21–22s per week to compensate for this increase in retail prices.[87] The increase in prices was not uniform. The diet of the more affluent, which included meat, fish, milk, butter, eggs and sugar, suffered the highest price increases; whereas, a family whose diet was restricted to cheaper staple foods experienced lower price increases; bread increased by only 55 per cent and potatoes by 59 per cent. Government price controls capped the increase in the price of bread with margarine and bacon continuing to be a cheaper alternative to butter and meat in the poorer districts.[88] Rationing towards the end of the war had little effect on labouring-class families since they could not, and never had been able, to afford the rationed foods and there was a plentiful supply of bread and potatoes.[89] The Sumner Committee concluded in June 1918 that the working classes were able to purchase food of the same nutritional value as in June 1914 and that the families of unskilled workmen were slightly better fed in 1918.[90] The impact of price inflation and rationing would have been felt more keenly in affluent households than in the poorer homes living on a bread and tea diet.

---

84 GCA, Govan Parish, Applications for Relief, D-HEW 17/754, 164604, 16 September 1914; D-HEW 17/754, 164615, 16 September 1914; D-HEW 17/803, 186220, 12 September 1917.

85 G. MacSporran, 'Glasgow and the Great War: A Study of Health and Wealth in an Industrial City' (PhD thesis, University of Stirling, 2018), 106, Table 1.

86 A. L. Bowley, *Wages and Income in the United Kingdom since 1860*, (Cambridge: Cambridge University Press. 1937), 31; Bowley, *Prices and Wages in the United Kingdom*, Table XXIII, 70.

87 J. M. Winter, *The Great War and the British People*. London: MacMillan, 1985), 231, 236.

88 Bowley, *Prices and Wages in the United Kingdom*, 42–45, 51–52; M. Ferguson, 'The Diets of Labouring Class Families during the Course of the War', *Journal of Hygiene* 18 (1920), 409–410.

89 Ferguson, 'The Diets of Labouring Class Families during the Course of the War', 409, 416.

90 Report of the Working Classes Cost of Living Committee (1918) Cd 8980, *Parliamentary Papers*, p. 9; I. Gazeley and A. Newell, 'The First World War and Working-class Food Consumption in Britain', *European Review of Economic History* 17 (2017), 88.

Professional and white-collar salaries and the hourly rates for skilled workers did not increase as sharply as the unskilled and semi-skilled in the war industries who were incentivised to maximise output. Soldiers' families, who were dependent on fixed separation payments, were particularly disadvantaged by rising prices. There was a corrosive difference in the same tenement close between those whose husband had volunteered and those who had stayed at home, as articulated by one individual:

> I am a soldier's wife which is a pity seeing the miserable pittance we get to keep body and soul together. If my husband had stayed at home and gone to some of the shipyards or munitions works then we would be getting pounds more per week.[91]

Families of enlisted men were forced to sell their possessions, move into cheaper rooms and apply for poor relief.[92] War widows' pensions were even lower averaging 13s. 6d. per week which only alleviated the most basic want while a bus conductress could earn £2 per week and a munitions worker, over £3 per week.[93] In summary, war conditions placed a premium on labour resources which had previously been undervalued, such as the unskilled, women and youths, with those closest to the manufacture of war materials benefiting the most. Others on a salary or fixed income suffered varying degrees of hardship which became more marked with time. The unskilled families suffered lower price escalation on their staple foods, but many could now afford an improved diet with more proteins and fat. The more affluent suffered higher price escalation with a possible degradation in their diet. The poor had indeed escaped from poverty.

Improved living standards in the poorest districts in New York between 1900 and 1914 led to a significant reduction in mortality rates. This was also evident in Glasgow during the war years. Children were the most vulnerable age-group, particularly infants up to one year old. Past progress in improving infant health had been slow; over the last four decades of the nineteenth century, infant mortality rates in Glasgow had reduced by only 10 per cent while the general death rate had reduced by 27 per cent.[94] Infant mortality rates in Glasgow during the war reduced by 15 per cent which was three to four times higher than the annual rate of decline in any period in the previous fifty years. The most striking

---

91 *Daily Record* (10 June 1918). Extract from a letter from an un-named 'Soldier's Wife'.

92 J. Lomas, 'Soldiering On: War Widows in First World War Britain', in M. Andrews and J. Lomas, eds, *The Home Front in Britain: Images, Myths and Forgotten Experiences since 1914* (Basingstoke: Palgrave Macmillan, 2014), 42–43.

93 Lomas,'Soldiering On: War Widows in First World War Britain', 49.

94 A. K. Chalmers, *The Health of Glasgow, 1818–1925* (Glasgow: Corporation of Glasgow, 1930), 189–190.

improvements were in the poorest districts; for example, a 31 per cent reduction in Whitevale and a 24 per cent reduction in Mile-end.[95] By 1919, the differential between infant death rates in the poor and affluent districts had been halved. Dr A. K. Chalmers, Medical Officer of Health for Glasgow, noted that small and light-weight children had malnourished and over-worked mothers and suggested that maternal health was a key factor. Chalmers noted that not all children were born with equal chances; a third of infant deaths were due to 'immaturity' which occurred mainly in the first week of life – a condition for which Chalmers stated that after-care can do little to remedy.[96] This is corroborated by health visitors' reports which recorded 88 per cent of babies being 'well' on their first visit in 1918 compared to 52 per cent in 1914.[97]

School-age children also became healthier during the war. The School Board of Glasgow reported a reduction in malnourished children from 11 per cent in 1914–15 to 4 per cent in 1916–17.[98] The Govan School Board commented in 1918 that children were cleaner and better clothed and that their nutrition had been well maintained during the war with a progressive increase in average weight and height.[99] Another indication of improved child health was the reduction in the incidence of rickets – a deficiency disease which was prevalent in the poorer communities. James Maxton, Independent Labour Party Member of Parliament and former teacher, recalled that, in the early 1900s, when he took his Bridgeton class for drill that 'thirty out of the sixty youngsters could not bring their heels and knees together because of rickety malformations'.[100] The Glasgow School Board reported a halving in the incidence of rickets during the war which the Board noted had been achieved despite a decrease in the consumption of milk, beef-fat, butter and eggs due to the war.[101]

The wartime improvement in health in the poorer areas was not restricted to children. The municipal districts in Glasgow in this period were, in the main, homogeneous with regards to socio-economic status. The district mortality

95 GCA, D-TC 7/11/3/14.22, *Reports of the Medical Officer of Health, 1914–19*, 30, Table VI; 37, Table XV.

96 GCA., D-TC 7/11/3/14.22, *Reports of the Medical Officer of Health, 1912*, 13, 16, 166.

97 GCA, D-TC 7/11/3/14.22, Report of the Medical Officer of Health, *1914–19*, 27, 39.

98 GCA, D-ED 9/1/33, *School Board of Glasgow, Annual Reports: Medical Inspection of Children, Year ending 30 June 1918*, 7.

99 GCA, D-ED 9/1/33, *Govan Parish School Board, Annual Reports: Medical Inspection of Children, Year ending 30 June 1915*, p. 15; *Year ending 30 June 1918*, 23, 28.

100 Speech by J. Maxton to the ILP Conference in 1927 quoted in G. Brown, *Maxton* (Edinburgh: Mainstream, 1986), 43.

101 GCA, D-ED 9/1/33, *School Board of Glasgow, Annual Reports: Medical Inspection of Children, Year ending 30 June 1915*, p. 8; *Year ending 30 June 1918*, 5; GCA, D-ED 9/1/33, *Education Authority of Glasgow (Previous School Board of Glasgow area), Annual Reports: Medical Inspection of Children, Year ending 31 July 1919*, 11.

rates, for all age groups, show that improved health was social-class specific. The poorest districts with the highest mortality rates benefitted from a ten per cent reduction in death rates between 1914 and 1918 compared to a five per cent increase in the more affluent districts. There was a clear pattern in the spectrum between poor and affluent in all districts: improving health during the war was inversely proportional to wealth.[102] This compares with the immediate pre-war period which had shown no reduction in overall mortality rates. All categories of diseases during the war showed a reduction in mortality rates which suggests a general improvement in health rather than a particular improvement in one category of disease. This occurred despite a deterioration in medical services with hospitals requisitioned for military use and fewer general practitioners.[103] Prior to the war, the residents of Calton, one of the poorest districts in Glasgow, were twice as likely to die as those in affluent Langside. By the end of the war, the health disadvantage of being poor in Calton had been halved. As with immigrant health in New York between 1900 and 1914, it is reasonable to conclude that this was due to improved living standards in the poorest districts in Glasgow.

The studies of New York between 1900 and 1914 and the war years in Glasgow have shown the extent to which health improved with increased wealth during periods of expanding economies with opportunities to secure higher earnings. The interwar years provide a stark contrast with much long-term unemployment and hardship which was prevalent in New York in the 1930s and for most of the interwar years in Glasgow. It could be expected that a reduction in living standards would have led to a deterioration in health. The response to mass unemployment will provide a useful insight into the changing attitudes towards the able-bodied poor and whether municipalities accepted responsibility for its less fortunate citizens.

The Great Depression: New York in the 1930s

The war years were a formative period for New York. The city was regarded by their metropolitan peers as 'un-American' due to the disparate and large immigrant enclaves which had sacrificed little of their ethnicity – in America, but not of America. After the outbreak of war, the anglophile political class in New York was concerned that the 'tinder box' mix of ethnicities with differing loyalties

---

102 See MacSporran, 'Glasgow and the Great War', 140–148.

103 A. G. V. Simmonds, *Britain and World War* One (Abingdon: Routledge, 2012), 181; J. Hogarth, 'General Practice', in G. McLachlan, ed., *Improving the Common Weal: Aspects of Scottish Health Services, 1900–1984*. Edinburgh: Edinburgh University Press, 1987), 172–177; J. Kinnaird, 'The Hospitals', in McLachlan. ed., *Improving the Common* Weal, 222–223.

could lead an outbreak of violence as witnessed in Europe.[104] This was most evident in East Harlem between the growing African American and Puerto Rican communities and the resident Italian population.[105] Tensions were exacerbated by the immediate decline in output and exports as European capital was withdrawn from New York with a consequent rise in unemployment. Food prices increased with accusations of hoarding, price fixing and a reluctance to sell between ethnic groups.[106] Such was the ensuing civil unrest that the authorities had to create city-operated markets to ensure a proper supply of food at market prices.[107] Former President Theodore Roosevelt addressed these racial tensions in a key-note speech in October 1915 stating that 'There is no room for hyphenated Americans in this country. The only man who is a good American is the man who is an American and nothing else'.[108] This set the tone for the political direction in New York for the rest of the war and was furthered by the German unrestricted submarine campaign and the discovery of the Zimmerman telegraph.[109] The entry of the United States into the war in 1917 was the final step towards the Americanisation of New York.[110] The war transformed the disparate communities in New York into a truly American metropolis and this process continued thereafter with restrictions in immigration in 1921 which reduced immigration from Southern and Eastern Europe by 80 per cent from pre-war levels but placed no restriction on immigration from Britain, Germany, Ireland and Scandinavia.[111] The discrimination against Jewish and Italian immigrants was enshrined in legislation supported organisations such as the Ku Klux Klan and the American Federation of Labour.[112] However, there was still a sense of cohesiveness and identification with fellow citizens which would prove to be essential to maintaining social order during the long years of the Great Depression in the 1930s.

---

104 Ross J. Wilson, *New York and the First World War* (Farnham: Ashgate, 2014), 39, 62, 66, 79.

105 Anbinder, *City of Dreams*, 481–484.

106 Wilson, *New York and the First World War*, 82–83.

107 Wilson, *New York and the First World War*, 84.

108 Wilson, *New York and the First World War*, 105–106.

109 Wilson, *New York and the First World War*, 110–120. The Zimmerman telegram was routed via German diplomatic channels to Mexico and proposed a military alliance 'to make war together' with the offer of New Mexico, Texas and Arizona being returned to Mexico. For more detail see Garrett Peck, *The Great War in America: World War 1 and Its Aftermath* (New York: Pegasus, 2018), 72–77.

110 Wilson, *New York and the First World War*, 138–139.

111 Anbinder, *City of Dreams*, 465–467. The Emergency Quota Act of 1921 was followed by the National Origins Act in 1924 which not repealed until 1964.

112 Anbinder, *City of Dreams*, 468.

The 1920s were years of economic growth and expansion. By the end of the decade, New York was an extraordinarily rich, diverse, and productive city with an unusually broad middle class. It was a white-collar city with high wages relative to the national average and a relatively small manufacturing sector. It was still ethnically diverse with 73 per cent of the population in 1930 having at least one parent born abroad.[113] In December 1928, President Coolidge's last State of the Union address reflected on the benign economy of the 1920s: 'No Congress of the United States ever assembled, on surveying the state of the Union, has met with a more pleasing prospect than which appears at this time. In the domestic field there is tranquillity and contentment' adding that that Congress should 'regard the present with satisfaction and anticipate the future with optimism'.[114] It had been a buoyant decade for Americans, as it had in New York, production and employment levels were high and rising with an increase in personal wealth evidenced by the increase in car production from 2.2 million in 1920 to 5.4 million in 1929.[115]

Much of this apparent wealth had been financed by debt. Three out of every five cars were bought on instalment credit as was other consumer durables; by 1929, credit had more than doubled to $3 billion.[116] Eighty per cent of American families had no savings whatsoever and had already 'spent' their future earnings on instalment credit. Some two per cent of families controlled two-thirds of America's savings.[117] They invested heavily in the bull market of the 1930s with the lure of easy profits leading investors to buy stocks on credit using the stock as collateral. Stock prices now no longer reflected the underlying values of investments rather they were set by speculative demand.

When stock prices stopped rising, the credit-fuelled bull market collapsed with investors, brokers and banks incurring severe losses.[118] Optimism was soon replaced with panic and despair as the stock market went into freefall on 28 October 1929, a process which continued to the summer of 1932 by which

---

113 Mason B. Williams, *City of Ambition* (New York: Norton, 2013), 75–80.

114 John Kenneth Galbraith, *The Great Crash, 1929* (London: Allen Lane, 2007), 30.

115 Galbraith, *The Great Crash*, 31; The production figure for 1920 was obtained from Martin V. Melosi, 'Automobile in American Life and Society' accessed from http://www.autolife.umd.umich.edu on 16 August 2023.

116 Robert S. McElvaine, *The Great Depression: America, 1929–1941* (New York: Times, 1993), 99, 40–41.

117 McElvaine, *The Great Depression*, 38.

118 See Galbraith, *The Great Crash*, 111–147, for an account of the stock market crash and 148–185 for the aftermath of the crash.

time the Dow Jones Industrial Average had lost 89 per cent of its peak value.[119] For most, who were non-investors, this was simply another boom and bust which would pass. However, in late 1930, the banking system started to collapse with six hundred banks closing in sixty days. The largest was New York's Bank of the United States which was the third largest bank in New York.[120] Consumers stopped spending, businesses could not get loans, bankruptcies followed, unemployment soared, and the American economy went into the downward spiral of the 1930s Great Depression.

The Great Depression in New York had a distinctive profile compared to other north-eastern cities.[121] Between 1929 and early 1933, the downturn was less severe than in other north-eastern metropolitan areas since it was less dependent on the manufacture of consumer goods which had suffered from an immediate drop in demand after the 1929 Crash. Even so, unemployment had risen in New York to 20 per cent of the work force although lower than Chicago at 28.9 per cent and Detroit at 32.4 per cent.[122] Some 1.5 million in New York were drawing emergency relief with 5,000 boys feral on the streets.[123] A mitigating factor to the contraction of credit after the 1929 Crash was the provision of non-banking credit among certain ethnic communities in New York. The large Jewish community, which accounted for 25 to 30 per cent of the population, provided some $25 million of non-formal credit during the Depression which facilitated the growth in the number of retail businesses.[124]

After 1933, there was a nation-wide gradual recovery but less so in New York due to the continued downturn in international trade which was a key part of the New York economy. There was also a shift in population and industry to the Southern and Western states which were becoming the locus for investment and growth in new industries, such as petro-chemicals, aeronautics and electrical engineering.[125] There was a second contraction between 1937 and 1938 which may have been due to fiscal tightening by the Federal Reserve. New York fared less well than other large metropolitan areas for the remainder of the decade.

---

119 Gary Richardson, *et al*, 'Stock Market Crash of 1929' accessed from http://www.federalreservehistory.org on 16 August 2023.

120 Aaron Gurwitz, *Atlantic Metropolis; An Economic History of New York City* (Cham, Switzerland: Palgrave, 2019), 406. The Bank of the United States failed with $160 million in deposits. Also see David M. Kennedy, *The American People in the Great Depression; Freedom from Fear, Part One* (New York: Oxford University Press, 1999), 65–69.

121 Aaron Gurwitz, *Atlantic Metropolis*, 401.

122 Gurwitz, *Atlantic Metropolis*, 403, Table 13.1.

123 Jules Stewart, *Gotham Rising; New York in the 1930s* (London; Tauris 2016), 23–24.

124 Gurwitz, *Atlantic Metropolis*, 417–418.

125 Gurwitz, *Atlantic Metropolis*, 421–425.

International trade continued to be 40 per cent below 1929 levels and its industries were no longer in growth sectors.[126]

It could be expected that health would deteriorate during the Depression and especially so in 1933 and 1937. Mortality rates in New York had reduced by a modest 13 per cent during the 'Roaring Twenties' to 11.3 deaths per 1,000 in 1929. Rates reduced by further seven per cent between 1929 and 1939 with mortality rates in 1933 and 1937 being lower than the pre-Depression level in 1928.[127] This reduction in the 1930s was evident across all age groups and all major categories of diseases, except for diabetes and certain cancers.[128] Life expectancy increased by just under 7 years during the 1930s to 62.5 years for males and 66.8 years for females.[129] The incidence of pulmonary tuberculosis, a disease of the poor, provides some indication of morbidity with new cases notified to the authorities in the 1930s reducing by 30 per cent.[130]

Manhattan, the most densely populated New York borough, provides a somewhat different perspective. Mortality rates remained static during the 1920s but increased by 12 per cent in 1930 and remained at this this higher level for most of the 1930s without a further spike in rates in 1933 and 1937.[131] The higher level was similar to the mortality rate in 1926 when there had been an outbreak of measles and influenza.[132] There is no evidence of a significant deterioration in health in New York during the Depression rather an improvement in City as a whole with increasing life expectancy but not in Manhattan where the death rate increased but only by the quantum of an outbreak of seasonal infectious disease. The difficult years of 1933 and 1937 passed without a noticeable deterioration in health.

The improvement in health in New York during the Depression, and the modest increase in Manhattan given the circumstances, could have been due to several factors, such as medical advances, changes in the age-composition of the population or relief measures which mitigated hardship. The general nature of the reduction in mortality in New York suggests that it was not due to a medical advance in one major disease. The age-composition changed marginally during

126 Gurwitz, *Atlantic Metropolis*, 420.

127 Rosenwaike, *Population History of New York*, 178, Table A-3.

128 Department of Health ('DoH'), The City of New York, 'Summary of Vital Statistics 1962, The City of New York', accessed from http://www.nyc.gov on 11 September 2023, p. 11, Tables 15 and 16.

129 DoH, 'Summary of Vital Statistics 1962', 11, Table 14.

130 DoH, 'Summary of Vital Statistics 1962', 12, Table 17.

131 National Center for Health Statistics, Centers for Disease Control and Prevention, 'Vital Statistics of the United States: 1890–1938: Mortality Statistics for 1930–1938', accessed from http://www.cdc.gov on 20 September 2023; 1931 Report, 7, Table L; 1933 Report, 15, Table 1B; 1937 Report, 49, Table 1; 1938 Report, 9, Table XIII.

132 DoH, 'Department of Health, Annual Report for 1926', accessed from http://www.babel.hathitrust.org on 20 September 2023, 149–150.

the 1930s with fewer children and more older adults but the change was not substantive.[133] It is probable that relief measures mitigated the impact of the Depression such that public health was broadly maintained during the 1930s. The Board of Health Annual Reports are not readily available for the 1930s so it is not possible to determine whether there were significant differences between affluent and poor districts. Another mitigating factor was the early charitable relief payments in 1930 of $4.5 million which increased to $21 million in 1932 with municipal relief payments which increased from $9 million to $21 million in the same period. These large sums, however, only provided the equivalent of one month's loss of wages for the eight hundred thousand unemployed in New York.[134] Due to the fall in tax revenues, this had to be financed by deficit spending supported by loans. Such was the burden of this relief expenditure that the City faced insolvency in early 1933.[135] Franklin Roosevelt, then Governor of New York State, instituted a temporary programme of work relief in 1931, the first State to do so, as a matter of 'social duty' to 'restore that close relationship with its people which is necessary to preserve our democratic form of government'.[136] This became the template for work relief when Roosevelt became president. Federal funding for relief wages was instituted after 1933 with a major step forward in the Emergency Relief Appropriation Act of 1935.[137] Some 250,000 were employed by 1936 on 'New Deal' relief schemes in New York.[138] The recession in 1937 and political opposition led to Roosevelt having to cut public spending which, after 1938, led to the demise of the 'New Deal'.[139]

The maintenance of health during a time of widespread hardship is a paradox which defies the drawing of simple conclusions. The breadlines along the Bowery in Lower Manhattan, the over-flowing night shelters and the race riots in Harlem were testimony to the depth of the Depression.[140] It would have been

---

133 DoH, 'Summary of Vital Statistics 1962', 12.

134 Kennedy, *The American People in the Great Depression*, 88. Also see James T. Patterson (2000) *America's Struggle against Poverty in the Twentieth Century* (Cambridge, Massachusetts: Harvard University Press, 2000), 55–56.

135 Gurwitz, *Atlantic Metropolis*, 415.

136 Kennedy, *The American People in the Great Depression*, 90–91; Williams, *City of Ambition*, 110–111.

137 *See* Kennedy, *The American People in the Great Depression*, 251–257 regarding the relief schemes.

138 Gurwitz, *Atlantic Metropolis*, 437.

139 Eric Rauchway, *The Great Depression and the New Deal* (New York; Oxford University Press, 2008), 115–118.

140 Stewart, *Gotham Rising*, 15, 23, 38–42. The riots in 1931 and 1935 were between African Americans and Filipinos. The Committee of Enquiry into the riots concluded that the

helpful to have had sight of the detailed health reports for municipal wards and more information on morbidity. Based on the information available, it suggests that the relief measures alleviated distress to the extent that life and limb were preserved. There was a stronger correlation between rising living standards and improvements in health in New York in the earlier years of the century. There remain unanswered questions which merit further research. For example, were there differences in health outcomes between ethnicities, how did the Lower East Side of Manhattan fare during this period, did morbidity rise such that there was widespread illness albeit not fatal? A comparison with Glasgow may provide a useful perspective.

Healthy or Hungry? Glasgow During the Interwar Years

Charles Webster debated whether the 1930s in Britain were a time of severe social deprivation or improving social and economic conditions.[141] This is relevant to Glasgow which had high unemployment for most of the interwar years. As with New York, the question to be addressed is whether the hardship of the interwar years led to a deterioration in health. Peace brought an end to the war economy in Glasgow with soldiers demobilised to an uncertain future and women and youths losing their munition wages with family incomes being significantly reduced. Although initial indications in 1919 were hopeful, the economy experienced a slump in the early 1920s with Glasgow's exporting staple industries becoming a weakness rather than a strength.[142] Shipbuilding was a key staple industry which stimulated, or otherwise, employment in other sectors in the local economy.[143] Output fell from 672,000 tons in 1920 to 175,000 tons in 1923 by which time 40 per cent of the shipbuilding workforce was unemployed.[144] Berth capacity had increased during the war on the Clyde, elsewhere within Britain, and in other maritime nations. The result was chronic over-capacity, which combined with little growth in international trade and a collapse in freight rates in 1920, led

---

'public health, safety and welfare in colored Harem have long been jeopardized by economic and social conditions, which the Depression has intensified'.

141 Charles Webster, 'Healthy or Hungry Thirties?', *History Workshop Journal* 13 (1982), 110.

142 Peter L. Payne, *Growth & Contraction: Scottish Industry, c. 1860–1990* (Economic and Social History Society of Scotland, 1992), 31.

143 Smyth, *Labour in Glasgow*, 21.

144 Hugh Peebles, *Warshipbuilding on the Clyde* (Edinburgh: John Donald, 2000), 165; Lewis Johnman and Hugh Murphy, 'An Overview of the Economic and Social Effects of the Interwar Depression on Clydeside Shipbuilding Communities', *International Journal of Maritime History*, 18, 1 (2006), 232, 239.

to redundant shipyards and cancelled contracts.[145] The Clyde yards had also lost profitable naval work, which was essential to their viability, as a result of the Washington Naval Treaty of 1921.[146] Between 1922 and 1927, unemployment in Britain's yards did not fall below 30 per cent with the highest levels being in 1922 and 1923.[147] Output increased again between 1928 and 1930 but collapsed again with the yards virtually empty between 1930 and 1936.[148]

Similar volatility is evident in the number of registered unemployed. After full employment at the end of the war, unemployment in all trades and industries in Glasgow had risen to 70,000 by the end of 1922, fell to 30,000 in 1927, and increased again to 120,000 from late 1930 to the end of 1935, then reduced to 80,000 until the end of 1938.[149] The deepest recession was in January 1933 when 41 per cent of adult males in Glasgow were unemployed with 136,000 on unemployment benefit and 114,000 on poor relief.[150] In December 1938 there were still 83,000 unemployed in Glasgow.[151] This indicates that there was high unemployment in Glasgow throughout most of the interwar years with particular hardship in the early 1920s and the early to mid-1930s. In contrast, the Midlands and South-East of England had much lower levels of unemployment due to expanding manufacture of consumer products.[152] Unemployment brought poverty to many districts in Glasgow as evidenced in 1922 when one in three schoolchildren were in receipt of free meals, clothing or boots and poor relief applications were 22 times the level at the end of the war.[153] Alec Glen, a doctor in the shipyard district of Govan, commented on the effect of poverty on the health of the poor:

> Food largely bread and carbohydrates and insufficiently clothed, especially in winter. Rickets widespread, tuberculosis rife, diphtheria, scarlet fever, whooping cough and even measles frequently fatal. The health of these people, particularly the women and children, was terribly neglected.[154]

---

145 Lewis Johnman and Hugh Murphy, *British Shipbuilding and the State since 1918; A Political Economy of Decline* (Exeter: University of Exeter, 2002), 11–16.

146 Peebles, *Warshipbuilding on the Clyde*, 91, 99.

147 Johnman and Murphy, *British Shipbuilding and the State*, 19.

148 Peebles, *Warshipbuilding on the Clyde*, 165–166.

149 Cunnison and Gilfillan, *The Third Statistical Account of* Scotland, 586, 923.

150 Smyth, *Labour in Glasgow*, 32–33.

151 Smyth, *Labour in Glasgow*, 203.

152 Noel Whiteside, *Bad Times: Unemployment in British Social and Political History* (London: Faber and Faber, 1991), 69.

153 GCA, D-ED 9/1/33, *Education Authority of Glasgow, Annual Report, 1920/21*, p. 10; GCA, D-HEW 17/873-907, Parish of Govan, Applications for Relief.

154 A. Glen, *In the Front Line: A Doctor in War and Peace* (Edinburgh: Birlinn 2013), 142.

With the scarcity of work, prejudice against the Irish, which had been prevalent for many years on Clydeside, now had a sharper edge.[155] Even the more enlightened now regarded the Irish as unwelcome intruders, even though most were native-born. The Church of Scotland promoted 'militant Protestantism' in its 1923 report, *The Menace of the Irish Race to our Scottish Nationality*, seeking to 'preserve the traditions, ideals, and faith of a great people'. Lord Scone, honorary president of the Scottish Protestant League, stated in 1928 that unemployment would be eradicated if only a half a million Irish could repatriated.[156] The cry of, No Popery, pervaded popular opinion and the interlinked Tory, Orange Order and Church organisations in the interwar years.[157] Sectarianism did not solve the problems of interwar Glasgow and some of the poorer districts, such as Calton, which were predominately of Irish descent, were particularly vulnerable to hard times having no savings and few possessions to pawn.[158]

Whether hardship led to a deterioration in health will be assessed by comparing the mortality rates for two municipal districts; Kelvinside which was a leafy, affluent district in the west end and Carlton which was one of the poorest districts in the inner-east side of the City.[159] These districts were typical of their socio-economic peer districts. Throughout the interwar period, mortality rates in Calton, with one exception, remained generally steady and did not increase above the 1919 level. Rates in Kelvinside, also with one exception, remained mostly steady during the 1920s but increased somewhat during the 1930s. The exception for both districts was a significant increase in mortality rates between 1928 and 1930 which peaked in 1929 at 40 per cent above the interwar average. It might be assumed that this was due to the deepening Depression, but this was not so. The increases in 1928 and 1930 were caused by outbreaks of measles.[160] The 40 per cent spike in 1929 was due to 'a sinister combination' of fog and low

155 Smyth, *Labour in Glasgow*, 201–203.

156 Tom Gallacher, *Glasgow: The Uneasy Peace, Religious Tension in Modern Scotland, 1819–1914* (Manchester: Manchester University Press, 1987), 134–137.

157 Gallacher, *Glasgow: The Uneasy Peace*, 144–150; see also Tom Gallacher, 'Protestant Extremism in Urban Scotland, 1930–39: Its Growth and Contraction', *Scottish Historical Review*, 64, 178 (1985), 143–167.

158 See Patricia Clark, *Calton Connections*, a private publication available at GCA, GC941443CAL for interesting background to life in Calton. She describes Calton as being 75 per cent Catholic Irish in 1921. It includes an interesting account of riots in May 1921.

159 These districts have been chosen since their boundaries were not affected by the boundary changes in 1920 which made many districts less homogenous with regards to their socio-economic status.

160 GCA, D-HE 1/1/25-32, *Report of the Medical Officer of Health for 1928*, 30; *Report of the Medical Officer of Health for 1930*, 63.

temperatures in the first quarter with an epidemic of influenza and associated pneumonia. Deaths at the extremes of life were unusually heavy and those with existing respiratory diseases were particularly vulnerable.[161] It is unlikely that this was due to the Depression since the increase in mortality was evident in affluent as well as poor districts and the death rates in the remaining quarters of the year were among the lowest recorded.[162] Furthermore, the highest level of unemployment during the Depression was in 1933 rather than 1929.

The Medical Officer of Health Report for 1933 contains some quite surprising information given the very poor economic position in that year. The Report noted that the overall mortality rate for Glasgow was the lowest on record, infant mortality was the second lowest on record, and the pulmonary tuberculosis death rate was also the second lowest on record. The Report cited 'agreeable weather conditions with no measles and less winter pneumonia' as the reasons for the lower mortality rates.[163] The mortality rate in Calton was no higher than the pre-depression level in 1920 and would remain so until 1938. The rate in Kelvinside in 1933 was higher but there had been a demographic change with an influx of working-class population into this 'residential' district.[164] The Report for 1936 continued to provide positive information on the decline of rickets, a deficiency disease, and the improving physique of children. The Report for 1938 reported the lowest overall mortality rate and infant mortality rate recorded. As already noted, there were still 83,000 registered unemployed in Glasgow in 1938.[165] These statistics indicate that the wartime gains in health were not reversed by the hardship of the interwar years and that health was maintained or improved, in terms of mortality and morbidity, during the Depression. Inclement weather and infectious diseases had more impact on public health than the longest and severest depression of trade in living memory.

Several reasons can be mooted for this paradox: supplementary nourishment for children and mothers, welfare payments and relief work. The wartime arrangements for feeding 'necessitous' children and mothers were greatly expanded on a scale which would not have been contemplated before the war.[166] The early 1920s were a particularly difficult period in Glasgow. In 1922, one million meals and

161 GCA, D-HE 1/1/25-32, *Report of the Medical Officer of Health for 1929*, 3–4.

162 GCA, D-HE 1/1/25-32, *Report of the Medical Officer of Health for 1929*, 4.

163 GCA, D-HE 1/1/25-32, *Report of the Medical Officer of Health for 1933*, 3–4.

164 GCA, D-HE 1/1/25-32, *Report of the Medical Officer of Health for 1933*, 273; GCA, D-HE 1/1/25-32, *Report of the Medical Officer of Health for 1938*, 34, 37, 51, 285, 292.

165 See footnote 146.

166 C. Rowan, 'Child Welfare and the Working-class Family', in M. Langan and B. Shwartz, eds, *Crises in the British State, 1880–1930* (London: Hutchinson, 1985), 227–230.

two million pints of milk were provided, free of charge, to mothers and children under the age of 5 years. By 1925, 1.6 million pints of milk were being distributed and dried milk given to 8,000 families with some 60,000 mothers and young children, in total, receiving assistance.[167] Poor relief payments also mitigated hardship. Insured workers qualified for limited unemployment relief which was their only support since the able-bodied were precluded from poor relief. However, legislation in 1921 allowed municipal authorities to give poor relief as a temporary measure to the able-bodied unemployed.[168] The benefit of up to 33 shillings a week, subject to scrutiny by a Poor Law Inspector, for a family with three children was set to be no more than required for necessary 'sustentation' and be distinctly less than relief wages.[169] A labourer had earned 46 shillings a week at the end of the war.[170] By 1924, nearly half of the working class in Glasgow had received relief with 70 per cent having been unemployed for over a year.[171] R. W. Peck, a senior Scottish civil servant, despaired that the labouring classes had benefitted most from the relief payments, rather than the more deserving skilled trades, and concluded that the most apparent evils of unemployment had been greatly mitigated 'and there is at any rate no actual starvation ... with a regular supply of food'.[172] Alec Glen, a general practitioner, provided an alternative account, describing how difficult it was for families to live on unemployment benefit of twenty-five shillings a week, paid for the first five weeks, and that unemployment and semi-starvation persisted in Govan throughout the 1920s.[173] This parsimonious level of poor relief continued into the early 1930s.[174] This became too great a burden on rate-payers and the contributions to the unemployment insurance fund had also become unsustainable with the government gradually assuming responsibility for the payment of unemployment relief after 1931 which was finally encapsulated in the 1934 Unemployment Act. The 'dole' was set to

167 GCA, D-HE 1/1/25-32, *Report of the* Medical Officer of Health for 1922, 35–37; GCA, D-HE 1/1/25-32, Report of the Medical Officer of Health for 1925, 55–57.

168 Ian Levitt, *Poverty and Welfare in Scotland, 1890–1948* (Edinburgh: Edinburgh University Press, 1988), 115. Legislation refers to The Poor Law Emergency Provisions (Scotland) Act, 10 November 1921.

169 Levitt, *Poverty and Welfare*, 116.

170 See MacSporran, 'Glasgow and the Great War', 106.

171 Levitt, *Poverty and Welfare*, 125, 131.

172 Lewis Johnman and Hugh Murphy, 'An Overview of the Economic and Social Effects of the Interwar Depression on Clydeside Shipbuilding Communities', *International Journal of Maritime History*, 18, 1 (2006), 233–234; Peck was Chief Inspector of the Scottish Board of Health.

173 A. Glen, *In the Front Line: A Doctor in War and Peace*, 137.

174 Levitt, *Poverty and Welfare*, 138.

provide the minimum relief possible which would avoid civil unrest in the febrile post-war climate of industrial unrest.[175] Unemployment reliefs were means tested which was deeply unpopular with claimants and payments were not generous.[176]

Government policy preferred rationalisation and retrenchment of businesses to providing relief wages. An official enquiry in 1931 concluded that relief work perpetuated casualism and cost £324 per person annum compared to £74 per annum unemployment relief. Official regulations encouraged job sharing through short-time or casual work while also claiming unemployment relief.[177] The National Shipbuilders Act of 1930 sought to reduce capacity by closing redundant or obsolete shipyards which, with the backing of the industry and banks, closed seven yards on the Clyde, mothballed two and placed quotas of another three shipyards. The 1935 British Shipping (Assistance) Act provided loans to owners to scrap old for new tonnage, but depressed shipping rates did not tempt owners to place orders on the Clyde with the north-east of England being the main beneficiary.[178] One government initiative did provide work on the Clyde. The construction of Hull Number 534 for Cunard, the future *Queen Mary*, was suspended at Clydebank in 1931 due to the owners' financial difficulties which affected 105,000 jobs at the yards and in the wider economy.[179] At the end of December 1933, the government took the unprecedented step of agreeing very generous assistance to allow Cunard to complete the vessel and to finance a second large liner, the *Queen Elizabeth*, on the basis that they would also amalgamate with the ailing White Star Line. Neville Chamberlain, then Chancellor of the Exchequer, stated that this was a 'matter of national interest' to retain the increasingly competitive North Atlantic trade routes and that unemployment was not a factor in providing assistance.[180]

---

175 Derek Fraser, *The Evolution of the British Welfare State: A History of Social Policy since the Industrial Revolution* (Basingstoke: Palgrave Macmillan, 2003), 201–202.

176 The National Archives, Cabinet papers, *1930s Depression and Unemployment*, accessed from http://www.nationaarchives.gov.uk/cabinetpapers on 31 August 2023; Whiteside, *Bad Times*, 75.

177 Whiteside, *Bad Times*, 72–74.

178 Anthony Slaven, *The Development of the West of Scotland*, 188–189; Johnman and Murphy, *British Shipbuilding and the State*, 52–53.

179 Johnman and Murphy, *British Shipbuilding and the State*, 41, 43. The estimate of 105,000 workers was made by the Engineering and Shipbuilding Trades Federation. They may have exaggerated to make a point. Three thousand workers at the shipyard were laid off when construction stopped.

180 Johnman and Murphy, *British Shipbuilding and the State*, 42–44. Construction commenced in May 1934.

While this provided jobs in Clydebank, it was not transformative and the issue of idle berths and surplus manpower continued up to 1939.[181]

Charles Webster, in addressing the 'Healthy or Hungry' question, concluded that there was no meaningful improvement in health with regard to mortality or morbidity for the disadvantaged during the depression and that class inequalities remained unchanged.[182] This would also be a reasonable conclusion for Glasgow. Inclement weather and infectious diseases would appear to have a greater impact than unemployment. The health profile during the interwar years did not differ between affluent and poor districts with health inequalities remaining unchanged.

Conclusion

This study into the relationship between health and wealth in Glasgow and New York between 1900 and 1938 has only been partially successful in reaching firm conclusions. There was a strong correlation in both cities between buoyant economies and improving health. The improvement in child health in New York between 1900 and 1914 was quite striking and reflected rising living standards as second, and succeeding, generations of immigrants progressed to more well-paid occupations. The large reservoir of unskilled labourers in Glasgow benefitted from the higher paid work in the war economy between 1914 and 1918, as did many women and youths with the improvement in health being most evident in the poorest districts. The 'indolent and squalid' poor in both cities took these opportunities to improve their standard of living and their health. It could be expected that hardship during the years of economic depression would have led to a significant deterioration in health, but the evidence suggests otherwise.[183] The Great Depression in New York during the 1930s led to unprecedented levels of unemployment which continued in varying levels of severity until 1938. Yet, mortality rates for New York remained static throughout these years. There was an increase in rates in Manhattan but no more than might be expected from poor

181 Johnman and Murphy, *British Shipbuilding and the State*, 59.

182 Webster, 'Healthy or Hungry Thirties?', 124–125.

183 Charles Webster commented that the 1930s depression in Britain 'must be regarded as a significant exacerbating factor tending to worsen still prevailing low levels of health'. See Webster, 'Healthy or Hungry Thirties?', 125. Also, Charles Webster, 'Health, Welfare and Unemployment during the Depression', *Past & Present* 109 (1985), 204–230. The decline in life expectancy in Glasgow identified in the 2021 report, *A Study of Changes in Health, Demographics, Socioeconomic and Environmental Factors in Glasgow over the last 20 Years*, is attributed to a reduction in living standards. See paragraph 1, footnote 1.

weather or cyclical infectious disease. Later reports suggest that life expectancy in New York increased during the Depression and some morbidity decreased, such as the incidence of pulmonary tuberculosis. The Depression in Glasgow lasted most of the interwar years also with high levels of unemployment yet the wartime improvements in the poorer districts, such as Calton, were largely maintained throughout the interwar years. The exception in 1929 was due to winter smog and a virulent outbreak of influenza and associated pneumonia rather than economic circumstances. The deepest year of the Depression was in 1933 yet overall mortality rates for adults and children in Glasgow for the year were among the lowest recorded. This paradox is difficult to account for since persistent poverty should have had a profound effect on public health. Perhaps, Glasgow and New York were different cities during the interwar years than in 1900 with more sympathetic attitudes towards the able-bodied unemployed which allowed measures to be put in place to alleviate hardship.

There had been significant changes in Glasgow and New York during the period of this study. In 1900, the cities attracted migrants seeking work or sanctuary. Cities were spaces where the individual found work and subsisted or failed and perished; the outcome being of little interest to the wider community. Poverty was regarded by 'respectable' society as being due to a lack of moral compass and that any help would simply perpetuate their indolence and degeneracy. Many of the poor were also 'alien', such as the Catholic Irish, Italians, Russian Jews, which added racial and religious prejudice to moral condemnation. The war years changed these attitudes. In New York, the 'hyphenated' immigrants in disparate ethnic enclaves became more assimilated; for example, Irish American immigrants became the New York Irish. This is a subtle but important difference. There were still ethnic tensions, but New Yorkers started to identify with each other as fellow citizens. This process of assimilation was less evident in Glasgow where long-standing prejudice against the Catholic Irish was exacerbated by the shortage of work and continued throughout the interwar years. However, attitudes in Glasgow had changed after the war towards citizens in distress, irrespective of their religion or ethnicity.

Glasgow would not have provided welfare or poor relief to the able-bodied unemployed before the war on a point of principle. Even charitable giving was restricted to the 'deserving' poor who were considered respectable but had fallen on hard times. The scale of assistance to 'necessitous' children and mothers in Glasgow in the early 1920s, together with poor relief to the unemployed, would have been inconceivable before the war. These initiatives were eventually subsumed into the national schemes for welfare payments, but they had been preceded by municipal initiatives to ease the hardship of the able-bodied unemployed. Charitable giving and municipal relief payments in New York also preceded the Federal 'New Deal' system of welfare payments and job relief. Such was the level of welfare assistance provided that the New York administration was pushed to the verge of bankruptcy. This largesse would also have been inconceivable before the war, again on a point of principle. Glasgow in 1920 and New York in 1930 had a greater sense of a social contract with their citizens than in 1900 with the intent to provide better health care and welfare for those in need. It was not entirely altruistic since there was a desire to maintain the social order and to avoid civil unrest and appeal to the newly enfranchised voters.

This study has shown a strong correlation between buoyant economies and improving living standards and health. The correlation between a deteriorating economy and poorer health is less clear, based on the source material available for this study. The contrast between the scale of the depression in Glasgow and New York and the maintenance of public health somewhat defies rational explanation. More research is necessary to explore this particularly with regard to the levels of mortality and morbidity in the poorer districts of both cities. However, based on the primary material available, it is reasonable to conclude that health was maintained during the Depression in both cities due to a more sympathetic and constructive attitude towards the able-bodied unemployed which allowed measures to be put in place to mitigate hardship. Between 1900 and 1938, Glasgow and New York had become metropolises which not only provided opportunities for personal advancement, but which had also adopted a sense of civic responsibility for the less fortunate in their midst.

Sectarianism in the City: A Comparison of Glasgow and New York in the Nineteenth Century

Cameron McKay

During the nineteenth century, the European tour was a rite of passage for elite Americans eager to emphasise their distinct cultural pedigree. Despite the appeal of more obvious tourist destinations such as Vienna and Florence, a surprising number of Americans found their way to Glasgow. For New Yorkers, the city held a strange appeal combining the sanctuary of the past with the unknown possibilities of modernity in a way that was alarmingly reminiscent of their own city. Perched on the western periphery of Europe, Glasgow is the very end of the Old World, while New York is the gateway to the New. Although Glasgow's origins date back to the sixth century, like New York it was not until the early modern era that she could convincingly be described as globally significant. As the world's gaze shifted from the Mediterranean to the Atlantic, the cities' similar geographical positions put them in opportune positions for the exchange of goods, ideas, and people. Their importance within the Atlantic world resulted in their size exceeding that of their respective capital cities, while also developing their own distinctive characteristics. While Edinburgh and Washington acted as their nation's political and legal centres, Glasgow and New York were hubs for trade and industry. One New Yorker who visited Glasgow was Justin D. Fulton, a Baptist pastor, whose pilgrimage to the city's Necropolis provided a near transcendental experience:

> As I stood on a beautiful summer morning, in front of the magnificent monument which the citizens of Glasgow have reared in memory of John Knox, the 'man who never feared the face of clay', and studied the face of the statue, so calm, so earnest, and beheld the Bible which his hand holds forth as the source of power that wrested Scotland from the dominion of the Pope and gave that land to Christ; as I gazed upon the tombs of the martyrs, and beheld the proofs of God's power in the changes wrought there and elsewhere in Britain, my thoughts winged their way westward and homeward. For the first time I was made to understand why Roman Catholic cathedrals and structures are being built in America.[1]

Fulton would later describe his religious epiphany in the 1887 book *Rome in America*. Fulton forebodingly warned that 'We are in a great fight at this great world-centre. Rome has in New York more brains, more culture, more money,

[1] Justin D. Fulton, *Rome in America*, (Boston: The Pauline Propaganda, 1887), 111.

and more hearty devotees than dwell in the eternal city.'[2] At the time of writing, New York had experienced nearly half a century of mass Catholic migration, an event which marked the beginning of the city's transformation from a bastion of WASP privilege to a culturally diverse global centre. Between 1815 and 1840 alone the Catholic population in New York grew from 15,000 to 90,000. Although Catholic immigrants came from all corners of Europe, it would be the Irish who were blamed for New York's changing religious demography. By 1845, half of the city's Catholic priests were Irish as were eleven of the sixteen parish churches.[3] The transition to a more pluralistic society would not be an easy one, with the Catholic Irish being scapegoated for the worst aspects of the modern city; namely criminality, overcrowding, political corruption, and public disorder. For evangelical Protestants like Fulton, Catholicism was more than an unfortunate superstition adhered to by backwards immigrants, but an existential threat to the American way of life. It is little wonder that the stony image of John Knox prompted such an emotional response in a mind so consumed with the onward march of Romanism.

Despite the sense of finality evoked by the mossy tombs of long dead reformers, religious conflict was alive and well in Glasgow at the time of Fulton's visit. One year prior to the publication of *Rome in America*, an anti-Home Rule meeting at Glasgow City Hall had resulted in a riot. At the head of an Orange band, a crowd of two thousand vandalised St Margaret's chapel in Kinning Park as well as a nearby Catholic school. Despite the chapel being situated next door to a police station no arrests were made.[4] That same year eight thousand Orangemen marched through Glasgow for the annual commemoration of the Battle of the Boyne. Unperturbed by the already inflammatory mood that year, Brother Chalmers L. Paton, Most Worshipful Grand Master for Scotland, informed his audience 'it had become more and more evident that times of trial were approaching for them – times to test the sincerity of their attachment to their principles, and to demand more than ordinary degree their maintenance of them and of the Protestant cause.'[5] The fiery words of the Grand Master were no sudden outburst buoyed by overexuberance and a large audience, but the culmination of a long-drawn ethno-religious battle waged in Glasgow, New York, and countless other cities across the Anglophone world.

[2] Ibid., xxxix.

[3] Hidetaka Hirota, 'Limits of intolerance: nativism and immigration control in nineteenth-century New York', *Journal of Ethnic and Migration Studies* 47/16 (2021), 3771–3787, at 3773.

[4] 'Orange Rowdyism in Glasgow', *North British Daily Mail* (24 April 1886), 4.

[5] 'Orange Demonstration in Glasgow', *Glasgow Herald* (12 July 1886), 9.

Sectarianism in New York and Glasgow shared many similarities which differentiated them from other cities. The natural indemnity towards Catholicism felt in both cities was motivated by the centrality of Protestantism in American and Scottish national identity. Glasgow and New York both represented a weakness in their respective nation's sense of homogeneity due to their religious and ethnic plurality, thus prompting a more forceful assertion of Protestant identity. Although anti-Irish sentiment in New York was seen as more racial, and in Glasgow more religious, the reality was that sectarianism drew on both strands of prejudice. Native hostility to Catholicism was not the only malefactor, however, and external pressures were also at play. The large number of Irish Protestants who emigrated to America and Scotland brought with them a culture of sectarianism. The importation of Orangeism gave native anti-Catholicism a firmer ideological basis, while providing a cultural outlet for sectarianism. All these factors combined against the backdrop of rapidly changing societies, which were still contending with the social upheavals of urbanisation. Battlelines were drawn over practically every aspect of civic life from education and employment to public order and politics. For two cities famed for their modernity and cosmopolitanism, New York and Glasgow saw some of the most protracted sectarian conflict of the nineteenth century.

Protestant Identity in Scotland and America

It is hard to imagine two nations more defined by Protestantism than Scotland and America. The Reformation had liberated Scotland from Rome and the regency of Mary of Guise, a revolution which was as much national as religious. The Presbyterian insistence on biblicism contributed to the establishment of the much-lauded parish school system, as well as the egalitarian ideal of the 'lad o'pairts' a concept not dissimilar from the 'American Dream'.[6] Protestantism would later serve the dual purpose of bringing the Scots into union with England, while simultaneously protecting their national characteristics via the maintenance of a separate state church.[7] The Union of 1707 allowed access to England's American colonies, an opportunity which allowed the spread of Scottish commerce as well as religious ideas. Scots in America, be they colonists, indentured servants, overseers, exiled Covenanters, tobacco merchants, or fur traders carried with

---

6 Rae Morton, 'Class in a 'Classless' Society: The Paradox of Scottish Egalitarianism', *Scottish Affairs* 75/1 (2011), 83–99.

7 Linda Colley, *Britons: Forging the Nation 1707–1837* (Yale University Press: New Haven and London), 12.

them the legacy of the Protestant Reformation. Glasgow herself would play no small role in claiming America for Protestantism. John Stirling, Principal of the University of Glasgow (1701–1727) and Moderator of the General Assembly of the Church of Scotland, was active in maintaining links with the American Presbyteries and the mother Church. During his principalship, twenty alumni of the university immigrated to America to serve as Presbyterian ministers. Of the two hundred Presbyterian ministers recorded in America in the first half of the eighteenth century, at least a third had a Scottish connection.[8] Although many Scots would remain loyal during the American Revolution, in New York the insurrection was blamed on a 'Whig triumvirate' of Presbyterian lawyers.[9] David Brown even suggests that the Declaration of Independence owes a debt to John Knox via his descendant the Paisley-born clergyman John Witherspoon.[10] The religious culture of ordinary Americans also retained a Calvinist flair, even as the Baptists made inroads into the old Presbyterian heartlands. The mass outdoor meetings that typified the revivalist movements of the nineteenth century drew upon the earlier traditions of the Presbyterian 'Holy fair'.[11] Rather than Wallace or Bruce, it was John Knox who resonated more with Americans than any other figure in Scottish history. Albert Bushnell Hart, the foremost American historian of his day, compared Knox favourably to the radical abolitionist John Brown, describing them as '-elemental forces, unpredictable, unaccountable, and beyond analysis'.[12] Scotland itself was presented to Americans as a sort of Protestant Mecca, whose religious history was intrinsically tied to their own. In 1917, the Scottish American magazine the *Caledonian* related to its readers the following description of St Giles Cathedral in Edinburgh: 'You approach the old Church from the Palace, at the foot of the mile-long hill that leads up to the Castle, and pass along the street, The Canongate. Every step taken recalls some heroic or patriotic memory; not a stone but was drenched again and again with blood and tears.'[13]

---

8 Henry Cowan, *The Influence of the Scottish Church in Christendom: Being the Baird Lecture for 1895, in Blythswood Parish Church Glasgow* (London: Adam and Charles Black, 1896), 149–150.

9 Joseph S. Tiedemann, 'Presbyterianism and the American Revolution in the Middle Colonies', *Church History* 74/2 (2009), 306–344.

10 David Brown, 'Scotland: religion, culture and national identity', *International journal for the Study of the Christian Church* 14/2 (2014), 88–99, at 91.

11 Michael S. Horton, 'At Least Weekly: The Reformed Doctrine of the Lord's Supper and of Its Frequent Celebration', *Mid-America Journal of Theology* 11/1 (2000), 147–169, at 160.

12 Albert Bushnell Hart, 'John Knox as a Man of the World', *The American Historical Review* 13/2 (1908), 259–280, at 259.

13 Charles Pettigrew, 'St. Giles and John Knox. Part I', *The Caledonian* (17April 1917), 25–28, at 25.

In contrast to the Catholic Irish, the Scots were welcomed as model immigrants. Bernard Aspinwall has argued that the Scottish work ethic, alongside their high level of education and strident Protestantism, allowed them to thrive in the United States. Although Scottish exceptionalism has long been debated, statistically at least, Scottish emigrants to the United States possessed relatively higher levels of literacy and had more savings than other migrants.[14] Despite his oft-quoted claim that 'there is no such thing as a hyphenated American who is a good American', Theodore Roosevelt was happy to boast of his mother's line descending from 'a lad from near Glasgow' who like thousands of 'enterprising Scotchmen have gone to the four quarters of the globe'. Roosevelt, like many of New York's Knickerbocker elite, was chauvinistically proud of his 'Holland, Huguenot, and Covenanting ancestors'.[15] For their part, Scots saw America as Protestantism realised; a righteous and godly 'city on a hill' built by the Calvinist doctrines of diligence, discipline, toil, and thrift. While travelling the United States in 1819, the Scottish economist James Flint advised prospective emigrants:

> In exchanging Britain for the United States, the emigrant may reasonably expect to have it in his power to purchase good improved land, and to bring it into a rude state of cultivation, with less capital unquestionably, than that employed in renting an equal proportion of good ground at home. He will not be burdened by an excessive taxation, nor with tithes, nor poor's rates; for there are no internal taxes paid to the government, no privileged clergy, and few people who live by the charity of others. His labour and his capital will be more productive, and his accumulation of property more rapid.[16]

Yet America was more to Scots than a lucrative economic opportunity. By 1854, the Glasgow-based newspaper *Christian News* proffered that 'It was a most favourable ordering of Divine Providence, that Protestantism should gain so extensive and permanent a footing in America, before Rome was permitted to make much effort to spread her pestiferous heresies in that fair land.'[17] Schrag has argued that the origins of American nativism lie in her puritan past. Free from the social and theological shackles of Europe, the pilgrims were faced with a vast nebulous to make a nation of. Limits needed to be put on who was American and who was not, and naturally this was limited to Anglo-Saxon Protestants and a few other

---

14 Bernard Aspinwall, *Portable Utopia Glasgow and the United States 1820–1920* (Aberdeen: Aberdeen University Press, 1984), 2, 251.

15 'Roosevelt Bars the Hyphenated', *New York Times* (13 October 1915), 1; Theodore Roosevelt, *Theodore Roosevelt: An Autobiography* (New York: MacMillan Company, 1913), 2–4.

16 James Flint, *Letters from America : containing observations on the climate and agriculture of the western states, the manners of the people, the prospects of emigrants, &c* (Edinburgh: W. & C. Tait, 1822), 148.

17 'Romanism in America', *Christian News* (7 October 1854), 186.

acceptable groups.[18] Protestantism would ease the differences between English, Scottish, and Dutch colonists to create a cohesive idea of America, which might otherwise be overwhelmed by rival claimants to the New World. Catholics would still be tolerated, but with the assumption they would become more like Protestants if treated reasonably. Despite Scotland's reputation for bigotry, the supposed inclusivity of American Protestantism was not without its admirers. In 1852, the liberal *North British Daily Mail* (an early incarnation of *Daily Record*) argued that 'Popery' had made little progress in America as Catholics had been treated 'kindly, leniently, and equitably'. The article continued 'Such is the thoroughly noble and enlightened spirit in which the American Protestants meet the invasion of Roman Catholic emigrants, which is continually darkening their land. They fill the social atmosphere with rays of light and freedom, and all inimical to these naturally pines and perishes.'[19] Although such attitudes were not uncommon in the 1850s, rapid urbanisation and mass Irish immigration would dilute the Protestant monopoly on the American dream and create a less tolerant attitude towards Catholicism.

The Coming of the Irish

Although native sectarianism needed little encouragement, the hostile reception granted to the Catholic Irish was partially the result of an earlier Irish migration. Prior to the famine, Protestants made up the majority of the Irish emigrants to both Scotland and America and still formed a significant minority amongst the Irish diaspora thereafter. Walker estimates that 25 per cent of Irish immigrants to Scotland between the eighteenth and nineteenth centuries were Protestants, albeit even this may be an undercount.[20] In America the 'Scots Irish', as they came to be known, were celebrated as model immigrants in stark contrast to their Catholic countrymen. In 1939, Henry Noble McCracken, president of Vassar College, was asked to address the Ulster-Irish Society of New York on his people's history. McCracken provided a metanarrative for the Ulster-Scots which intrinsically linked their own story to that of America's manifest destiny. 'Religion, education and government: on all these the Ulster Irish laid strong hands and wrought mightily. But even more significant were the contributions

---

[18] Peter Schrag, *Not Fit for Our Society: Immigration and Nativism in America* (University of California Press, Berkley, Los Angeles, London, 2010), 27–28.

[19] 'Romanism', *North British Daily Mail*, (10 July 1852), 2.

[20] Graham Walker, 'The Protestant Irish in Scotland', in T. M. Devine, ed., *Irish Immigrants and Scottish Society in the Nineteenth and Twentieth Centuries* (Edinburgh: John Donald Ltd., 1991), 63–90, at 68–69.

to industry and invention. No wonder that in his westward trek he stopped to invent the harvester that made the great western farms a reality. His energy was really prodigious. The forests fell, the stumps were pulled, the rivers stemmed.'[21] The reception given to the later Catholic arrivals can in part be explained by the Irish Protestant influence on Scotland and America. As we shall see, in both Glasgow and New York Irish Protestants adapted their sectarian cultural practices in a way that was acceptable to the host society. Although there were always plenty of native Scots willing to fill its ranks, it was Irish Protestants who were the backbone of the Orange Order in Scotland. Kauffman's analysis of Orange Order membership rolls in Scotland between 1860 and 1991 identified a clear geographical correlation with the Protestant Irish diaspora. The percentage of Irish Protestants within a county's population was the strongest indicator of Orange Order membership density, even more so than the number of Catholics.[22]

The influx of thousands of Catholic Irish during the Great Famine would drastically change the reputation of the Irish diaspora in New York and Glasgow. Civic life would be indelibly changed with the arrival of a people whose alienness was at odds with existing social and cultural norms. However, one should be careful of assuming that native responses to the famine Irish were universally hostile. Devine argues that although relief responses in Glasgow were mixed, overall, the Irish were treated little different from Scottish paupers, although this was hardly a great mercy.[23] Nonetheless, it is agreed that there was a hardening of attitudes as the scale of famine migrants increased, putting further pressure on already unstable urban communities. Between 1845 and 1851 some 1.5 million Irish men, women, and children travelled to the United States. The one hundred thousand Irish who came to Scotland were in relative terms small, but for a country of only 2.8 million with no significant Catholic population since the Reformation, it represented a lasting demographic effect which caused major societal changes.[24] By the dawn of the twentieth-first century more than 800,000 Scots, some 16 per cent of the population, were Catholic, not drastically less than the 22 per cent

---

21 Henry Noble MacCracken, 'Address to the Ulster-Irish Society of New York, 1939', in J. J. Lee, and Marion R. Casey, eds., *Making the Irish American History and Heritage of the Irish in the United States* (New York: New York University Press, 2006), 286–288, at 288.

22 Eric Kauffmann, 'The Orange Order Since 1860: A social analysis', in Martin J. Mitchell, ed., *New Perspectives on the Irish in Scotland* (Edinburgh: John Donald, 2008), 157–190, at 170.

23 T. M. Devine, 'The Great Irish Famine and Scottish History', in Martin J. Mitchell, ed., *New Perspectives on the Irish in Scotland* (Edinburgh: John Donald, 2008), 20–30, at 27.

24 Devine, 'The Great Irish Famine and Scottish History', 20.

of Americans who identify as Catholic.[25] New York was the main epicentre of Irish emigration with over a quarter of a million Irish-born residents by 1870. Although the Irish also settled outside of New York, they tended to live in large cities, with 44.5 per cent of the Irish-born population living in America's fifty biggest cities.[26] The transportation of a predominantly rural people to a rapidly expanding urban environment would prove traumatic for both the new arrivals and the host society. Given that the Irish were largely left to fend for themselves, they would create their own self-enclosed social worlds which provided everything from education and social provision to sport and recreation. In Glasgow in particular the Catholic influence on the city's education and charities can still be seen to this day, albeit this has led to accusations of insularity amongst the Catholic community.[27] Aspinwall has gone so far as to describe the social function of the Catholic Church in Glasgow as a 'state within a state'.[28]

More worryingly the very presence of the Irish threatened the dream of a Protestant New World. In his religious survey of America in 1845, the Presbyterian clergyman Robert Baird estimated that there were 1.3 million Roman Catholics in America, most of whom were Irish and German immigrants, or former French and Spanish subjects from the newly acquired territories.[29] Writing in 1855, after a decade of mass Irish immigration, Baird had increased his estimate to over 3 million Catholic Americans. Baird insisted, perhaps for his own peace of mind, that the number of actual communicants was much lower at between 120,000 and 140,000.[30] The increase in the Catholic population tied into wider fears over Irish immigration. Catholic and Irish would become synonymous terms in both Scotland and America, while Protestant invariably meant 'native'. Glasgow and

---

25 T. M. Devine, 'The End of Disadvantage? The descendants of Irish-Catholic immigrants in modern Scotland since 1945', in Martin J. Mitchell, ed., *New Perspectives on the Irish in Scotland*, (Edinburgh: John Donald, 2008), 191–207, at 191; https://www.britannica.com/topic/Roman-Catholicism/Roman-Catholicism-in-the-United-States-and-Canada.

26 Kevin Kenny, *The American Irish: A History* (Pearson Education Ltd: Harlow, 2000), 105.

27 Tom Gallagher, *Glasgow: The Uneasy Peace Religious tension in Modern Scotland* (Manchester: Manchester University Press, 1987), 33.

28 Bernard Aspinwall, 'The welfare state within the state: the Saint Vincent De Paul Society in Glasgow, 1848–1920', *Studies in Church History* 23/1 (1986), 444–59; Bernard Aspinwall, 'The Catholic minority experience in Scotland: the poorhouse view 1850–1914', *Immigrants & Minorities* 31/2 (2013), 127–145.

29 Robert Baird, *Religion in America, or, An account of the origin, progress, relation to the state, and present condition of the evangelical churches in the United States : with notices of the unevangelical denominations* (New York: Harper & Brothers, 1845), 271.

30 Robert Baird, *State and prospects of religion in America: being a report made at the conference of the Evangelical alliance, in Paris, August 25th, 1855* (New York: Robert Carter & Brothers, 1856), 29.

New York possessed large Protestant Irish populations, as well as an ethnically diverse Catholic community, but it was the Catholic Irish who bore the brunt of sectarian and anti-Irish prejudice. Italian Americans, particularly those from the *Mezzogiorno*, experienced similar levels of discrimination to the Catholic Irish and never enjoyed the consolation prize of political influence. Yet anti-Italian sentiment, even at its most vitriolic, rarely used the language of sectarianism. Indeed, Protestant missionaries often regarded Italians as hopeful targets for conversion, whereas the Catholic Irish seemed wholly irredeemable.[31] Likewise, Scottish Italians, alongside other predominantly Catholic ethnic minorities such as Poles and Lithuanians, were rarely victimised by Scotland's culture of sectarianism.[32]

Unlike, Irish Protestants who were usually well received, the Catholics who arrived during the famine years were seen as a social problem and drain on civic resources. In Glasgow, in the winter of 1847 an estimated 49,993 destitute Irish arrived at the Broomielaw, with one soup kitchen in St Enoch's square feeding 4,000 to 5,000 immigrants per week.[33] *Glasgow Herald* complained in 1849 that 'Irish pauperism costs £30,000 p.a. irrespective of disease, degradation, and crime, which are constant attendants of these people.'[34] Similar tales could be found in New York, as lacking the support networks of friends and family, destitute Irish immigrants quickly crowded the city's public institutions. Between 1849 and 1859 three-fourths of foreign-born patients at Blackwell Island Insane Asylum were foreign-born, two-thirds of which were Irish.[35] Yet the resentment towards the famine Irish went beyond mere concerns over public money. Rather than victims fleeing starvation, the Catholic Irish were cast as slavish adherents of Rome sent to destroy America. L. W. Granger, a vocal Know Nothing activist, directed his vitriol at the Catholic Irish in 1851 thus:

> With this tide of immigration, rolls on in rapid succession, battalions of Romish Priests, to first plant upon our soil, its accursed institution. In the larger cities of the Union, they fill our jails, poor-houses and prisons, and sow among us the seeds of death in its vilest forms. They are told, (through their Clergy,) that they must not be content with

31 Philip S. Rose, *The Italians in America*, (New York: George H. Doran Company, 1922), 42, Enrico Sartorio, *The Social and Religious Life of Italians in America*, (Boston: Christopher Publishing House, 1918), 103–104.

32 Kay Goodall, Peter Hopkins, Simon McKerrell, John Markey, Stephen Millar, John Richardson, Michael Richardson, *Community Experiences of Sectarianism* (Edinburgh: Scottish Government Social Research, 2015), 25.

33 Devine, 'The Great Irish Famine and Scottish History', 25–26.

34 'Irish Treatment of Irish Paupers', *Glasgow Herald* (19 March 1849), 2.

35 Alan M. Kraut, 'Illness and Medical Care among Irish Immigrants to Antebellum New York', in Ronald H. Bayor and Timothy J. Meagher, eds., *The New York Irish* (Baltimore: John Hopkins University Press, 1996), 153–168, at 159.

> the security the laws guarantee to them in America, but that they must wage a ceaseless warfare with their institutions if they refuse to give them a due proportion of all public moneys calculated to advance their interest and religion.[36]

Although Granger's view undoubtedly represented the extreme end of the spectrum, New York and Glasgow's experience of the famine created a lasting impression of the Catholic Irish. In the face of inadequate social provision, which was no better equipped to aid natives, it was easier to blame the Catholic Irish for their situation. The memory of the famine generation would become the basis for sectarian and anti-Irish bigotry throughout the nineteenth century.

Why the Catholic Irish attracted such a hostile reaction, as well as the longevity of this peculiar Scottish prejudice, has long been debated. Ewen Cameron argues that historians have tended to view the discrimination directed at the Irish in Scotland as more religious than racial in character.[37] Gallagher has suggested that the lack of a distinct Scottish ethnic identity, due to a prevailing sense of Britishness, lessened racial prejudice against the Irish in Scotland.[38] Indeed British historians such as Sheridan Gilley, tend to congratulate the British for never succumbing to the sort of visceral racism which characterised nineteenth-century America.[39] In contrast, Finn states that sectarianism in Scotland is intrinsically tied to nineteenth-century ideas regarding race, with the Catholicism of the Irish being cited as evidence of racial degeneracy. The belief in Scottish egalitarianism, as well as our 'colour-coded' understanding of race, has disguised the racialisation of the Irish.[40] The animosity of nineteenth-century Scots towards the Catholic Irish was rooted in a self-consciousness regarding their own Celtic origins. In one letter to the *National Observer* in 1895 the writer complained that in their efforts to denigrate Irish Home Rule, the English made unfair generalisations about all Celtic people. The writer compared Lord Salisbury's 'characteristic disquisition on the Celtic fringe' with the attitude of Governor Ben Tillman of South Carolina towards Black voters. Albeit Tillman was a white supremacist and self-confessed lyncher, the writer continued, 'The Celtic "Macs" of Scotland

---

36 L. W. Granger, *Wide-awake! Romanism: its aims and tendencies. The sentiments of a 'Know-nothing'* (Detroit: Published by the Proprietor, 1854), 14.

37 Ewen Cameron, *Impaled Upon a Thistle: Scotland since 1880* (Edinburgh: Edinburgh University Press, 2010), 137.

38 Gallagher, *Glasgow: The Uneasy Peace*, 34.

39 Kevin Kenny, 'Race, Violence, and Anti-Irish Sentiment in the Nineteenth Century', in J. J. Lee and Marion R. Casey, eds., *Making the Irish American History and Heritage of the Irish in the United States* (New York: New York University Press, 2006), 364–378, 368–369.

40 Gerry P. T. Finn, 'A Culture of Prejudice: Promoting Pluralism in Education for a Change', in T. M. Devine, ed., *Scotland' Shame? Bigotry and Sectarianism in Modern Scotland* (Edinburgh and London: Mainstream Publishing, 2000), 53–88, at 54–56.

swarm in every colony and are among the most successful wherever you go. But all this does not stop the average English journalist from keeping as part of his stock in trade the customary generalisations about the "indolent" and "impossible" Celt'.[41] *Glasgow Courier* proffered in 1851, that 'To say that the Celtic race must be ill-conditioned, revengeful, and miserable, is indeed harsh and unnecessary; but no one can deny that had the native Irish been as orderly, as submissive, as averse to bloodshed, and as incapable of conspiracy as the English, it would not be long Eire be as comfortable and happy.'[42] Kidd argues that as scientific racism began to take hold, Scots attempted to cast off their Celtic origins in favour of a more Anglo-Saxon inheritance. Some Lowland Scots even went so far as to claim that their genetic inheritance was more Germanic than that of the English.[43] Writing from Glasgow in 1899, 'Gothic Gael' insisted that 'The so-called Scots of Ireland never conquered Scotland. Therefore, I conclude the primitive Gothic element preponderates all over Scotland.' The anonymous writer went on to appropriate pseudo-scientific arguments to prove that the Scots were even more Germanic than their English neighbours. 'The heads of the Scotch, taking Scotland all over, have much more the oval Gothic shape about them than the Saxon English, who have a much more rounded shape.'[44] Given the dubiousness of attempts to categorise the Irish as racially separate from Scots and Americans, emphasising their Catholicism was useful way to mark them as different.

In so stratified a society as the nineteenth-century American city, the Catholic Irish transcended accepted hierarchies, as they could not easily be excluded by the traditional markers of ethnicity. African Americans and East Asians were easily identifiable by their non-white appearance; Italians, Hispanics, Jews, and Slavs by their respective languages and obviously foreign cultures. Surnames could also be used to identify outsiders who might try to 'pass' within a generation or so, hence the tendency to Anglicise foreign sounding names. All of these methods of exclusion were less effective in othering the Irish. The Catholic Irish were little different from other northern Europeans and were more upwardly mobile than other minorities. In Scotland the ambiguity of the Irish was compounded by the fact that many Celtic family names were not denominationally exclusive. James E. Handley suggests that one would be surprised to 'scan at random the school registers and learn thereby the proportion of Protestant Ryans and Regans

---

41 'F.J.', 'Saxon and Scot', *National Observer* (23 November 1895), 51–52.

42 'The Late Murder in Ireland', *Glasgow Courier* (17 December 1851), 6.

43 Colin Kidd, 'Race, Empire, and the Limits of Nineteenth-Century Scottish Nationhood', *The Historical Journal* 46/4 (2003), 873–892.

44 'Gothic Gael', 'Letter to the Editor', *Highland News* (7 October 1899), 9.

and Catholic Robertsons and Ritchies'.[45] The Catholic Irish then represented a more subversive threat than other immigrant groups as they were scarcely different from other northern Europeans, thereby challenging notions of racial superiority. The Catholic Irish would need to be firmly differentiated from the native white ascendancy if the ideal of Protestant America was to be preserved. With respect to New York, Gorn argues that the threat to native privilege posed by rapid urbanisation, falling wages, and the deskilling of jobs resulted in an aggressive form of working-class masculinity.[46] Nativist street gangs such as the Atlantic Guards, the Plug Uglies, and most notably, the Bowery Boys defended the privileges of true-born Americans with violence and intimidation. From this culture of street sectarianism developed oath bound anti-Catholic fraternal societies such as the Loyal Orange Institution of the United States, the Order of the Star Spangled Banner, and the Junior Order of United American Mechanics. In turn these oath bound societies would remerge as overtly political movements. The Order of the Star Spangled Banner would evolve into the Know Nothings and their political wing the Native American Party.[47] The American Protective Association (APA) would develop from the American Orange Order, although the lines between the two were often blurred.[48]

From the mid-1830s onwards, Romanism was presented as the antithesis of the American way of life and the Irish its unquestioning foot-soldiers. New York was thought to be particularly vulnerable to the Catholic onslaught given the extent of Irish political power in the city. The inventor and painter Samuel Morse was one of the first to warn of the dangers of Catholic political power. Under the nom de plume 'Brutus', Morse constructed a sweeping Catholic conspiracy against the United States involving Austria, Prince Metternich, the Papacy, and the Jesuits.[49] The following year Morse would run for mayor of New York on a Native American ticket, the political arm of the Know Nothings, but would come last with only 1,490 votes.[50] Although Morse was an eccentric who fell on the paranoid fringe of anti-Catholic prejudice, even moderates found it difficult

45 Handley, *The Irish in Modern Scotland*, 325.

46 Elliot J. Gorn, 'Good-Bye Boys, I Die a True American': Homicide, Nativism, and Working-Class. Culture in Antebellum New York City', *The Journal of American History* 74/2 (1987), 388–410.

47 Sabrina P. Ramet, and Christine M. Hassenstab, 'The Know Nothing Party: Three Theories about its Rise and Demise', *Politics and Religion* 6/3 (2013), 570–595, at 571.

48 W. J. H. Traynor, 'Policy and Power of the A.P.A', *The North American Review* 162/475 (1896), 658–666.

49 Brutus, *Foreign Conspiracy Against the Liberties of the United States* (New York: Leavitt Lord & Co, 1835).

50 Louis Dow Scisco, *Political Nativism in New York State*, (Ams Press: New York, 1968), 29.

to reconcile Catholicism with American values. Robert Baird, a Presbyterian clergyman, was more conciliatory towards individual Catholics but not their Church and clergy. Writing in 1844, Baird countered the 'assertion that has often been made by the opponents of the Roman Catholics in United States, that they can never be safe citizens of the republic, and the predominance of the church would overthrow our political constitution'. Baird pointed out that there were many patriotic Catholic Americans, and it was only the Catholic clergy who hated 'republican institutions'.[51] Despite their views Morse and Baird were not pariahs excluded from intellectual life, indeed both were elected to the American Philosophical Society in 1848.[52] Although sectarianism was more proletarian in Glasgow, anti-Catholicism was not entirely absent from the city's intellectual elites. In 1850, Sir Archibald Alison the younger used his inaugural speech as Lord Rector of the University of Glasgow to address the intolerance of the Catholic Church.[53] Indeed it was not until after the Second World War that Irish Catholics attended the university in large numbers, with the number of Catholic students trebling between the mid-1950s and early 1970s.[54] One of the most visceral opponents of the Catholic Church in America was the *Methodist Review*, edited by the theologian and anti-slavery campaigner John McClintock. The review's diatribes against Catholicism went beyond mere ecclesiastical debates, with regular articles attacking the creeping threat of Romanism. In 1855, the review reproduced an article by the Huguenot evangelical Napoleon Roussel comparing criminal statistics in Protestant and Catholic nations. The review passed judgement that Roman Catholicism was the foremost enemy of progressivism and good government:

> The sum of all knowledge is acquaintance with God and his works; and the sum of all virtue, because of all the commandments, is love to God and our neighbour. And as from these all good springs, it follows that whatever country has most of them must be most prosperous, exalted and happy. Now, will any person deny that the great scheme carried out by the Catholic priesthood has been precisely the reverse of the principles we have just now stated?[55]

The writer then defended Protestant ascendancy, asking their readers to 'Look at Ireland as compared to Scotland, look at the United States compared with South

51 Baird, *Religion in America*, 271.
52 https://search.amphilsoc.org/memhist/search?year=1848;year-max=1848;smode=advanced;startDoc=1
53 James E. Handley, *The Irish in Modern Scotland* (Cork: Cork University Press, 1947), 94.
54 Gallagher, *Glasgow: The Uneasy Peace*, 240.
55 Napoleon Rousel, 'The Relations of Romanism and Protestantism to Civilisation', *Methodist Quarterly Review* XXXVIII/July (1855), 408–418, at 415–417.

America, look at Belgium compared with Holland.'[56] The inclusion of South America in this comparative list demonstrates the interaction between sectarianism and American colonial thought. America's Protestant mission was easily incorporated into the ideologies of Manifest Destiny and the Monroe Doctrine. Guardino argues that the Mexican-American War (1846–48) saw anti-Catholicism implemented to justify American expansionism in the south-west.[57] As America's ascendancy as a major power became increasingly tied to the Protestant cause, it was easy and useful to portray Catholics as a dangerous fifth column. Writing in the *New York Tribune* in 1886 the Rev John Lee claimed, 'That the Papal Syllabus – which every Roman Catholic is required to believe-condemns the teachings of the Constitution of the United States, no intelligent Romanist can deny.' In an attempt to prove Catholic treachery, the reverend cited a letter from Pope Pius IX to Jefferson Davis offering 'perfect friendship' to the Confederate president.[58]

The Politics of Sectarianism

Despite the similarities between the Irish experience in New York and Glasgow, politics was one area of divergence. In New York the Catholic Irish quickly ingratiated themselves into the Democratic party-political machine, whereas Glasgow's Irish struggled to gain a foothold in local politics until after the First World War. In both cities' sectarianism was a defining factor in local politics, exasperating existing political issues while also hindering attempts at co-operation between competing interest groups. Given some of the stereotypes surrounding the Irish, New York's political scene typified by its factionalism, rowdiness, and abundant use of violence, was one of the few areas where the new arrivals were readily accepted. Anbinder notes that the Catholic Irish's first foray into politics was within the notorious Five Points neighbourhood, were they quickly gained control of the area's saloons, grocery stores, and fire department. The success of local politicians was largely dependent on their effective use of violence on election days, either by intimidating voters to make the right decision or by fighting off the supporters of other candidates.[59] Given the prevalence of faction fighting in rural nineteenth-century Ireland, emigrants would be more than

---

56 Ibid., 417.

57 Peter Guardino, '"In the Name of Civilization and with a Bible in Their Hands:" Religion and the 1846–48 Mexican-American War', *Mexican Studies/Estudios Mexicanos* 30/2 (2014), 342–365.

58 John Lee, *Religious Persecution. An Examination of Cardinal Manning's Letter in the New York Tribune, July 3, 1886* (Chicago: Cranston & Stowe, 1887), 8, 81–83.

59 Tyler Anbinder, "We Will Dirk Every Mother's Son of You": Five Points and the Irish Conquest of New York Politics', in Kevin Kenny, ed., *New Directions in Irish-American History* (University of Wisconsin Press: Madison, 2003), 105–122.

capable of holding their own in the rough and tumble of New York politics. The ability of the Irish political bosses to mobilise their voters effectively made them kingmakers during local elections. While touring North America in the 1850s, Scottish author Charles Mackay made the likely apocryphal claim that 'during hot election contests in the State or the municipality of New York, when the whole male immigration, landed in the morning from a Cork of Liverpool vessel, has voted ere the afternoon for one "ticket" or the other.'[60]

As early as the 1850s, the Catholic Irish were seen as the harbingers of the jobbery and corruption that afflicted New York politics. Tammany Hall, the great centre of New York's Democratic political machine, was accused of being under undue Irish influence.[61] The Angus-born geologist Sir Charles Lyell never failed to encounter anecdotal evidence of Irish venality during his travels in America. According to Lyell, the corruptibility of Irish voters was blamed for everything from Henry Clay's latest failed presidential bid to the inability of the municipal authorities to remove pigs from the streets of New York.[62] Although the Irish infiltration of New York's political scene offered many advantages, it also fuelled further resentment against the community, with a common accusation being that the Irish held a disproportionate amount of influence. In reality, the Irish were just one interest group within the well-oiled political machine that was Tammany Hall. The low socio-economic position of the Catholic Irish meant their votes could be more easily bought, with Tammany's patronage of plum municipal jobs being particularly enticing. MacRaild has argued that the factionalism of migrants, as well as the ease at which they could be influenced, made the Catholic Irish easy targets for New York's political bosses. Macraild estimates that in the 1860s the Tweed ring provided 754 jobs to the Irish political lobby. Despite being more numerous than the Irish, New York's German community could only squeeze fifty or so positions from the Tammany patronage machine.[63] The Catholic Irish also had no choice but to engage in underhand political tactics to survive such a hostile environment. Hirota has argued that the mobilisation of the Irish vote was so effective it prevented legislators from enacting anti-immigration laws despite strong nativist demands to do so.[64]

---

60 Charles Mackay, *Life in America: or Sketches of a Tour of the United States and Canada in 1857–8 Vol 1* (London: Smith Elder & Co., 1859), 178.

61 Oliver E. Allen, *The Tiger: The Rise and Fall of Tammany Hall* (Addison-Wesley Publishing Company: New York, 1993), 83

62 Charles Lyell, *A Second Visit to the United States of North America Vol 1* (New York: Harper & Brothers Publishers, London: John Murray, 1849), 189–190.

63 Donald M. MacRaild, 'Crossing migrant frontiers: Comparative reflections on Irish migrants in Britain and the United States during the nineteenth century', *Immigrants & Minorities* 18/2–3, (1999), 40–70, at 56, 61.

64 Hirota, 'Limits of intolerance.'

For old stock Protestants, the success of the Catholic Irish in local politics was an affront to their long-held monopoly on power. It was during his first term in the New York Assembly that Theodore Roosevelt first encountered the Irish political machine. Roosevelt confided to his diary 'There are some twenty-five Irish Democrats in the house, all either immigrants or sons of emigrants, coming almost entirely from the great cities-New York, Brooklyn, Albany, Buffaloe. They are a stupid, sodden vicious lot, most of them equally deficient in brains and virtue.' He continued that the 'average Catholic Irishman of the first generation as represented in this Assembly, is a low, venal, corrupt and unintelligent brute.'[65] The Glasgow press relished the opportunity to report on the corruption and political skulduggery of Tammany Hall in contrast to their own city's conscientious administration. In 1887, *Greenock Telegraph* reported that over the preceding decade Tammany Hall had gifted the Catholic Church real estate worth three and a half million dollars and a further six million in cash.[66] By 1897, *Daily Record* could smugly comment that 'The interest with which the New York Mayoralty contest is being watched in this country is sterling proof, if such be wanted, of the influence of good government on the masses.'[67]

Unlike their counterparts on the other side of the Atlantic, Glasgow's Catholic Irish never enjoyed the same levels of influence over local politics. Although native sectarianism no doubt played a part in the political alienation of the Catholic Irish, there were other factors that inhibited organisation. For most of the nineteenth century, the Catholic Church in Scotland did not actively encourage political engagement and seemed content to 'render unto Caeser'. This would change in the social convulsions of the later nineteenth century which forced the Church to address temporal matters. Pope Leo XII's encyclical *Rerum Novarum*, although condemnatory of socialism, addressed the issues faced by the working class and supported the rights of workers to organise trade unions. Gilley has argued that Leo XII's critique of socialism was aimed at the revolutionary and anti-clerical variety found on the continent. British socialism, however, could be more easily melded with Christian values thus allowing an avenue for Catholic involvement.[68] Organising Glasgow's Catholic Irish into a coherent voting block proved much harder than on the other side of the Atlantic. By 1883, Glasgow's three hundred strong Jewish community already had a councillor. The Irish would

65 Theodore Roosevelt, *A Most Glorius Ride: The Diaries of Theodore Roosevelt 1877–1886*, Edward P. Kohn, ed., (Albany: State University of New York Press, 2015), 213.

66 'The Secret of Dr McGlynn's Persecution', *Greenock Telegraph and Clyde Shipping Gazette* (22 August 1887), 2.

67 'Tammany on Trial', Daily Record(1 November 1897), 4.

68 Sheridan Gilley, 'Catholics and Socialists in Scotland', in Roger Swift and Sheridan Gilley, eds., *The Irish in Britain: 1851–1939*(Pinter Publishers: London, 1989), 212–238, at 212–213.

have to wait another decade before one of their own was elected to the council, and even then, they would have to settle for a Protestant Ulsterman, who was at least a Home Ruler.[69] This is not to say that comparisons were entirely lacking. As in New York, a common accusation towards the Catholic Irish was their lack of class consciousness and perceived political slavishness. MacRaild has argued that as the diaspora in Britain had better links to Ireland than their American cousins, they focused on the much bigger prize of Home Rule as opposed to making a foothold in local politics. Although this made the Irish natural allies of Gladstonian Liberals, it also alienated them from the rising labour movement.[70] The early electoral failures of the Scottish Labour Party, such as Keir Hardie's defeat in the 1888 Mid-Lanarkshire by-election, were blamed on the Catholic Irish voting Liberal. Irish nationalism may have been at the forefront of diaspora politics, but the Catholic Irish electorate was too small to seriously hinder labour. To take the example of the 1888 by-election, even if the constituency's entire Irish electorate had voted Labour Hardie would still have placed last.[71] Many urban working-class men did not have the vote in Britain until the Representation of the People Act 1918, meaning the Catholic Irish vote was of little consequence. The Irish in New York were a more effective voting block as the franchise was less restrictive even by American standards. Prior to mass Irish immigration, New York had already dropped property requirements for white male voters in 1821.[72] The relative absence of anti-Catholicism amongst Glasgow's elites compared with its prevalence amongst New York's upper-class, can in part be explained by the Irish diaspora in Scotland never forming a serious challenge to the political status quo.

Orangeism

Ulster migrants, both Catholic and Protestant, brought with them the religious schisms which had divided them at home. This included the various folkish manifestations of sectarianism adopted by both communities, such as ribbonism and other secret societies. Ironically, the Orange Order would become one of Ireland's first cultural exports, with lodges being founded not only in Scotland and America, but also England, Canada, Australia, New Zealand, and South Africa.[73]

---

[69] Gallagher, *Glasgow: The Uneasy Peace*, 62.

[70] MacRaild, 'Crossing migrant frontiers', 63.

[71] J. J. Smyth, *Labour in Glasgow, 1896–1936: Socialism, Suffrage, Sectarianism* (Edinburgh: Birlinn Ltd, 2000), 186, 194.

[72] Hirota, 'Limits of intolerance', 3777.

[73] *Report of the Proceedings of Thirteenth Triennial Session of the Grand Orange Council of the Loyal Orange Association of the World, Held in the City of Dublin, Ireland, July 15*th *and 16*th *1903* (Glasgow: Office of the Imperial Grand Secretary, 1903), 10.

By the 1900s, the global presence of the order lead to the Imperial Grand Orange Council issuing travel certificates which permitted members entry to other lodges around the world.[74] In both New York and Glasgow, Orangeism crystallised impulsive bouts of native anti-Catholicism into a more definable cultural and political programme. After its foundation in Ireland in 1795, the Orange Order already had a presence in New York by the 1820s.[75] One encyclopaedia of American fraternities estimated that by the end of the nineteenth century, the Loyal Orange Institution had around one hundred thousand members across the United States.[76] The order adopted the rituals of already well-established fraternities such as the freemasons, indeed, the lines between New York's masonic and Orange lodges were often blurred. Despite its name, the Prince of Orange No.16, New York City, was a masonic lodge.[77] The Orange Institution drew together the various sporadic forms of popular anti-Catholicism in New York into a more cohesive outlet. Orangeism also brought its own heritage, institutions, and organisational structure, thereby elevating bigotry to legitimate cultural expression.

By the 1870s the annual 12th of July parades in New York were becoming more violent. During the American Civil War, the Draft Riots of 1863 had saw predominantly Irish rioters burn down public buildings, two Protestant churches, and the Colored Orphan Asylum. The legacy of these earlier riots created a less tolerant attitude towards public disorder, especially when it was the Irish who were seen as the instigators. MacRaild has argued that even into the 1840s African Americans and the Irish co-existed and even intermarried in New York's Sixth Ward. These two marginalised groups would not, however, unite to find common cause. Conservative Catholics, such as Archbishop John Hughes, viewed closer ties with African Americans as a hinderance to their own attempts elevate their community's social standing. On the slavery issue Irish Catholics were at best ambivalent and at worst fearful that free Blacks would be unwelcome competitors in the labour market.[78] Where exactly the Catholic Irish stood within America remained unresolved even after the Civil War. Antebellum New York would become a battleground between Catholic and Protestant Irish over which community could more convincingly call themselves American.

---

74 Ibid., I.

75 Michael A. Gordon, *The Orange Riots: Irish Political Violence in New York, 1870 and 1871* (Ithaca and London: Cornell University Press, 2009), 22.

76 Albert C. Steven, *The Cyclopaedia of Fraternities,* (New York: E. B. Treat and Company, 1907), 91.

77 Stephen H. Tyng, *Address at the Installation of Officers of Prince of Orange No.16, New York City, December 29, A.L. 5866* (New York: Baldwin and Jones Printers, 1867).

78 MacRaild, 'Crossing migrant frontiers', 50.

In 1870, matters came to a head when Catholic Irish protestors attacked a picnic organised by the Orangemen following their parade. Gordon has estimated that eight people were killed in the 1870 riots, with a further fifteen confirmed injuries, but only six arrests.[79] The 1870, incident would be a mere pre-cursor to the violence that occurred the following year. In 1871, Tammany Hall banned the Orangemen from marching to prevent further disorder but later backtracked. Good government reformers were putting increasing pressure on Boss Tweed and there were accusations that the ban was pandering to the Irish. The riots occurred in the wake of the Paris Commune a few months earlier and elite New Yorkers were incensed that Tammany had surrendered to mob rule. The Orangemen would be allowed to march but under a heavy escort of police and militiamen. The Orange parade was met by hundreds of counter-protestors organised and drilled by the Ancient Order of Hibernians.[80] Following reports of gunshots the troops panicked and shot into the crowd and surrounding buildings. When the smoke cleared over one hundred and sixty civilians had been killed, alongside three soldiers, and two police.[81] The city police and militia did at least achieve their aim of protecting the Orangemen, as only one of their ranks appears to have been injured.[82]

The prevailing attitude amongst New York's press is interesting in that they viewed the rioting as essentially an Irish problem as opposed to a solely Catholic one. Within this context of a nation still mending the wounds of the Civil War, neither the Protestant Orangemen nor their Catholic Irish opponents seemed particularly American. One political cartoon which captured the public mood portrayed a disapproving Lady Liberty commanding Orange and Green rioters to 'Fold those rags! I'll have but one flag here.'[83] Despite a few lapses of sensationalism, the *Sun* had the foresight to mollify the inflammatory situation, reiterating that not all Irish Catholics were culpable for the disorder that occurred. One day after the riot the paper reminded its readers that Archbishop McCloskey and the rest of the Catholic clergy had 'denounced and forbidden' any attempt at stopping the parades by force. The rioters were merely 'grog shop and bar-room ruffians, men with no religion or principles of any kind'. As noble as the newspapers efforts were, the *Sun* was perhaps overly optimistic in their claim that 'We do not doubt that the Irish Catholics of this city would,

---

[79] Gordon, *The Orange Riots*, 121–123.

[80] Edwin G. Burrows and Mike Wallace, *Gotham: A History of New York to 1898*, (Oxford University Press: New York, 1999), 1003–1005.

[81] Gordon, *The Orange Riots*, 225–229.

[82] Burrows and Wallace, *Gotham*, 1008.

[83] Gordon, *The Orange Riots*, 162.

if necessary, turn out under arms to defend the right of Orangemen to walk through the streets with their banners and music.'[84] *New York Herald* had a reputation for non-partisan reporting, but its tendency towards melodrama often made immigrants an easy target. True to form the paper favoured neither the Orange nor the Green but instead framed the riots as conflict between the Irish and ignoring native anti-Catholicism. An article published five days after the 1871 riots stated 'that in every large city in the world where Irishman of the opposite creed do congregate peace is disturbed, property is imperilled, life is endangered once a year. This is true in Belfast and Dublin. It is true in Glasgow and Liverpool. It is true in New York, in Boston, in Chicago, in Saint Louis, in San Francisco. It is not less true in one less whit in Melbourne and Sydney.' In apparent exasperation the writer pleaded ignorance claiming that 'The secret of this antagonism we do not pretend to know.'[85] The *Herald's* stance was interpreted by the Irish as anti-Catholic resulting in one of the more humorous responses to the Orange Riots. The paper's editor, James Gordon Bennett Junior, was portrayed in a cartoon featured in *Irish World* as leading a march of simian-like Orangemen. Bennett was lampooned wearing a kilt and tam o'shanter while playing the bagpipes, a reference to his family's Scottish origins.[86] Ironically Bennett Senior, the *Herald's* founder, had been born in Banff, and not uncommon for that region, was a Roman Catholic.[87]

Those who sought to defend the Orangemen placed the parades within wider debates over freedom of speech and the right to free assembly. Rev. Hugh Smith Carpenter of Westminster Presbyterian Church sermonised to the Brooklyn Polytechnic Institute 'You are all aware that the matter of immediate issue on 12th of July, was the bare right of procession, the simple freedom of festive celebration.' Carpenter elaborated that 'Free song is a style of free speech. Free step is comprehended in free agency. A free banner with its devices and mottoes, is unquestionably no more invidious, than a free newspaper.' Carpenter was careful to draw a distinction between Catholicism and what he termed Romanism, even going so far as to say that it was better to be a good 'Papist' than a bad Protestant. Carpenter nonetheless drew upon common fears of the Catholic Irish, deriding them as venal savages. 'This large band of ruthless, heartless, and imbruted Celts,

84 'Deep Wrong to the Catholic Irish', *Sun*, (13 July 1871), 2.

85 'Religious and Political Reforms-Progress and Triumph of Popular Ideas', *New York Herald* (17 July 1871), 4.

86 Gordon, *The Orange Riots*.

87 James L. Crouthamel, *Bennett's New York Herald and the Rise of the Popular Press* (New York: Syracuse University Press, 1989), 4.

must no longer be bought by party politics, nor as an organic nucleus, a separate nationality, kept in untamed bands like tribes of Indians.'[88] J. T. Headley, variously a Presbyterian clergyman, historian, Know Nothing, and former New York Secretary of State, framed the decision to ban the Orange parades as intolerant and un-American. 'Processions of all kinds and nationalities were allowed on the streets, and to forbid only one, and that because it was *Protestant*, was an insult to every American citizen.'[89]

At the heart of the debate over the Orange parades was the battle over which Irish tradition could most convincingly claim the mantle of patriotism. During the nineteenth century, it became a popular belief that the Ulster-Scots were 'to a man' on the side of the patriots during the American Revolution. This belief although undoubtedly exaggerated was not entirely inaccurate, with even George III subscribing to the belief that the revolution was 'a Presbyterian war'.[90] Nonetheless, it was difficult to bridge the gap between Orangeism and modern American patriotism. In the wake of the Fenian Raids of the 1870s, the Canadian lodges refined the previously malleable definition of Protestant loyalism to a more definite commitment to the British Empire. The *Constitution and laws of the Loyal Orange Association of British America* (1878) stated that 'In short the Orange Constitution, like a glorious moral luminary, intended to pour its refulgence, not one part only of the ample circumference of the British Dominions, but simultaneously on every portion, equally enlightening the whole periphery.'[91] One year later the Loyal Orange Association implemented an opening prayer to be used by all Canadian lodges which gave homage to Queen Victoria and the preservation of her realms.[92] A book of Orange songs and toasts published in

88 Hugh Smith Carpenter, *Understanding of the Times: A Sermon in Relation to the Recent Riot, preached by Rev. Hugh Smith Carpenter at the Polytechnic Institute, Brooklyn, Sunday Evening July 16, 1871* (Brooklyn: Eagle Print, 1871), 8, 16, 19.

89 J. T. Handley, *The Great Riots of New York, 1712 to 1873: Including a full account of the Four Days' Draft Riot of 1863* (New York: Charles Scribner & Co, 1873), 294.

90 James G. Leyburn, 'Presbyterian Immigrants in the American Revolution', *Journal of Presbyterian History* 54/1 (1976), 9–32, at 24.

91 Loyal Orange Association of British North America, *The Constitution and laws of the Loyal Orange Association of British America* (Belleville: Loyal Association of British America, 1878), 4.

92 Loyal Orange Association of British North America, *Forms to Observed in Private Lodges of the Loyal Orange Association of British America* (Ottawa: Loyal Association of British America, 1879), 5.

Toronto in the 1850s featured several anti-American verses. One of which, *The Flaunting Flag of Liberty* included the lines:

United States! your banner wears
Two emblems: one of fame;
Alas! the other that it bears
Reminds us of your shame!
The white man's liberty in types,
Stands emblazoned by your stars;
But what's the meaning of the stripes?
They mean the Negroes' scars.[93]

This created obvious problems for the American lodges, as how could one be simultaneously loyal to the British crown and the American republic? A short history of the Orange Order published in America and Canada in 1898 addressed this very paradox. The anonymous historian included the caveat that 'the obligation taken in the United States is of course one of unswerving loyalty to that country, and there are no more loyal and law-abiding people within the Union than the Orangemen, who in the dark days of the rebellion and in other times of trouble, fought and died like heroes for the Star-Spangled Banner.'[94] During the 1871 riots it was reported that the Orangemen had saluted the statue of George Washington on Fifth Avenue, while the band playing the *Star Spangled Banner.*[95] When the Belfast Member of Parliament, William Johnston, addressed New York's Orangemen one year after the riots he endorsed their claim to be loyal Americans. Johnston stated, 'It had been alleged against the Orangemen living in the United States that they were a British faction established in the midst of a republic.' He continued that 'If that was so he would not be here tonight. He would not encourage Orangemen, Protestants, to be disloyal to the constitution which sheltered and protected them.'[96] In 1889, the American Order asked its members to join New York's civic parade for the bicentennial of Washington's inauguration.[97] Orangemen were also present during a parade in Philadelphia in 1879 during a visit from Ulyesses S. Grant, and again during the inaugural

93 William Shannon, *The United Empire Minstrel, A Selection of the Best National, Constitutional, and Loyal Orange Songs and Poems* (Toronto: Henry Rowsell, 1852), 13.
94 *The History of the Orange Order* (William Banks: Toronto, 1898), 39.
95 'The Hibernian Mob', *Sun* (13 July 1871), 2.
96 'Johnston, of Ballykilbeg', *New York Herald* (13 August 1872), 10.
97 'Meetings', *World* (29 April 1889), 4.

memorial parade for the deceased president at New York in 1897.[98] The Great Reproachment between the United States and Britain towards the end of the century may have given the American Orangemen an easier time. America's triumph over Catholic Spain during the Spanish-American War was reported to be well received by Canadian Orangemen.[99] Perkins has argued that Britain welcomed America's arrival to the imperial table, viewing her ascension as a validation of Anglo-Saxon superiority.[100] The Loyal Orange Lodge of the United States actively portrayed themselves as a fraternal society for respectable patriotic Americans. An advert published in *American* in 1894 sought to correct 'the false impression that enemies are conveying in the minds of men who are unacquainted with Orange principles'. The advert stated that they were a fraternal society who promoted 'frugality and industry'. The order supported its members as well as their dependents, and as a result, 'Orangemen seldom become a public charge or seldom accept pauper bread.' Prospective members were expected to be of Protestant stock, sound health, and law-abiding.[101]

Following the 1870 riots the Orange Order in America tried to exert their influence in more subtle means. The American Protective Association was founded in 1887 as an anti-Catholic secret society with alleged ties to the Orange Order. W. J. H. Traynor, the leader of the APA during the 1890s, denied that there was a strong Orange influence, admitting that only one of the founding members had been an Orangeman. Traynor may have been a referring to himself as he was a Supreme Grand Master in the Order.[102] Scisco has suggested that the APA's membership in New York was predominantly Protestant Irish, suggesting the likely possibility of an Orange connection.[103] By the 1890s the American lodges had adopted a more explicitly nativist stance. Orangemen were required to be American citizens, while it was official lodge policy that immigration should be restricted, and the period of naturalisation extended.[104] American labour organisers feared that the APA was being used as a cat's-paw to divide the working class. Eugene V. Debs, who would later run for president five times under a socialist

98 'Grant', *New York Herald* (17 December 1879), 3; 'To Give the City the Tomb', *Sun*(22 April 1897), 5.

99 R. S. Pennefather, *The Orange and the Black: Documents in the History of The Orange Order Ontario and the West 1890–1940* (Toronto: Orange and Black Publications, 1984), 3–4.

100 Bradford Perkins, *The Great Rapprochement; England and the United States, 1895–1914*, (Atheneum: New York, 1968), 87.

101 'Loyal Orange Institution', *American* (14 September 1894), 6.

102 Traynor, 'Policy and Power of the A.P.A', 660; 'Not so Many Fools', *Buffalo Courier Express* (9 June 1892), 4.

103 Scisco, *Political Nativism in New York State*, 68.

104 'Loyal Orange Institution', *American* (14 September 1894), 6.

ticket, went so far as to publish a warning against the APA in 1894. Debs, who was himself of Huguenot stock, charged the APA with trying to destroy organised labour by creating division. In the face of a unified working class, the APA had instigated 'the plan to *bomb* their ranks with dynamite bigotry. The fires of hell never burn more fiercely than when fanned by the breath of fanatics'.[105]

The strength of Orangeism in Scotland meant that the trials of the American lodges were viewed with interest and sympathy. The Order had a presence in Scotland since the late 1790s, but it was largely confined to the smaller industrial communities of Lanarkshire and Renfrewshire. Glasgow itself did not possess an Orange Lodge until 1860, but in less than twenty years the city had as many as one hundred lodges with a total membership of between fourteen and fifteen thousand.[106] The Orange Riots of 1871 were well covered by the Scottish press, with most accounts portraying the Orangemen favourably. Reports were not confined to the Glasgow area either, with papers across Scotland reporting on the events of 1870–71.[107] *Renfrewshire Independent* described 'pale but determined' Orangemen carrying the stars and stripes with inscriptions such as 'True Sons of Liberty Lodge 221' and 'American freemen, fall in'. Their opponents were a 'mob' of 'armed and scowling Hibernians' who were, nonetheless, cowed by a strong show of force.[108] *North British Daily Mail*, meanwhile, was quick to reiterate that it was the Catholic rioters who fired the first shots and that the troops had only acted in defence.[109] *Glasgow Herald* portrayed the attack on the Orangemen as a wider Catholic conspiracy as opposed to a spontaneous act of intra-communal violence. The rioters were described as 'ribbonmen' in reference to the secret society who defended the Catholic Irish peasantry from Orangemen and landlords in rural Ireland. 'Roman Catholic' and 'Hibernian' secret societies were also accused of conducting military drills in preparation of the parade. More worryingly, the 69th Regiment of the National Guard 'the Fighting Irish' were said to planning to intervene on the side of the rioters.[110] These fears were largely unfounded as Catholic Irish police and soldiers were widely credited for being on the side of

---

105 Eugene V. Debs, 'The American Protective Association', *Locomotive Firemen's Magazine* 18/3 (1894), 280–282.

106 Gallagher, *Glasgow: The Uneasy Peace*, 26.

107 'Desperate Fighting Between Catholics and Orangemen in New York', *Dundee Courier* (13 July 1871), 3; 'The Riots in New York', *Inverness Advertiser* (18 July 1871), 3; 'The Riots in New York', *Falkirk Herald* (20 July 1871), 3.

108 'The New York Riots', *Renfrewshire Independent* (29 July 1871), 3.

109 'The Orange Riots in New York', *North British Daily Mail* (15 July 19), 5.

110 'Great Riot Between Orangemen and Catholics in New York', *Glasgow Herald* (14 July 1871), 5.

law and order. Even the Know Nothing J. T. Handley acknowledged the 'almost universal faithfulness of the Roman Catholic Irish police to their duty'.[111]

In Glasgow, Orange and Green marches provided flashpoints for intra-communal violence, but never to the scale of New York. Paradoxically, Gallagher has noted that the two defining characteristics of sectarianism in Scotland is its longevity but also its 'relative' lack of serious violence. He identifies several factors unique to Scotland which actually dampened sectarian tension rather than fuelling it. The Scottish economy of the 1840s and 1850s was relatively buoyant and could easily absorb unskilled Irish labourers without threatening local workers. The Great Disruption also resulted in the Church of Scotland being more preoccupied with internal schisms than the existential threat of the Catholic Irish.[112] Nonetheless, this trend should not be exaggerated as violence and sectarianism inevitably went hand-in-hand even if it never reached North American standards. Perhaps the most serious rioting occurred in 1880 during simultaneous Orange and Home Rule demonstrations across the west of Scotland. Rioters armed with pikes and pistols fought running battles resulting in the stabbing of a detective, the shooting of two Orangemen, and twenty-five arrests. Remarkably no one was killed.[113] Generally speaking the annual Orange marches passed without major incident. Gallagher has suggested that the senior leadership of the order tended to keep a lid on the more extremist elements.[114] Another factor may have been that native Protestant supremacy was more secure in Scotland, meaning that an organised show of force would have served little purpose for either side. Orange marches may even have provided an outlet for intercommunal tension that, although still odious to some, could be contained and conducted with a reasonable degree of orderliness. In 1885, *Glasgow Herald* reported that although there had been rioting in Belfast on 12th of July, the Orange marches in Glasgow and Ayrshire had passed 'quietly'. During his address to marchers that year, Provincial Grand Master George MacLeod even 'cordially admitted there were many Romanists who were good men'.[115] As was the case in New York, Glasgow's Orangemen were keen to cast themselves on the side of law and order. Following rioting in Partick 1875 during a Home Rule procession, the Grand Orange Lodge of Scotland held an enquiry into allegations that their members had instigated the disorder. The accusation that an Orangeman had commenced the riot by pulling down a

111 Handley, *The Great Riots*, 304–305.
112 Gallagher, *Glasgow: The Uneasy Peace*, 33–36.
113 'Riots in Glasgow', *North British Daily Mail*, (16 August 1880), 5.
114 Gallagher, *Glasgow: The Uneasy Peace*, 295–297, 329.
115 'Orange Celebrations', *Glasgow Herald* (13 July 1885), 8.

green flag was found to be untrue, while the only action the Orangemen took against the Home Rulers was done 'at the request of the police' who were being overwhelmed by the mob.[116] Regardless of the veracity of their version of events, this was a clear attempt to distance the Order from the sort of violence associated with Orange parades in New York.

Conclusion

In 1895, over 1,500 Orangemen accompanied by one hundred mounted policemen marched up Fifth Avenue for the 12th of July parades. Although the Brooklyn parade was less impressive with only sixty-one Orangemen turning out, clearly Orangeism was alive and well in New York at the close of the nineteenth century. Although there were reports that the singing of the 'Protestant Boys' grated some members of the public, the event passed by peacefully without a repeat of the events of the 1870s.[117] Perhaps the immense violence of the earlier riots and the outcry that followed convinced both communities to grudgingly accept the other's presence. Even as late as 1922, three thousand men, women, and children were reported to have taken part in an Orange march in Harlem, but again there were no significant disturbances.[118] The Orange Order in America would, however, never again replicate its fin de siècle heyday. Ironically the Order's quest to appeal to respectable American citizens was its undoing. Alcohol had been banned at the annual Boyne parades much to the chagrin of some members. In 1914, Master William A. Dunlap suspended some 17 lodges totalling 2,000 members due to holding a 12th of July picnic where liquor had been purveyed.[119] Post-Second World War the few references of the American Orange Order were in the obituaries of its aging membership.

At the turn of the century, anti-Catholicism was becoming a niche prejudice in New York as more pressing racial issues came to the fore. By the early 1890s, more than 400,000 immigrants were still entering the port of New York every year at a rate of over 1,000 per day.[120] The new arrivals were predominantly Italians and eastern Europeans, many of them Jews. Coupled with African American

---

116 'Commission of Inquiry at Partick by the Grand Orange Lodge of Scotland', *Glasgow Herald* (8 September 1875), 4.

117 'Orangemen Celebrate', *Sun* (13 July 1895), 3.

118 'Orangemen Hold Parade', *New York Herald* (13 July 1922), 6.

119 'Suspends 2,000 Orangemen', *Sun* (15 July 1913), 3.

120 *Immigration Investigation. Report of the House Committee on Immigration and Naturalization under the Joint Resolution of Senate and House January 29 1892* (Washington: Government Printing Office, 1892), IV.

migration from the south, the Catholic Irish had risen several strata in the American hierarchy. The Draft Riots of the Civil War, as well as their continued support of the Democratic party, illustrated the Irish commitment to maintaining the status quo, as opposed to finding common cause with other marginalised groups. As the Irish nationalist movement grew in New York, which included branches of the Ancient Order of Hibernians as well as the more radical fenians and Clan na Gael, it was the Catholic Irish who could claim the mantle of 'Irish American'. On the centenary of the American Revolution, the *Irish World* could confidently claim that 'The cause of America in 1776 is the cause of Ireland in 1876.'[121] The revival of the Irish question as well as the rise of Ku Klux Klan did briefly reignite anti-Catholicism in the 1920s. Although assertively Anglo-Saxonist and Protestant, the KKK did not seriously hinder the upwards progress of the Catholic Irish. In an America moving increasingly towards isolationism many moderate Protestants sympathised with the cause of Irish freedom, having little desire to prop up the British Empire after the disillusionment of the First World War.[122] Perkins argues that few Americans sympathised with Ulster's resistance to Irish Home Rule and refused to believe Protestants would be discriminated against in a Catholic majority Ireland.[123] The Johnston-Reed Act of 1924 limited immigration to 165,000 entrants per year and put severe restrictions on southern and eastern Europeans, Africans, as well as an outright ban on Asians. Yet the yearly quota for arrivals from the Irish Free State was the third highest of any nation, exceeded only by Great Britain and Germany.[124] White Christian America could not afford to dilute its majority by being picky about who could join their club. For their part, Irish Americans were happy to accept the improvement in status while retaining their own cultural identity.

Sectarianism took a more vitriolic turn during the interwar years in Glasgow, as many of the factors that had eased sectarian tensions in the nineteenth century were less visible. Scotland's changing role from an integral partner of the British imperial project to a peripheral fringe of the United Kingdom, was hardly conducive to Catholic assimilation. The Great Depression and the downturn in global shipbuilding meant that skilled Protestant workers lost many of their privileges and forced them to compete with Catholics for jobs.[125] The Church of Scotland

121 T. W. Moody, 'Irish American nationalism', *Irish Historical Studies* 15/60 (1967), 438–445

122 Edward Cuddy, 'The Irish Question and the Revival of Anti-Catholicism in the 1920's', *The Catholic Historical Review* 67/2 (1981), 236–255.

123 Perkins, *The Great Rapprochement*, 285.

124 Mae M. Ngai, *Impossible Subjects Book Subtitle: Illegal Aliens and the Making of Modern America*, (Princeton: Princeton University Press, 2004), 28.

125 Gallagher, *The Uneasy Peace*, 134–135.

Act 1921 would set the course for reunification with the United Free Church in 1929, thus partially resolving the internal conflict that had been waging in the Church since the Great Disruption. With the bulk of the seceders brought back into the fold, the Church could focus on another internal enemy: the Catholic Irish. In 1923, the Church and Nation Committee produced a report entitled *The Menace of the Irish Race to our Nationality*, which accused the Irish of lowering wages, criminality, and drunkenness.[126] Although many Americans could look on with sympathy to the cause of the Irish freedom, most Scots had too much of a vested interest to see the secession of southern Ireland as anything other than a further weakening of the Union. The fact that Glasgow was the epicentre for Irish republican activity during the Easter Rising and beyond only increased suspicion against the Catholic community.[127] The decline of the Liberals and the collapse of the middle ground also saw sectarianism enter Sottish politics in a far more explicit way. Alexander Ratcliffe's anti-Catholic Scottish Protestant League, although founded in Edinburgh, would make its first real political breakthrough in Glasgow. By 1931, SPL candidates were taking council seats from both the Independent Labour Party and the Conservatives.[128] Although the success of Ratcliffe's SPL, as well as John Cormack's Edinburgh-based Protestant Action, would be short lived, it is nonetheless curious that anti-Catholicism became more prevalent in Scottish politics as its influence was declining in the United States. Yet the resolution of New York's sectarian problems was not celebrated by all. In 1935, *Vanguard*, the newspaper of the SPL, reported on a letter it had received from a Scotswomen living in New York. The woman, a native of Fife, thanked the paper for the work of the SPL and expressed her opinion that Popery was 'the foulest stench belched out of hell'. The paper was happy to learn that there remained in New York those who had not abandoned the Protestant cause:

> New York is not so very far from Glasgow after all, and it is cheering for us to know in that Rome-ridden city, the centre of American corruption and political fraud, we have readers who think of us and pray for us in this great work of Protestantism.[129]

---

126 Elinor Kelly 'Challenging Sectarianism in Scotland: The Prism of Racism', *Scottish Affairs* 42/ (2003), 32–56, at 34.

127 Cameron McKay, 'In Glasgow we made bombs': the role of Irish-Scots in the Easter Rising', *Scottish Labour History* 51/1 (2016), 79–94.

128 Tom Gallagher, 'Protestant Extremism in Urban Scotland 1930–1939: Its Growth and Contraction', *The Scottish Historical Review* 64178, Part 2 (1985), 143–167.

129 "Belched out of Hell", *Vanguard*, (11 December 1935), 5.

PART III

Imaginings

A Glasgow Imaginarium: Portable Emotions, Experiences and Meanings

Stephen Bowman

'It had slipped and shattered in a misty fusion of unrelated images … He was telling a story, some mythic memory of antique weal …'

Lewis Grassic Gibbon, 'The Woman of Leadenhall Street', in *Smeddum: A Lewis Grassic Gibbon Anthology* (Edinburgh: Canongate, 2001), 439.

Imagine a building filled with Glasgow. This chapter is that building, an 'imaginarium', as curated by me. I've collected a miscellany of things for you to peruse: fragments of my memory, snippets from the rest of this book, and other people's recollections and perceptions. I have been directly inspired by Walter Benjamin's work on nineteenth-century Paris, though my aims are a little different to his. Benjamin hoped that his *Arcades Project* would help the twentieth century wake up from the 'dreamworld' of 'commodity fetishism' borne of the nineteenth century.[1] Given we are yet to emerge from the phantasmagoria Benjamin described, we are as well to lay aside our matter-of-fact Glaswegian empiricism for a moment and pay attention to the ways in which the city's dreamworlds collide. After all, such worlds are surrealist individual and collective syntheses of past and present emotions, experiences, and meanings.[2] Many of the emotions, experiences, and meanings presented in this short chapter are my own (and offer an account of my interest in producing this book), but they are also historically contingent and may be yours too. They have been generated by my own experience of passing time and filtering it through the city of Glasgow. They are also generative of each other and shaped by contestable readings of history. The imaginarium seems all

1 Simon Gunn, 'City of Mirrors: *The Arcades Project* and urban history: Roundtable: Walter Benjamin's Arcades Project', *Journal of Victorian Culture* 7/2 (2002), 263–275.

2 The most famous example of thinking creatively about one's own relationship to a city is Italo Calvino's book *Invisible Cities* (1974). In a recent edited collection on Calvino's work, Ursula Lang considers Glasgow alongside Calvino's imagined city of Leonia, both of which are defined by their relentless 'making and remaking'. See Ursula Lang, '"Submerging the City in Its Own Past": Tracing Glasgow's Architectures of Inhabitation', in Benjamin Lindner, ed, *Invisible Cities and the Urban Imagination* (Cham: Palgrave Macmillan, 2022), 175–184.

a jumble, but it might be helpful for you to know that everything is where it is for a reason. It might also help if I provided you with something of a road map through my own thinking. You should proceed in the assumption that (as I argue elsewhere in this book) the 'imagined community' of the city is constructed by the individual's engagement both with that which is forever lost in time and that which remains, including the very physical and extant traces of the past in the ever-changing built environment.[3]

It is difficult to make sense of cities. These atomising, collective, attractive, repellent places leave only shattered and often unrelated fragments of meaning in their wake. As a result, I return to Benjamin, who urged us to take these fragments – the 'detritus' of a past awaiting recognition in the now – and display them side by side, as he did with the material he collected on nineteenth-century Paris.[4] John Dos Passos also developed creative ways to capture the urban essence in his historical novels, including 1925's *Manhattan Transfer*, which presents a multitude of fictional narratives and perspectives about 1920s and 1930s New York and intersperses these with select quotations from real newspapers.[5] Such 'literary montages', built from the remains of another time, are 'tools' to summon the past – its emotional aspects, people's experiences of it, and the meanings attached to it – and reveal its relationships with the present.[6] With this in mind, and like Allan Pred's Benjamin-inspired study of nineteenth-century Stockholm, this chapter merges various approaches to engage with the multifaceted nature of the historical urban experience, frequently 'blurring the "social scientific" and the "humanistic" … blurring the "academic" and the "artistic"' and 'juxtaposing conventional and unconventional forms'. It is a creative history exploring the human and autobiographical elements of writing about Glasgow's transatlantic past.[7]

---

3 See also Tom Hulme, *After the Shock City: Urban Culture and the Making of Modern Citizenship* (Woodbridge: Royal Historical Society, 2019), 8.

4 Walter Benjamin, 'First Sketches', *The Arcades Project*, translated by Howard Eiland and Kevin McLaughlin (Harvard: Harvard University Press, 2002).

5 Jay McInery, 'Introduction', in John Dos Passos, *Manhattan Transfer* (London: Penguin Modern Classics, 2000), 7–11.

6 Katie Barclay and Jade Riddle, 'Urban Emotions and the Making of the City', in Barclay and Riddle, eds, *Urban Emotions and the Making of the City* (New York: Routledge, 2021), 13–14.

7 Allan Pred, *Lost Words and Lost Worlds: Modernity and the Language of Everyday Life in Late Nineteenth-Century Stockholm* (Cambridge: Cambridge University Press, 1990), xv; Alison Twells, Will Pooley, Matt Houlbrook, and Helen Rogers, 'Undisciplined History: Creative Methods and Academic Practice', *History Workshop Journal*, advanced e-publication (6 October 2023), https://doi.org/10.1093/hwj/dbad012, accessed 8 December 2023; Stephen Bowman, Rosie Al-Mulla, Sarah Bromage, Katharina Pruente, and Duncan Armstrong, '"An Unusual Period of Unspecified Length": A Creative Oral History of the Covid-19 Pandemic', in Andrew Smith, ed., *Paper Trails: The Social Lives of Archives and Collections* (UCL Digital Press, 2024), https://ucldigitalpress.co.uk/BOOC/Article/3/148/, accessed 10 July 2024.

Alasdair Gray's *Lanark* contains what has become a much-quoted line of dialogue by the protagonist Duncan Thaw, who explains that few people appreciate Glasgow's importance and beauty because 'nobody imagines living here'. This he contrasted with other cities, including Florence, Paris, London, and New York: '[n]obody visiting them for the first time is a stranger because he's already visited them in paintings, novels, history books and films.'[8] Gray's book was published in 1981 and was in part an autobiographical tale of the author's own formative youth spent in the city in the 1950s. What Gray wrote in the 1970s about the 1950s was fundamentally true. It still rings true today, demonstrated ironically enough by the decision to locate the 2024 film version of Gray's novel *Poor Things* not in Glasgow but in London. Even so, and as Gray himself knew, Glasgow did and does exist in people's imaginations. We have Gray to thank for stimulating many of these imaginations, not only through his fiction but his wider public art projects too, including his paintings of Glasgow people and places exhibited as the *Continuous Glasgow Show* at the People's Palace in the city's east end in 1978. Duncan Thaw may have said that Glasgow only existed in a 'music hall song and a few bad novels', but this was only ever a half truth. I was born in Glasgow, and my immediate family are mostly from the city, but I was brought up and have lived most of my adult life in one of its satellite towns. Self-evidently, a globally important transatlantic Glasgow has loomed large in my historical imagination and this chapter both demonstrates and seeks to examine this personal conundrum. Nor I am the only person whose work has been shaped by transatlantic Glasgow. Two famous Scottish musicians have also reflected on imagining Glasgow in relation to North America, especially New York. Discussing the inspirations behind their 1984 hit song about Glasgow, 'Tinseltown in the Rain', the *Blue Nile*'s Paul Buchanan said that the band wanted to convey the notion that 'Tinseltown' is 'whatever your dream is … whatever you lost'. They were inspired by the 'universal nature of cities', reflecting that 'Glasgow's not the same scale as New York, but if you just shrunk it down to a corner, it could be.'[9] Meanwhile, Sharleen Spiteri of Glasgow band *Texas* has said that the success of her collaborations with Staten Island hip-hop artists Wu-Tang Clan is partly due to the 'drive' the two groups' 'shared' that comes 'with being from those places'.[10]

---

8 Alasdair Gray, *Lanark: A Life in 4 Books* (Edinburgh: Canongate, 1981), 243.

9 Paul Buchanan quoted in Wyndham Wallace, 'Making The Blue Nile: A Walk Across The Rooftops', *Classic Pop* (4 November 2021), https://www.classicpopmag.com/2021/11/making-the-blue-nile-a-walk-across-the-rooftops/, accessed 17 June 2024.

10 Sharleen Spiteri quoted in Stevie Chick, '"Sharleen is my homegirl" – how Texas and Wu-Tang Clan became pop's weirdest pals', *The Guardian* (15 December 2020), https://www.theguardian.com/music/2020/dec/15/sharleen-spiteri-homegirl-texas-wu-tang-clan-became-pops-weirdest-pals, accessed 17 June 2024.

Glasgow's Garden Festival in 1988 is one of my earliest childhood memories. This was just before Glasgow was named European City of Culture in 1990. I can also recall a childhood visit to the newly opened Glasgow Royal Concert Hall that year and in subsequent years with my proudly Glaswegian grandparents, now gone. Ian Spring's contemporaneous comment that he did not 'give much of a damn about a new opera hall' did not and does not speak for me.[11] My sense of the city's physical scale and historical depth was enhanced when it became the UK City of Architecture and Design in 1999. By then, I was going through my adolescence and two of my grandparents were dead. The city is a monument to being-no-more for people transformed.[12] A week or so after my Royston-born maternal grandfather Joseph's funeral in February 1998, my Gorbals-born paternal grandfather Hugh took me, aged 12, to the Odeon cinema by the River Clyde to see the newly released James Cameron film *Titanic*, the music from which we would later use during the funeral of my grandmother and Joseph's wife Betty in 2006. Seeing the film at that precise point in my life in 1998 – when it served as punctuation to the decline and passing of the older generation of my family – was more of a formative experience for me than it is probably fashionable for a professional historian to admit to, even decades later. But it seems clearer now that a number of different processes were in operation to create my own Glasgow imaginary which, if not necessarily without basis in fact, was fundamentally partial and romanticised. Cameron's film tells the story of the sinking of RMS *Titanic* on its maiden voyage from Southampton to New York in 1912 through the eyes of a young first-class passenger, played by Kate Winslet, who has a romance with a steerage passenger, played by Leonardo DiCaprio. It was a cultural phenomenon upon release and remained the highest-grossing film of all time until 2010.

There were reasons for the film's success other than the pop culture appeal of its lead actors and its aggressively marketed soundtrack. These centred on the film's engagement with – and interpretation and presentation of – the historical past.[13] Cameron himself described interest in the history of the *Titanic* as a 'form of consensus hallucination', and it is clear that his film was a product and an inducer of an hallucinatory state.[14] As Terry-Chandler argues, Cameron's film

---

[11] Ian Spring, *Phantom Village: The Myth of the New Glasgow* (Edinburgh: Polygon, 1990), 4.

[12] Benjamin, 'First Sketches', *The Arcades Project*, 833.

[13] Jeff Smith, 'Selling My Heart: Music and Cross-Promotion in *Titanic*', in Kevin S. Sandler and Gaylyn Studlar, eds, *Titanic: Anatomy of a Blockbuster* (New Brunswick: Rutgers University Press, 1999), 46–63.

[14] Cameron quoted in Fiona Terry-Chandler, 'Vanished Circumstance: Titanic, heritage, and film', *International Journal of Heritage* Studies 6/1 (2000), 67–76, 75.

depicts RMS *Titanic* as 'beautiful yet also powerfully symbolising the engineering achievements of the male world and containing the sumptuous consumables of the female ... Here is a re-creation of a beautiful Edwardian past – evoking the glamour of the material culture onboard'.[15] This is a Benjaminian phantasmagoria by another name: not of the nineteenth century but of the early twentieth, and it intoxicated the late 1990s like a drug.[16] The steel-built ship itself was successor to the world borne of nineteenth-century commodity capitalism and the iron arcades and was fetishised by Cameron's lens, which lingered on the material objects that he believed embodied the Edwardian aesthetic. Indeed, a number of these objects were genuine relics of the period, most notably some of the clothing worn by the actors. Benjamin teaches us, however, that such objects have 'lost ... the logic of their original place in the market'. They are simply the detritus of a past age, unable to provide unvarnished access to the dreamworld from which they originated.[17] The realism of Cameron's film is therefore a mirage, and it is impossible for *Titanic* the movie to separate itself from the nineteenth-century and early twentieth-century milieu it seeks to depict. In Benjaminian terms, there was no awakening from the spell.

The Odeon where I saw *Titanic* is part of an entertainment and retail park established at Springfield Quay on the southside of the River Clyde and is therefore intrinsically connected to a locale that not only built transatlantic ocean liners but was also the point of departure and arrival for passenger and freight shipping to North America in the nineteenth and early twentieth centuries. Perhaps some of the steamship passengers Kevin James wrote about in his chapter for this volume – including the Albany jeweller Robert Dayton Williams in 1870 – had passed through this part of the city. The transatlantic connection is built into the surrounding streets. Near the Odeon, but on the other side of the river just off the Broomielaw, sits Washington Street. An unassuming street now largely made up of commercial properties, Washington Street is named after the first President of the United States because its one-time owner, the Leicester-based Mary Reid, was an admirer of Charles James Fox, the British statesman who was sympathetic to the American revolutionaries' cause in the 1770s and 1780s. Reid died in 1839, though not before declining to sell her land on Washington

15 Ibid., 75.

16 See Scott McCracken, 'Random Patterns, Flashes of Insight: Walter Benjamin's *Arcades Project*, Roundtable: Walter Benjamin's Arcades Project', *Journal of Victorian Culture* 7/2 (2002), 279: As McCracken explains, Benjamin 'argues that the experience closest to that of nineteenth century urban life is the drug experience.' In light of this, Cameron's notion of 'hallucination' becomes even more striking.

17 Ibid., p. 279.

Street to the Clyde River Trustees, who offered to buy it from her for £8,000 in 1814/15 so they could build more docks to support the city's ever-increasing shipping traffic.[18] I was not aware of such historical details as a 12-year-old, but I know now that my engagement with the history of Glasgow – from walking its gridded streets with their tall buildings and dingy alleyways reminiscent of Gotham City, to my enjoyment of the archival papers from the 1890s and 1900s that I first used as an undergraduate History student – started under the influence of a dreamscape that Walter Benjamin could identify and grapple with, but which Hollywood could only perpetuate. I had probably already understood Glasgow as a nineteenth- and twentieth-century city, but my youthful filmgoing resulted in my historicising of it in transatlantic terms. It meant that when I did first go to New York – on a research trip as a PhD student – I was primed to make the historical and emotional connection with Glasgow. This translocal entanglement of history and popular culture was something that Anne Massy and Mike Hammond also observed in young peoples' views about the *Titanic* movie in the city of Southampton, a place with very tangible connections to the ship itself. There, where many cinema goers saw the film at a riverside leisure complex built in very close proximity to where *Titanic* set sail in 1912, Cameron's *Titanic* was read with a 'parodic self-awareness and a burgeoning sense of local identity, the latter instigated by the film'.[19] The result is this chapter: a self-indulgent essay exploring my own 'burgeoning sense of [*trans*]local identity' and how it shaped my historical interest in Glasgow.[20]

Even if the authors have not made it explicit, many of the chapters in this volume also have autobiographical underpinnings and are interpretations of Glasgow's history at least partly built from individual life stories. During a

---

18 'Old Glasgow and its environs', *Glasgow Herald* (29 October 1864), 2; In 1931, the US Consulate in Glasgow wrote to the Town Clerk seeking information about why this street and another in Govan were called 'Washington Street'. See G. E. Chamberlin, American Consul General, Glasgow, to David Stenhouse, Glasgow Town Clerk, 21 May 1931, Records of the American Consulate, Glasgow, Scotland, Vol. 7, 1931, RG84 State Department Records, US National Archives and Records Administration, Archives II, College Park, Maryland (NARA II); Glasgow Town Clerk Depute to G. E. Chamberlin, 28 May 1931, Records of the American Consulate, Glasgow, Scotland, Vol. 7, 1931, RG84, NARA II.

19 Anne Massey and Mike Hammond, '"It was True! How Can You Laugh?" History and Memory in the Reception of *Titanic* in Britain and Southampton', in Sandler and Studlar, eds, *Titanic*, 261.

20 In my view, 'translocalism' is about exchange and construction of historical and cultural discourses and memories between inter-connected local (that is to say, sub-national) places. I am exploring this concept in other aspects of my work. See also Clemens Greiner and Patrick Sakdapolrak, 'Translocality: Concepts, Applications and Emerging Research Perspectives', *Geography Compass* 7/5 (2013), 373–384.

planning meeting for *Portable City* held in July 2023 for example, Tahitia McCabe spoke of her 'personal lived experience as an American living in Glasgow' and remembered arriving in the city for the first time in the early 2000s and being conscious of 'just how much it was like [her] hometown of Portland, Oregon'. Like Portland, Glasgow is 'an old Victorian city on a river, a place that felt that it was a bit down-at-heel but coming back up again'. Tahitia said she 'felt immediately at home' and that this shaped her approach to her history writing:

> Part of what I'm interested in with my chapter on American migrants to Glasgow in the late nineteenth century is whether they had the same sense of feeling that Glasgow was natural and homelike ... It is very autobiographical for me. Understanding the people who came before me living in Glasgow and what they felt and their sense of community, and contrasting that to how I now live as a modern American living in Glasgow with lots and lots of connections. For example, I belong to the American Women's Club, and we have monthly meetings. We have a sense of ourselves and having an American community, and I'm just very curious about who the people were who came before me, and did they have the same experience as I am having. It's also helping me to feel more of a part of Glasgow by learning more about the history of Glasgow.., so it's helping me put down stronger roots into the community.[21]

This calls to mind a genre of urban writing – 'spatial autobiography' – that Evelyn Schulz has found in Tokyo. Such works are characterised by 'scaling down Tokyo and splitting it into manageable pieces' offering 'interpretations of Tokyo's history comprised of individual experiences'. Writing in this way further decentres the 'master narrative of nation building, progress, and growth' and, as Schulz points out, is characteristic of Benjaminian 'porosity' where 'porous spaces of private and public life enter the realms of history and collective memory'.[22] In Benjamin's words:

> [s]treets are the dwelling place of the collective. The collective is an eternally unquiet, eternally agitated being that – in the space between building fronts – experiences, learns, understands, and invents as much as individuals do within the privacy of their own four walls.[23]

Taking the autobiographical turn to urban history also provides an opportunity to think more sensitively about the embodied aspects of experiencing, understanding, and analysing city life. Though such an approach naturally invites a deeper

---

21 Tahitia McCabe, audio recording of *Portable Cities* roundtable made by Stephen Bowman, University of Stirling, 12 July 2023.

22 Evelyn Schulz, 'Mapping Environments of Memory, Nostalgia, and Emotions in "Tokyo Spatial (Auto)biographies"', in Barbara E. Thornbury and Schulz, eds, *Tokyo: Memory, Imagination, and the City (Lanham: Lexington Books, 2018)*, 77.

23 Benjamin, M. The Flâneur, M3a, 4, *Arcades Project*, 423.

engagement with how a city 'felt' to people in the past, my main interest here is in reflecting upon the emotional and emotive dimension to academic research and writing itself.[24] The historian may enter into a constructive emotional dialogue with the primary sources, but what about the emotions and experiences that the historian brings to that dialogue in the first place? As Katie Barclay argues, academic historians are increasingly exploring 'emotion as a productive lens of analysis, a dimension of cognition and decision-making, and something to be embraced, rather than avoided'.[25]In urban history writing, such emotional sensitivity encourages us to pay attention to the fact that a city is the sum of its parts and that these parts are defined by an interplay between the individual and the collective, and between the human and the (sometimes very local) built environment. In other words, people and place, past and present, and history and the self, are irrevocably linked. Writing about New York, Colson Whitehead said:

> Our streets are calendars containing who we were and who we will be next. We see ourselves in this city every day when we walk down the sidewalk and catch our reflection in store windows, seek ourselves in this city each time we reminisce about what was there fifteen, ten, forty years ago, because all our old places are proof that we were here. One day the city we built will be gone, and when it goes, we go. When the buildings fall, we topple, too.[26]

This seems an echo of the Benjaminian notion that:

> [b]eing past, being no more, is passionately at work in things. To this the historian trusts for his subject matter. He depends on this force, and knows things as they are at the moment of their ceasing to be.[27]

Becoming aware of passings lends a melancholy air and an emotional impetus to the historian's work. Indeed, this realisation is what has underpinned some of the most adventurous forms of history writing, including the Benjamin-inspired Michael Lesy's 1973 *Wisconsin Death Trip*, which explores life and death in a small Wisconsin town in the nineteenth century through creative uses of historical newspaper reportage and photographic sources. Lesy's montages accentuate the morbid features of the everyday and evidence a contemporary fascination with

---

24 Nicolas Kenny, *The Feel of the City: Experiences of Urban Transformation* (Toronto: University of Toronto Press, 2018), 17–18.

25 Katie Barclay, 'State of the Field: The History of Emotions', *History* 106/371 (2021), 456–466, 456.

26 Colson Whitehead, *The Colossus of New York* (New York: Doubleday, 2003), 9.

27 Benjamin, 'First Sketches', 833.

reports and depictions of death. A very few other writers have followed Lesy's controversial lead, though B. J. Hollars' 2014 book experimenting with real and fabricated reports of drownings near another Wisconsin town at the end of the nineteenth century and beginning of the twentieth is one example. Lesy and Hollars were at least partly interested in the role that emotions – especially feelings of pastness – can play in navigating historical sources. Lesy later reflected on his work and admitted that 'I'd like to say I knew what I was doing and why I was doing it ... But I didn't. What I knew was what I felt, and what I felt was that I was descending into darkness.'[28] Lesy was not referencing the darkness of the modern city but the darkness of death. The physical reality of death (loss, absence) exists typically unacknowledged in all historical study but its emotional dimensions also envelope an urban history written by people with a personal attachment to the city being studied. Glasgow is a city in which many of my relatives were born, lived, worked, and died. To paraphrase Whitehead, people and places topple together.

Passings and pastness underpin Benjamin's observation that the 'unfathomability of the moribund arcades is a characteristic motif'.[29] Death came to these nineteenth-century urban spaces as it did to the people who used them. This fact, and all facts like it, is emotive. This is why Benjamin included in his *Arcades Project* a dreamlike section of writing by the Swedish author and playwright August Strindberg (b. 1849-d. 1912) that depicted a 'brightly lit' but eerily empty arcade:

> Then he went on into the arcade ... There was every possible kind of shop, but not a soul to be seen, either behind or before the counters. After a while he stopped in front of a big window in which there was a whole display of shells. As the door was open, he went in. From floor to ceiling there were rows of shells of every kind, collected from all the seas of the world. No one was in, but there was a ring of tobacco smoke in the air ... So he began his walk again, following the blue and white carpet. The passage wasn't straight but winding, so that you could never see the end of it; and there were always fresh shops there, but no people; and the shopkeepers were not to be seen.[30]

There are Glaswegian examples of Benjamin's 'characteristic motif', for example in work by Glasgow writer James Cowan. Cowan used his daily lunchbreaks to stroll the city, publishing accounts of his expeditions in the *Glasgow Evening*

---

28 Michael Lesy, *Wisconsin Death Trip* (Albuquerque: University of New Mexico Press, 1973/2000); Lesy quoted in B. J. Hollars, *Dispatches from the Drownings: Reporting the Fiction of Nonfiction* (Albuquerque: University of New Mexico Press, 2014), xx.

29 Benjamin, H. The Collector, H1a, 3, *Arcades Project*, 205.

30 Strindberg, *Märchen* (Munich and Berlin, 1917), 52–53, 59, quoted in Benjamin, H. The Collector, H1a, 3, *Arcades Project*, 205.

Citizen during the 1930s under the pseudonym 'Peter Prowler'.[31] He published a collection of these accounts with some additions in book form in 1951. In 1932, this Scottish flâneur haunted the city's streets and moribund arcades. Cowan described the Argyll Arcade, which still exists today, and the Queen Arcade, now gone. He was also interested in two other arcades: the Union Arcade and another unnamed premises between Waterloo Street and Bothwell Street. To Cowan, each was 'a sort of phantom'. The Union Arcade was planned in the 1840s but never built, and he had no memory of the unnamed premises despite his familiarity with the area during his youth and having read accounts of it. He wrote: 'I wonder if this has anything to do with the haunting feeling I often have that I used to know another Glasgow arcade which I cannot now locate. I keep hoping that I may rediscover it some day.' Some of Cowan's readers wrote to the *Evening Citizen* with information about arcades he had failed to remember. He later visited a 'queer old arcade' in Virginia Street and 'had the feeling that it might be the one I was unable to recall'.[32] Cowan had a certain preoccupation not only with changes to the built environment but also with the way these changes made him feel. Elsewhere, he describes Bothwell Street (which, by the 1930s, contained some of Glasgow's most American-looking buildings) as his 'street of dreams' and wrote about 'six old arches' near Bishop Street on the southern part of Bothwell Street that were the leftovers of an abandoned building project by prominent businessman and town councillor James Scott (d. 1884). Cowan wrote that the 'six old arches remain as a melancholy reminder of what might have been' and that they remained 'curiously perched on the edge of an abyss, apparently unconnected with anything, and seemingly having no useful purpose'.[33] Cowan's phantom arcade and his melancholy arches (which would be demolished in 1944) were 'monument[s]' of 'being-no-more'. His is the voice of a person grappling with his own mortality and relationship to urban modernity.[34]

James Cowan's reflections encapsulate those aspects of the modern condition that are, in Svetlana Boym's words, 'contradictory, critical, ambivalent and reflective on the nature of time', combining 'fascination for the present with longing

---

31 James Cowan, *From Glasgow's Treasure Chest* (Glasgow, 1951), 3–6; Little else is known about James Cowan, but thanks are due to the Glasgow painter David R. Warrilow who is familiar with the work of 'Peter Prowler' and recalled meeting with Cowan's daughter some years previously to discuss her father's writing, and who provided me with additional clarification during one of my visits to the Mitchell Library in Glasgow.

32 Cowan, *Glasgow's Treasure Chest*, 69.

33 Cowan, *Glasgow's Treasure Chest*, 242–243; For Scott's biography, see 'Death of Mr James Scott', *Glasgow Herald* (25 April 1884), 6.

34 Benjamin, 'First Sketches', 833.

for another time'.[35] This short chapter has been similarly absorbed in the compelling nature of time and preoccupied by the relationships between the present and a lost past. The quote at the top of this chapter – taken from Lewis Grassic Gibbon's 1936 short story about the final days of a lonely prehistoric human, 'The Woman of Leadenhall Street' – is a reminder of the fragmented nature of history and memory and of the reliance of both on feelings of nostalgia and pastness. This chapter has itself been a 'misty fusion of unrelated images', or an imaginarium: a creative merging of other parts of this book, autobiographical details, materials from the secondary literature, antiquarian texts, and historical newspapers. It has also been a 'story' based partly on my own 'mythic memory of antique weal', shaped by emotional remembrances from my childhood and a subjectivity that have inscribed particular and personal meanings onto the built environment. Acknowledging the emotional and autobiographical aspect of writing history in this way also encourages us to seek out the emotional aspect of the past itself even when this is not immediately obvious. Glasgow's historical portability relied on the transfer and exchange of people and ideas between Glasgow and North America (and indeed elsewhere), but this was a messy process that was experienced at the level of the individual life and its attendant events, emotions, and passings. The historical record – with which we are all necessarily in emotional dialogue – shows how even the melancholy arches on Glasgow's street of dreams contained within them the essence of this portability. One of the architects employed by James Scott to redevelop Bothwell Street was a man named Alexander Kirkland. The 1884 book *Glasgow Past and Present* – another of the countless nineteenth-century publications documenting the city's rise – described Kirkland's Bothwell Buildings as 'a chaste and elegant range of warehouses and offices' but also noted proudly that the architect was by then the Chief Commissioner of Buildings in Chicago.[36] Kirkland had emigrated to the US in 1868, initially settling in Jefferson, Wisconsin, before moving to Chicago three years later. While in Chicago he became 'one of the leading architects' in the United States and served as president of the city's St Andrews Society. Death would come to Kirkland in 1892, by which point he had returned to Wisconsin. Here is evidence of the melancholy air and emotional impetus to urban history.

35 Svetlana Boym, *The Future of Nostalgia* (New York: Basic Books, 2001), 22.

36 John Carrick, 'Notes on Dean of Guild Court Records', Note R (31 December 1849, Vol. 1. page 156), *Glasgow Past and Present, Illustrated in Dean of Guild Court Reports and In the Reminiscences and Communications of Senex, Aliquis, J.B., Etc, Volume 1* (Glasgow, 1884), lxx; The Chicago Daily Tribune described Kirkland in 1881 as the 'Superintendent of Public Buildings and City Building Inspector.' See 'Alexander Kirkland', *Chicago Daily Tribune* (1 January 1881), 6.

Alongside James Cowan, Robert Dayton Williams, Mary Reid, and my own memories, Alexander Kirkland passes into my Glasgow imaginarium. In the final analysis, the idea of Glasgow as a 'portable city' is constructed as much at an emotional level as it is a result of migration patterns and modern economics.

> 'Awakening as a graduated process that goes on in the life of the individual as in the life of generations. Sleep its initial stage. A generation's experience of youth has much in common with the experience of dreams. Its historical configuration is a dream configuration. Every epoch has such a tide turned towards dreams, the child's side.'
>
> Walter Benjamin, K, Dream City and Dream House, Dreams of the Future, Anthropological Nihilism, Jung, K1, 1, *Arcades Project*, 388.

Glasgow and the British Empire

Craig Lamont

Every city has an origin story. For Glasgow, it was the arrival of St Kentigern (or Mungo) around the year 550 which marked the earliest civic developments. The present Glasgow Cathedral – dedicated to St Mungo – dates to the twelfth century. Around the same time an annual fair was established, and the tradition of the 'fair fortnight' in the form of a local holiday is maintained (albeit on a limited basis) to this day. The 'miracles' of St Mungo are well enshrined in civic insignia and rhyming folklore: restoring life to a robin; restarting a fire with a hazel branch; retrieving a lost ring from the mouth of a fish. These, with the bell he allegedly brought from Rome, comprise the 'bird that never flew, the tree that never grew, the bell that never rang, and the fish that never swam'. The retention of these origin story icons in everyday imagery help to build Glasgow's unique cityscape. Following the Reformation, a burgeoning community changed the face of Glasgow from a small religious hub to an ambitious mercantile town. The population rose from around 7000 in 1600 to around 12,000 in 1700. In 1736 the first history of Glasgow was published,[1] and by the middle of the century trade with the Americas – tobacco, sugar, rum – increased the city's financial standing. The population was doubled. The slave economy that kept these trading efforts going have only been brought to the fore in Scottish Studies in the last few decades. As a result of the revolt of the American colonies in 1775, Glasgow could no longer use the former British routes for the tobacco trade, but cotton and textile production – again dependent on slaves – soon brought new fortunes. By 1801 the population was over 77,000 and Glasgow had become even more central to British trading efforts and led the way in several heavy industries such as coal mining and iron founding. From 1807 the abolitionist movement swept Britain; slavery was eventually abolished in 1833, though the families and estates were compensated handsomely by the government. For sure, the trade carried on following the end of the Napoleonic Wars (1803–15), at which point the British Empire became the foremost global power. From about 1820 Glasgow became known in the press as 'the second city in the empire', an epithet which has been inscribed time and again.[2]

---

1 John M'Ure, *A View of the City of Glasgow* (James Duncan, Glasgow: 1736).

2 Craig Lamont, *The Cultural Memory of Georgian Glasgow* (Edinburgh: Edinburgh University Press, 2021), 169.

During these processes Scotland's fabric was being pulled in various directions by the forces of Empire which this chapter will explore with a particular focus on Glasgow. For example, the infamous clearance of people for sheep walks – and better profits from the land – in Sutherland between 1809 and 1821 saw the expulsion of around 15,000 Highlanders. Waves of emigration linked to the clearances are one of the major aspects of the Scottish diaspora, found especially in the communities of Scotland's cities and in North America. Meanwhile, steam power was realised with the launching of the *PS Comet* (1812), a steamboat going between Glasgow and Greenock on the (still relatively shallow) Clyde. By 1831 the population of Glasgow was calculated at around 202,000. The next year saw the Scottish Reform Act which would change electoral history. Much of the agitation for change came from civil unrest in weaving and artisan communities in Glasgow and beyond.

More change would soon affect Glasgow in the 1840s, when large numbers of immigrants from the Scottish Highlands and Ireland arrived, largely due to famine. Now generally viewed as passive acts of atrocity in the form of mismanagement by the British government, the failure of crop farming comes into sharp focus in Glasgow, whose economy depended more and more on people, trades, and machinery. Anticipating the Improvement Acts that would go some way to addressing Glasgow's population and structural congestion, 1859 marked the completion of a massive engineering and aqueduct network which supplied Glasgow with fresh water from Loch Katrine. It was 14 October, and the water was released with a lever by none other than Queen Victoria: one of many symbolic moments for Glasgow and the mode of imperial celebration. This war of improvement in Glasgow was concurrent with war in the wider empire. Colin Campbell, later 1st Baron Clyde was born in Glasgow in 1792, and in November 1857 he led the repression of an Indian Mutiny in Lucknow. Campbell is one of many 'soldier heroes' celebrated throughout Britain, helping reinscribe the moral values best suited to imperial pride. The Improvement Act of 1866 saw more civic change in Glasgow, including slum clearances which would go on to define similar imperial projects overseas. While the slums were being cleared, the River Clyde was undergoing new and extensive improvements to bring larger vessels into the heart of the city. For the duration of the eighteenth, and most of the nineteenth century, ships could only sail as far as Greenock and Port Glasgow. This brought about a significant warehouse economy for Glasgow's increased stake in imperial commerce. But in the second half of the nineteenth century, this changed dramatically. Glasgow became the true centre of shipbuilding and was therefore (now undisputedly) the 'second city in the empire'.

Glasgow's connections to North America grew considerably during this time. In *Portable Utopia* – which the present collection responds to – Bernard Aspinwall provides numerous flattering portrayals of Glasgow's 'American' qualities. For example, Aspinwall says 'Glasgow was probably the greatest of all nineteenth-century cities,' adding that in that century Glasgow grew 'at an American pace'.[3] Elsewhere, Jackson and Munn have illustrated the growth of shipping lines which connected Glasgow and North America, such as the Allan Line founded in Greenock but moving to Glasgow in 1846, and the Anchor Line to New York in 1856.[4] Indeed, improvements to shipping and navigation helped boost emigration and export to North America during the 1860s and 70s. These tropes of civic pride found new audiences, most notably during a series of 'International' Exhibitions between 1888 and 1938, all of which positioned Glasgow as the chief imperial hub outside London.[5] C. A. Oakley's *The Second City* (1946) not only gathers up many of the above histories but marks the moment when Glasgow's imperial garb became less viable, less vibrant. But this is true more widely, as the British Empire's grip of the globe began to weaken following the Second World War. After the Partition of India in 1947, a queue of British colonies looking to mark their independence, as the United States of America had in 1776, grew in length. Today, the British Empire is more prevalent in cultural memory than in daily life. Parades and royal visits to the Commonwealth of Nations revitalise these memories and bring debates to the fore. But in looking back across the successive waves of Britain's imperial influence, Glasgow's role – for better and worse – cannot be underestimated.

There are several notable scholarly works which cover very good ground on this, especially a raft of new publications in the 1990s: *Glasgow, vol. I: Beginnings to 1830* (1995) edited by Devine and Jackson, the follow-up *Glasgow, vol. II: 1830–1912* (1996) edited by Fraser and Maver, and *Imperial Cities* (1999) edited by Driver and Gilbert, which includes MacKenzie's seminal chapter on Glasgow. Indeed, the bibliography of texts bringing Glasgow into imperial contexts is vast and diverse. Devine's *The Tobacco Lords* (1975) for instance is one of the earliest works, an important starting gun for the present field of study. But as MacKenzie notes, there

---

3 Bernard Aspinwall, *Portable Utopia: Glasgow and the United States, 1820–1920* (Aberdeen: Aberdeen University Press, 1984), xi.

4 Gordon Jackson and Charles Munn, 'Trade, Commerce and Finance', *Glasgow Volume II: 1830 to 1912* eds. W. Hamish Fraser and Irene Maver (Manchester and New York: Manchester University Press, 1996), 52–95, 65.

5 For more on these exhibitions, *cf.* Craig Lamont, 'Cultural Memory and Nationalism at Scotland's International Exhibitions: 1886–1938', *Studies in National Movements* 12 (2023), 71–100: https://doi.org/10.21825/snm.90192

are 'only two oblique references to slaves or slavery' in Devine's book.[6] In *Britain's Slave Empire* (2000) by James Walvin, Glasgow is brought into the British context, perhaps building on the rejuvenation of Glasgow studies in the mid-1990s, which also included *The Glasgow Enlightenment* (1995) edited by Hook and Sher. Most recently, Mullen's *It Wisnae Us* (2009) and *The Glasgow Sugar Aristocracy* (2022) have elucidated the full extent of Glasgow's late eighteenth-century complicity with slavery, pushing the discussion of local agents of Empire even further. As well as this new wave of Glasgow histories (see also Fry 2017 and Lamont 2021), Glasgow's imperial connections feature often in MacKenzie's *A Cultural History of the British Empire* (2022). Studies like these have traced Glasgow's impact on the world, but they are also mindful of the British Empire's impact on Glasgow.

The British Empire shaped Glasgow not only financially, but also aesthetically and in terms of the memorialisation efforts in city spaces. Perhaps the best built example of this takes the form of the Nelson monument in Glasgow. For the Rev. Dr William Ritchie, it was a question of honour. 'Render therefore honour to whom honour is due', as preached Ritchie from Romans 13:7 in August 1806 before a large procession made their way to the foundation stone of the monument for Horatio Nelson (1758–1805) in Glasgow Green.[7] The subscribers to the monument were accompanied by the Lord Provost, the Glasgow Troop of Light Horse, the Commissioners of Police, the Faculty of Physicians and Surgeons, and several other high office bearers from Glasgow's old and elite establishments. Several masonic lodges were represented, completing this highly ceremonial demarcation of Glasgow's place in the British imperial nation. Vessels with naval flags were at the Broomielaw by the time the procession reached the Green, and around 80,000 spectators are reported to have attended. Bearing in mind Glasgow's population was only 77,000 as of 1801, this remarkable congregation of spectators for a soldier with no local connection represent a new mode in civic and national pride. This Glasgow landmark was the first structural commemorative act for Nelson, followed by a whole raft outside London in Birmingham, Liverpool, and Edinburgh.[8] As Dawson says, Nelson's life was celebrated across many media, especially in print: broadside ballads, chapbooks, romances, and biographies.[9] For Glasgow's elite, Nelson was the prototypical British hero.

6 John M. MacKenzie, '"The Second City of the Empire": Glasgow – imperial municipality', in Felix Driver and David Gilbert, eds, *Imperial Cities: Landscape, Display and Identity* (Manchester and New York: Manchester University Press, 1999), 205–237, 219.

7 *Caledonian Mercury* (4 August 1806), 3.

8 Lamont, *Georgian Glasgow*, 157.

9 Graham Dawson, *Soldier Heroes: British Adventure, Empire and the Imagining of Masculinities* (London and New York: Routledge, 1994), 62.

A royal salute of 21 guns marked the close of the ceremony.[10] When the column was completed in 1807, workmen at the summit of 145ft, reportedly gave three cheers. The ships returned with their flags, and another crowd had gathered.[11] These types of commemoration became much more commonplace in the nineteenth century following the Napoleonic Wars, with British heroes and values being consecrated more widely. It is interesting to compare this wave of valorisation with an event in New York in the summer of 1776, when the equestrian statue of George III was pulled down, destroyed, and later cast into over 42,000 bullets for the revolutionary army.[12] One being the home-soil cultivation of national pride; the other being the destruction – and weaponisation – of a symbol of foreign oppression. Both commemorative moments, in line with historic conflicts, represent the fall and rise of the British Empire. To mark its subsequent (second) fall we could consider the destruction of the Nelson column (1809) in Dublin in 1966, fifty years after the Easter Rising. Depending on the city, and the historical moment, we can observe a vast array of imperial echoes.

This chapter will focus specifically on Glasgow's crucial role in the growth of the British Empire and its own civic development, driven by the dual processes of civic improvement and cultural expression. In the next section, I will trace origins of Glasgow's entry into the imperial system and chart the meteoric rise of the city merchants. After this, I will examine the nineteenth century in more detail, looking at various civic improvements, imperial monuments, literary boosterism, and the coming of the International Exhibitions in which Glasgow set out its stall. In the final section I offer a reading of more events, monuments, and debates around the nomenclature of Glasgow. It will be shown that centuries of imperial development are firmly embedded in the cultural memory of the city: a legacy which we are still coming to terms with.

Waves of Empire: Beginnings to C. 1803

England's empire across the Atlantic had been expanding since the early sixteenth century. According to Devine and Rössner, attempts by Scots to establish a presence in America were low-key: with fewer than 200 Scots in the English colonies

---

10 *Caledonian Mercury* (4 August 1806), 3.

11 *Morning Post* (15 August 1807), 3.

12 Wendy Bellion, 'A Toppled Statue of George III Illuminates the Ongoing Debate Over America's Monuments', *Smithsonian Magazine* (28 January 2022), https://www.smithsonianmag.com/history/a-toppled-statue-of-george-iii-epitomizes-the-ongoing-debate-over-americas-monuments-180979463/, accessed 20 October 2023.

before 1640.[13] Fry has suggested that Glasgow's trading links with these colonies were given a 'boost' after 1651, owing to the English occupation of Scotland and the protection offered by Cromwell. This, and the chaos of Civil War, encouraged Glasgow's town council to plan ahead for more trading with the New World. In 1668 they bought land and established what became known as Port Glasgow: a new harbour for ocean-going vessels.[14] Between 1667 and 1700 the city also constructed four sugar refineries, appointed a Professor of Navigation (1681), and established a navigation school (1695).[15] During this period also, Scots colonies were set up in East New Jersey and South Carolina (1684). In the latter case, it was Glasgow merchant Walter Gibson (later Lord Provost), who transported Covenanting exiles across the Atlantic. 'Stuarts Town' did not last long: Spanish and English opposition to Scottish incomers put a quick end to the scheme.[16] In cases like this we can see how the fallout of religious struggle creates opportunities for emigration, negotiated by the powerful class of merchants; the same men who later occupy high office and influence the fate of the nation. Gibson was the first in a large wave of Glasgow Provosts with these imperial links, many of whom had connections with the Atlantic slave economy, as Mullen notes in his 2022 report.[17] As the century came to a close, four Lord Provosts subscribed to the Company of Scotland Trading to Africa and the Indies (also known as the Scottish Darien Company).[18]

The disastrous impact of the scheme to establish a new colony in Darien on the Isthmus of Panama is one of the crucial turning points in Scottish and British history. In the vocabulary of Scotland's past the word Darien has been likened to a 'scar on the memory of the Scots'.[19] The severe financial fallout is well-known as one of the pivotal reasons why the Union of Scotland and England in 1707 was expedited after almost a century of debate. Of course, the opening up of the formerly English colonies which brought Glasgow's merchants unprecedented opportunities became a success story for the city in material terms. One of the

13 T. M. Devine and Philipp R. Rössner, 'Scots in the Atlantic Economy, 1600–1800', in John M. MacKenzie and T. M. Devine, eds, *Scotland and the British Empire* (Oxford: Oxford University Press, 2011), 30–53, 30.

14 Michael Fry, *Glasgow: A History of the City* (London: Head of Zeus, 2017), 7; Devine and Rössner, 'Scots in the Atlantic Economy', 37.

15 Lamont, *Georgian Glasgow*, 114.

16 Ibid., 116.

17 Stephen Mullen, *Glasgow, Slavery and Atlantic Commerce: An Audit of Historic Connections and Modern Legacies* (Glasgow, City Council: 2022): https://www.glasgow.gov.uk/index.aspx?articleid=29117, accessed 20 October 2023.

18 Ibid.

19 Lamont, *Georgian Glasgow*, 116.

best reflections of this is John Galt's *The Entail* (1822), a novel which follows Claud Walkinshaw, whose father dies and loses the family fortune during the ill-fated Darien scheme. Galt is one of the chief writers of the nineteenth century as far as Glasgow is concerned, and in *The Entail* Claud's quest to recover his family's wealth as a merchant 'coincides with the development of Glasgow as a prosperous community'.[20] But how did Glasgow come to flourish, exactly?

Following the Union of 1707, Glasgow's growth was slow and steady. As an imperial city of ambition, this period saw the rise of the mercantile elite. For decades the merchants of the English port cities of Bristol and Liverpool saw the Glasgow merchants as a nuisance to their hitherto unchallenged trading, accusing firms of avoiding tax duties. Nonetheless, trading increased and by 1735 Glasgow 'had forty-seven vessels trading abroad'. By 1741 the warehouses and storage 'cellars' at Port Glasgow for the unloading of tobacco were filling up.[21] The tobacco trade was 'fully developed' by the 1750s, by which point the merchants had perfected their system of using bonds to offset crushing customs duties. The system of re-exporting also kept the city connected with its older European networks of trade. An advert in the *Caledonian Mercury* tells us that 'the *Matty* and *Cochran* are safely arrived in Virginia' in August 1750, and that ships arrived in Greenock carrying sugar and rum from Jamaica and tobacco from Virginia, as well as several others carrying salt, oatmeal and other goods. Bale goods were also dispatched to Virginia via two ships, and no less than six ships carrying tobacco were sent to France.[22] In this mode of trading, Glasgow merchants' revenues reached incredible heights, and so they became more visible, working their way into the collective memory of Glasgow's newfound fame. But who were they?

One of the early 'tobacco lords' was Andrew Cochrane (1693–1777). He served as Lord Provost three times between 1744 and 1761 and established the Political Economy Club (c. 1743). Often referred to as 'the Cochrane Club', the society comprised mostly merchants, but some elite professionals took part in debates, including Adam Smith, whose intimate view of Glasgow's growth at this point is clearly a crucial inspiration for his future landmark text *The Wealth of Nations*

20 Mark Schoenfield and Clare A. Simmons, 'Introduction', in Schoenfield and Simmons, eds, *John Galt, The Entail: or The Lairds of Grippy* (Edinburgh: Edinburgh University Press, 2022), xxix.

21 George Eyre-Todd, *History of Glasgow, Volume III* (Glasgow: Jackson, Wylie & Co., 1934), 179.

22 *The Caledonian Mercury* (16 August 1750), 3.

(1776).[23] Cochrane also established the Glasgow Arms Bank in 1750 with John Murdoch, his successor as Lord Provost. It is likely that the ship advertised in the *Caledonian Mercury* was for this Cochrane, and in Glasgow today we have Cochrane Street as well as a handsome memorial inside Glasgow Cathedral. Archibald Ingram (1699–1770) followed a similar pattern to Cochrane in maintaining Atlantic trading routes from a position of political power. These are but two prominent names in the first generation of 'tobacco lords', a community no greater than around 160 men.[24] In Glasgow's cultural memory of these individuals there is perhaps no one more (in)famous than John Glassford. Glassford Street is named for once being the site of the Shawfield Mansion, built in 1711 and commemorated in *The Glassford Family Portrait* (c. 1767). The *Portrait* depicts opulence, fashion, taste, and family life in Glasgow's upper classes during this fruitful period of civic growth. It has become something of a touchstone for discussions of slavery, given the presence of a Black servant boy at the edge of the painting.[25] Glassford was one of the most successful of Glasgow's merchants, running three separate companies 'at the pinnacle of the Virginia-Clyde tobacco commerce in 1775'.[26] William Cunninghame of Lainshaw (1731–1799) was another major player, and was himself resident in Virginia in the late 1740s.[27] One of the main reasons for the historic glossing of Glasgow in the slave trade is that the merchants were absentee planters or owners, and although there are plenty of documented cases of runaway slaves in the city,[28] there was little other than the *Glassford Portrait* to offer a visual connection between Glasgow's powerful few and the system of slavery across the Atlantic. Cunninghame did leave behind one of the most important built reminders of slave-related wealth, however, in the form of his former mansion, built c. 1778, which now forms the core structure for the Gallery of Modern Art. Around this time, the changing face of the British Empire was beginning to impact more than just the wealthy few.

The major event which ended this unprecedented upward trajectory for these merchants was the American War of Independence (1775–1783). It was at this point when several major trading firms began to dwindle, some into bankruptcy.

---

23 Ralph McLean, 'Professors, Merchants, and Ministers in the Clubs of Eighteenth-Century Glasgow', in Mark C. Wallace and Jane Rendall, eds, *Association and Enlightenment: Scottish Clubs and Societies, 1700–1830* (Lewisburg, PA: Bucknell University Press, 2021), 85–100, 86.

24 Mullen, *Glasgow, Slavery*, 31.

25 Lamont, *Georgian Glasgow*,106.

26 Mullen, *Glasgow, Slavery*, 22.

27 Mullen, *Glasgow, Slavery*, 95.

28 *Runaway Slave in Britain*: https://www.runaways.gla.ac.uk/.

In establishing independence from Britain, the thirteen colonies which would become the United States of America were no longer open for exploitation by Glasgow, or indeed any British city. Crucially, the end of the war also marked the establishment of the Glasgow Chamber of Commerce, which brought trade with the newly independent USA back onto the table, albeit under different terms.[29] This solution served to revitalise dwindling trade, but the political schism only revealed Glasgow's deep-seated loyalty to the British establishment. The two-time Lord Provost Robert Donald (1724–1803), himself a tobacco merchant, was granted permission by George III to 'raise a regiment of a thousand men at the expense of the City' during the early years of the conflict.[30] The formation of the Glasgow Regiment marks an early example of the powerful, colonial powers installing a potent sense of British national pride in the citizenry. It is worth noting that this same Hanoverian identity was on show during the Jacobite occupation of Glasgow in 1745, which mustered very little for the travelling rebel army. Erected in 1735, the equestrian statue of William of Orange in Argyle Street (now placed near Cathedral Square), was an expression of Protestant and royalist pride commissioned by James Macrae (1677–1744), who rose up the ranks of the British East India Company. One year later M'Ure's *History of Glasgow* was published, containing poetic dedications to William and Mary. Later, Glasgow's public displays of affection for the great and good were often brought forth by the public at large. But these early consecrations of identity and loyalty do paint a picture of Glasgow's position in the mid-to-late eighteenth century. Meanwhile, as stated above, the New York statue of George III was destroyed and repurposed for ammunition. For Jones, the war with America 'awakened a new, uniquely British political consciousness in Glasgow', providing 'Glaswegians with the opportunity to patriotically affirm their rights and liberties as established members of the British Empire'.[31] It might be more accurate to say '*re*awakened' and '*re*affirm', for these British, Hanoverian loyalties were inscribed well before the revolt. Given the hammer-blow to the city's mercantile class, though, the war did prove to be a turning point. Following the establishment of the Glasgow Regiment, citizens were reportedly 'animated by the zeal for their excellent constitution'

---

29 R. H. Campbell, 'The Making of The Industrial City', *Glasgow Volume I: Beginnings to 1830* (Manchester and New York: Manchester University Press, 1995), 184–213, 192.

30 John Strang, *Glasgow and its Clubs* (London and Glasgow: Richard Griffin and Co., 1857), 192.

31 Brad A. Jones, 'The American Revolution, Glasgow, and the Making of the Second City of the Empire', in Simon P. Newman, ed., *Europe's American Revolution* (Basingstoke: Palgrave Macmillan, 2006), 1–25, 1–2.

and 'subscribed most liberally'.[32] Soon, Glasgow's identity would be called into question as another imperial stand-off unfolded.

The French Revolution and its political fallout swept the British Isles, agitating labouring classes into protest. Following the Calton weavers' strike in 1787, Glasgow's artisan community was awakened to social injustices like never before. Events in France, and the growth of Jacobin clubs and societies debating class injustices, would change the face of Britain's democratic constitution in the coming decades. Meanwhile, the Forth and Clyde Canal was opened (1790), allowing for the improved transportation of goods from Glasgow to the east of Scotland. Several colonial merchants contributed to the development of this landmark engineering moment, including Archibald Spiers (1758–1832), Chairman of the Committee for the Canal.[33] As Glasgow and other British centres of commerce expanded their networks and wealth, the sense of British pride among the people was still palpable. Just as Glaswegians had subscribed to fight the Americans in the 1770s, so too were they prepared to defend against a potential French invasion in the 1790s. Support was not unequivocal, as Wold shows in his study of Scotland during this period, especially following the Militia Act of 1797. But Glasgow held onto its powerful imperial identity. An article printed in the *Glasgow Courier* in December 1792 asserted that Scotland 'was currently in a better situation than ever before in her history'.[34] Radical support dwindled around this time, as the Clerk of Session, George Home, boasted in a letter to his cousin in London, that clubs 'now consist only of the very refuse of the People'.[35]

In terms of industry, Glasgow was fast becoming the leader in cotton. According to Cooke, there had been 'an almost complete switch' in Glasgow between 1780 and 1791 'from the production of linen or cotton/linen combinations' to 'pure cotton muslins'.[36] As of 1791 it was estimated that there were 15,000 cotton looms in west central Scotland.[37] Cotton, like tobacco, was intrinsically linked to an enslaved workforce in the West Indies, representing a shift in Glasgow's imperial exploitation in the march towards industrialisation.[38] In Galt's *Bogle Corbet* (1831), we follow the story of the titular character from his earliest childhood memories

---

32 Ibid., 14.
33 Mullen, *Glasgow, Slavery*, 115.
34 Atle L. Wold, *Scotland and the French Revolutionary War, 1792–1802* (Edinburgh: Edinburgh University Press, 2015), 204.
35 Ibid., 138.
36 Anthony Cooke, *The rise and fall of the Scottish cotton industry, 1778–1914* (Manchester and New York: Manchester University Press, 2010), 24.
37 Campbell, 'The Making of the Industrial City', 199.
38 Mullen, *Glasgow, Slavery*, 32.

as a child in Jamaica to his life in Glasgow and his emigration to Canada. In Glasgow, one of Corbet's acquaintances declares 'Let Glasgow flourish by the weaving of cotton.'[39] Galt's penchant for weaving metaphors to describe civic growth has been explored elsewhere,[40] but this example from *Bogle Corbet* aligns with Graham's notion that the city's civic growth created a more secular society. Describing the early eighteenth century, Graham says 'These were the days when the motto of the city was "May Glasgow flourish by the preaching of the Word" – leaving it for commercial bailies in another and more secular century to dock it [...] considering that a means of "flourishing" far inferior to cotton, shipping, soft goods, and hardware.'[41] This march towards modernity with a more skilled labour force and new industries was often celebrated, and linked positively to Empire. Poetry of the day was reflective of the city's newfound status. Lines published in *The Glasgow Museum* in 1773 declared:

> That Glasgow on the base of commerce rose
> A noble fabric, all the world knows.
> She bids her sons to fly from pole to pole.
> Where Sol enlightens or where ocean roll,
> And in her fleets bring to their native strand,
> The arts and treasures of each foreign land.[42]

The imagery of a city being elevated – physically in stature and infrastructure – by its traders, is important in any discussion of Glasgow and Empire. And there are more, subtler markers in other poems such as John Mayne's *Glasgow: A Poem*, first printed in 1783. The opening declaration ('Hail, Glasgow! fam'd for ilka thing') is followed by typical civic boosterism, this time following the Standard Habbie, or Burns stanza rhyme. The city's merchants and professional classes are mentioned, along with the 'pride wafted' on the Clyde as trade from 'the Indies and America' brought about new wealth. A new edition of Mayne's poem was printed in 1803, boasting 53 new stanzas, packed full of yet more Glaswegian

---

39 John Galt, *Bogle Corbet; or, The Emigrants* v. 1 (London: Henry Colburn & Richard Bentley, 1831), 32.

40 Lamont, *Georgian Glasgow*, 123.

41 Henry Grey Graham, 'Tobias Smollett', *Scottish Men of Letters in the Eighteenth Century* (London: Adam & Charles Black, 1908), 299.

42 Richard B. Sher, 'Images of Glasgow in Late Eighteenth-Century Popular Poetry', in Andrew Hook and Sher, eds, *The Glasgow Enlightenment* (Phantassie, East Lothian: Tuckwell Press, 1995), 190–213, 207.

characteristics, including the figures of the Scottish Enlightenment at Glasgow, the weaving and spinning of 'the muslin robe', and new celebrations of industry and commerce.[43] This was all building towards another watershed moment in the age of the British Empire. The Napoleonic Wars were more than just a continuation of Britain's long war with France; they marked a new age for Empire defined by the grandeur of war and heroism. In the *Caledonian Mercury* of 12 September 1799, a 'Gentleman in Glasgow' wrote the following verses 'on receiving the intelligence of the surrender of the Dutch fleet', also known as the Vlieter incident:

How oft, since Old Neptune to Britons resign'd,
His chariot and sceptre, have our en'mies combin'd,
That chariot and sceptre, from us to obtain;
How oft fought us for them – how oft fought in vain,
For our ships ay were oak, invincible our men,
They always were steady,
Ready, boys, ready,
O'er Ocean our Empire t'assert and maintain.[44]

Clearly echoing the famous song *Rule, Britannia* by the Scottish poet James Thomson, this is an example of Glasgow's civic pride, specifically connecting Glasgow's access to the seas with the Empire's naval might. It also anticipates a rapidly growing cult obsession with 'soldier heroes' in Glasgow, and Britain more generally.

This section has brought together the key moments in Glasgow's rise, from its pre-Union beginnings to the height of slave-produced wealth and the establishment of a mercantile elite. Not only the individuals, but the literature and the objects which reflect these processes have been brought to the foreground in order to produce a clearer view of this period. In the next section we will look at a new era in Glasgow's history, an age in which soldier heroes offer inspiration for the ever-swelling population, and the efforts at home – and abroad – to improve the city's infrastructure.

43 John Mayne, *Glasgow: A Poem* (1803). Online edition: https://xtf.lib.virginia.edu/xtf/view?docId=chadwyck_ep/uvaGenText/tei/chep_2.1234.xml;brand=default, accessed 20 October 2023.

44 'Verses Written by a Gentlemen in Glasgow', *Caledonian Mercury* (12 September 1799), 4.

Consecrating the Empire: Heroes and Crowds in the Nineteenth Century

Glasgow's shape and size would undergo vast changes as the century progressed. To imagine the public memorials as a topographical map of civic self-portraiture, William of Orange in the city centre had been joined by Nelson in Glasgow Green. The Hunterian Museum (1807), located initially on the Old College campus on the High Street represented another monument, enshrining the rich scientific and medical history of Glasgow rather than any one person. Though named for William Hunter (1718–1783) and his vast medical and antiquarian objects moved back from London, the site was as much for Glasgow's enlightenment as it was for Hunter: portraits of Cullen, Smollett and Hutcheson[45] in the Museum were soon joined by a statue of Watt in 1833. The next public memorial in Glasgow would be the first in George Square, now the chief civic space. The monument to Sir John Moore (1761–1809), was unveiled on 18 August 1819. Unlike Nelson, or indeed William of Orange, Moore was Glaswegian by birth. He was the son of John Moore the author, physician, and correspondent of Robert Burns. At a ripe age, Moore became part of the new Glasgow regiment that fought in the American Wars. He was quickly promoted through the ranks, and in 1808 led forces against Napoleon in the Peninsular War. In this new century, Glasgow's unshakeable British loyalty was cemented, and, upon his death on the battlefield in Corunna (1809), Moore became Glasgow's first 'soldier hero'. But as McKenzie has shown, the subscription plans and even the design negotiations were not straightforward.[46] Also, George Square was in its infancy during this period: as contemporary depictions of the Moore monument show, it is more reasonable to say that the square grew around Moore than saying he was placed in a site of high importance. In other words, Moore's bronze likeness set the standard for the other statues (including Watt, Burns, Gladstone) that would follow.

In choosing the material for the Moore statue, a symbolic circle which opened with the pulling down of George III's statue in New York was closed. There, the melted remains of the monument were made into bullets. In Glasgow, the statue 'was cast from three tons of bronze salvaged' from captured canons at the end of the Napoleonic Wars. What is more, the final subscription amount (just shy of £3,600) could not all be spent on the statue, and so the surplus was used 'to repair the damage caused by lightning striking the Nelson Monument' in 1810.[47]

---

[45] Lamont, *Georgian Glasgow*, 74.

[46] Ray McKenzie et al., *Public Sculpture of Glasgow*: Public Sculpture of Britain, Vol. 5 (Liverpool: Liverpool University Press, 2002), 121.

[47] Ibid., 122.

Two heroes for the price of one. But in fact, there are two more. All told, they represent Glasgow's ultimate saluting of the British Empire in the form of soldier heroes. The equestrian monument to Arthur Wellesley, the Duke of Wellington (1760–1852) was inaugurated on 8 October 1844 in Exchange Square, in front of what is now the Gallery of Modern Art. Wellington was immortalised for defeating Napoleon at Waterloo, though, like Nelson who won at Trafalgar, he had no connection to Scotland. Glasgow at this point in its imperial construction has two types of absentee memory-subjects: the merchants who seldom visited their plantations and whose enslaved workforce laboured out of sight; and the English soldier heroes whose statues took permanence where they never did in life. McKenzie relates how the art critics disputed Marochetti's appointment as the sculptor and how the statue was 'wantonly defaced' in its first year.[48] We can safely assume some public ambivalence, even aggression, towards the monument. But McKenzie also notes the support of business firms and wealthy individuals, and that 'within a few months a fund of nearly £10,000 had been raised', making this 'by far the largest, as well as most speedily gathered, private subscription for any monument in Glasgow in the nineteenth century'.[49] Toasts and festivals for Wellington had taken place mostly in England, and these were reported in the Scottish presses. The memory-makers in this instance do not necessarily represent the feeling of Glasgow's common citizen, not that they ever did. Instead, a deputation consisting of the Lord Provost 'and the noblemen and gentlemen of the counties in the west of Scotland' addressed Wellington at his house in April 1840, to ask his permission to meet with the artist they would select.[50] Here we have a living subject consecrated in Glasgow's public sphere on behalf of the city's ongoing imperial narrative. Not just his likeness, but – crucially – his values are invoked by Walter Buchanan in his poem 'Royal Exchange, Glasgow, 1894'. Fifty years after the monument appears, Buchanan describes the subject as more graceful than a Roman, with a 'calmly serious face', 'unmoved' by the weather, and whose 'high ideals' (especially duty) he invites us to share.[51], As the co-editor of the present volume so aptly suggested, we might well consider Buchanan's work a poorer version of Russian writer Alexander Pushkin's poem *The Bronze Horseman* (1833/37), which depicts St Petersburg's statue to Peter the Great. Though much shorter and less ambiguous about his equestrian subject

48 Ibid., 339.
49 Ibid., 337.
50 *Morning Post* (13 April 1840), 4.
51 Walter Buchanan, 'Royal Exchange, Glasgow, March 1894', *The Glasgow Ballad Club: Ballads and Poems by Members of the Glasgow Ballad Club, Second Series* (Edinburgh, 1898), 153–155.

than Pushkin, Buchanan does reveal the mode of expected remembrance in Glasgow for these types of monuments.

The other major figure here is the monument to the aforementioned Lord Clyde (1792–1863). This statue was inaugurated on 5 August 1868, beside the monument to Clyde's fellow Glaswegian Sir John Moore. He was known as the conqueror of the Indian Mutiny, a victorious epithet that put Clyde in league with those other soldier heroes whose fame often obscures the heinousness of the British imperial hand. Both Moore and Clyde were involved in large-scale bloody repressions on behalf of the British state.[52] It is only recently that these narratives have been brought out of the shadows cast by the greatness of the statue's subjects. In terms of Glasgow's imperial aesthetic, however, it is worth noting that the placement of Clyde beside Moore was not the only suitable suggestion. As McKenzie states, a proposal was made to erect Clyde beside Wellington in the Exchange Square, and to move Moore to the same site to form a triumvirate of 'Britain's greatest military leaders'.[53] This scheme was never realised, but standing these two Glasgow-born soldier heroes side by side was a powerful statement of British imperial pride in its own right.

Not everyone subscribed to Glaswegian imperial sentiment. Following the radical rising of 1820, James Wilson of Strathaven, and later John Baird and Andrew Hardie were executed for treason. Their attempt to overthrow the government with armed force did not muster the numbers they had hoped, but the spirit of dissent was awakened. From around 1816, support had been growing in Glasgow at Thrushgrove, comprising land owned by the radical businessman James Turner. Around 40,000 people turned up to petition parliament for political reform.[54] A monument to Hardie and Baird was erected there in 1832. It is not extant, but a replacement monument was erected in Sighthill cemetery in Glasgow in July 1847. According to the radical newspaper *The Northern Star*, the remains of Hardie and Baird were exhumed in Stirling and marched to Glasgow, and, after stopping briefly in Thurshgrove, reinterred in Sighthill. Unlike the private subscriptions for the memorialisation of the British military elite, this commemoration of two executed radicals was enacted by 'the working men of Glasgow, the men who toll and think'.[55] The writer in *The Northern Star* claims that no 'withered cheek will

---

52 Lamont, *Georgian Glasgow*, 161.

53 McKenzie, *Public Sculpture*, 137.

54 Craig Lamont, 'Remembering the Radical War: Monuments, markers and commemorations', in Gerard Carruthers, Kevin Thomas Gallagher, Craig Lamont and George Smith, eds, *1820 Scottish Rebellion: Essays on a Nineteenth-Century Insurrection* (Edinburgh: John Donald, 2022), 213–235, 214.

55 Ibid., 220.

be moistened with tears' for the memory of George IV, or statesmen like Lord Castlereagh (1769–1822). In Alasdair Gray's *Lanark* (1981), the author sketches out this history and connects it to imperial Britain:

> So Baird, Hardie and Wilson were arrested, tried and hung, and the bloody tide of revolution receded. Then one day the government noticed it could give the vote to almost everyone without losing power. The unemployed got assisted passages to Canada, Australia, Asia and Africa, where they prospered by grabbing land from the natives. Britain became an empire, everyone lived happily ever after, and a monument was erected to Baird and Hardie and Wilson who had died to make us free.[56]

This deliberately slapdash, conversational passage reflects the tediousness of lives lost in the struggle for human rights. The imperial forces carry on regardless, and tokenistic sympathies are paid to those who 'toll and think' – to cite the radical newspaper – and suffer for it. The portrayal of Glasgow is found often in *Lanark* to be disorienting, with histories thrown together as successive generations set their eyes on new priorities. Much earlier, there was a sense of this in Galt's *Annals of the Parish* (1821), in which Glasgow's imperial wealth overflows into to the fictional parish of Dalmailing. The novel is set between 1760 and 1810, and, as McIlvanney says, is most effective in portraying the 'inability' of the parish to 'contain and make sense' of the changes brought about by Empire.[57]

The 1820s and 30s saw a great number of societal questions unravelling. The abolitionist movement was growing at around the same time as the concessions being mooted for Roman Catholics were being opposed. For all that the opening of the Roman Catholic St Andrew's Chapel (now Cathedral) on Clyde Street in 1816 should represent a huge change in Glasgow's religious demographic, the centuries-old sectarian divide was still palpable. The King's Visit to Scotland in 1822, in which the tartan regalia previously banished after Culloden was transferred symbolically onto George IV, was contemporaneous with the beginnings of Irish famine.[58] The *Glasgow Herald* printed notice of the distresses in Ireland, but supplemented news with anti-Irish tracts taken from around Britain.[59] In February 1829 a flyer was published by a William Dorsey, looking for the citizens of Glasgow to petition parliament on Roman Catholic Concessions. 'Let it not be said,' the flyer stated, 'that the second city in the Empire, with a population

---

56 Alasdair Gray, *Lanark: A Life in Four Books* (Edinburgh: Canongate, 1981/2007), 337.

57 Liam McIlvanney, 'The Glasgow Novel', in Gerard Carruthers and McIlvanney, eds, *The Cambridge Companion to Scottish Literature* (Cambridge: Cambridge University Press, 2012), 217–32, 221.

58 *Glasgow Herald* (24 June 1822), 2.

59 *Glasgow Herald* (12 August 1822), 1.

of upwards of 200,000 was amongst the last, to step forward in defence of its religion'. The statues of Knox in the Necropolis and William of Orange in Argyle Street are cited as models for Glasgow to follow in defending their Protestant faith.[60] William Smeal, who had founded the Glasgow Anti-Slavery Society in 1822, invited Frederick Douglass to speak to a gathered crowd in 1846. Douglass, whose free name is derived from the hero of Walter Scott's *Lady of the Lake* (1810), was born into slavery in Maryland as Frederick Augustus Washington Bailey. His presence in Glasgow, and Edinburgh, during these years speaks to the ongoing social reform and campaigning which animated public life. Following the peak of the Great Famine, or *Gorta Mór,* in 1847, the immigration of the Irish into Glasgow was noted by John MacGregor (1797–1857), MP for Glasgow.[61] By 1849, some of the journalism printed in the *Glasgow Herald* was laced with hateful suspicion for the Irish in general.[62] While it is not the purpose of this chapter to focus on anti-Irish sentiment, it is worth noting that racism and xenophobia was exhibited often in anti-Catholic and pro-slavery publications, and in the periodical presses. Indeed, it is tempting to trace such Social Darwinism to the colonial activities of the previous century, and to consider how these developed alongside the immense increase in population Glasgow experienced through immigration. As Tomlinson has shown, shared anti-Irish and white supremacist attitudes were harboured well into the twentieth century, often by teachers who made assumptions about the mental capacity of particular groups. Views like these were given weight by psychologists such as Hans Eysenck, who, as late as 1971, suggested that '"Negroes and the Irish" had lower mental capacities due to crimes committed against their ancestors.'[63]

According to Devine and MacKenzie, 'two-thirds of all British iron-built tonnage was produced on the Clyde between 1851 and 1870.'[64] A supplement on Glasgow printed in *The Graphic* in 1880 offers an illustrated tour of the city's chief spaces. The growth of trade and shipbuilding are given due praise, and the 'older Glasgow, ignorant of chemicals and steam engines', is relegated to the best-forgotten past. The new water supply from Loch Katrine, opened in 1859, is also noted, quoting Scott's famous line ('the land of the mountain and the flood') from *The Lay of the Last Minstrel* (1805). A rather bleak picture is painted of Glasgow – again in part connected to Irish immigration – in the throes of

---

60 Poster, Glasgow University Special Collections: Sp Coll Bh12-y.25/100.
61 *Warder and Dublin Weekly Mail* (24 February 1849), 1.
62 *Glasgow Herald* (22 October 1849), 2.
63 Sally Tomlinson, *Education and Race from Empire to Brexit* (Bristol: Policy Press, 2019), 86.
64 T. M. Devine and John M. MacKenzie, 'Scots in the Imperial Economy', 227–254, 237.

squalor and poverty, in a section on the City Improvement Act of 1866. This highly expensive endeavour is one of the key moments in which Glasgow received the imperial treatment while simultaneously posturing as a centre of the Empire. Following a delegation to Paris to witness Haussmann's renovation of Paris, civic leaders addressed Glasgow's sanitation and overcrowding head-on.[65] In the same year, Marochetti's equestrian statue of Prince Albert was inaugurated in George Square. Permission was granted by Queen Victoria to relocate her own equestrian monument from St Vincent Place – where it had been since 1854 – putting Victoria and Albert side by side in George Square. In other words, the city leaders were reinscribing loyalism in the first year of the Improvement works. Before long, city rebuilding efforts in Glasgow became the standard method deployed in other imperial cities. As MacKenzie has shown, improvements in Bombay, Calcutta, Rangoon, Singapore, Lagos and Dehli between 1898 and 1937 followed the Glasgow model. 'What had started out as a highly discriminatory class order of residential accommodation, water supply and sanitation', MacKenzie says, 'had become a racial one overseas'.[66] As reports in London showed, Glasgow was still being 'improved' in this manner into the twentieth century. In February 1904, journalists noted that 'Glasgow has still dark spots and unwholesome areas to conquer': a plainly imperial evocation in which the reader might confuse a flourishing British city with a distant outpost of the Empire.[67]

The 1880s marked a new period of civic boosterism for Glasgow. The largest built manifestation of this was the completion of the new Town Hall (or City Chambers) in 1888. John Carrick, leader of the city improvements in the crumbling and overcrowded High Street and Old Cross, singled out George Square as the ideal location. As Groten has recently shown, George Square was already furnished with the new post office (1876) and the Merchant's House (1877), and an array of statues from Sir John Moore to Victoria and Albert.[68] The final design by John Young was inspired by the ancient cities of Italy and can be seen today in its classical renaissance splendour. The pediment of the building was originally meant to convey Glasgow allegorically, with the River Clyde and a fleet of ships 'sending her manufactures and arts to all the world'. But the opportunity of the

---

65 'Improvements in Glasgow', in Michelle Allen-Emerson, ed., *Sanitary Reform in Victorian Britain: Sanitary Reform and Urban Development* (New York: Routledge, 2013), 225–228, 226.

66 John M. MacKenzie, *The British Empire Through Buildings: Structure, Function, Meaning* (Manchester: Manchester University Press, 2020), 186.

67 *Tower Hamlets Independent and East End Local Advertiser* (6 February 1904), 6.

68 Miel Groten, 'Glasgow's new town hall: imperialism, nationalism and civic pride, 1877–1889', *Urban History* 48 (2021), 644–662, 649.

upcoming golden jubilee for Victoria changed the course of this, with Young opting instead for 'a most important imperial memorial' depicting the Queen 'surrounded' by well-wishing subjects from Scotland, Ireland and Wales, as well as Britain's colonies.[69] These figurative well-wishers represent people from India, China, Canada, and Africa – 'symbolised by a white man having his arm round the neck of a negro'.[70] As Goten put it, 'Cities all over Britain and the empire were falling over each other to erect monuments to Victoria in 1887,' and indeed Glasgow already had, but 'none had the Glasgow elite's opportunity to associate their city government with the monarchy so explicitly and to transform their monument to municipal rule into a monument to imperial rule at the same time.'[71] During the Queen's visit in August 1888, George Square – 'the Valhalla' of Glasgow as it was denoted in the press[72] – was awash with flags, flowers, and symbolic heraldry of the four nations, with a particular focus on the royal equestrian statues. The newly built City Chambers were 'unadorned, so that Her Majesty might see' the new structure in its full glory.[73]

The Queen's procession was conveyed from George Square to Kelvingrove Park, where the Glasgow International Exhibition was taking place. Following the layout and intention of the 1886 Edinburgh exhibition, Glasgow used this opportunity to further consecrate its imperial centrality. Besides the vast temporary structure in vogue since the Great Exhibition in London in 1851, Glasgow had a replica of the Bishop's Palace, lost to time since the 1790s, and a huge number of cultural and historical artefacts pertinent to Scotland. For the most part though, the experience was in line with several British exhibitions in gathering an imperial aesthetic, representative of British India as much – if not more – than the architectural style of the host city. One of the crowning objects in the Exhibition was the three-storey terracotta Doulton Fountain. As Spooner has said, the fountain's prime location, size, and four figurative groups (Canada, Australia, India and South Africa) beneath the likeness of Queen Victoria is 'a clear celebration of Britain's imperial achievements'.[74] At the close of the exhibition the fountain was dismantled and in 1890 it was reconstructed in its present location in Glasgow

---

69 Ibid., 653.

70 *Glasgow Herald* (21 January 1887), 7; Mullen, *Glasgow, Slavery*, 48.

71 Groten, 'Glasgow's new town hall', 653.

72 *Glasgow Herald* (23 August 1888), 4.

73 Ibid.

74 Rosemary Gall Spooner, 'Close encounters: international exhibitions and the material culture of the British Empire, c.1880–1940' (2016), 138: PhD thesis: https://theses.gla.ac.uk/7386/, accessed 20 October 2023.

Green, with speeches on the greatness of Britain's Empire.[75] By the end of the nineteenth century, Glasgow had conceptualised itself as a crucial component of empire. In its buildings, its public statues, and its first international exhibition, the city had become diffused with imperial symbols and iconography, from the pediment on the City Chambers to the Doulton Fountain in Glasgow Green. When a second, larger exhibition was staged in 1901, Glasgow 'extolled Britain's world supremacy, a claim substantiated by technological virtuosity and colonial domination'.[76]

As the twentieth century wore on, Britain's grip on the globe was gradually loosened. In the first few decades, and especially during the First and Second World War, Glasgow remained committed to the ongoing proliferation of British national – and imperial – pride. But, as the next section will show, this process typifies a new age of Glasgow's diminishing relationship with empire. Most of the statues and street names remain intact, but there has been a shift in civic awareness. Where once these markers were intended to reflect greatness and inspire pride, they are now often criticised and sometimes scorned. While this is not unique to Glasgow, it is worth studying Glasgow in what we might consider the 'shadow of empire', where the bombastic crowds and civic pride have given way to something more mournful and divisive.

Nostalgia and the Shadow of Empire

In the closing passage of *The Second City*, Oakley laments that Glasgow's heyday has passed, that a city of 'unlimited opportunity' had slipped, in the 1930s, into a 'pretty wretched condition'.[77] The devastation of war had damaged Britain's global economic interests. This was obvious in Glasgow's 1938 'Empire Exhibition', held in Bellahouston Park. The aims of the exhibition set out in the official guide-book are telling. They include: 'stimulating work and production', 'fostering Empire trade and a closer friendship among the peoples of the British Commonwealth of Nations', and 'to emphasise to the world the peaceful aspirations of the peoples of the British Empire'.[78] As in previous imperial shows, there were regional pavilions and visitor attractions connecting Glasgow with Canada, Australia, New Zealand, South Africa and other colonial African zones such as Southern

---

75 McKenzie, *Public Sculpture*, 169.

76 John E. Findling, eds., *Historical Dictionary of World's Fairs and Expositions, 1851–1988* (Greenwood, CT; London: Greenwood Press, 1990), 172.

77 C. A. Oakley, *The Second City* (London and Glasgow: Blackie & Son Ltd., 1946), 338.

78 These 'Objects of the Exhibition' were printed in a list in the *Official Guide* (1938), 66.

Rhodesia. The exhibition also featured a Highland Clachan and Irish weaving cottages, which pitted the modern progress of Glasgow (via the Empire) against these poor, antiquated, even primitive Gaelic landscapes.[79] Of course, within a year of the exhibition saw the beginning of the Second World War, and the beginning of the end of the British Empire proper.

Throughout the twentieth century, though, imperial ideologies continued on, casting a shadow from the monolithic nineteenth century. A good example of this is the popular, mass-celebration event known as 'Empire Day', which commenced on 24 May 1903. From this date – the late Queen Victoria's birthday – to the 1950s, Empire Day events in Britain and in the colonies helped proliferate national pride during difficult financial periods. Much work has been done to analyse the impact of Empire Day in different social groups, across divisions of class, and in schools and youth movements.[80] The concept was ushered in by Reginald Brabazon, Lord Meath (1841– 1929), to propagate the 'magnificence and power of the Empire'.[81] In 1909 *The Scotsman* reported that several colonies and dependencies participated loyally in celebrations. For the first time, Glasgow joined in. Union flags and Scottish standards were on display 'over the principal buildings', the national anthem played in theatres, and several corporations celebrated with banquets, toasting the royal family and the Empire. As the report noted, the 'main purpose' was 'to train the rising generation in the virtues of loyalty and patriotism'.[82] It was an attempt to harness the obvious anxieties about the future and combine local and national pride under a well-worn banner. It became an annual event in Glasgow, and in 1911 it was reported that schoolchildren were addressed on the subject of Empire as a matter of course.[83] By 1930 the movement had become more popular, with processions of around 1000 children converging at the Cenotaph in George Square. The Cenotaph was unveiled in 1924 and became a prime 'site of memory' for the easily achieved connection between civic spaces and their own unique war memorials, especially during remembrance services.[84] In these interwar years, the true extent of Britain's imperial force was transformed into moral lessons on peace and community,

79 Lamont, 'Cultural Memory and Nationalism.'
80 Brad Beavan, *Visions of Empire: Patriotism, Popular Culture and the City, 1870–1939* (Manchester: Manchester University Press, 2015), 150–1.
81 Ibid., 142.
82 *The Scotsman* (25 May 1909), 4.
83 *The Scotsman* (25 May 1911), 6.
84 Lamont, *Georgian Glasgow*, 159.

often delivered by former soldiers anxiously awaiting the next war.[85] Clearly, the aim was to teach children that the Empire bestowed freedom on its subjects, and was nothing less than 'a living example to the world' on the global prosperity and peace that Britain had achieved. When we consider these events with VJ Day celebrations, it is easy to understand what Macwhirter calls 'the high noon of unionism' in Glasgow. The Clydebank Blitz of March 1941 proved that Glasgow, even as it suffered financially, was crucial to Britain.[86] Another good example of youth mobility in memory-making and identity-forging is the Boys' Brigade (BB). Founded in Glasgow in 1883, MacKenzie has noted that the BB was 'a specifically Christian organisation, closely involved with mainly Protestant and dissenting churches', and that the military aesthetic and practice (uniforms, ranks, drillings) developed at home were easily reproduced in BB Companies throughout the Empire in the first years of the twentieth century.[87]

This new focus on youth brings us into the realm of memory and nostalgia. For sure, most of this chapter has been concerned with the imperial force driving Glasgow's growth and connections overseas, and the focus on cultural memory has shown that the city today remains firmly imperial in its aesthetic. Yes, Wellington is better known for his traffic cone than his military prowess, but he nonetheless remains part of Glasgow's cultural identikit – right beside shipbuilding and titan cranes. Nostalgia for the Empire has become a more common topic in recent years. Sanghera's *Empireland* and Mitchell's *Imperial Nostalgia* (both 2021) and Woods' *Rule Nostalgia* (2022) are prime examples of the turn in imperial historiography, away from glorification and towards interrogation. Sanghera, for example, highlights that the might of Britain's army during global conflict was itself a global force: comprising support (soldiers, supplies, navigation) from all British colonies. This multicultural might is rarely noted.[88] One previous study cited by Sanghera is Heather Streets' *Martial races* (2010), which examines the 'biological or cultural disposition to the racial and masculine qualities necessary for the arts of war' in groups such as Scottish Highlanders, Punjabi Sikhs, and Nepalese Gurkhas. More recently in Scotland we have Jackie Kay's poem 'The Look of Loss' (2018) – about Arthur Roberts, the Black Scottish soldier during the

85 In the coverage of Empire Day events (*The Scotsman*, 24 May 1937, 9) and their build-up (*The Scotsman*, 16 May 1937, 11), army personnel addressed youthful crowds about the Empire.

86 Iain Macwhirter, *Road to Referendum* (Glasgow: Cargo, 2014), 110.

87 John M. MacKenzie, *A Cultural History of the British Empire* (New Haven, CT.: Yale University Press, 2022), 64.

88 Sathnam Sanghera, *Empireland: How Imperialism Has Shaped Modern Britain* (London: Penguin, 2021), 198.

First World War, and the work of Colourful Heritage, who will soon inaugurate Scotland's first British Indian Army (BIA) memorial in the grounds of Kelvingrove Art Gallery and Museum, in Glasgow. New memorials like this help promote a more diverse cultural memory where the British Army is concerned, reshaping the old civic topography represented by a select few soldier heroes.

'The imaginary of empire', says Mitchell, 'was suffused, at the moment of its creation, with a mood of mourning and elegy, a sense of itself as already yearning back towards a glorious past'.[89] We see this in Glasgow, in the earliest built manifestations of imperial pride: monuments to heroes inaugurated with a particularly Protestant – often masonic – ceremony. There was no space in the ceremony, or in the resulting 'object' of remembrance, for anything but glory and respect. It was not until around 1990 – when Glasgow's civic heritage was festooned with City of Culture status – that working-class groups began to question the nomenclature of areas such as 'Merchant City'. The phrase had been used by Gomme and Walker in *Architecture of Glasgow* (1968), but in the 1990s it was officialised, as Magdin (2021) has shown, to 'increase civic pride and attract human and capital investment', and to create a 'new image' of Glasgow's historic centre distinct from the crumbling reminders of deindustrialisation.[90] The socialist Workers City movement produced a book, *The Reckoning: Beyond the Culture City Rip Off* (1990). The editor, Farquhar McLay, remembers his uncle giving him a couple of tips on being a working man: 'There's nae use in me fullin your heid wi a lot o damned nonsense aboot whit's in front o ye. Ships that saved the Empire and aa that rubbish. That's what they gie ye in the schuil but it's crap, it's aa crap. Never mind the bluidy Empire, you mind No. 1.'[91] The advice to forget the empire was borne of an insecurity and anxiety for the conditions of workers and the power structures in modern Britain. It is interesting that the 'bluidy Empire' as celebrated in the classroom bears no resemblance to the realities of the working class.

In H. V. Morton's *In Search of Scotland* (1929), we find all the language of Glasgow's most commonly perceived strengths. Anticipating Oakley's nostalgia for Glasgow of the turn of the century, Morton cites the 'transatlantic alertness'

---

89 Peter Mitchell, *Imperial Nostalgia: How the British Conquered Themselves* (Manchester: Manchester University Press, 2021), 57.

90 Rebecca Magdin, 'Recognising Emotions within Urban Development', in Katie Barclay and Jade Riddle, eds, *Urban Emotions and the Making of the City: interdisciplinary perspectives* (London and New York: Routledge, 2021), 143–163, 157.

91 Farquhar McLay, 'Working at it', in Farquhar McLay, ed., *The Reckoning: Beyond the Culture City Rip Off* (Glasgow: Clydeside Press/Workers City Movement, 1990), 113–120, 117.

and the 'self-centred' greatness of Glasgow.[92] His description of a ship being launched on the Clyde is a celebration of the city's industrial golden age, and at all times it is intrinsically linked to the concept of the waiting empire. All this retrospective city-scaping during national economic decline. In his next chapter, we meet a commissionaire at the steelworks in Motherwell who keeps a picture of Lord Roberts (1832– 1914) on the wall of his office.[93] This man, Morton tells us, marched with Roberts to Kandahar. Private expressions of imperial or national pride are common in the text, but it does form an important distinction between those private, generational memories and those cultural memories in the form of monuments bestowed upon a city. When Roberts died in 1914, a committee planned for a statue to be erected, and a Lord Roberts 'day' was organised with the assistance of 4,000 volunteers including the Boys Brigade to raise funds.[94] It was unveiled in 1916, becoming a new landmark in the officialised British cityscape of Glasgow. Over a century later, in 2017, a petition was posted online to remove the 'racist, colonial statue'.[95] This was slightly ahead of its time and did not garner much support. The social awareness of statues and their implied celebrations of imperial atrocities reached a tipping point in 2020, and the Colston statue toppling in Bristol has come to symbolise this. As a result, the UK Government issued 'Guidance for custodians on how to deal with commemorative heritage assets that have become contested' in October 2023.[96] Clearly, the questions of memory, history and identity are far from settled. As for Glasgow, the city continues to consider its imperial past. The University and the City Council have been praised for leading the way in some cases of reparative justice, symbolically in renaming of buildings and financially by way of scholarships. Nostalgia has become less acceptable in Glasgow, and the place of the British Empire continues to spark debate.

This chapter has outlined the impact of the British Empire on Glasgow's civic imagery, or 'cityscape' to cite the term used by Fuhrer et al. who investigated 'the process through which an image of a city or an urban landscape is imaginatively

92 H. V. Morton, *In Search of Scotland* (London: Methuen, 1931 [1929]), 250.

93 Ibid., 260.

94 McKenzie, *Public Sculpture*, 232.

95 Lamont, *Georgian Glasgow*, 161; McKenzie, *Public Sculpture*, 204.

96 Report: https://www.gov.uk/government/publications/guidance-for-custodians-on-how-to-deal-with-commemorative-heritage-assets-that-have-become-contested, accessed 20 October 2023.

constructed'.[97] For sure, Glasgow remains imbued with the visual language of its origin story: St Mungo and his miracles, both officially and colloquially. The bird, the bell, the fish, the tree. At the height of Empire, we might think of another symbolic tree: the one felled in Galt's novel *Bogle Corbet* (1831) in the new Canadian town, named 'Stockwell' after the Glasgow street, which the emigrant community see as a connection to their home city.[98] Finally, and more immediately, we might consider the tree from a less nostalgic perspective. Recent scholarship has made it clear that Glasgow's flourishing was connected to many of Empire's atrocities: violence, genocide, and slavery. In his 'Seeds of Antiracist Education' video-poem, Tawona Sithole recites the African proverb: 'what forgets is the axe, but the tree that was cut does not forget.'[99] In Glasgow today, the axe and the tree are being given their place together.

---

97 Therese Fuhrer, Felix Mundt and Jan Stenger, 'Introduction', Fuhrer, Mundt and Stenger, eds, *Cityscaping: Constructing and Modelling Images of the City* (Berlin: Walter de Gruyter GmbH, 2015), 1.

98 Lamont, *Georgian Glasgow*, 128.

99 Tawona Sithole, *Seeds of Antiracist Education* –Building Racial Literacy Programme: https://www.youtube.com/watch?v=BlQE3vEaDvs, accessed 20 October 2023.

People Make Glasgow Portable – and Portable People Make Glasgow: The Case for Translocal Scottish Diaspora Studies

Tanja Bueltmann

In the summer of 1842, Gorbals-born Allan and his wife Joan from Duddingston near Edinburgh, sat in a small printing shop in Chicago, Illinois, folding recently printed volumes of Scottish folk songs. Allan, so an acquaintance recounted, 'stitched every copy'.[1] This Allan thus engaged in helping prepare Scottish folks songs for distribution in the US was Allan Pinkerton, one-time saviour of Abraham Lincoln, Civil War spy, and the founder of Pinkerton National Detective Agency – the first 'private eye'.[2] The story of how a boy from Glasgow made it to what was to become one of America's greatest cities to then establish such an illustrious life post-migration begins in the Gorbals at the corner of Muirhead Street and Rutherglen Loan in Glasgow 'this Scotch city of brawn and capital', but the Gorbals 'the abode of swarms of those whose fortunes and surroundings are equally meager and lorn'.[3] When Allan was born in 1819, the family struggled to make ends meet; his father had died when Allan was a young boy. It was partly because of these circumstances that Allan started working as soon as he was able, eventually becoming a cooper. It was this work that led to him becoming active in the Chartist movement, travelling throughout the UK to take part in meetings and protests.[4] This activism, Allan's story goes, was what eventually made him

---

1 *The Indiana State Sentinel*, 'A Detectives Early Life', 25 September 1889; see also Stephen Winick, 'Hidden Folklorists: Allan and Joan Pinkerton', Library of Congress blog (18 May 2017), https://blogs.loc.gov/folklife/2017/05/hidden-folklorists-allan-and-joan-pinkerton/, accessed 12 February 2024.

2 For a general background on Pinkerton and the agency he established, see S. Paul O'Hara, *Inventing the Pinkertons or, Spies, Sleuths, Mercenaries, and Thugs. Being a Story of the Nation's most Famous (and Infamous) Detective Agency* (Baltimore: Johns Hopkins University Press, 2016); the logo of Pinkerton's Agency showed an eye, see https://blogs.loc.gov/manuscripts/2023/10/the-eye-that-never-sleeps-pinkertons-national-detective-agency-records/, accessed 6 February 2024.

3 Both quotes from 'A Detectives Early Life', *The Indiana State Sentinel* (25 September 1889).

4 See for instance Robert McCrie, 'Allan Pinkerton (August 25, 1819–July 1, 1884): Founder of the Security Services Industry', *Journal of Applied Security Research* 5 (2010), 543–552.

'an outlaw with a price on his head',[5] emigration emerging as his best recourse to escape from what seemed certain punishment in Glasgow. By that point in the early 1840s, Allan was already married to Joan, the two thus making their way across the Atlantic together. Following early struggles in their new home, Allan and Joan settled in the township of Dundee,[6] where Allan initially set up a cooperage, but then – largely by accident – became involved in police work, which eventually led to him establishing his own detective agency in the 1850s. His expertise in detective work became so well-regarded that Allan was made President Lincoln's chief intelligence agent during the Civil War, once providing information that helped foil an assassination plot on the President-elect in Baltimore in early 1861.[7]

While an impressive story of a Scottish immigrant building a life across the Atlantic – of a 'portable' Glaswegian's pioneering spy and detective work that would shape policing and intelligence services in the US and globally for decades to come – Allan's life in the US, ultimately, tells a much more complex story than this potted introductory sketch reveals. It is a story that raises questions about the portability of people, their ideas and values, made in one locale and transported to another to shape it, and how we can best understand such patterns of transfer and exchange. For how could a man who had been active in the Chartist Movement in Scotland be the same man who was instrumental in repressing organised labour in the US, including, for instance, the Molly Maguires?[8] This is a question we will return to. Before we do, however, let us first reflect on the idea of portability itself, which, in one way or other, has been central to all chapters in this volume.

Portability is a key concept in studies focused on transnationalism, referring to the ability of people to carry not just themselves, but also other aspects of their lives, their knowledge, practices and values, across national borders. From the visitors who chose to come to Glasgow that James explores in his chapter to those who embarked on overseas trips to promote the city like Glasgow, as Marie Kane did as goodwill ambassador examined in Taylor's chapter, portability

5 'A Detectives Early Life', *The Indiana State Sentinel* (25 September 1889).

6 Named after Dundee, New York, which, in turn, was named after Dundee in Scotland. For details on the naming, see Henry Gannett, *The Origin of Certain Place Names in the United States*, 2nd *edition, Department of the Interior, Bulletin No. 258* (Washington: Government Printing Office, 1905), 110; see also 'A Glasgow Man's Enterprise in the United States', *Glasgow Herald* (3 January 1868).

7 'A Glasgow Man's Enterprise in the United States', *Glasgow Herald* (3 January 1868).

8 For general context on the Molly Maguires, see Kevin Kenny, *Making Sense of the Molly Maguires*, 25th *Anniversary Edition* (Oxford: Oxford University Press, 2023).

is intrinsically connected with movement and agency of people. Trade links, participation in the British Empire, and the establishment of shipping routes that connected the city to the world were key factors in advancing this portability, alongside, of course, the migration of people themselves – both in terms of outmigration from Glasgow and immigration to the city. What makes the concept of portability particularly important and interesting, therefore, is that it has no directional limitation: it is through people that places become portable but, at the same time, portable people contribute to making places. Ultimately, it is this people-centred portability that lies at the heart of this collection. As a result, Glasgow is a place we can define with the help of three reference points of portability: the city's reaching out, its opening up, and its connectedness – all of which have been explored in the chapters of this collection. Glasgow's reaching out, most notably through imperial endeavours, is the most complex parameter explored as this reaching out could be intensely negative for the places that were being reached, emphasising that portability is neither equitable nor just by default. The consequences of these types of connections still shape the city now. Glasgow's links with the slave trade are the most notable example, the wealth that flowed from the business of exploiting human beings remaining visible in Glasgow's cityscape to this day. Developments like the 1938 Empire Exhibition examined by Taylor, meanwhile, sought to provide a more positive reading of the city's position and capabilities, quite literally reaching out for investment. Secondly, however, Glasgow's own opening up has a long trajectory, first receiving those who moved from other parts of Scotland and nearby Ireland, to the arrival of immigrants from a wider range of places, including smaller immigrant communities like that of Americans that McCabe explores. In this collection New York has been a particular focus of the connectedness that stemmed from these processes of reaching out and opening up. It is a connectedness facilitated by transport links but evident in a range of developments, including the parallel developments and historiographies this collection has explored, particularly in the chapters by Bowman, Smyth, McSporran and McKay.

Consequently, the discussions in this collection can indeed be appropriately situated in the context of transnationalism, as the editors have set out in the introduction. What the collection also highlights, however, is that it can be critical to look beyond the nation: as important to our understanding of Glasgow's portability as the transnational perspective is, many of the links explored in this collection can also be conceptualised as translocal and can, in fact, be better described as such. Framed in the most basic terms, translocality refers to the connections and relationships that exist between two or more places, challenging the idea of bounded localities. Viewed in that way, translocality shares characteristics with the concept of transnationalism, but is different in its reference point, which is not the nation, but specific locales that are connected. This focus reveals the degree to which people – their active agency – are a bridge between specific places and how they enable exchange and transfer between them. As Conradson and McKay observe, 'many of the events and communities that shape our sense of self are connected to particular places'[9] and it is this connection that shapes their agency. Consequently, portable people draw on that locally rooted agency too when they transfer their ideas and values, bringing them to another place. In highlighting the diverse ways in which a specific locale can shape this agency and the developments that flow from it, this collection thus provides important new insights in how a translocal perspective enhances our understanding of exchange and links across borders through a place-specific perspective that does not give primacy to the nation.

Let us briefly revisit each chapter in this collection to demonstrate why this matters, and why it makes a difference to how local comparisons, in this case primarily relating to urban histories, can be strengthened when they are recognised as forms of exchange that exhibit parallel characteristics but also a distinctiveness that relates to their respective locale. A translocal lens helps us to uncover that dialogue between the parallel and the distinctive. Critically, as James's chapter highlights, this dialogue is not limited to a static location: even the journey between two places can enable a specific translocal spatial framing. There is a translocal connection for non-permanent migrants and, as is captured in the evidence James presents, in that specifical locations could serve very distinct roles – like the example of 'entering Europe by the Glasgow door'. Travellers were not the only agents of translocal connections, however. As Taylor's examination of the 1938 Empire Exhibitions demonstrates, this role could also be fulfilled by organisations – the Scottish Development Council in this case, though we also get another example of the translocal agency of Marie Kane who was specifically tasked with facilitating exchange and connections. Both forms of agency were intended to generate investment, but there were other ways in which translocality mattered, particularly in relation to peace and soft diplomacy that centred, for instance, on links between Glasgow and New York. What a translocal focus can help achieve, we are beginning to better understand thanks to these considerations and Bowman's discussion of the parallel historiographies of New York and Glasgow, is how important it is to mitigate against exceptionalism. Bigger urban centres were often faced with similar problems; identifying parallels and studying

9 David Conradson and Deirdre McKay, 'Translocal Subjectivities: Mobility, Connection, Emotion', *Mobilities* 2/2 (2007), 167–174.

them in their specific local environment and then a translocal comparison helps identify what were perhaps more universal responses and what was distinctive to a specific locale. The chapters by Smyth, McSporran, and McKay all demonstrate this very well. Smyth offers an immediate translocal comparison through the lens of the wash-house and keeping clean in the city, documenting how a translocal perspective helps address that urban histories are not well-examined within the context of the nation because it is usually the specific locale that shapes distinctive responses. Similarly, Smyth demonstrates that while there are common patterns in the development of Glasgow and New York, for instance the correlation between economic growth and health improvements, other developments were the result of distinct local issues or questions. In New York, for instance, there had been a better assimilation of Irish immigrants, while Catholic Irish remained more at the margins of society in early twentieth-century Glasgow. Such distinct developments, as McKay's chapter shows in-depth, is a direct result of the different ethnic make-up and subsequent pressures and problems in New York and Glasgow. New York had become increasingly diverse due to the changing background of new immigrants arriving in the city, contributing to a decline in some sectarian practices as the societal fault lines, as it were, no longer lay there. In Glasgow, meanwhile, there were no such changes and sectarianism became more vitriolic during the interwar years, for example. A translocal perspective enables us to understand such dynamics. Ultimately, they are the result of people moving, so it is also important that we shed new light on translocal migration. McCabe's chapter does this for a group – American immigrants in Glasgow – that neither made up a large proportion of the city's immigrant community, nor was particularly distinctly positioned given shared language and a degree of shared culture. Moreover, a majority were effectively return immigrants with Scottish roots. Nevertheless, better understanding such communities and how they enabled translocal exchange is important as it helps shed more light on the matrix of connections that underpinned that translocal exchange. The matrix of connections does not only exist across space, however, but can also be found across time as Bowman's imaginarium reminds us. Moreover, the emotional dimensions that make a place deserve to be captured through our history and memory – collective and individual and however fragmented they may sometimes be. In fact, it is in addressing this fragmentation where a translocal approach can again provide depth and detail. Translocality offers one more piece in the puzzle, as it were. And that puzzle is one, of course, that becomes even more complex when we recognise how Glasgow's civic imagery and its very cityscape, shaped so fundamentally by the gains made from the exploitation of enslaved Black people, clashes with the atrocities committed in the name of that trade. Lamont's chapter, the final in this collection, thus provides an important reminder that Glasgow's history, the city's experiences and its own understanding of itself, do not exist in isolation. Translocal perspectives of the kind espoused in this collection provide important new insights in the interconnectedness of Glasgow. That is also why, in combination, all chapters highlight why, at the end, it is worth pausing over the wider contribution that this collection can make both in opening up translocal perspectives in their own right, but also in helping us consider how this collection can help move forward debate in Scottish diaspora studies, providing an inroad into how diaspora too goes beyond the nation.

Putting the Translocal into Scottish Diaspora Studies

The concept of transnationalism has shaped the discussion of globally linked processes, activities and the flow of people for several decades, making important contributions to our understanding of how connected the world can be across national boundaries.[10] It allows us to reflect on types of relationships that transcend borders, but also the diverse exchange patterns that underpin such relationships, as we have seen throughout this collection. Critically, over time the ways in which this can happen has changed, with new technologies and improvements in long-distance travel having contributed to enabling an increasingly globalised world. The concept of diaspora has its own place in these links and the process of movement and exchange that underpin them, connecting different national/ethnic groups cross-border. This happens, in part, through enabling structures such as those I have examined in my own work, or institutions such as churches, for example.[11] Importantly, however, transnationalism and diaspora are not synonymous even though both can serve as 'research lenses through which to view the aftermath of international migration'.[12] Despite this, we can often find a 'conceptual conflation and overuse'.[13] In part, this is the

---

[10] M. Kearney, 'The Local and the Global: The Anthropology of Globalization and Transnationalism', *Annual Review of Anthropology* 24 (1995), 547–565; Steven Vertovec and R. Cohen, eds, *Migration, Diasporas and Transnationalism* (Cheltenham: Edward Elgar, 1999); Steven Vertovec, *Transnationalism* (London and New York: Routledge, 2009).

[11] See for instance Tanja Bueltmann and Donald M. MacRaild, *The English Diaspora in North America: Migration, Ethnicity and Association, 1730s–1950s* (Manchester: Manchester University Press, 2016); Valerie Wallace, *Scottish Presbyterianism and Settler Colonial Politics: Empire of Dissent* (Cham: Palgrave Macmillan, 2018).

[12] Thomas Faist, 'Diaspora and Transnationalism: What kind of dance partners?', in Rainer Bauböck and Thomas Faist, eds, *Diaspora and Transnationalism: Concepts, Theories and Methods* (Amsterdam: Amsterdam University Press, 2010).

[13] Vertovec, *Transnationalism*, 17.

result of both concepts drawing on the nation as their reference point, reinforcing it as the key focus in exploring patterns of cross-border links. It is also the result, however, of the traditional diaspora focus, which was primarily associated with the forced dispersal of people, their exile and subsequent trauma, of having to leave places without a nation to return to – theirs became an imagined homeland, most notably in the case of the Jewish diaspora. While exile and trauma can be core markers of diaspora, definitions have expanded.[14] Some of my own work documents, for example, how characteristics of diaspora can be established even in English communities abroad – 'even' because these communities tended to be seen as oppressors rather than the oppressed, so do not fit the traditional diaspora markers.[15]

Situated within this wider context, a translocal perspective can serve as a way to refine and enhance how we view cross-border connections and, most critically, diverse forms of exchange, including not just their reach in terms of localised and global scales, but also the level of analysis as locality can improve understanding across macro-, meso-, and micro-levels.[16] This matters because despite the increased transnational and global nature of links, research documents that there can still be a localised spatial rooting in both the experiences of people who have moved, but also in other types of links that stretch from place to place.[17] During Scotland's UEFA EURO 2024 matches in Germany, for example, localised reference points immediately facilitated a deep connection between Scotland fans and the city of Cologne, where the Scotland team played its match against Switzerland. In particular, this was the result of the local football club – F. C. Köln – adopting the melody of Runrig's song *Loch Lomond* for their club's anthem, 'Mer stonn zo dir, *FC* Kölle', but specifically also the actions of the fans.[18] While this may seem a trivial example, it is one that shows the importance of local experiences in shaping perceptions of and connections between people, even those who

---

14 See for example Robin Cohen, *Global Diasporas: An Introduction* (London and New York: Routledge, 2008).

15 For wider context to this discussion, see Tanja Bueltmann, David T. Gleeson and Donald M. MacRaild, 'Invisible Diaspora? English Ethnicity in the United States before 1920', *Journal of American History* 33:4 (2014), 5–30.

16 Vertovec, *Transnationalism*, 20.

17 For example W. Kokot, 'Culture and Space – anthropological approaches', *Ethnoscripts* 9 (2007), 10–23; D. Ley, 'Transnational spaces and everyday lives', *Transactions of the Institute of British Geographers* 29 (2004), 151–164.

18 In particular this relates to this story: 'Viral video shows Tartan Army in Cologne helping elderly woman', *Glasgow Times* (19 June 2024), https://www.glasgowtimes.co.uk/news/24398918.viral-video-shows-tartan-army-cologne-helping-elderly-woman/.

have never met.[19] An obvious thought for leaders of Cologne should be if they can make this a translocal link with a Scottish city, a new kind of city twin-ship grounded in a shared translocal experience. Moreover, it is of course also worth emphasising that various forms of connections have existed long since before nations and nation states became the core reference point for investigations.[20] Ultimately, the key point is this: many of the links, forms of engagement and exchange traced in this collection, while well-situated in a transnational framework, also document deeply translocal links as we have seen. Translocality thus offers a way to refine how we capture place-based developments and patterns relating to mobility – of both people and ideas; of practices and services – enabling us to better conceptualise and examine the interconnected nature of place-based characteristics through people and their agency. This is what makes it of interest too to Scottish diaspora studies.

Translocality is a concept that has been drawn upon, particularly in social and cultural studies, as well as in human geography and postcolonial studies, for some time. It is, therefore, not a new idea in itself and has seen extensive debate covering themes relating to how it sits alongside other concepts focused on processes connected to globalisation and transnationalism. Despite this wider interest in the concept, there has been no sustained engagement with it in Scottish diaspora studies. This is interesting to note for several reasons, but particularly because the importance of translocality is certainly recognised in diaspora studies generally.[21] Where more closely aligned work exists, it focuses, however, on the British diaspora as a whole and offers a more narrow colonial perspective to engage with for understanding translocality.[22] What this edited collection does, as has now

---

19 This ties in with Benedict Anderson's ideas on 'imagined communities', see *Imagined Communities: Reflections on the Origin and Spread of Nationalism* (London and New York: Verso, 1991).

20 Vertovec, *Transnationalism*, 3.

21 See for example Roger Ballard, 'The Dynamics of Translocal and Transjurisdictional Networks: A Diasporic Perspective', *South Asian Diaspora* 1/2 (2009), 141–66; Hariz Halilovich, 'Trans-Local Communities in the Age of Transnationalism: Bosnians in Diaspora', *International Migration* 50/1 (2012), 162–178; Andreas Hepp, 'Localities of Diasporic Communicative Spaces: Material Aspects of Translocal Mediated Networking', *The Communication Review* 12/4 (2009), 327–48; Michael Rios and Joshua Watkins, 'Beyond "Place": Translocal Placemaking of the Hmong Diaspora', *Journal of Planning Education and Research* 35/2 (2015), 209–19; Martin Slama, 'Translocal Networks and Globalisation within Indonesia: Exploring the Hadhrami Diaspora from the Archipelago's North-East', *Asian Journal of Social Science* 39/2 (2011), 238–57.

22 See Silke Stroh, 'Theories and Practices of Transmigration: Colonial British Diasporas and the Emergence of Translocal Space', in Marga Munkelt, Markus Schmitz, Mark Stein and Silke Stroh, eds, *Postcolonial Translocations: Cultural Representation and Critical Spatial Thinking* (Leiden: Brill, 2013), 293–320.

become clear, is demonstrate why it is important for Scottish diaspora studies to rise to this evident engagement gap and consider what insights the translocal characteristics of the Scottish diaspora and Scotland's connected place in the world – viewed through a localised lens – have to offer. Links with and through Glasgow examined here are, of course, only one potential such translocal prism.

In part, the engagement gap that exists is likely to stem from the dominant focus on 'the nation' as the main reference point in Scottish diaspora studies. This has been the case in much of my own work too, for instance, so I am fully appreciative of the rationale behind this focus: the key anchor in the lives of most diasporan Scots who actively express their identity or draw on networks and ethnic associations in their new lives abroad, for instance, remains Scotland as the nation they left. Moreover, homeland connections back to Scotland are also normally framed around the nation as a whole, for instance at events such as annual St Andrew's Day celebrations, where speeches to 'old Scotia' abound. Similarly, where particular ideas were transferred across borders, for instance around higher education, they also tended to flow from the level of national practice.[23] Translocality matters because, alongside these perspectives, it can open up a new way of engaging with what we might call the conditions of diasporas: they are shaped not only by the national background of immigrants, but also their place-based rooting in a specific locale. As Oakes and Schein observed, translocality 'draws our attention to multiplying forms of mobility [...] without losing sight of the importance of localities in peoples' lives'.[24] With that in mind, translocality focuses on agency to capture the experiences of migrants,[25] covering too precisely the kind of portability that this collection has examined. In doing so, argue Oakes and Schein, translocality 'deliberately confuses the boundaries of the local in an effort to capture the increasingly complicated nature of spatial processes and identities, yet insists on viewing such processes and identities as place-based rather than exclusively mobile, uprooted or "travelling"'.[26] Translocality, then, is about local-to-local connections that operate within a transnational space that is connected in many other ways. The key point is that, despite the overarching transnational connection, the local is not ignored or detached from it. With this

23 For examples see Tanja Bueltmann, Andrew Hinson and Graeme Morton, *The Scottish Diaspora* (Edinburgh: Edinburgh University Press, 2013).

24 Tim Oakes and Lisa Schein, 'Translocal China: An Introduction', in Tim Oakes and Lisa Schein, eds, *Translocal China: Linkages, Identities, and the Reimagining of Space* (New York: Routledge, 2006), 1.

25 Katherine Brickell and Ayona Datta, 'Introduction: Translocal Geographies', in Katherine Brickell and Ayona Datta, eds, *Translocal Geographies: Spaces, Places, Connections* (London and New York: Routledge, 2011), 3.

26 Oakes and Schein, 'Translocal China', 20.

in mind, Brickell and Datta help us better understand what this might mean in practice, thinking of translocality as 'a form of "grounded transnationalism" – a space where deterritorialized networks of transnational social relations take shape through migrant agencies'.[27] The local focus helps to better capture and better understand the underpinning agency in the lived everyday experience of migrants, their behaviours and impacts.

In order to develop such a perspective, we need to 'move beyond the focus on the primacy of national space [...] mapping out how other spaces and places can become significant during the process of migration and movement'.[28] This is something that this collection offers us, even if not intentionally from the outset, capturing a range of localised experiences 'as the product of flows of people, things, ideas, that is, the global connections between sites'.[29] Here, it really is about the 'placeness' of Glasgow and how it was portable. In some respects, this was the result of wider processes, most notably British imperial links. As Lamont's chapter shows, however, even these wider connections could result in very specific place-based impacts, in this case in the visible imperial markers throughout the city. Elsewhere, we have direct links from one specific place to another – links that, as Bowman's first chapter shows, have long since contributed to the imagining of translocal links. But such more abstract parallel imaginings are only one example as Smyth, MacSporran and McKay's chapters highlight. From shared conversations about public services to welfare provision and the experiences of sectarianism, all of these links are embedded not just transnationally, but translocally in the specific context of Glasgow (and New York in these instances). The most immediate connecters were, of course, the people – agents of portability, as discussed – who enabled engagement and exchange. From the leisure travellers in James' chapter who recognised 'sacred historic ground' upon arrival to the American immigrants making home in Glasgow that McCabe writes about, they were the crucial human links. As Taylor demonstrates, at times their link function between places was invested with discrete roles, such as the ambassadorial functions we learn were pursued by Kane in relation to the 1938 Empire Exhibition. Despite such examples of concrete experiences, localised exchanges can go beyond a physical location and also related to the ways in which local characteristics are expressed in collective memory, however. Moreover, places

27 Brickell and Datta, 'Introduction', 3.

28 Ibid., 4.

29 Michael Burawoy, *Global Ethnography: Forces, Connections, and Imaginings in a Postmodern World* (Berkeley, Los Angeles and London: University of California Press, 2000), 29.

themselves are not passive, but are shaped by a range of agents and that of course includes those who are not migrants but already live in the respective locale, as well as the structures within which all residents of a place operate – though this may not be the same for all as there are, of course, also place-based differences *within* a city such as Glasgow.

Situated within this broader context, translocality thus becomes a relational dimension that is created as a result of mobility of some people and/or ideas, and the engagement that flows from it. Critically too, such links can be spatial. Consider, for instance, Glasgow's Tobacco Merchant's House. The house received its name from one of its first inhabitants, Robert Findlay, who was a prominent merchant with ties to both the Virginian tobacco trade and the West India trade in the late eighteenth century. The Tobacco Merchant's House is now the last surviving Georgian villa built by tobacco and West Indian merchants in Glasgow's Merchant City. A translocal approach can help us explore what role such spaces played as the homes of merchants who were engaged in transatlantic slaving economies. For instance, how could such spaces, as both a physical and social space, link into slaving economies? There is significant potential in adopting a translocal perspective to explore such questions and the present collection helps bring out why such a translocal perspective can be so compelling: it has revealed not only 'local-to-local relations', but also specific localised forms of 'transnational urbanism', which reflect the limitations of a transnational perspective given the place-based and place-linked nature of these developments.[30] Recognising this within the wider framework of diaspora studies thus enables appreciation of the interconnected global and local dynamics in place-based contexts. Importantly, this also reflects that translocality is neither static nor bounded,[31] and a broad range of dynamics can intersect, including factors such as a migrant's socio-economic background, class and/or gender could be pivotal in shaping outcomes. In essence, what we can find are essential different scales of connectedness. Yet while these exist, a critical point identified by Verne is that 'a translocal perspective focuses the same time on both "what flows through places" and "what is in them"'.[32]

Drawing on these characteristics of translocality, it is clear that it can greatly enhance how we explore not just the general connectedness and exchange between places as a result of portability, but also consider it in the context of

30 M. P. Smith, *Transnational Urbanism: Locating Globalization* (Malden: Blackwell Publishers, 2001).

31 J. Verne, *Living Translocality: Space, Culture and Economy in Contemporary Swahili Trade* (Stuttgart: Franz Steiner Verlag, 2012).

32 Verne, *Living Translocality*, 19.

Scottish diaspora studies to advance our understanding of ongoing place links, capturing layers of place-specific portability through the agents of mobility. While diaspora encapsulates a transnational focus connecting homeland with diaspora communities abroad, as well as across diaspora communities, translocality adds specific place-to-place connections and exchange. In combination, they reveal a global system of interactions and exchange that recognises diverse layers. This enables consideration of how localised contexts, and everyday behaviours and practices in these localised contexts, shape that system of interactions.[33] In essence, the nation loses its primacy – and this is a good thing in terms of how it broadens the scope of Scottish diaspora studies. Critically, this can also have the positive benefit of challenging perspectives of exceptionalism that sometimes shape public discourse in particular. While the Scottish diaspora, and Scotland itself, certainly show distinct characteristics, exceptional they are, for the most part, really not.[34]

Another benefit is that a translocal perspective can help expand what is best described as the tangibility of diaspora: diaspora is not just a word or an abstract concept, but something that can be recognised by the communities themselves and measured by researchers. Translocality can enhance such assessments by providing the place-specific angle, helping us to capture and better understand the 'renewed importance of place and locality'.[35] Moreover, we can use a translocal diaspora framework to classify types of diaspora links. As Busumtwi-Sam and Anderson suggest, translocality can help consider links horizontally within a locality; laterally across localities in one country and/or across national boundaries; but also vertically in terms of diasporic flows that direct back to the locale in the home country.[36] As a result, a translocal diaspora framework can help mitigate some of the issues Brubaker and others set out as main challenges inherent in the

---

33 See also Clemens Grainer and Patrick Sakdapolrak, 'Translocality: Concepts, Applications and Emerging Research Perspectives', *Geography Compass* 7/5 (2013), 373–384.

34 An area where this has already been challenged quite well is around Scotland's involvement in the slave trade: while there were substantial numbers of abolitionists in Scotland, we now know that Scotland, and Glasgow specifically, still benefitted significantly from the slave trade.

35 Margit Fauser and Gery Nijenhuis, 'Migrants' Transnationality, Societal Transformation, and Locality: An Introduction', *Population, Space and Place* 22/4 (2015), 336–342, quote on 336.

36 James Busumtwi-Sam and Robert Anderson, '"Trans-local" Diaspora and Development: A concept and research note', Simon Fraser University, 10 October 2010; available online here: https://www.sfu.ca/diasporas/pdf/Translocal_Concept_Note_Oct_10_2010.pdf.

diaspora concept in their rejections of it.[37] There is a final point worth mulling over and that is Scotland's position as a nation without a state,[38] giving focus to localised reference points people can identify that do not have to involve questions about how they relate to the British state. In part this is possible due to the 'mutually constituent' nature between the local and the global,[39] facilitated here through people: the nation is not a prerequisite for global connections. For many, therefore, a focus on a specific place or even locale within it, offers a better way to capture negotiations of their own identity and heritage, and how these are transported across borders. It is important to recognise, however, that there is no 'one' translocal experience as translocality can have different manifestations, real or imagined. Let us consider three examples at the end of this discussion.

Let me first turn to my own investigations – the study of ethnic associations – in which I became very aware of the limitations of a transnational focus: at a minimum, the nation was often only one layer in how Scottish emigrants negotiated their links (and their identity) across borders. Consequently, a focus on trans*national* connections can potentially hide more than it reveals. I sought to address this issue by looking at the localised referents, as I called them, in ethnic associational culture.[40] Such localised referents were regularly employed in diaspora communities around the world. But to understand the potential that lies in a translocal perspective we do not even have to look abroad as Glasgow offers fascinating insights into this in the context of even just Scotland's internal diaspora, i.e. Scots who migrated to Glasgow from other parts of Scotland. As is documented in the records of one ethnic association established with a localised referent, namely the Glasgow Dumfriesshire Society, a number of such groups were set up in the city throughout the late eighteenth and nineteenth centuries, including the Perthshire Society, the Angus and Mearns Society, and a number of associations with local roots in the Highlands, such as the Skye Association. Most of these ethnic associations were primarily concerned with providing relief or support for those who hailed from the same area of Scotland that they

---

[37] Rogers Brubaker, 'The "Diaspora" Diaspora', *Ethnic and Racial Studies*, 28/1 (2005), 1–19; also Cairns Craig, *Intending Scotland: Explorations in Scottish Culture since the Enlightenment* (Edinburgh: Edinburgh University Press, 2009).

[38] See also David McCrone, *Understanding Scotland: The Sociology of a Nation* (London: Routledge, 2001), 37.

[39] Table 1 in Victor Roudometof, 'The Glocal and Global Studies', *Globalisations* 12/5 (2015), 782.

[40] See Chapter 6, especially complexity two, in Tanja Bueltmann, *Clubbing Together: Ethnicity, Civility and Formal Sociability in the Scottish Diaspora to 1930* (Liverpool: Liverpool University Press, 2014), 193–224; complexity two is discussed from 201 onwards.

represented, having moved to Glasgow.[41] It is interesting to see the establishment of the Dumfriesshire Society given the area's relative proximity to Glasgow. However, despite being quite close, the actions of all the groups established, including the Dumfriesshire Society, document core diaspora characteristics. By the late 1870s, for instance, the Society had a healthy fund of over £1,000 from the contributions of over 400 members.[42] The money served to sustain a charitable fund and enabled the provision of two university bursaries per year, documenting how charity and education were important to the Society.[43] The express purpose of bursaries was to support talented young people from Dumfriesshire.[44] While considering this internal diaspora in terms of local referents in ethnic associational culture, adopting a translocal perspective in the assessment of this ethnic association can help explore how any returnees from Glasgow to Dumfriesshire capitalised on the education received. In essence: what knowledge etc was transferred back, if any? Among the groups in Glasgow that were catering for Highland Scots, Gaelic societies played a particularly important role, combining support provisions with language maintenance and cultural pursuits. A Gaelic Society was set up in Glasgow in 1887, making clear that those who spoke Gaelic were rooted in different local traditions and thus needed to ensure that these were maintained so 'that the future generation should not lose touch with their country's past'.[45] Cultivating Gaelic thus became the core focus, but this was entwined with the hope of 'fostering a Celtic spirit among the Highlanders to Glasgow'.[46] Education underpinned these activities, with lectures an soirees with talks a common approach to promoting the Gaelic language.[47] These types of ethnic associational activities in Scotland's internal diaspora highlight that localised roots could trump other associational remits. But for Scotland's internal diaspora this of course also just made perfect sense, as the migrants who were establishing associational structures had not left the nation – making reference to localised roots was basically their only option. However, the same approach of local rooting was also pursued by Scots abroad, who did thus operate transnationally and translocally. Gaelic and Highland

41 Based on details extracted from Glasgow Dumfriesshire Society Annual Report, 1900, 8. Dumfriesshire Society Records are held at Glasgow University Archive.

42 Report of the Glasgow Dumfriesshire Society (Glasgow: Robert Anderson, 1881), 3.

43 Rules included in Appendix, *Glasgow Dumfriesshire Society: Report &c* (Glasgow: Robert Anderson, 1900), 85.

44 Ibid., 4–5.

45 *Transaction of the Gaelic Society of Glasgow, volume 1, 1887 to 1891* (Glasgow: Archibald Sinclair, 1891), ii–iii.

46 Constitution and Rules, in ibid., v.

47 For example P. McNaughton, *Lecture on the Importance of the Gaelic Language to Highlanders* (Edinburgh: McLauchlan & Stewart, 1885).

societies were particularly common.[48] In New Zealand, for example, a Caithness, Sutherland, Orkney, and Shetland Association was founded in the 1870s. By 1876, the Association reportedly had a membership of 79 and its pursuits were focused on directly attracting new immigrants to New Zealand, for instance from the Fair Isle, then supporting the newly arrived immigrants.[49] As the Association's first report a year earlier makes clear, such endeavours were a result of opening up 'communication with the kindred associations in the Home country' to discuss enabling emigration from the 'native counties' the association was catering for. It was, therefore, specifically this local rooting that drove associational activity, and then became distinctly translocal.[50]

Such patterns of translocal links are not just traceable historically, however. In my recent research on Scots in continental Europe, which included a survey of current Scottish immigrants resident there, the importance of translocal links in their own identity negotiation became evident. Notably, the survey conducted reveals that among those Scots currently resident in an EU/EEA country or Switzerland, 32.8 per cent noted that they still relate to a local identity in Scotland even though they no longer life there: they thus effectively made their identity translocal as it still shapes their thinking of themselves.[51] This is tied up with perceptions of where home is, which is also very (trans-)localised for a number of respondents: they do not think of Scotland, but of the specific place they are from, in combination with the place in continental Europe that they now live in. As one respondent observed, 'Greece is not my home. Glasgow is my home. I've lived in many other cities, including in different EU countries, but Glasgow is my home.'[52] For this respondent, Glasgow emerged as the translocal home in their frequent moves. For others, the local aspect came out strongly upon their (temporary) return. As another respondent explained, for example, they 'feel at

48 See for instance Tanja Bueltmann, *Scottish Ethnicity and the Making of New Zealand Society* (Edinburgh: Edinburgh University Press, 2011), 75ff.

49 *Otago Witness* (29 January 1876).

50 *Otago Daily Times* (20 January 1876); this also explains that the association had initially been the Caithness and Sutherland Association, but that immigrants from the other locations then approached the association to see if they could join.

51 Tanja Bueltmann, 'Identity, Belonging and Representation Post-Brexit among British Citizens in the EU/EEA and Switzerland', University of Strathclyde (2023), https://strathprints.strath.ac.uk/83699/, 39.

52 Survey response 201 R_qyA33ouRgTqMiit; collected as part of the above research entitled 'Transeuropean Scots: Scotland's European Diaspora Post-Brexit in Longitudinal Perspective'. The study was funded by the Royal Society of Edinburgh with a Personal Research Fellowship.

home walking around Glasgow'.[53] Again a specifically translocal diaspora framework can help us better understand such patterns, in this instance in identity negotiation.

Considering the specifically translocal connections between people and places and how they might enhance Scottish diaspora studies also, finally, brings us back across the Atlantic to Allan Pinkerton. For many, Pinkerton is a former radical Scottish Chartist who supported abolition and pioneered detective work. For others, however, as Jeffreys-Jones explains, he 'abandoned the radical principles he held in Scotland', undermining workers in America by effectively becoming 'a pillar of the repressive American establishment'.[54] There are complexities in Pinkerton's story that make it difficult to ascertain with certainty which interpretation is more accurate. For instance, Pinkerton's own personal archive was destroyed when a fire at the Pinkerton Detective Agency tore through the building, making it impossible to establish his personal views in more detail. What we can say, however, is that the answer to what appears as a change in Pinkerton's position – from supporter of workers to their persecutor – most likely lies in his local experiences in Glasgow. As Jeffreys-Jones also queried, 'did he abandon the cause of his Gorbals comrades at the moment when he sailed down the Clyde for America'?[55] The key question worth probing here is which behaviour was actually a continuity: we are inclined to assume that Pinkerton, as a Chartist, was fighting for workers and thus, the break in continuity can be seen in him then supporting their repression in the US instead. What, however, if it was actually that repression that represents more of a continuity with Pinkerton's upbringing and activity in Glasgow? Maybe he had become familiar with, or even learned of, strike-breaking and other ways to undermine labourers there, and it is this aspect that constitutes the real translocal continuity. In a letter sent to Alexander Macdonald in 1869, Pinkerton wrote about labour relations, noting that 'capital has invariably preyed upon the labouring classes', supporting their 'right to organize'. However, he also made reference to arbitration as a 'new idea' that might be 'more effective than any resort to force'.[56] It is also worth highlighting his views on the informer, some of which potentially imply that he may have had knowledge of the informer's position from his own experiences. In any case, it

---

53 Survey response 499 R_1mykW3XzKesyTWl, ibid.

54 Rhodri Jeffreys-Jones, 'Allan Pinkerton: Informed Scot or Scottish Informer?', *Journal of Historical Studies* 42/2 (2022), 198.

55 Ibid.

56 All quotes from ibid., 203.

is noteworthy that even though he had set out that such systems were outdated, he nonetheless commenced work of 'anti-union espionage'.[57] The development of his own American identity may have played a key role in these patterns and actions around the Molly Maguires. As Pinkerton himself explained in 1878, 'I have been a poor lad in Scotland, buffeted and badgered by boorish masters … [but] In American citizenship there exists all the essentials to make success in the life of every man not only possible, but probable.'[58]

The question remains, however, whether Pinkerton really changed from the days of his Gorbals' youth. While it is clear that he did reject labour violence, 'his agency by the 1870s peddled in force and violence [… and] These had been the preferences of the physical-force Chartists'[59] that Pinkerton himself had followed in his youth. This might provide further evidence Pinkerton may not actually have broken with his local roots but continued them. This, Jeffreys-Jones muses, may also explain some of Pinkerton's behaviour after leaving Scotland: 'he may have fled his native country not in fear of the authorities, as he claimed, but because his former comrades had found him out as an informer and were out to get him.'[60] Again it is difficult to establish this with certainty, but there is some evidence that points in this direction, for instance a letter Pinkerton had sent to acquaintances in Scotland shortly before Pinkerton's agency went after the Molly Maguires. As Pinkerton explained:

> Ah! The misery I think of since I have left Scotland, I cannot tell, I can scarcely survive it, the misery and wretchedness of the Gorbals. It is terrible to think of, and only think, what I escaped, when I was a young man, when the Chartists, engulfed me into the glorious Battle, with them, and then I fought it to the last and then left my Country.[61]

If nothing else, considering these references and inconsistencies in Pinkerton's story does at least raise the question of whether he did perhaps actually learn detective work in Glasgow. Was he perhaps 'actually an informer and agent provocateur',[62] and could this explain his anti-union activities in the US? It may never be possible to fully understand this story, but what is clear is that a translocal perspective that really considers the specific Glasgow context of Pinkerton's life in comparison with his actions in the US provides likely the most fruitful angle

57 Ibid., 204.
58 Allan Pinkerton, Strikers, Communists, Tramps, and Detectives (New York, 1878), x–xi.
59 Jeffreys-Jones, 'Allan Pinkerton', 205.
60 Ibid.
61 Ibid., 206, original in Library of Congress.
62 Jeffreys-Jones, 'Allan Pinkerton', 213.

to do so. As Jeffreys-Jones surmises in his conclusion, for example, his 'familial intimacy with the Glasgow police gave him the opportunity to inform without leaving a trace' and if these indeed were his Scottish values, then they appear to have made it across the Atlantic. It is because of this level of detail and richness that a translocal perspective can offer – alongside a transnational one where desired – that this collection, which has demonstrated many other such links, serves as an important call for historians of the Scottish diaspora to seriously consider translocality.

Selected Bibliography

Abrams, Lynn, Kearns, Ade, Hazley, Barry, and Wright, Valerie, *Glasgow: High-Rise Homes, Estates and Communities in the Post-War Period* (Oxon: Routledge, 2020).

Anbinder, Tyler, *City of Dreams: The 400-Year Epic History of Immigrant New York* (New York: Mariner, 2017).

Anderson, Benedict, *Imagined Communities: Reflections on the Origin and Spread of Nationalism* (London and New York: Verso, 1991).

Aspinwall, Bernard, 'The Catholic minority experience in Scotland: the poorhouse view 1850–1914', *Immigrants & Minorities* 31/2 (2013), 127–145.

Aspinwall, Bernard, 'The welfare state within the state: the Saint Vincent De Paul Society in Glasgow, 1848–1920', *Studies in Church History* 23/1 (1986), 444–59.

Aspinwall, Bernard, *Portable Utopia: Glasgow and the United States, 1820–1920* (Aberdeen: Aberdeen University Press, 1984).

Auletta, Ken, *The Streets were Paved with Gold: The Decline of New York – an American Tragedy* (New York: Random House, 1979).

Barclay, Katie, 'State of the Field: The History of Emotions', *History* 106/371 (2021), 456–466.

Benjamin, Walter, *The Arcades Project*, translated by Howard Eiland and Kevin McLaughlin (Harvard: Harvard University Press, 2002).

Berman, Marshall, *All That Is Solid Melts Into Air: The Experience of Modernity* (London: Verso, 1982),

Berry, Stephen, R, *A Path in the Mighty Waters: Shipboard Life and Atlantic Crossings to the New World* (New Haven: Yale University Press, 2015).

Blake, Angela, M, *How New York Became American, 1890–1924* (Baltimore: Johns Hopkins University Press, 2006).

Bowman, Stephen, 'The Scottish-American Association, 1919–1923: A Study in Failure', *Journal of Scottish Historical Society* 39/2 (2019) 166–192.

Breitenbach, Esther, 'Pro-Empire Sentiment in Twentieth Century Scotland Before Decolonisation', in Stephanie Barczewski and Martin Farr, eds., *The MacKenzie Moment and Imperial History* (Basingstoke: Palgrave MacMillan, 2019).

Brickell, Katharine, Datta, Ayona, 'Introduction: Translocal Geographies', in Katherine Brickell and Ayona Datta, eds, *Translocal Geographies: Spaces, Places, Connections* (London and New York: Routledge, 2011).

Britton, Sarah, 'Urban Futures/Rural Pasts: Representing Scotland in the 1938 Glasgow Empire Exhibition', *Cultural and Social History* 8/2 (2011), 213–232.

Brown, Stewart, J. '"Outside the Covenant": The Scottish Presbyterian Churches and Irish Immigration, 1922–1938', *Innes Review* 42/1 (1991), 19–45.

Bueltmann, Tanja, MacRaild, Donald, M. *The English Diaspora in North America: Migration, Ethnicity and Association*, 1730s–1950s (Manchester: Manchester University Press, 2016).

Burk, Kathleen, *The Lion and the Eagle: The Interaction of the British and American Empires 1783–1972* (Bloomsbury Publishing Plc, 2019).

Cameron, Ewen, A. 'Glasgow's going round and round: some recent Scottish urban history', *Urban History*, 30/2 (2003) 276–287.

Cameron, Ewen, *Impaled Upon a Thistle: Scotland since 1880* (Edinburgh: Edinburgh University Press, 2010).

Carruthers, Gerrard, MacDonald, Catriona, M. M. 'Fictive Pasts and Past Fictions', *The Scottish Historical Review* 92/234 (2013), 137–166.

Chalmers, A. K. *The Health of Glasgow, 1818–1925* (Glasgow: Corporation of Glasgow, 1930).

Checkland, S. G., *The Upas Tree: Glasgow, 1875–1975* (Glasgow: University of Glasgow Press, 1976).

Crawford, Robert *On Glasgow and Edinburgh* (Cambridge, MA: Harvard University Press 2013).

Damer, Seán, *From Moorepark to 'Wine Alley': the rise and fall of a Glasgow Housing Scheme* (Edinburgh: Edinburgh University Press, 1989).

Davies, Andrew, 'The Scottish Chicago? From "Hooligans" to "Gangsters" in Inter-War Glasgow', *Cultural and Social History* 4/4 (2007), 511–527.

Devine T. M., MacKenzie, John, M. 'Scots in the Imperial Economy', in John M. MacKenzie, and T. M. Devine, ed., *Scotland and tahe British Empire, Oxford History of the British Empire Companion Series* (Oxford, Oxford University Press, 2011).

Devine, T. M., *To the Ends of the Earth, Scotland's Global Diaspora, 1750–2010* (London: Allen Lane, 2011).

Dollan, Patrick, *A Tale of Two Cities, Glasgow-New York* (Glasgow, 1940).

Duranti, Marco, 'Utopia, Nostalgia and World War at the 1939–40 New York World's Fair', *Journal of Contemporary History* 41/4 (2006), 663–683.

Deborah, Dwork, 'Health Conditions of Immigrant Jews on the Lower East Side of New York, 1880–1914', *Medical History*, 25 (1981), 28–29.

Evans, N. J., 'The Emigration of Skilled Male Workers from Clydeside during the Interwar Period', *International Journal of Maritime History* 18/1 (2006), 255–280.

Ewen, Shane, *What is Urban History?* (Cambridge: Polity, 2016).

Fry, Michael, *Glasgow: A History of the City* (London: Head of Zeus, 2017).

Gallagher, Tom, *Glasgow: The Uneasy Peace* (Manchester: Manchester University Press, 1987).

Gilley, Sheridan, 'Catholics and Socialists in Scotland', in Roger Swift and Sheridan Gilley, eds., *The Irish in Britain: 1851–1939* (Pinter Publishers: London, 1989).

Gilroy, Paul, 'The Black Atlantic as a counterculture in modernity', in Susan Manning and Andrew Taylor, eds, *Transatlantic Literary Studies: A Reader* (Edinburgh: Edinburgh University Press, 2007).

Goodman, David, 'Loving and Hating Britain: Rereading the Isolationist Debate in the USA', in Kate Darian-Smith, Patricia Grimshaw and Stuart

McIntyre, eds, *Britishness Abroad Transnational Movements and Imperial Cultures* (Melbourne: Melbourne University Press, 2007).

Gottmann, Jean, 'Megalopolis or the Urbanization of the Northeastern Seaboard', *Economic Geography* 33/3 (1957), 189–200.

Graham, Eric, J, *Clyde Built: Blockade Runners, Cruisers and Armoured Rams of the American Civil War* (Edinburgh: Birlinn Limited, 2006).

Gray, Alasdair, *Lanark: A Life in 4 Books* (Edinburgh: Canongate, 1981).

Groten, Miel, 'Glasgow's new town hall: imperialism, nationalism and civic pride, 1877–1889', *Urban History* 48/4 (2020), 1–19.

Gurwitz, Aaron, *Atlantic Metropolis; An Economic History of New York City* (Cham: Palgrave, 2019).

Handley, James, E. *The Irish in Modern Scotland* (Cork: Cork University Press, 1947).

Harper, Marjory, Evans, Nicholas, J. 'Socio-economic Dislocation and Inter-war Emigration to Canada and the United States: A Scottish Snapshot', *The Journal of Imperial and Commonwealth History* 34/4 (2006), 529–552.

Huyssen, Andrea, *Present Pasts: Urban Palimpsests and the Politics of Memory*, (Stanford: Stanford University Press, 2003).

Jackson, Gordon, Munn, Charles, 'Trade, Commerce and Finance', in W. H. Fraser and Irene Maver, eds, *Glasgow, vol. 2, 1830–1912* (Manchester: Manchester University Press, 1996).

Jeffreys-Jones, Rhodri, 'Allan Pinkerton: Informed Scot or Scottish Informer?', *Journal of Historical Studies* 42/2 (2022), 197–216.

Jenkinson, Jacquline. *Black 1919: Riots, Racism, and Resistance in Imperial Britain* (Liverpool: Liverpool University Press, 2009).

Johnston, Ronald, *Clydeside Capital, 1870–1920: A Social History of Employers* (East Linton: Tuckwell Press, 2000).

Kauffmann, Eric, 'The Orange Order Since 1860: A social analysis', in Martin J. Mitchell, ed, *New Perspectives on the Irish in Scotland* (Edinburgh: John Donald, 2008).

Keating, Michael, *The City That Refused to Die: Glasgow: The Politics of Urban Regeneration*, (Aberdeen: Aberdeen University Press, 1988).

Kennedy, Charles, *The American Consul: A History of the United States Consular Service, 1776–1924*, (Washington, D.C.: Bloomsbury Academic, 2015), 101–102.

Kennedy, David. M, *The American People in the Great Depression; Freedom from Fear, Part One* (New York: Oxford University Press, 1999).

Kenny, Kevin, *The American Irish: A History* (Pearson Education Ltd: Harlow, 2000).

Kenny, Nicholas, Madgin, Rebecca, eds, *Cities Beyond Borders: Comparative and Transnational Approaches to Urban History* (London: Routledge, 2015).

Kenny, Nicholas, *The Feel of the City: Experiences of Urban Transformation* (Toronto: University of Toronto Press, 2018).

Kidd, Colin. 'Race, Empire, and the Limits of Nineteenth-Century Scottish Nationhood', *The Historical Journal* 46/4 (2003), 873–892.

Lamont, Craig. *The Cultural Memory of Georgian Glasgow* (Edinburgh: Edinburgh University Press, 2021).

Lesy, Michael. *Wisconsin Death Trip* (Albuquerque: University of New Mexico Press, 1973/2000).

Lindner, Christoph, *Imagining New York City: Literature, Urbanism, and the Visual Arts, 1890–1940* (Oxford: Oxford University Press, 2015).

MacKenzie, Angus, '"Public-spirited men": Economic Unionist Nationalism in Inter-War Scotland', *Scottish Historical Review* 96/1 (2017), 87–109.

MacKenzie, John M., '"The Second City of the Empire": Glasgow – imperial municipality', in Felix Driver and David Gilbert, eds, *Imperial Cities: Landscape, Display and Identity*, (Manchester: Manchester University Press, 1999).

MacRaild, Donald, M, 'Crossing migrant frontiers: Comparative reflections on Irish migrants in Britain and the United States during the nineteenth century', *Immigrants & Minorities* 18/2-3 (1999), 40–70.

MacRaild, Donald, M. Ellis, Sylvia, Bowman, Stephen, 'Interdependence Day and Magna Charta: James Hamilton's public diplomacy in the Anglo-world, 1907–1940s', *Journal of Transatlantic Studies* 12/2 (2014), 140–162.

Madgin, Rebecca, 'Recognising Emotions within Urban Development', in Katie Barclay and Jade Riddle, eds, *Urban Emotions and the Making of the City: Interdisciplinary Perspectives* (New York: Routledge, 2001).

Maver, Irene *Glasgow* (Edinburgh: Edinburgh University Press, 2000).

McIlvanney, Liam, 'The Glasgow Novel', in Gerard Carruthers and McIlvanney, eds, *The Cambridge Companion to Scottish Literature* (Cambridge: Cambridge University Press, 2012), 217–32.

Morton, Graeme, *Unionist Nationalism: Governing Urban Scotland 1830–1860* (Edinburgh: Tuckwell Press, 1999).

Muir, James, Hamilton, *Glasgow in 1901* (Glasgow, 1901).

Mullen, Stephen, *Glasgow, Slavery and Atlantic Commerce: An Audit of Historic Connections and Modern Legacies* (Glasgow, City Council: 2022).

Munro, Forbes, Slaven, Tony, 'Networks and Markets in Clyde Shipping: The Donaldsons and the Hogarth, 1870–1939', *Business History* 43/2 (2001), 19–50.

Nenadic, Stena, 'The Victorian Middle Classes', in W. Hamish Fraser and Irene Maver, eds, *Glasgow, Volume II: 1830–1912* (Manchester University Press: Manchester, 1996).

Ngai, Mae, M. *Illegal Aliens and the Making of Modern America* (Princeton: Princeton University Press, 2004).

O'Hara, Paul, *Inventing the Pinkertons or, Spies, Sleuths, Mercenaries, and Thugs. Being a Story of the Nation's most Famous (and Infamous) Detective Agency* (Baltimore: Johns Hopkins University Press, 2016).

Oakley, C. A. *The Second City* (Glasgow, 1946).

Peat, A. 'Scottish Internationalisms at the 1938 Empire Exhibition: Between Britain, Europe, and Empire', *Open Library of Humanities* 6/1 (2020), 21.

Ramet, Sabrina, P, Hassenstab, Christine, M, 'The Know Nothing Party: Three Theories about its Rise and Demise', *Politics and Religion* 6/3 (2013), 570–595.

Reitano, Joanne, *The Restless City: A Short History of New York from Colonial Times to the Present* (New York: Routledge, 2018).

Riddell, John F, *Clyde Navigation: A History of the Development and Deepening of the River Clyde* (Edinburgh: John Donald Publishers, Inc., 1979).

Riddell, John, F, 'Glasgow and the Clyde', in Peter Reed, ed, *Glasgow: The Forming of the City* (Edinburgh: Edinburgh University Press, 1993).

Robinson, Jennifer, 'Johannesburg's 1936 Empire Exhibition: Interaction, Segregation and Modernity in a South African City', *Journal of Southern African Studies* 29/3 (2003), 759–789.

Rodgers, Daniel T., *Atlantic Crossings: Social Politics in a Progressive Age* (Cambridge MA: Belknap Press of Harvard University Press, 1998).

Roger, Richard, 'The Labour Force', in W. Hamish Fraser and Irene Mavor, eds, *Glasgow, Volume II: 1830–1912*, (Manchester: Manchester University Press, 1996).

Roper, Tony, *I'll No Tell Ye Again: My Autobiography* (Edinburgh: Black and White Publishing, 2014).

Russell, James, B, *Life in One Room* (Glasgow: 1888).

Sanghera, Sathnam, *Empireland: How Imperialism Has Shaped Modern Britain*, (London: Penguin, 2021).

Scisco, Louis, Dow, *Political Nativism in New York State* (New York: Ams Press, 1968).

Scott Morton, Fiona, 'Entry and Predation: British Shipping Cartels 1879–1929', *Journal of Economics and Management Strategy* 4/6 (1997), 679–724.

Serrano, Montes, C, 'The Empire Exhibition of Scotland, 1938: the image and representation of an ephemeral modernity', *Expresión Gráfica Arquitectónica* 25/39 (2020), 32–45.

Shadow, George, *Midnight Scenes and Social Photographs Being Sketches of Life in the Streets, Wynds, and Dens of the City* (Glasgow, 1858/1976).

Shaw, Albert, *Municipal Government in Great Britain and Municipal Government in Continental Europe* (New York: The MacMillan Company, 1895).

Shefter, Martin, 'New York's National and International Influence', in Shefter, ed., *Capital of the American Century: The National and International Influence of New York City* (New York: Russell Sage Foundation, 1993).

Smyth, James, *Labour in Glasgow 1896–1936: Socialism, Suffrage and Sectarianism* (East Linton: Tuckwell Press: 2000).

Smyth, James, 'Resisting Labour: Unionists, Liberals and Moderates in Glasgow between the Wars', *The Historical Journal* 46/2 (2003), 375–401.

Smyth, James, 'The Power of Pathos: James Burn Russell's Life in One Room and the Creation of Council Housing', *The Scottish Historical Review* 98/1 (2019), 103–127.

Spring, Ian. *Phantom Village: The Myth of the New Glasgow* (Edinburgh: Polygon, 1990).

Steinberg, Mark, D, *Petersburg Fin de Siècle: The Darkening Landscape of Modern Times, 1905–1917* (New Haven: Yale University Press, 2011).

Taylor, Avram, '"Are you a Billy, or a Dan, or an old tin can?": street violence and relations between Catholics, Jews, and Protestants in the Gorbals during the inter-war years', *Urban History* 41/1 (2014), 124–140.

Treble, J. H, *Urban Poverty in Britain 1830–1914* (London: Batsford Academic, 1979).

Walker, Graham, 'The Protestant Irish in Scotland', in T. M. Devine, ed., *Irish Immigrants and Scottish Society in the Nineteenth and Twentieth Centuries* (Edinburgh: John Donald Ltd., 1991).

Webster, Charles. 'Healthy or Hungry Thirties?', *History Workshop Journal* 13/3 (1982), 110–192.

Weir, Molly, *Shoes Were for Sunday, in Molly Weir's Trilogy of Scottish Childhood*, (Edinburgh: Lomond Books, 2000).

Whiteside, Noel, *Bad Times: Unemployment in British Social and Political History* (London: Faber and Faber, 1991).

Winter, J. M, *The Great War and the British People* (London: MacMillan, 1985).

Withers, Charles, 'The demographic history of the city, 1831–1911', in W. Hamish Fraser and Irene Maver, eds, *Glasgow, Volume II: 1830–1912* (Manchester: Manchester University Press, 1996).

Yablon, Nick, *Untimely Ruins: An Archaeology of American Urban Modernity, 1819–1919* (Chicago: University of Chicago Press, 2009).

Zola, Emille, *L'Assommoir* (Oxford: Oxford University Press, 2009).

Notes on Contributors

Dr Stephen Bowman is Lecturer in History at the University of Stirling. He has interests in the historical cultural and political connections between Scotland and the US, including through his work on urban history and his Royal Society of Edinburgh-funded project on the cultural memory of Scot's born 'father' of the US Navy John Paul Jones. His book *The Pilgrims Society and Public Diplomacy, 1895–1945* was published by Edinburgh University Press in 2018, and he has also published with the *Journal of Transatlantic Studies*, the *Journal of Scottish Historical Studies*, and *History Scotland*. In addition, Stephen has interests in the field of 'creative history', and led the research, writing, and production of one of the first scholarly historical treatments of the COVID-19 pandemic: the film and article '"An Unusual Period of Unspecified Length": A Creative Oral History of the Covid-19 Pandemic' published in 2024 by UCL Press in *Paper Trails: The Social Life of Archives and Collections.*

Professor Tanja Bueltmann is Professor in International History at the University of Strathclyde. Her main research interest is in immigrant community life, especially ethnic associational culture. She has primarily focused on the Scottish and English diasporas, but the scope of her research has widened to include broader aspects of immigrant collective action over time. Her current project is entitled 'Transeuropean Scots: Scotland's European Diaspora Post-Brexit in Longitudinal Perspective' and was funded by the Royal Society of Edinburgh.

Professor Kevin James holds the Scottish Studies Foundation Chair and is Professor of Modern Scottish History at the University of Guelph. A graduate of McGill University, where he obtained the highest standing in Arts in his graduating year, and of Edinburgh University, where he held a Commonwealth Scholarship, Kevin has held grants and fellowships in Scotland, Ireland, Canada and the United States, and has collaborated in research partnerships around the world. A specialist in modern Scottish tourism and travel history, Kevin is also Director of the University's Centre for Scottish Studies.

Dr Craig Lamont is Lecturer in Scottish Studies at the University of Glasgow. Dr Lamont is an expert in cultural memory studies, print culture, Glasgow, and Scottish literature. His monograph, *The Cultural Memory of Georgian Glasgow* (2021), is an adaptation of his award-winning PhD thesis. He has edited on the scholarly editions of Allan Ramsay, Robert Burns, and John Galt, and continues to publish on cultural memory, slavery, and Glasgow.

Dr Graham MacSporran is a graduate of the University of Stirling and is now an independent researcher. His doctoral thesis explored the relationship between changes in living standards and health in Glasgow during the First World War, with particular reference to the health of the poorest in society in this period. He continues to research changes in public health in Glasgow between 1900 and 1939.

Tahitia McCabe is the Knowledge Exchange Fellow for the Postgraduate Genealogical, Palaeographic and Heraldic Programme and the Lead Tutor for the PG Certificate Programme at the University of Strathclyde. She holds a BFA (Bachelor of Fine Arts) in costume design and a BA in History from Southern Oregon State College and an MLS (Master's in Library Science) from Syracuse University in upstate New York. Tahitia also holds a Postgraduate Diploma in Genealogical, Palaeographic and Heraldic Studies from the University of Strathclyde. As an immigrant herself, migration is one of her key research interests and she is currently focusing on Americans in Scotland during the nineteenth century. She is a member of the New England Genealogical Society, the Association of Professional Genealogists, the National Genealogical Society, and a Fellow of the Royal Society of Arts.

Dr Cameron McKay is an assistant director and faculty member at Arcadia University's Edinburgh Centre, having previously worked at the University of Stirling and the University of Edinburgh. He has published articles in *Scottish Labour History*, *History Scotland*, *Scottish Church History*, and *Historical Research*. His book *Crime and the First World War in Scotland* was recently published as part of the *Scottish Historical Review's* monograph series.

Dr James Smyth retired from his position as Senior Lecturer in History at the University of Stirling in 2024. His original research was in the history of labour politics in the late nineteenth and early twentieth century, but he has developed interests into family life and labour, the small firm in the nineteenth century, business and politics in the twentieth century, housing and neighbourhood identity, and public health. He has held awards from the Economic and Social Research Council, the Joseph Rowntree Foundation, and the Wellcome Trust. More recently he developed interests in historical public health and climate in Glasgow, New York, Chicago, Paris, and Liverpool.

Dr Kieran Taylor is Lecturer in Education at Queen Margaret University. His doctoral research at the University of Stirling examined the relief of Belgian Refugees by Glasgow Corporation during the First World War. His research interests relate to migration, politics and change in Scottish society. His recent research has examined the ways in which the state, local government and education services interact with migrants. He is a member of the Scottish Catholic Historical Association and the Cultural History of Glasgow Network. He has held awards from the British Academy and is currently researching the experience of unaccompanied asylum-seeking children in Scotland.

Index

The City as Place

Emotions, Experiences, and Meanings

The purpose of this series is to examine the city as a lived place. Specifically, we are interested in the ways in which the city is invested with meaning through everyday lived experiences. The series is particularly interested in submissions that focus on the perceptual and felt dimensions of urban places through exploring the experiential, emotional, sensory, and affective dimensions that contribute to how people behave in, feel about, and move around in cities. Books in this series will interrogate the relationship between people and place through a focus on the diverse ways in which subjective and intimate feelings are fundamental constituents of the urban experience. We encourage authors to examine the city as a lived place from a range of different perspectives, and to be inclusive of individual and collective voices in the city to better understand the historical development and contemporary evolution of diverse urban settings.

Some of the questions we seek to explore through the series include, but are not restricted to:

- How is the city experienced, by whom, and how does this change over time?
- Who shapes the experience of the city and for what reasons?
- How do individual and shared joy, fear, pride, nostalgia, disgust, or other emotions, shape the meanings attributed to urban spaces?
- How does the lived experience of, and emotional connections to, urban places inform the way particular spaces within cities are preserved and memorialized, or alternatively demolished and redeveloped?
- In what ways is our understanding of the lived experience of the city sharpened through the lens of comparative, transnational, and global approaches?

The series seeks to examine the real and the imaginary, the representational and the non-representational, the historical and the contemporary, the remembered and the recreated in all historical periods including research on the twenty-first-century city. The series is open to work covering all geographic areas, and we encourage authors, where possible and relevant, to situate their studies in comparative, transnational, or global perspectives. Books may be published in English or in French.

Vol. 1 Laura Bowie
The Streets Echoed with Chants:
The Urban Experience of Post-War West Berlin
2022. ISBN 978-1-78997-581-9

Vol. 2 Stephen Bowman and Kieran Taylor (eds)
Portable City:
Modern Glasgow's Transatlantic Connections
2026. ISBN 978-1-80374-281-6

www.ingramcontent.com/pod-product-compliance
Ingram Content Group UK Ltd.
Pitfield, Milton Keynes, MK11 3LW, UK
UKHW021852100926
8556IPUK00020B/1189

9 781803 742816